Gregory of Nyssa and the Grasp of Faith

Union, Knowledge, and Divine Presence

MARTIN LAIRD

OXFORD
UNIVERSITY PRESS

OXFORD

UNIVERSITY PRESS

Great Clarendon Street, Oxford OX2 6DP

Oxford University Press is a department of the University of Oxford.
It furthers the University's objective of excellence in research, scholarship,
and education by publishing worldwide in

Oxford New York

Auckland Cape Town Dar es Salaam Hong Kong Karachi Kuala Lumpur
Madrid Melbourne Mexico City Nairobi New Delhi Shanghai Taipei Toronto

With offices in

Argentina Austria Brazil Chile Czech Republic France Greece
Guatemala Hungary Italy Japan Poland Portugal Singapore
South Korea Switzerland Thailand Turkey Ukraine Vietnam

Oxford is a registered trade mark of Oxford University Press
in the UK and in certain other countries

Published in the United States
by Oxford University Press Inc., New York

© Martin Laird 2004

British Library Cataloguing in Publication Data
Data available

Library of Congress Cataloging in Publication Data
Data available

Typeset by SPI Publisher Services, Pondicherry, India
Printed in Great Britain on acid-free paper by
Biddles Ltd., King's Lynn, Norfolk

ISBN 978-0-19-926799-6 (Hbk.)
978-0-19-922915-4 (Pbk.)

OXFORD EARLY CHRISTIAN STUDIES

General Editors

Gillian Clark   Andrew Louth

THE OXFORD EARLY CHRISTIAN STUDIES series includes scholarly volumes on the thought and history of the early Christian centuries. Covering a wide range of Greek, Latin, and Oriental sources, the books are of interest to theologians, ancient historians, and specialists in the classical and Jewish worlds.

Titles in the series include:

For my parents
Dorothy and Bob Laird

ACKNOWLEDGEMENTS

This study is a revised version of a doctoral thesis presented to the University of London (Heythrop College). It began life, however, during fruitful years of study and research in Rome at the Institutum Patristicum Augustinianum, and I remain indebted to engaging lectures and guidance by, especially, Professor Salvatore Lilla, Dom Jean-Robert Pouchet, Professor Manlio Simonetti, and Dom Basil Studer. Towards the end of this stay in Rome I came across two people who were kind enough to guide my research on Gregory of Nyssa: Professor Mariette Canévet, University of Strasbourg, and the Revd Dr Anthony Meredith, SJ, Heythrop College, University of London. Whilst lecturing each spring at the Gregorian University, Rome, Mlle Canévet was incredibly generous with her time and spirit over several years. Her sharing with me her deep familiarity with Gregory and her willingness to read and comment on every word of the original version of this study have left me a burden of gratitude which is a privilege to bear. Anthony Meredith took me in off the streets of London and answered some initial queries I had. After I moved from Italy to England, these encounters became official supervisory sessions from which I profited immensely (and with much humour amongst Farm Street Jesuits), but more importantly I learnt from him how scholarship could be an expression of *fides quaerens intellectum*.

I am happy to thank the British Library, where most of this work was composed (initially in the Round Reading Room in Bloomsbury and then its new location near King's Cross); Heythrop College Library, London; the Bodleian Library, Oxford; and Dom Henry Wansbrough, Master of St Benet's Hall, Oxford, for providing a most congenial environment during a final year of preparation.

For the revised version of this thesis, I have first to thank its examiners, Dr Graham Gould, King's College London, and the Most Revd Dr Rowan Williams, (now) Archbishop of Canterbury, for their helpful and encouraging comments. As General Editor of Oxford Early Christian Studies, Professor Andrew Louth was most encouraging and generous at every step along the way. The anonymous reader for Oxford University Press, whose blood pressure I fear I raised at not a few points, did me the kind service of a thorough and challenging reading. Lucy Qureshi at the Press is a delight to know; long may she continue there.

Material from the following chapters has appeared elsewhere in revised form: from Chapter 3 as ' "By Faith Alone": A Technical Term in Gregory of Nyssa', *Vigiliae Christianae* 54 (2000), 61–79; from Chapter 6 as 'Apophasis and Logophasis in Gregory of Nyssa's *Commentarius in Canticum canticorum*', *Studia Patristica* 34 (2001), 126–32; from Chapter 7 as 'Gregory of Nyssa and the Mysticism of Darkness: A Reconsideration', *Journal of Religion* 79 (1999), 592–616.

Unless otherwise noted, translations of ancient and modern sources are my own. Especially in the case of ancient sources, I have usually consulted one or more of the translations listed in the bibliography. I have also consulted the Revd Professor Richard Norris's as yet unpublished translation of Gregory of Nyssa's *Homilies on the Song of Songs*. My heartfelt thanks to him for allowing me to read a draft of his translation.

Villanova University has been my academic community and home for the last few years, and I wish particularly to acknowledge the collegial support and valued friendship of Dr Christopher Daly, Dr Kevin Hughes, and Dr Thomas Smith, as well as that of the Department of Theology and Religious Studies.

For more years than I can count, my at times gypsy lifestyle has been grounded by the friendship of many. I wish especially to acknowledge Lord and Lady Buxton, the Honourable Michael Coll, John FitzGerald, OSA, Richard Jacobs, OSA, Mary Grace Kuppe, OSA, Betty Maney, Pauline Matarasso, Gerald Nicholas, OSA, Ben O'Rourke, OSA, Martha Reeves, Polly Robin, Raymond Ryan, OSA, Werner Valentin, my confrères at St Monica's Priory, Hoxton Square, London, and last but not least Tom and Monica Cornell of The Catholic Worker, Marlboro, New York, who are the kitchen table in my life.

CONTENTS

ABBREVIATIONS

ANRW	*Aufstieg und Niedergang der Römischen Welt*
CUF	Collection des Universités de France
FC	Fathers of the Church
GCS	Griechischen Christlichen Schriftsteller
GNO	Gregorii Nysseni Opera
LCL	Loeb Classical Library
LNPF	A Select Library of Nicene and Post-Nicene
	Fathers of the Christian Church
PG	Patrologiae Graeca
SC	Sources Chrétiennes
SCBO	Scriptorum Classicorum Biblioteca Oxoniensis

Frequently cited texts of Gregory of Nyssa

Contra Eunom.	*Contra Eunomium Libri*
De anima et res.	*De anima et resurrectione*
De beat.	*De beatitudinibus*
De hom. op.	*De hominis opificio*
De orat. dom.	*De oratione dominica*
De virg.	*De virginitate*
De vita. Greg. Thaum.	*De vita Gregorii Thaumaturgi*
In Cant.	*Commentarius in Canticum canticorum*
In Eccl.	*In Ecclesiasten*
In inscrip. Psalm.	*In inscriptiones Psalmorum*
Orat. cat.	*Oratio catechetica*
Vita S. Mac.	*Vita S. Macrinae*

Introduction

Faith the Christian Foundation

'But the Law has found its fulfilment in Christ, so that all who have faith will be justified.' So proclaimed Paul to the Christians at Rome.[1] 'If you declare with your mouth', he continues, 'that Jesus is Lord, and if you believe with your heart that God raised him from the dead, then you will be saved.'[2] That faith, and not obedience to the Law, could open the doors of justification and salvation, Paul insisted, was nothing new, and he looks to Abraham as one who embodied this faith: 'Abraham put his faith in God and this was reckoned to him as uprightness.'[3] Indeed the Letter to the Hebrews provides a salvation history that focuses on acts of faith from Abel and Enoch through Abraham, Moses, and the prophets.[4] What is true of Abraham is true of all believers: 'it is people of faith who receive the same blessing as Abraham, the man of faith'.[5]

Faith as a doorway to God is foundational for Christianity from the beginning, but as Christianity began to move out and engage the Hellenistic culture in which it was immersed, this emphasis on faith as somehow providing access to God seemed to generate more heat than light. It was not that *pistis* meant nothing to a philosophical culture permeated by the spirit of Plato. It did indeed mean something, and Plato's Allegory of the Line is often taken as the *locus classicus* in this regard:[6] caught up in sense impression, faith was associated with a very low and unreliable form of knowledge. As E.R. Dodds observed long ago in his Wiles Lectures: 'Had any cultivated pagan of the second century been asked to put in a few words the difference between his own view of life and the Christian one, he might reply that it was the difference between *logismos* and *pistis*, between reasoned conviction and blind faith. To anyone brought up on classical Greek philosophy, *pistis* meant the lowest

---

[1] Rom. 10: 4 (*The New Jerusalem Bible*).   [2] Rom. 10: 9.
[3] Rom. 4: 3; cf. Gal. 3: 7 and Gen. 15: 6.   [4] Heb. 11.
[5] Gal. 3: 9.   [6] *Republic* 511e.

grade of cognition.'[7] It was clearly not the case that Greek philosophy did not value the divine; Neoplatonism was especially concerned with divine union. What was required for this, however, was not faith but the non-discursive reaches of the intelligence. This is in many ways a suitable place to situate the subject of the present study of Gregory of Nyssa.

While Gregory of Nyssa spoke of faith in a variety of senses, this study will focus on a particular, indeed technical, use of the term *pistis*. We shall see that Gregory of Nyssa ascribes to faith qualities which Neoplatonism would reserve to the crest of the wave of *nous*. Indeed, for Gregory of Nyssa, faith becomes a faculty of union with God, who is beyond all comprehension, beyond the reach of concept, image, word. To speak of union with God beyond noetic activity is something with which Neoplatonism is very familiar, though it would not until Proclus see that faith had a role in this apophatic union. But Gregory does see the role of faith in union with God, and to develop his views on this matter he grounds himself not in Plotinus or Porphyry but in certain biblical figures who embody faith, especially Abraham, Moses, the bride of the Song of Songs, and Paul.[8]

Philo, Clement of Alexandria, and Origen had done much in their own Middle-Platonic context to show that biblical faith could be taken with epistemological seriousness. For Philo faith was the 'queen of virtues'[9] and he could ascribe to faith the capacity to unite with God: 'What then is the cementing substance? Do you ask, what? Piety, surely, and faith: for these virtues adjust and unite (ἐνοῦσιν) the intent of the heart to the incorruptible Being: as Abraham when he believed is said to "come near to God" (Gen. 18: 23).'[10] Clement of Alexandria attempted to give a thorough explanation of faith to assuage the objections of both Greek philosophy and the Gnostics, who considered their *gnosis* higher than simple faith. For Clement faith became the acceptance of the first principles of knowledge that cannot be proved, but without which there

---

[7] E. R. Dodds, *Pagan and Christian in an Age of Anxiety* (Cambridge, 1965), 120–1.

[8] More on Gregory's relationship to aspects of Neoplatonism in Chapter 4.

[9] Philo, *Abr.* 46. 270 (LCL, Philo vol. vi, trans. F. Colson). See H. Wolfson, *Philo: Foundations of Religious Philosophy in Judaism, Christianity, and Islam*, vol. ii (Cambridge, Mass., 1968), 215–18. For a philological study of faith in Philo, see D. Lindsay, *Josephus and Faith: Πίστις and Πιστεύειν as Faith Terminology in the Writings of Flavius Josephus and in the New Testament* (Leiden, 1993), 53–73.

[10] Philo, *Mig.* 24. 132 (LCL, Philo vol. iv, trans. F. Colson and G. Whitaker).

could be no *gnosis*.[11] In his *Contra Celsum* Origen is keen to refute Celsus'
accusation that Chrisitans accept things on faith without the support of
reason.[12] Origen concedes that faith is 'useful for the multitude, and that
we admittedly teach those who cannot abandon everything and pursue a
study of rational argument to believe without thinking out their
reasons'.[13] He insists, however, that this is not the ideal and that faith
with the support of reason is better than faith alone: 'it is in harmony
with scripture to say that it is far better to accept doctrines with reason
and wisdom than with mere faith'.[14] But Origen is not always on the
defensive about faith. Commenting on Luke 8. 48, 'My daughter your
faith has saved you,' Origen likens philosophers to physicians who
attempt but fail to heal humanity. 'But upon touching the fringe of
Jesus' garment, who alone is the physician of souls and bodies, [human-
ity] is healed on the spot by the fire and warmth of faith. If we look to our
faith in Jesus Christ and consider how great is the son of God and touch
something of him, we will see that in comparison to the fringes in him we
have touched but a fringe. But all the same the fringe heals us and
enables us to hear Jesus say: "Daughter, your faith has saved you".'[15]
As much as Origen values the reasoned argument of philosophy, he can
speak of faith as providing something that philosophy alone cannot
provide. Faith mediates real contact with Jesus and brings healing.[16]

These brief glimpses of Philo, Clement, and Origen represent the
early Christian concern to integrate the epistemological concerns of
their philosophical-cultural *milieux* into a viable understanding of how
Christian faith could lead to an experience of God. While Gregory of

---

[11] See esp. Clement of Alexandria, *Stromateis* ii, trans. J. Ferguson, FC 85 (Washington,
DC, 1991). On faith and knowledge in Clement see E. Osborn, *The Philosophy of Clement of
Alexandria* (Cambridge, 1957), 127–45 and S. Lilla, *Clement of Alexandria: A Study of
Christian Platonism and Gnosticism* (Oxford, 1971), 118–42; see also J. Moingt, 'La Gnose
de Clément d'Alexandrie dans ses rapports avec la Philosophie', *Recherches de Science
Religieuse* 37 (1950), 398–421; 37 (1950), 537–64; 38 (1951), 82–118; R. Mortley, *Con-
naissance religieuse et herméneutique chez Clément d'Alexandrie* (Leiden, 1973), 109–25;
R. Berchman, *From Philo to Origen: Middle Platonism in Transition* (Chico, Calif., 1985), 176–9.
[12] For a broad survey of Middle-Platonic pagan criticism of Christianity see S. Benko,
'Pagan Criticism of Christianity during the First Two Centuries AD', in *ANRW* ii. 23/2,
1055–1117; see also R. Wilken, *The Christians as the Romans Saw Them* (New Haven, 1984).
[13] Origen, *Contra Celsum* 1. 10, trans. H. Chadwick (Cambridge, 1965), 13.
[14] Ibid. 1. 13 (Chadwick, 16).
[15] Origen, *In Lucam* fragmenta (M. Rauer (ed.), 240. 25–35); trans. R. Daly in H. von
Balthasar, *Origen, Spirit and Fire: A Thematic Anthology of His Writings* (Washington, DC,
1984), 94.
[16] See F. Bertrand, *Mystique de Jésus chez Origène* (Paris, 1951), 121–40, esp. 130–2.

Nyssa is very much heir to this Alexandrian tradition, he writes in a Neoplatonic-cultural context which is much less hostile towards faith. Curiously, late Neoplatonism begins to look very much like a religion, not least in the way in which it came to value faith and revelation. Dodds remarks, 'pagan philosophy tended increasingly to replace reason by authority—and not only the authority of Plato, but the authority of Orphic poetry, of Hermetic theosophy, of obscure revelations like the *Chaldaean Oracles*'.[17] It is worth considering this rise of faith in late Neoplatonism, not to suggest that this was a direct influence on what Gregory claimed of faith as a faculty of union, but rather to show that the theological culture of late antiquity, *for both Christianity and late Neoplatonism*, saw immense, religious possibility in faith. The exaltation of faith was part of the spirit of the age.

Faith in Late Neoplatonism: Porphyry, Iamblichus, and Proclus

One of the defining features of late Neoplatonism was its increasing religiosity and the manner in which it too came to extol faith. This is not without a certain irony; philosophical Hellenism in general had previously derided faith as among the lowest forms of cognition: 'it was the state of mind of the uneducated, who believe things on hearsay without being able to give reasons for their belief'.[18] But after Plotinus especially, Neoplatonism 'became less a philosophy than a religion, whose followers were occupied like their Christian counterparts in expounding and reconciling sacred texts. For them too *pistis* became a basic requirement.'[19] A propos of late antiquity as a whole, Dodds remarks: 'The entire culture, pagan as well as Christian, was moving into a phase in which religion was to be co-extensive with life, and the quest for God was to cast its shadow over all other human activities.'[20] Dodds has suggested that this was in large part a parallel response from both Christians and pagans to the anxiety that marked the age, an age 'so filled with fear and hatred as the world of the third century, any path that promised escape must have attracted serious minds. Many besides Plotinus must have given a new meaning to the words of Agamemnon in Homer, "Let us flee to our own country" '.[21]

An approach altogether different from Dodds's reduction of religious aspiration and expression to anxiety-response is taken more recently by

---

[17] Dodds, *Pagan and Christian*, 122.   [18] Ibid., 121.   [19] Ibid., 122.
[20] Ibid., 101.   [21] Ibid., 100–1.

Jay Bregman. Bregman sees in later Hellensim the interaction of three distinct dynamics. First, is 'the Classical tradition of Greek customs, language, institutions and literature, an element of which nevertheless involved acknowledgment of the gods and religious practice'.[22] Second, the Greek philosophical tradition, in the light of which the entire cultural heritage was to be interpreted, 'as in the Neoplatonism of Plotinus and Porphyry, in which the highest activities are contemplation, *unio mystica* and *amor intellectus dei*'.[23] Third, Bregman says, is 'the theurgic Neoplatonism of Iamblichus, Julian's guru, and Proclus, where rites and religious *practice* are basic and essential . . .'.[24] This is not to suggest that genuinely devout religious practice did not exist among non-Christian Hellenists until the late Neoplatonism of the fourth and fifth centuries; for certainly it did, as H.-D. Saffrey has sensitively demonstrated.[25] What Bregman usefully highlights, however, is a cultural trend in late Neoplatonism which witnesses the coming together of the classical philosophical patrimony and religious piety, indeed faith, what Gregory Shaw has aptly termed, 'the platonizing of popular religion'.[26] This can be sufficiently demonstrated by surveying some of the key moments in late Neoplatonism's change in attitude towards religious practice in general and towards the role of faith in particular; for 'no religion can dispense with *pistis*'.[27]

Plotinus would seem to have had precious little time for faith. Its epistemological possibilities were advanced but little beyond that accorded it by Plato's Allegory of the Line.[28] While not disparaging it outright, for Plotinus, faith would have negligible relevance to the ascent to the One, the flight of the alone to the alone. As Rist has put it: faith for Plotinus is 'conviction derived from the experience of the senses'.[29] With his disciple Porphyry, however, things begin to change.

A committed critic of Christianity, Porphyry was quick to deride the irrational faith of Christians.[30] This allegedly irrational faith, however, is

---

[22] J. Bregman, 'Elements of the Emperor Julian's Theology', in J. Cleary (ed.), *Traditions of Platonism: Essays in Honor of John Dillon* (Aldershot, 1999), 339.

[23] Ibid.   [24] Ibid.

[25] H. Saffrey, 'The Piety and Prayers of Ordinary Men and Women in Late Antiquity', in A. Armstrong (ed.), *Classical Mediterranean Spirituality* (New York, 1986), 195–213.

[26] G. Shaw, *Theurgy and the Soul: The Neoplatonism of Iamblichus* (University Park, Pa., 1995), 231.

[27] Dodds, *Pagan and Christian*, 123.   [28] *Republic* 511e.

[29] J. Rist, *Plotinus: The Road to Reality* (Cambridge, 1967), 234; for some nuanced meanings of faith in Plotinus see also 235–9.

[30] See A. Meredith, 'Porphyry and Julian against the Christians', *ANRW* ii. 23/2, 1120–49, esp. 1125–37; see also Wilken, *The Christians as the Romans Saw Them*.

not Porphyry's final word on the possibilities of faith. In his later years
Porphyry writes a letter to his wife Marcella that reveals both a respect
for traditional religious practice and an acknowledged role for faith in a
relationship with God.[31] Writing to console his wife during an extended
absence, Porphyry encourages Marcella to 'disregard the irrational confusion caused by passion and consider it no small thing to remember the
divine doctrine by which you were initiated into philosophy "for deeds
provide the positive demonstrations of each person's beliefs" and
"whoever has acquired certainty must live in such a way that he himself
can be a certain witness to the beliefs which he speaks about to his
disciples"'.[32] At first glance one might take the language of philosophical initiation to refer only to the type of philosophical life to which
Porphyry would have been exposed by Plotinus, but Porphyry goes on
to speak of traditional religious practice and honouring God in a manner
that gives greater credence to traditional religion than Plotinus would
have accorded it. 'For this is the principal fruit of piety: to honour
the divine in the traditional ways, not because He needs it but because
He summons us by his venerable and blessed dignity to worship him.
God's altars, if they are consecrated, do not harm us; if they are
neglected, they do not help us.'[33] Moreover, not only does Porphyry's
philosophical piety include traditional Hellenic religious practice
according to ancestral custom, but Porphyry can also speak quite positively of the role of faith in a relationship with God. 'Let four principles
in particular be firmly held with regard to God: faith, truth, love, hope.
For it is necessary to have faith that conversion toward God is the only
salvation.'[34] This text has been much commented upon. Rist claims that
the triad 'faith, truth, and love' marks a clear influence of the *Chaldaean
Oracles* and constitutes, moreover, the first sign of direct influence of the
Chaldaean Oracles to date.[35] Citing A.H. Armstrong, Rist says that faith in
Ad Marcellam is ' "Platonic firm rational confidence" '.[36] Dodds was less

[31] The attitude towards religion is so devout as to prompt some to suggest the unlikely
case that Porphyry had been positively influenced by Christians; for a review of this
opinion see *Porphyry the Philosopher: To Marcella*, trans. K. Wicker (Atlanta,1987), 4.

[32] *Ad Marcellam* 8. 137–50; critical text and translation by K. Wicker, *Porphyry the
Philosopher*, 52–3.

[33] *Ad Marcellam* 18. 294–9 (Wicker, 60), translation by Wicker, 61.

[34] *Ad Marcellam* 24. 376–9 (Wicker, 66), translation by Wicker, 67; Porphyry goes on to
speak likewise on truth, love, and hope.

[35] Rist, *Plotinus*, 239. Rist bases himself on H. Lewy, *Chaldean Oracles and Theurgy:
Mysticism, Magic and Platonism in the Later Roman Empire* (Cairo, 1956, new edition by
M. Tardieu, Paris, 1978), 144–5.

[36] Ibid.; see A. Armstrong, 'Platonic *Eros* and Christian *Agape*', *Downside Review* 79
(1961), 105–21, at 116 n. 5.

certain that this triad came from the *Chaldaean Oracles*, but does think it a
good deal more likely than Harnack's suggestion of the influence of
1 Cor. 13: 13 on Porphyry.[37] For our purpose, however, of indicating late
Neoplatonism's gradual exaltation of faith, it is worth pointing out at
least three things. First, Porphyry places faith in the context of a
relationship with God. Second, while Porphyry does not suggest that
union with God is mediated by faith (something which Plotinus would
never have advocated, but which Proclus will indeed claim), it is nevertheless necessary, 'the first condition of the soul's approach to God'.[38]
Third, what Porphyry has to say about both faith and the 'ancestral
custom' of religious practice, provides a good place to take a sort of
cultural pulse. For we see here an example of the cultural tendencies
announced earlier by Bregan: the tendency in later Hellenism to interpret
religious practice in the light of philosophy. In *Ad Marcellam* Porphyry is
not simply advocating ancient religious practice; the letter is an instruction in the life of philosophy. What is noteworthy about Porphyry's
positive views on faith and religious practice expressed here is that he
sees them as ideal preparation for the life of philosophy. 'Porphyry
remains the philosopher as he integrates the search for personal salvation into the metaphysical structure of Neoplatonism'.[39] This adds some
precision and a slight corrective to Dodds's general observation that
after Plotinus Neoplatonism became less a philosophy than a religion.
Religious rites and practices did not replace Neoplatonism, but were
integrated into Neoplatonism's description of the philosophical life for
late antiquity. Porphyry, at least in *Ad Marcellam*, provides a clear pulse in
this Platonizing of popular religion, but Iamblichus and Proclus provide
a yet stronger pulse.

There is a certain urgency in Iamblichus' defence of theurgy.[40] Porphyry was not always so tolerant of theurgic rites, and in many ways the
views of religious practices expressed to his wife represent a softening of
the rather more critical and suspicious views expressed in the Letter to
Anebo or in *De abstinentia*. Following Plotinus, Porphyry held that divine

---

[37] Dodds, *Pagan and Christian*, 123 n. 2; Dodds emphasizes that, in contrast to the
Chaldaean Oracles, 'Porphyry's *pistis* is a state of mind, not a cosmological principle' (ibid.).
For a succinct overview of those who argue a Christian influence on Porphyry see *Porphyry
the Philosopher*, trans. Wicker, 28–9, n. 23.

[38] Dodds, *Pagan and Christian*, 122.

[39] *Porphyry the Philosopher*, trans. Wicker, 13. Wicker concurs with A. Smith, *Porphyry's
Place in the Platonic Tradition* (The Hague, 1974), 145.

[40] P. Hadot reminds us that the term 'theurgy' was coined by the author (or authors)
of the *Chaldaean Oracles*; see P. Hadot, *What is Ancient Philosophy?*, trans. M. Chase
(Cambridge, Mass., 2002), 170.

union was achieved through νοῦς. 'The philosopher...is detached
from exterior things...and has no need of diviners or the entrails of
animals.... Alone and through himself, as we have said, the philosopher
will approach the god...'.[41] Theurgic rituals, according to Porphyry, did
not lead to divine union but served only to purify the lower soul.[42] This
was cause for concern on the part of Iamblichus, his former pupil.[43] As
Peter Brown has put it: 'The austere philosophical transcendentalism of
Porphyry threatened to deny that the gods were available on earth and
hence to deny that heaven was accessible to men through the traditional
rituals.'[44] 'This doctrine', says Iamblichus, 'spells the ruin of all holy ritual
and all communion between gods and men achieved by our rites, by
placing the physical presence of the superior beings outside this earth.'[45]
By exalting the role of theurgic rituals, however, Iamblichus was not
abandoning the Platonism in which he was schooled, but adapting it in
such a way that the ancient religious customs served a vital function in the
life of the philosopher.

Gregory Shaw claims that Iamblichus' *De mysteriis*, written in response
to Porphyry's Letter to Anebo, is late antiquity's best example of
the changes that were coming about in traditional pagan worship.
'Iamblichus thoroughly revised and defended pagan divinational practices by placing them within the theoretical framework of Platonic and
Pythagorean teachings...'.[46] This, combined with the growing authority
of the *Chaldaean Oracles*,[47] resulted in the theurgic rites that gave further
shape to the religious complexion of Neoplatonism in the fourth century
(and beyond). But why did Iamblichus see a philosophical need for
theurgy and how did theurgy fulfil that need?

Iamblichus had taken a different view from both Plotinus and Porphyry regarding the structure of the soul. For Plotinus and Porphyry, the

[41] Porphyry, *De abstinentia* II. 52. 2–4, in *Porphyre: De l'abstinence*, ed. J. Bouffartigue and
M. Patillon (Paris, 1977), quoted in G. Shaw, 'Divination in the Neoplatonism of
Iamblichus' in R. Berchman (ed.), *Mediators of the Divine: Horizons of Prophecy, Divination,
Dreams and Theurgy in Mediterranean Antiquity* (Atlanta, 1998), 240.
[42] Shaw, 'Divination', 240.
[43] See ibid., 230–1 for a concise summary of Iamblichus' fundamental disagreement
with Porphyry.
[44] P. Brown, *The Making of Late Antiquity* (Cambridge, Mass., 1978), 100–1.
[45] Iamblichus, *De mysteriis* I. 8 (28. 6), ed. E. des Places (Paris, 1966), 55, quoted in
Brown, *The Making of Late Antiquity*, 101.
[46] Shaw, 'Divination', 228.
[47] J. Dillon, 'Iamblichus of Chalcis', *ANRW* II. 36/2, 868–9, at 878; more on the
Chaldaean Oracles in Chapter 4.

essence of the soul was undescended in body and, hence, never lost its divine status. Porphyry was not being flippant when he stated in *De abstinentia*, 'the philosopher will approach the god'.[48] The statement reveals his understanding of the nature of the soul, whose essence, undescended in the body, remains eternal and well placed 'to approach the god' without mediation by theurgy. Not so for Iamblichus; the essence of the soul is descended in the body, with the result that, of the soul's two functions—animating the body and uniting with the divine—the soul can only perform the former. It is the precise role of theurgy to make up for what soul cannot do, by allowing the gods to come to soul and use it as their instrument.[49] Ancient rituals such as divination became for Iamblichus theurgic rites, divine works that did far more than merely cleanse the lower soul (something which Porphyry admitted).[50] Theurgic rituals 'bridged the gap between the soul's *ousia* and *energeia*: it allowed the divinity of the soul to be experienced immediately as divine but at the cost of its singular self-consciousness'.[51]

Because of Iamblichus' understanding of the structure of soul, we can see more clearly how vital a role something like divination can now be seen to play. Iamblichus says, 'only divination, therefore, in uniting us with the gods, truly enables us to share in the life of the gods, and since it participates in the foreknowledge and thought of the Divine, we ourselves may truly attain to divinity by means of it; and divination is the authentic guarantee of our good, since the blessed Intellect of the gods is replete with good of every kind'.[52] With Iamblichus the old rites, with their entrails and oracles and sacrifices, can no longer be said to be mere superstition; they are the means of uniting with the divine. Iamblichus has given them an anthropological grounding in the structure of the soul itself, which makes them crucial for the life of the philosopher.[53]

Amongst those inspired by Iamblichus, Julian the Emperor must be reckoned the most famous in the fourth century. A convert to Iamblican Neoplatonism through Maximus of Ephesus, Julian 'was the most

[48] *De abstinentia* II. 52. 2–4; cf. Plotinus, *Ennead* II. 9. 2.

[49] See Shaw, 'Divination', 240–8; Hadot, *What is Ancient Philosophy?*, 171; see also L. Siorvanes, *Proclus: Neo-Platonic Philosophy and Science* (Edinburgh, 1996), 191.

[50] See R. T. Wallis, *Neoplatonism*, 2nd edn. (London, 1975), 107–10.

[51] Ibid., 245.

[52] Iamblichus, *De mysteriis* X. 4 in *Les Mystères d'Egypte*, ed. E. des Places (Paris, 1966), quoted in J. Gregory, *The Neoplatonists: A Reader*, 2nd edn. (London, 1999), 152.

[53] See Shaw, *Theurgy and the Soul*, 231: 'Iamblichus provided a theoretical justification for well-known religious practices of the Greco-Roman world.'

enthusiastic fourth-century religious Hellene',[54] and theurgy, according to Rowland Smith, 'is the most strikingly fourth-century feature in the devotional and intellectual make-up of the man'.[55] Some scholars see Julian establishing an Hellenic church 'with its own orthodoxy and priestly hierarchy under his direction' very much driven by Iamblican theurgy.[56] Rowland Smith, however, while acknowledging Julian's personal debt to theurgic Neoplatonism, nevertheless cautions strongly against exaggerating its influence on his public religious programme.[57] To whatever degree, great or little, theurgic Neoplatonism affected the Empire during his brief reign, Julian remains an important example of how the Iamblican reforms of Neoplatonism were still very much alive. As Philip Rousseau has recently put it: 'Especially among the followers of Iamblichus, [Julian] harnessed the energies of a generation that had already steeled itself in the face of Constantine's tolerance and conversion...'[58]

If the Iamblican theurgic reforms of the fourth century were in a large measure responsible for late Neoplatonism's sustained religious complexion, we might well expect to see the role of faith also come to the fore. While we have seen Porphyry speak of faith sympathetically, it is really Proclus we must turn to in order to see the positive regard in which late Neoplatonism came to hold faith.

If indeed Porphyry was the first Neoplatonist to give evidence of the growing influence of the *Chaldaean Oracles*, he was clearly not the last.[59] Iamblichus 'turned them into the ultimate theological authority',[60] and Proclus on several occasions refers to the famous Chaldaean triad of faith, truth, and love. Saffrey maintains that the entrance of the *Chaldaean*

[54] Bregman, 'Elements of Julian's Theology', 337.

[55] R. Smith, *Julian's Gods: Religion and Philosophy in the Thought and Action of Julian the Apostate* (London, 1995), 112.

[56] Bregman, 'Elements of Julian's Theology', 337; for similar views see also J. Bidez, *La Vie de l'Empereur Julien* (Paris, 1930); G. Bowersock, *Hellenism in Late Antiquity* (Cambridge, 1990); P. Athanassiadi-Fowden, *Julian and Hellenism* (Oxford, 1981).

[57] Smith, *Julian's Gods*, 110–13: 'Iamblican theurgy impinged on him deeply, to be sure; but it was a part of his personal credo, not the whole of it. It belonged principally to the philosophic piety of the private man...' (113); see also 220–4. Bregman, 'Elements of Julian's Theology', 348 n. 30, would seem to take exception to Smith but does not attempt to counter all Smith's claims.

[58] P. Rousseau, *The Early Christian Centuries* (London, 2002), 197.

[59] Rist, *Plotinus*, 239.

[60] H. Saffrey, 'Neoplatonist Spirituality II: From Iamblichus to Proclus and Damascius' in A. H. Armstrong (ed.), *Classical Mediterranean Spirituality* (New York, 1986), 253.

Oracles into Neoplatonism had two important consequences. First, it gave rise to what Iamblichus developed as theurgy.[61] Second, the *Chaldaean Oracles* became a theological authority that gave Neoplatonists a new way of reading Plato. Appearing probably in second-century Syria, the *Chaldaean Oracles* were thought to be the transmissions of a medium in communication with Plato.[62] 'Since the *Oracles* were Platonic, Plato himself became a god capable of proffering oracles; his writings thus became the revelation of a sublime doctrine, a truly "holy scripture".'[63] One can see how Iamblichus' theory of the descended soul accommodates within Neoplatonism this new need for revelation: because the soul is fully descended, it cannot save itself; the philosopher stands in need of divine assistance. These Platonic oracles supplied such guidance, which Iamblichus worked into his theurgic rites. While Proclus certainly continued to see a role for theurgy within fifth-century Neoplatonism, he is particularly useful for seeing the role which faith comes to play in the soul's search for divine union in the context of theurgy.[64]

Proclus ascribes to faith qualities which Plotinus and Porphyry would never have done. More than conviction derived from either the senses or intellect, faith becomes for Proclus a faculty of divine union beyond the level of intellect. His clearest statement of this is to be found in the *Platonic Theology*. With the Chaldaean triad of love, truth, and faith in the background, Proclus discusses how each is a means of contact with the divine. Love establishes contact with Beauty and truth with Wisdom, but, 'What', he asks, 'will unite us with the Good? What will still all activity and movement? . . . In a word, it is the Faith of the gods which, by means beyond description, brings all the ranks of gods and *daemons*, and the blessed among souls, into union with the Good. For the Good must be sought not by knowledge and its imperfection, but only by surrender to the divine radiance.'[65] As the means of union with the Good, this faith has a certain pride of place: 'Neither Beauty nor Wisdom nor any other property of Being is for all things so worthy of Faith, so secure, so indubitable, so incomprehensible to the sequential

---

[61] Ibid.

[62] Ibid. For a more in-depth treatment see H. Saffrey, 'Les néoplatoniciens et les *Oracles Chaldaïques*', *Revue des Etudes Augustiniennes* 27 (1981), 209–25.

[63] Saffrey, 'Neoplatonist Spirituality', 254.

[64] For a helpful examination of differences between Iamblichan and Proclan theurgy, see A. Sheppard, 'Proclus' Attitude to Theurgy', *Classical Quarterly* 32 (1982), 212–24.

[65] Proclus, *Platonic Theology* I. 25, ed. H. Saffrey and L. Westerink, *Théologie Platonicienne* (Paris, 1968), 110, 1–10; translation by Gregory, *The Neoplatonists: A Reader*, 170.

movement of thought, as is the Good.'[66] It is clear that Proclus is not using faith in the sense that Plato and Plotinus used it.[67] Faith is not, as Siorvanes has put it, 'the absence of demonstrable argument or truth'.[68] Because the Good is beyond discursive knowing, the means of contact must be non-discursive. This is what Proclus sees in faith. For Proclus faith is an unknowing that is higher than knowing that unites with the Good, that is beyond the grasp of all noetic activity. What makes possible this union with the Good is precisely the role of theurgy: 'theurgy leads to a supra-intellectual faith which reaches God'.[69]

With Proclus, then, we see most clearly the religious possibilities that late Neoplatonism came to see in faith. Clearly this is not the inferior knowledge described by Plato in the Allegory of the Line; nor is it just the rational faith that Porphyry came to see as 'a fundamental requirement of the philosopher'.[70] Proclus asks: 'What is the cause of this initiation except that faith? For on the whole the initiation does not happen through intellection and judgement, but through silence which is unifying and is superior to every cognitive activity. Faith imparts this . . .'[71]

Since at least Plato, the approach to the divine has been through love and truth. Why has Proclus seen in faith a third possibility for the philosopher, a possibility on a par with, if not nobler than, love and truth? Three reasons suggest themselves for consideration. One important reason is that the *Chaldaean Oracles* has upgraded faith by incorporating it into the triad along with love and truth. Thanks to the *Chaldaean Oracles*, which is considered Platonic revelation, faith has become a category whose importance is guaranteed by such revelation. Given this, the exalted understanding of faith, tied to higher theurgy, should be understood as a development *within* Platonism.[72] Second, this exalted role of faith corresponds to the changes regarding the soul wrought by Iamblichus. A fully descended soul stands in need of assistance to realize

[66]   Proclus, *Platonic Theology* I. 25, ed. H. Saffrey and L. Westerink, *Théologie Platonicienne* (Paris, 1968), 110, 1–10; translation by Gregory, *The Neoplatonists: A Reader*, 170.

[67]   Indeed Proclus distances himself from just this understanding at I. 25 (Saffrey and Westrink, 110, 17–22).

[68]   Siorvanes, *Proclus*, 191–2.

[69]   Ibid., 192; see 192–9 for an account of Proclus' range of views on theurgy; see also Sheppard, 'Proclus' Attitude to Theurgy', 219, and Rist, *Plotinus*, 244.

[70]   Rist, *Plotinus*, 238; Porphyry thought the Christians exemplified irrational faith, which 'does not find God' (Rist, *Plotinus*, 238).

[71]   Proclus, *Platonic Theology*, IV. 31 quoted in Siorvanes, *Proclus*, 193.

[72]   L. Rosán, *The Philosophy of Proclus* (New York, 1949), 215 n. 152, suggested that Proclus' emphasis on faith might reflect a Christian influence.

its divine nature; 'it has to be "lifted up" by divinity itself'.[73] The revealed text of the *Chaldaean Oracles*, along with its theurgy that led to faith,[74] was this divine assistance that lifted the soul to salvation. Finally, for Neoplatonism generally, and certainly for Proclus, the One is beyond all noetic activity. Because of faith's ties to theurgy, plus the fact that faith itself does not require the grasp of comprehension, faith seems an obvious virtue to develop when speaking of the approach to and union with the One.

While Christianity has espoused the way of faith from the beginning, late Neoplatonism eventually came to do something similar, as Dodds has observed. As to why, Dodds points to the anxiety of the age and ultimately prefers to see it 'as an illustration of the old and true saying that "we grow like what we hate"'.[75] I have suggested that changes within Neoplatonism regarding the fallen nature of the soul, ushered in most notably by Iamblichus, are a significant factor in explaining the religious character that late Neoplatonism took on. Pierre Hadot has recently observed: 'For Neoplatonism and Christianity, the two spiritual movements which dominated the end of antiquity and opposed each other, man cannot save himself by his own strength but must wait for the divine to take the initiative.'[76] For both traditions, the fallen state of the human requires that the divine take the initiative, what Christians would call grace and revelation. Hadot, moreover likens, late Neoplatonist reliance on 'the material and sensible rites' of theurgy to the Christian need for 'the mediation of the incarnate Logos and the sensible signs of the sacraments in order to enter into contact with God'.[77] Interesting as these and other parallels are, in the course of this study of what Gregory of Nyssa had to say about Christian faith as a means of union with God we shall see striking differences.

The exaltation of faith by both Christians and late Neoplatonists was part of the theological climate of late antiquity generally, but despite some interesting parallels between Gregory and Neoplatonism regarding how faculties of union work, there is important divergence regarding faith. Commenting on the difference between Christian faith and Proclan faith, Rist says: Πίστις then in Proclus is not very like the Christian's faith, for there is no real parallel between the Christian's faith in

---

[73] Siorvanes, *Proclus*, 191.

[74] For a good discussion of higher and lower theurgy in Proclus see Sheppard, 'Proclus' Attitude to Theurgy'.

[75] Dodds, *Pagan and Christian*, 123.   [76] Hadot, *What is Ancient Philosphy?*, 171.

[77] Ibid.

Christ and the Neoplatonist's reliance on the *Chaldaean Oracles*.[78] Rist
does not elaborate on Christian faith, but as for Gregory of Nyssa's
special account of it, we shall see emphases that will ultimately distinguish it sharply from the late Neoplatonist account of it. Gregory will
emphasize, among other things, the sacramental origins of faith and
highlight, whether boldly or with characteristic subtlety, the developmental character of faith and the transformation of soul as a result of the
union mediated by faith. But most of all Gregory presumes in faith a real
relationship with the Incarnate Word, immanent in creation, in sacred
scripture and in the person of Jesus of Nazareth. To this faith of
Abraham, Moses, the bride, and Paul let us now turn.

<hr>

[78] Rist, *Plotinus*, 245.

The Exaltation of Faith:
The State of Current Research

Faith in Gregory of Nyssa: the Critical Heritage

In his recent book on Gregory of Nyssa, Bernard Pottier[1] notes the centrality of faith in the thought of the fourth-century Cappadocian.[2] Moreover, he identifies faith as the heart of Gregory's mystical theory.[3] Nor is Pottier a solitary voice in drawing attention to this fact. For indeed, since the beginning of the twentieth century, scholars of Gregory of Nyssa have noted the importance of faith in his thought.

Not least among these scholars is the eminent figure of Hans Urs von Balthasar, whose pioneering work, *Présence et Pensée: Essai sur la philosophie religieuse de Grégoire de Nysse*, was one of the first twentieth-century studies

---

[1] B. Pottier, *Dieu et le Christ selon Grégoire de Nysse: Etude systématique du 'Contre Eunome' avec traduction inédite des extraits d'Eunome* (Namur, 1994), 215.

[2] For a general orientation to the fourth-century Roman province see A. Di Berardino, 'La Cappadocia al tempo di Basilio', in *Mémorial Dom Jean Gribomont*, Studia Ephemerides Augustinianum 27 (Rome, 1988), 167–82. J. Daniélou, *Le IVième siècle: Grégoire de Nysse et son milieu* (Paris, 1965). B. Gain, *L'Eglise de Cappadoce au IVe siècle d'après la correspondance de Basile de Césarée (330–379)*, Orientalia Christiana Analecta 225 (Rome, 1985). A.H.M. Jones, *The Cities of the Eastern Roman Provinces* (Oxford, 1937). R. Heine, 'Cappadocia', in *Encyclopedia of the Early Church*, ed. A. Di Berardino, trans. A. Walford (Cambridge, 1992), s.v. J-R. Pouchet, *Basile le Grand et son univers d'amis d'après sa correspondance: Une stratégie de communion*, Studia Ephemerides Augustinianum 36 (Rome, 1992). P. Rousseau, *Basil of Caesarea*, Transformation of the Classical Heritage 20 (Berkeley, 1994).

[3] Pottier, *Dieu et le Christ*, 215: 'La thème de la foi est central dans la pensée de Grégoire, et rien de ce qui concerne la connaisance de Dieu ne peut se traiter sans l'aborder. L'approche mystique à laquelle nous invite Grégoire, est d'abord une approche par la foi, car la foi est le cœur de la mystique'. Throughout this study all translations of ancient and modern languages are my own unless otherwise indicated.

to sound the depths of Gregory's thought.[4] Von Balthasar is perhaps the first to identify the exalted epistemological status which Gregory accords faith.[5] Commenting on Gregory's interpretation of Abraham as he set out from his homeland, not guided by any of the representations of God present to his mind, von Balthasar says that true knowledge takes place beyond all light in a divine night. This night, says von Balthasar, is faith which performs two functions: it mediates the approach to God and unites the mind to God.[6]

Von Balthasar's overall treatment of faith in Gregory of Nyssa is very sparse indeed. Nevertheless, he prompts one to consider the question of faith in the context of the more searching question of what mediates between *intellectus* and God. Hence, while he does not pursue the question of the role of faith in Gregory's thought, he has framed the question for us: what mediates between mind and God?

Jean Daniélou, whose pioneering work, *Platonisme et théologie mystique: doctrine spirituelle de saint Grégoire de Nysse*, has in many ways set the stage for the study of Gregory's mystical doctrine, likewise sees the role of mediation and union played by faith in the celebrated text on the migration or ascent of Abraham.[7] Faith makes present what escapes the grasp of discursive knowledge. Such knowledge, says Daniélou, is 'opposed to the simplicity of faith which alone introduces the things of God to the mind'.[8] Hence, he detects another function of the mediational role of faith: not only does faith unite the mind to God, it also gives to the mind something of what it 'knows' of God. This point should be stressed, says Daniélou, as a characteristic of Gregory's thought.[9]

But perhaps Daniélou's outstanding contribution in this regard is his designation of faith as an organ or faculty of knowledge. Like von

---

[4] Hans Urs von Balthasar, *Présence et Pensée: Essai sur la philosophie religieuse de Grégoire de Nysse* (Paris, 1942).

[5] von Balthasar, *Présence et Pensée*, 67.

[6] Ibid., 73–4.

[7] *Contra Eunom.* II. 84–93, GNO I. 251–4. Both von Balthasar and Daniélou have in mind the important text on the migration of Abraham from the *Contra Eunomium*, GNO I. 251–4, a text which we shall have occasion to consider in greater detail in Chapter 3.

[8] J. Daniélou, *Platonisme et théologie mystique: Essai sur la doctrine spirituelle de saint Grégoire de Nysse*, 2nd edn. (Paris, 1953), 143: '... opposée à la simplicité de la foi qui seule introduit à l'intelligence des choses de Dieu'. Daniélou is speaking specifically of *curiositas* (πολυπραγμοσύνη).

[9] Ibid.: 'Cette vue majeure devait être mise en relief, car elle caractérise la pensée de Grégoire'.

Balthasar Daniélou also focuses on the migration of Abraham and sees in it three clearly indicated levels, indeed a 'hierarchy of three orders of knowledge'.[10] Each level of knowledge has a particular organ or faculty of knowledge proper to it. Hence, when Abraham goes beyond Chaldaean philosophy, the father of the faith is going beyond that level of knowledge concerned with appearances. The particular faculty concerned with the level of sense-knowledge is, according to Daniélou, αἴσθησις.[11] Next Abraham passes beyond the level of knowledge concerned with abstract realities such as God's power, goodness, or infinity. Daniélou calls this symbolic philosophy and aligns it with the faculty of φαντασία καταληπτική.[12] Finally the patriarch, having been purified of all conjectures and concepts, arrives at pure faith. Daniélou calls this apophatic philosophy, and the relevant faculty of knowledge is precisely πίστις.[13] Hence, Daniélou sees in the migration of Abraham three levels, and 'each of these levels corresponds to a particular faculty: αἴσθησις, for appearances, φαντασία καταληπτική, for abstractions, πίστις, for realities'.[14]

Daniélou detects in the bride's apprehension of the Beloved another important example of Gregory's notion of faith. In Homily 6 on the Song of Songs, the bride embarks on one of her many ascents. Not unlike Abraham she leaves behind all creatures and forsakes all manner of comprehension. Having done so she finds her beloved by faith. This finding by means of faith renders the bride's heart a divine dwelling place.[15] Daniélou observes that faith is operating at a level beyond the

---

[10] Ibid., 146.

[11] Ibid. Cf. *Contra Eunom.* II. 89, GNO I. 252. 24–8. One should distinguish this sense of the term αἴσθησις from its reserved sense found in the well-known text in Homily 11 on the Song of Songs (*In Cant.* XI, GNO VI. 324. 10–11). See the observations of Daniélou, *Platonisme et théologie mystique*, 195–7, and especially those of M. Canévet, 'La Perception de la présence de Dieu: A propos d'une expression de la XIe *Homélie sur le Cantique des Cantiques*', in *Epektasis: Mélanges Patristiques Offerts au Cardinal Jean Daniélou*, ed. J. Fontaine and C. Kannengiesser (Paris, 1972), 443–54.

[12] Ibid. Cf. *Contra Eunom.* II. 89, GNO I. 253. 1–10; it should be noted that the phrase 'φαντασία καταληπτική' itself does not appear in the text in question. While the distinct level of knowledge which Daniélou wishes to establish seems arguable, Gregory uses a rather more general phraseology and, with respect to a *precise* faculty of knowledge, somewhat elliptical: καὶ πᾶν τὸ καταλαμβανόμενον ὑπὸ τῆς ἰδίας δυνάμεως (GNO I. 253. 9–10). Φαντασία καταληπτική, however, is used three times in the *Contra Eunom.* (I. 364, GNO I. 134. 22; III. 7. 16, GNO II. 220. 23–4; III. 8. 3, GNO II. 238. 19) and twice in the *Commentarius in Canticum canticorum* (*In Cant.* I. GNO VI. 35. 7 and *In Cant.* XII, GNO VI. 357. 6).

[13] Ibid.; cf. *Contra Eunom.* II. 89, GNO I. 253. 10–17.   [14] Ibid.

[15] *In Cant.* VI, GNO VI. 183. 5–13.

grasp of concepts, hence in darkness, and mediates contact between the soul and God.[16] Only in this 'pure faith can one mysteriously touch the one who remains ever hidden in darkness'.[17]

Whereas von Balthasar designated the roles of union and mediation in Gregory's use of faith, Daniélou goes beyond this to highlight the epistemological function of faith and to identify the apophatic as its proper area of concern: the realm of apophatic philosophy is that of faith.[18]

In 1955 Walther Völker published his important contribution to the study of Gregory of Nyssa.[19] As in the two previous studies, relatively little ink is spilt on the notion of faith in Gregory. This would apparently be justified in the eyes of the German scholar, for there are very few precise ideas regarding the topic in question. The most one could hope for, then, would be a few general observations.[20]

As Völker pointed out in his book on Philo, faith is not a technical term in the Alexandrian Jew but a word with a wide range of meaning. Völker would wish to argue the same for Gregory of Nyssa.[21] For in Gregory's written corpus faith is used, according to Völker, in a variety of senses such as 'credibility', 'fidelity', 'demonstration', and even the 'profession of faith'.[22] But in general faith signifies the relationship between a person and God in such a way that presents no particular problem for interpretation.[23] Philo, however, is more interested in how faith arises. Gregory, by contrast, is much less interested in this question. Only once, says Völker, does Gregory observe that faith comes from free decision.[24] Moreover, Völker suggests that Gregory leaves to one side both the question of whether faith is the gift of divine grace as well as the relationship between faith and grace. Furthermore, the relationship between faith and knowledge, especially the Aristotelian-Stoic

---

[16] Daniélou, *Platonisme et théologie mystique*, 195.   [17] Ibid.

[18] Ibid., 146: 'Le domaine de la philosophie apophatique est proprement celui de la foi.'

[19] Walther Völker, *Gregor von Nyssa als Mystiker* (Wiesbaden, 1955).

[20] Ibid., 140.

[21] Ibid.: 'Könnten wir bei Philo beobachten, daß das Wort πίστις kein fester terminus technicus ist, sondern in verschiedenen Bedeutungen verwandt wird, so ist Gregor wenig interessiert'. Cf. idem, *Fortschritt und Vollendung bei Philo von Alexandrien* (Leipzig, 1938), 244 n. 1.

[22] Ibid.

[23] Ibid.: 'Aber im allgemeinen meint es doch das Verhältnis des Menschen zu Gott, so daß sich für die Interpretation kaum Schwerigkeiten ergeben dürften'.

[24] Ibid. Völker supports this observation with *Orat. cat.* xxxvi. 2 and suggests that Gregory is following Clement; see *Stromateis* v. 3. 2 (SC 278, 28).

doctrine, is altogether absent from Gregory of Nyssa. Even though the rationalism of Eunomius had given him the opportunity to address this issue, Gregory fails to do so in any detail.[25]

Nevertheless, Völker does acknowledge that Gregory accords faith a high epistemological status, placing it beyond the level of discursive reason.[26] He also admits that faith has various levels of meaning, beginning with adhesion or consent to doctrine handed down, which ultimately grows and develops into a means of union with God, as seen in the well-known migration of Abraham.[27] Indeed faith is of capital importance whether in the realm of knowledge or in the realm of the virtues. In this Gregory is more or less in harmony with the Alexandrian tradition. Yet Völker acknowledges that when Gregory attributes to faith capabilities which exceed those of the mind, he parts company with the Alexandrian tradition.[28]

In concluding his brief examination of faith in Gregory of Nyssa, Völker says that if one considers Gregory's views on faith in the context of his overall doctrine on perfection, one is convinced of the organic unity that occupied his interior life.[29] Indeed Gregory sees in faith the seed from which everything develops.[30]

With the publication of Mariette Canévet's study of Gregory of Nyssa the question of faith in Gregory's thought crosses a new threshold.[31] In her study of the linguistic strategies and symbolism in the writings of Gregory of Nyssa, she builds on the insights of what previous scholars have said about faith but identifies other important characteristics as well.

Like von Balthasar, Daniélou, and Völker, Canévet observes that Gregory situates faith in an epistemological and apophatic context. Focusing her comments on an important passage in Homily 3 on the Song of Songs, where the soul arrives at an understanding of what cannot be grasped except by faith,[32] Canévet says that as attached as

---

[25] Ibid., 141.

[26] Ibid. Völker relies on *De vita Greg. Thaum.*, GNO x. i. 10. 5–7.   [27] Ibid.

[28] Ibid., n. 7: 'In dieser hohen Wertung des Glaubens verläßt Gregor die Bahnen der christlichen Alexandriner.' In making this observation Völker has in mind an important passage from Homily 3 on the Song of Songs (*In Cant.* III, GNO VI. 87. 5–9), particularly the phrase διὰ μόνης πίστεως.

[29] Ibid., 143.   [30] Ibid.

[31] M. Canévet, *Grégoire de Nysse et l'herméneutique biblique: Étude des rapports entre le langage et la connaissance de Dieu* (Paris, 1983); see also idem, 'Grégoire de Nysse (saint)', in *Dictionnaire de Spiritualité*, s.v. Grégoire de Nysse, vol. VI (Paris, 1967), 971–1011, esp. 994–6.

[32] *In Cant.* III, GNO VI. 87. 2–8.

Gregory is to apophatic vocabulary and to the ungraspable nature of God, he does know the vocabulary of grasping. This grasping is accomplished beyond all concepts by the sole mediation of faith.[33]

Moreover, while this grasping by means of faith is not on the level of discursive thought, it is nevertheless a form of knowledge.[34] Like Völker, Canévet sees that the mediation of faith is also accompanied by divine indwelling. The *locus classicus* in this regard is the bride in Homily 6 on the Song of Songs, who, having found the Beloved by means of faith, becomes a dwelling place for God.[35] For Canévet, then, this grasping by faith results in the indwelling of the Word in the soul.[36]

But to say that faith is beyond thought should not imply that it has nothing whatever to do with discursive thought. For this '*intuition de la foi*', as Canévet terms it, attempts to translate itself into concepts even though the infinity of the divine essence be incompatible with the finite character of discursive thought.[37] According to the French scholar this is the significance of the drops of the night on the locks of the Beloved in Homily 11 on the Song of Songs.[38] In this rather cryptic text Gregory says it is not possible for the soul entering the Sanctuary to encounter torrential showers of knowledge; rather one must be content if truth but bedew one's knowledge with thoughts delicate and indistinct, these rational drops being distilled through the saints and inspired ones.[39]

Canévet says that this particular thought is often referred to by Gregory as 'that which is produced in us'.[40] As evidence she proposes David, who is 'obliged to write the Psalms because he cannot otherwise teach us the knowledge of the mysteries which is produced in him, coming from God'.[41] While indeed the divine nature cannot be grasped by the mind, one must attempt 'to unveil the intuition (ὑπόνοιαν) of

---

[33] Canévet, *Grégoire de Nysse et l'herméneutique biblique*, 62.

[34] Ibid, 63: '... cette saisie devient réellement une connaissance, car c'est la foi qui sert de médiation dans la quête apparemment vaine de l'essence divine: à travers les mots, les pensées, l'âme se tend vers Dieu: c'est la foi qui l'unit à Lui.'

[35] *In Cant.* VI, GNO VI. 183. 7–12.

[36] M. Canévet, *Grégoire de Nysse et l'herméneutique biblique*, 63: 'La saisie par la foi n'est donc pas de l'ordre de la pensée: elle consiste en l'inhabitation du Verbe dans l'âme.'

[37] Ibid.: 'cette connaissance essaie cependant de se traduire en pensées, bien que l'infinité de l'essence divine soit incompatible avec le caractère défini de nos concepts'.

[38] Ibid.

[39] *In Cant.* XI, GNO VI. 325. 21–326. 5.

[40] Canévet, *Grégoire de Nysse et l'herméneutique biblique*, 64; see *Contra Eunom.* II, 578, GNO I, 395, 2–3: ... τὴν ἐγγενομένην ὑμῖν περὶ τοῦ θείου ὑπόνοιαν.

[41] Ibid., 64. Canévet is citing *Contra Eunom.* II. 394, GNO I. 341. 20–1.

God which is produced in us'.[42] This thought, says Canévet, is like an image or imitation of the one whom we seek and which is produced in us. While it resembles what we seek it does not manifest directly its form (which no eye has seen) but as through a mirror it produces a reflection of that which is sought.[43] Finally, Canévet says, 'the intuition is obliged to enter into definite concepts in order to be expressed'.[44]

The contribution of Canévet to the understanding of faith in Gregory of Nyssa can be summarized as follows. She would seem to be in basic agreement with von Balthasar, Daniélou, and Völker that faith is properly understood in the context of Gregory's epistemology and characteristically comes into play at the zenith of an apophatic ascent. In such an apophatic context faith can be observed to do two things: faith unites and mediates.[45] While Canévet has not, as has Daniélou, described faith as an organ or faculty of knowledge, her observations would seem to harmonize well with Daniélou's. For Canévet too, faith is a faculty which unites and mediates.

But that which carries the discussion of faith across the threshold of debate into a new level of discussion is, first, her observation that Gregory's faith can somehow manage paradoxically to grasp the ungraspable. Moreover, this intuitive grasping on the part of faith constitutes in some sense knowledge of God. Second, the intuition of faith is characterized by a dynamic tendency to translate itself into concepts in order to be spoken.

In her study of grace and freedom in Gregory of Nyssa, V.E.F. Harrison likewise addresses the notion of faith.[46] At the outset of her concise treatment of faith Harrison situates the theme in its proper epistemological context. Like the other scholars we have considered, she sees the journey of Abraham as being a text of great importance[47] and observes that faith comes not at the beginning of the Patriarch's journey but at the conclusion of various stages of increasing

---

[42] Ibid. Canévet is citing *Contra Eunom.* II. 578, GNO I. 395. 2–3.

[43] Ibid. Canévet is citing *In Cant.* III, GNO VI. 86. 14–18.

[44] Ibid.: 'L'intuition est enfin obligée d'entrer dans des concepts définis pour être dite'.

[45] Each of these scholars has based his or her views largely on two texts of crucial importance to the matter in question: the migration of Abraham in *Contra Eunom.* II, GNO I. 252–3 and the experience of the bride, particularly in *In Cant.* VI, GNO VI. 182. 4–183. 13.

[46] V. Harrison, *Grace and Human Freedom according to Gregory of Nyssa,* (Lewiston, NY, 1992).

[47] *Contra Eunom.* II. 84–93, GNO I. 251–4.

knowledge.[48] In other words, faith comes into play at the apex of an epistemological ascent, 'a pilgrimage of the mind'.[49]

Harrison would query those scholars who claim there is no knowledge of God in Gregory and who conclude that there is only faith as a sort of consolation prize. According to Harrison these scholars would view Abraham's experience as a vain quest for the impossible (i.e. knowledge of God), a quest which Abraham ultimately abandons, settling for faith.[50] The Orthodox scholar has specifically in mind Barmann and Heine.

Barmann thinks Gregory contrasts faith with knowledge. 'When knowledge fails faith provides a kind of possession or presence of what cannot be possessed by knowledge.... [F]aith brings not knowledge but darkness.'[51] According to Heine, Gregory teaches that 'man does not relate to God primarily by knowledge,... but by faith which reaches out beyond knowledge'.[52]

According to Harrison both Barmann and Heine fail to pay sufficient attention to the Eunomian context and therefore miss an important point: 'It is not all knowledge but knowledge in the Eunomian sense that Gregory contrasts with faith. Abraham really does know God as he manifests himself in his creative activity. Only when Abraham tries to reach beyond this to the divine essence does he find not knowledge but faith.'[53]

Having argued for the epistemological status of faith, she identifies the function of faith as that of bridging the ontological gulf between the created and the uncreated. Faith 'brings us into a relation with the divine essence'.[54] In saying this Harrison joins the ranks of von Balthasar, Daniélou, Völker, and Canévet, all of whom acknowledge that faith performs this function of union.

Franz Dünzl's study of the *Commentarius in Canticum canticorum* devotes several pages to the theme of faith.[55] Following Völker, Dünzl maintains that Gregory departs from the Alexandrian understanding of faith as

[48] Harrison, *Grace and Human Freedom*, 64.   [49] Ibid.   [50] Ibid., 66–7.

[51] B. Barmann, 'The Cappadocian Triumph over Arianism' (Ph.D. thesis, Stanford University, 1966), 396–7.

[52] R. Heine, *Perfection in the Virtuous Life: A Study of the Relationship between Edification and Polemical Theology in Gregory of Nyssa's 'De Vita Moysis'* (Cambridge, Mass., 1975), 144. It should be noted that on 146 Heine quotes *Contra Eunom.* II. 91, GNO I. 253. 25–8.

[53] Harrison, *Grace and Human Freedom*, 67.

[54] Ibid.

[55] F. Dünzl, *Braut und Bräutigam: Die Auslegung des Canticum durch Gregor von Nyssa* (Tübingen, 1993).

something which must be surpassed through knowledge.[56] Nor is faith some sort of 'alternative or corrective to theology'.[57] Dünzl would agree with others, especially with Canévet, that faith is the means of becoming 'beast of burden and dwelling place of God'.[58] Faith transcends both thought and speech, but in this process theology is neither absolutized nor negated.[59] Thought, which by nature seeks to grasp, seeks God who cannot be grasped. Faith resolves this aporia: the 'grasp of faith'[60] does not violate divine incomprehensibility. Faith does not render thought superfluous because the thought's seeking implies a continuous process of detachment.

Dünzl's treatment, then, acknowledges not only the exalted status of faith in Gregory of Nyssa, but also the harmonious relationship with thought which faith nevertheless transcends.

One of the more sustained treatments of faith to date has been Bernard Pottier's recent study of the *Contra Eunomium*. Just as thought has priority over language in Gregory of Nyssa, so, according to Pottier, faith has priority over knowledge.[61] While Pottier would seem to agree with Harrison that the movement into faith is a movement of the mind,[62] Pottier goes on to suggest that, even though faith and know-ledge are epistemological categories,[63] there is a marked discontinuity between knowledge and faith. While Gregory's earlier writings, says Pottier, may well have allowed for more of a continuity between the two, the controversy with Eunomius marks a threshold in the Cappado-cian's thought, beyond which 'thought is more radically refused access to the encounter with God'.[64] For this reason, then, Pottier says that 'the passage from knowledge to faith appears as a rupture'.[65] For Pottier the

---

[56] Ibid., 295–6.   [57] Ibid., 296.

[58] Ibid.: 'Gregor sieht in der πίστις vielmehr das (einzige) Mittel, "Jochtier" und "Wohnung" Gottes zu werden.'

[59] Ibid.   [60] Ibid., 297: 'Zugriff des Glaubens'.

[61] Pottier, *Dieu et le Christ*, 207. In an overall positive review of Pottier's book, C. Kannengieser laments that Pottier's treatment of the priority of faith over thought is '*trop discret*'; see *Revue des Études Augustiniennes* 42 (1996), 181–4, at 182.

[62] Harrison, *Grace and Human Freedom*, 64, describes the ascent to faith as a 'pilgrimage of the mind'; Pottier, *Dieu et le Christ*, 207, describes it as 'la recherche de Dieu par l'esprit humain...'.

[63] Pottier clearly says so on 214: 'Πίστις et γνῶσις deviennent ainsi deux catégories à teneur épistémologique...'.

[64] Ibid., 'Il semble que avec la polémique eunomienne, "la critique du langage...est devenue extrême", et la rencontre de Dieu, refusée plus radicalement à la pensée.' Pottier cites M. Canévet, *Grégoire de Nysse et l'herméneutique biblique*, 52.

[65] Ibid., 207: 'Le passage de la connaissance à la foi... se donne comme une rupture.'

'radical metaphysical rupture between the created and Uncreated' is the model for the distinction between faith and knowledge.[66] Harrison, by contrast, would seem to be more cautious, and probably more accurate, when she says that in this pilgrimage of the mind faith 'surpasses' knowledge.[67] Nevertheless, Pottier's observation leads him to assert that there is a certain development in Gregory's thought: 'before the *Contra Eunomium*, God is accessible by thought; with the *Contra Eunomium*, God is rigorously unknowable for thought; in the mystical works, while commenting on the journey of Abraham, of Moses, or of the bride in the *In Canticum*, Gregory maintains the positive encounter with God beyond all thought'.[68]

Pottier summarizes Gregory's doctrine as follows: 'The general teaching of Gregory is that the knowledge which does not attain to *what* God is, comes to us through the energies, but that faith, in the night, touches God as he is—but it is not knowledge.'[69] Moreover, faith is oriented towards (*acheminée vers*) this 'beyond knowing'.[70]

A final work to be considered in this survey of research on Gregorian faith is that by Claudia Desalvo.[71] Desalvo is aware of the immediate epistemological implications of Gregory's concept of God as infinite. Since God cannot be grasped by concepts, there must be a new cognitive approach, an approach which Gregory identifies as faith.

The value of Desalvo's treatment lies in her illustration of the epistemological innovation involved in Gregorian faith. Desalvo observes how Gregory has made, by his exaltation of faith, some dramatic adjustments to the traditional Platonic levels of knowledge. Gregory has removed faith from the sphere of opinion and placed it at the top of the noetic sphere, above knowledge.[72] This departure of Gregory, she claims, is not surprising, for he grounds his epistemology in his ontological distinction between infinite creator and finite creature,[73] an

---

[66] Ibid., 214. Pottier clearly says so on 214: 'Πίστις et γνῶσις deviennent ainsi deux catégories à teneur épistémologique ...'.

[67] Harrison, *Grace and Human Freedom*, 69. I will have more to say about the continuity and discontinuity between faith and knowledge in Gregory of Nyssa.

[68] Pottier, *Dieu et le Christ*, 207–8.

[69] Ibid., 209: 'La doctrine générale de Grégoire est que la connaissance qui n'atteint pas *ce que* Dieu est, nous vient par les énergies, mais que la foi, dans la nuit, touche Dieu tel qu'il est—ce n'est pourtant pas une connaissance.'

[70] Ibid.

[71] Claudia Desalvo, *L' 'oltre' nel presente: La filosofia dell' uomo in Gregorio di Nissa* (Milan, 1996), 215–35.

[72] Ibid., 223; see *Republic* VI. 511 d–e.

[73] For a concise statement of this distinction see *In Cant.* VI, GNO VI. 173–4.

ontological presupposition which Plato did not share. For Gregory, faith opens up a new cognitive path.

In her survey of representative texts, then, she can identify two levels of Gregorian faith. One level is characterized by an awareness of the ontological limits of our cognitive capacity. According to Desalvo, faith does not constitute a cognitive step towards the divine but rather a renunciation of knowledge. Nevertheless it stays within the limits of discursive reason and does not attempt to cross over the boundary between finite creature and infinite creator. Desalvo considers this to be a philosophical concept of faith. But Desalvo also acknowledges a higher level of faith. More than just a renunciation of knowledge, faith opens the way to union with God. This is not simply a recognition of the infinity and unknowability of God but is also the way of uniting with God, towards whom the energy of reason tends. Since God is infinite, the cognitive journey opened up by faith is also without limit; it is epistemology rooted in ontology.

New Directions

This survey of research on the topic of faith in Gregory of Nyssa yields a fairly homogenous consensus based on a more or less fixed collection of texts. Faith performs functions of mediation between the mind and God and is the faculty that unites one to God. Although Gregory himself does not explicitly say that faith is a faculty or *dynamis*, the fact that it performs functions of mediation and union leads us to agree with Daniélou that to conceive of faith as a faculty is helpful in viewing Gregory's largely idiosyncratic way of speaking of faith in certain epistemological and apophatic contexts.

While von Balthasar was amongst the first to observe the exalted epistemological role of faith and to identify these functions of mediation and union seen in the famous ascent of Abraham in the *Contra Eunomium*, he seems either to have changed his mind or to have lost sight of this observation when speaking of Denys the Areopagite and Maximus the Confessor in a subsequent essay, 'Fides Christi'. In this essay von Balthasar says that

to an ever increasing extent in the philosophy of late antiquity, the *excessus*, beyond all γνῶσις, which is the true organ for the encounter with God, bears the name πίστις. But this πίστις and the apophatic approach of a 'philosophical' theology keep their connection with Christian theology because of the work of Dionysius the Areopagite and Maximus the Confessor. They accomplished this so thoroughly that it was put in the very centre of theology and—as high scholasticism shows—Christian thought can no longer ignore their legacy.[74]

The statement is curious indeed. Not that Denys and Maximus did not consider faith 'the true organ for the encounter with God',[75] but that von Balthasar would seem to give them credit and not Gregory of Nyssa. While indeed it may be argued that Denys and Maximus the Confessor have exerted greater influence on the West, it would seem that von Balthasar's own research suggests that Gregory of Nyssa would be the one responsible for the aforementioned. For before either Denys or Maximus it was Gregory of Nyssa who broke with the great master Origen and the general thrust of the Alexandrian tradition by overcoming knowledge through faith.

Not only is there consensus that faith performs this mediation and union, but, beginning with Canévet, who is in turn followed by Dünzl, there are other important characteristics: though faith is beyond concepts it tends to translate itself into concepts. Hence, David is obliged to write the Psalms and the bride is obliged to speak to her maiden companions of her ineffable encounters with the Beloved.

If these various components constitute the basic parameters of the *status quaestionis* concerning faith, how could one propose to advance the question? Several possible new directions present themselves for consideration.

(A) Von Balthasar makes an explicit connection between faith and darkness.[76] Von Balthasar is but one of the many scholars who have highlighted Gregory's 'mysticism of darkness'. While we agree with the connection between faith and darkness, we feel the need to adjust the view that Gregory's mystical theology is fundamentally a mysticism of darkness. We say *adjust* rather than *correct*. For while Gregory's view of the spiritual life involves without doubt what can be called a mysticism of darkness (but only when the scriptural texts upon which he is commenting dispose him to do so), it is only part of the picture. Indeed text after text, especially in the *Commentarius in Canticum canticorum*, suggests that Gregory's mystical theology is no less one of light than

[74] 'Fides Christi', in *Spouse of the Word: Explorations in Theology II*, trans. E. Oakes (San Francisco, 1991), 76 f.

[75] See *De div. nom.* VII. 4.

[76] von Balthasar, *Présence et Pensée*, 73–4, where he identifies πίστις with θεία νύξ.

one of darkness, and that faith, in the exalted sense with which the present study is concerned, has to do with both light and darkness.

A celebrated and beautiful passage from the Homily 11 on the Song of Songs depicts the spiritual life as a progressive movement into darkness.[77] This text has led scholars to conclude that Gregory, in contrast to Origen, conceives the spiritual life as a movement into the divine darkness.[78] But our reading of Gregory of Nyssa suggests this estimation is in need of redress. For there are any number of texts, in fact the majority of relevant texts, which speak of the spiritual life in the language of light and of movement into light. Nor are these texts necessarily about less advanced stages of the spiritual life, for many of them refer to the very divinization of the soul. A passage from Homily 5 on the Song of Songs, which speaks of divine indwelling as the work of the Holy Spirit in the decidedly luminous imagery of daylight pouring forth its rays and removing the shadows of life, is but one of numerous examples.[79]

Perhaps more representative of Gregory's thought on the subject is an equally beautiful, yet more succinct, description of the spiritual life. In Homily 12 on the Song of Songs Moses ascends through various stages, enters a cloud, and then enters the darkness where God is. But Moses then becomes like the sun, unable to be approached by others.[80] Moses enters the darkness where God is but becomes light; he stays in the darkness of unknowing but is deified in light. This text, with its interplay of both light and darkness, seems to me to be more representative of the subtle word-play, of the consistent intermingling of the luminous and the obscure and especially of Gregory's ubiquitous liking for the oxymoronic throughout the broad sweep of the *Commentarius in Canticum canticorum*.[81] If indeed Gregory of Nyssa is a mystic of darkness, he is no less one of light.

(B) From the outset of our survey we have seen that the exalted role of faith has been placed in rather bold epistemological relief by virtually all the scholars we have considered. Desalvo has noted how this is an intended departure from the general lines of Platonic epistemological

---

[77] *In Cant.* XI, GNO VI. 322–4.

[78] See for example A. Louth's helpful presentation of Gregory's mystical theory in *Origins of the Christian Mystical Tradition: From Plato to Denys* (Oxford, 1981), 80–97.

[79] *In Cant.* XI, GNO VI. 169.

[80] *In Cant.* XII, GNO VI. 355. 11–14.

[81] Harrison takes a similar view; see *Grace and Human Freedom*, 72–3 and 86–7.

tradition based on Gregory's ontological distinction between infinite creator and finite creature.[82]

Going back to Plato himself, we see that faith was amongst the lowest forms of knowledge possible and to be superseded by progressively higher forms of knowledge.[83] The *Republic* provides the *locus classicus*. At the end of Book VI Plato presents his well-known Allegory of the Line. Here (511d–e) faith has no access to ultimate truth, being limited to common sense assurance about things. Access to ultimate truth is attained by ἐπιστήμη in the sphere of νόησις. For Gregory of Nyssa, by contrast, it is faith which has access to ultimate truth. This is indeed a radical departure from Plato, and Desalvo has done well to point out that Gregory has grounded this new epistemological view of faith in ontology; I wish to build on this and take it further by claiming, with the migration of Abraham as the case in point, not only that Gregory's epistemology is rooted in his ontology, as Desalvo has shown, but that this epistemology is rooted in exegesis. Indeed Desalvo has hinted at this. I wish to make it more explicit by showing that Gregory's important treatment of the migration of Abraham is from beginning to end guided by Gregory's reading of Paul.

(C) We may ask, moreover, what is the relationship between faith and the mind? Völker, in agreement with von Balthasar and Daniélou, acknowledges the mediational role of faith but then goes on to suggest that, as in Philo, faith is not a technical term, but rather a word with a wide range of meanings such as credibility, fidelity, demonstration. But in general faith signifies the relationship between God and the human person. Völker's position, however, would seem to be open to considerable question.

The word 'faith' occurs with relative frequency in Gregory's writings.[84] There is indeed a wide range of meaning. But the clear *minority* of these occurrences demonstrates faith in this exalted sense of a faculty which mediates and unites the mind to God. The vast majority displays a variety of general meanings such as notional assent,[85] considered

---

[82] Desalvo, *L' 'oltre' nel presente*, 223–4; this point has likewise been made by A. Meredith, *The Cappadocians* (London, 1995), 67 and 88–9.

[83] Dodds, *Pagan and Christian*, 120–3.

[84] For example, the *Thesaurus Linguae Graecae* produces some 350 matches for the forms of πιστεύω and for πίστις (and its oblique forms) in the *Contra Eunomium*, 68 matches in *De vita Moysis*, and 137 matches in the *Commentarius in Canticum canticorum*.

[85] e.g. *Contra Eunom.* 1. 23. 1, GNO 1. 88. 23; 219, GNO 1. 90. 14; 220, GNO 1. 90. 24.

opinion,[86] or an item of faith or creed.[87] Only the minority of occurrences reveals faith in its exalted role of that which bridges the gap between mind and God, and it is with this sense that the present study will concern itself.

Furthermore, Völker claims that Gregory does not use faith in a technical sense. I would suggest quite the opposite—that this is a helpful way to view Gregory's reserved use of faith and the role this reserved use plays in his thought as a whole. Virtually all the significant uses of faith in this exalted sense occur either as an object of the preposition *dia* or as the instrumental dative. Gregory does this often enough to lead one to the conclusion that he employs faith as a technical term denoting that faculty of union which bridges the gap between the mind and God and which mediates knowledge (in a qualified sense).[88] We see this clearly, for example, in Homily 3 on the Song, where Gregory speaks of the soul which is led through conceptions to an understanding of the ungraspable by faith alone and which establishes in itself a nature that transcends intelligence.[89] Faith is used in the dative singular in this same epistemological sense in Homily 6, where the bride searches for the Beloved in darkness and finally finds him 'by means of faith'. Immediately after this Gregory uses the same instrumental sense of faith when the bride says that she will never let go of the Beloved once he has been found by the grasp of faith.[90]

---

[86] e.g. *Contra Eunom.* I. 376, GNO I. 137. 22; 384, GNO I. 139. 16; 406, GNO I. 145. 18.

[87] e.g. *Contra Eunom.* I. 122, GNO I. 64. 9; 127, GNO I. 65. 18; 137, GNO I 68. 15.

[88] Speaking of πίστις in this same exalted sense in *De vita Greg. Thaum.*, GNO x. i. 10. 5–7, R. Hübner, in his book *Die Einheit des Leibes Christi bei Gregor von Nyssa* (Leiden, 1974), 189, says that 'Glaube hat in diesen Aussagen sicherlich eine sehr viel umfassendere Bedeutung.... Glaube kann auf diese Weise ein weites Bedeutungsfeld haben.' Our contention, while acknowledging that Gregory speaks of faith in a variety of senses, will maintain that when Gregory speaks of πίστις as something above intelligence he is not using it in a general or wide sense at all, but rather in a quite specific, indeed technical, sense.

[89] *In Cant.* III, GNO VI. 87. 5–8: τὴν οὖν διὰ τῶν τοιούτων νοημάτων χειραγωγουμένην ψυχὴν πρὸς τὴν τῶν ἀλήπτων περίνοιαν διὰ μόνης πίστεως εἰσοικίζειν ἐν ἑαυτῇ λέγει δεῖν τὴν πάντα νοῦν ὑπερέχουσαν φύσιν. Several other texts employ the formulation διὰ μόνης πίστεως: *Contra Eunom.* I. 371. 4, GNO I. 136. 17; *Contra Eunom.* III. 8, GNO II. 243. 11; and *De hom. op.*, PG 44, 208B; and *In Cant.* III, GNO VI. 87. 15 shows divine indwelling being mediated διὰ πίστεως.

[90] *In Cant.* VI, GNO VI. 183. 7–9: καὶ πᾶσαν καταληπτικὴν ἔφοδον καταλιποῦσα, τῇ πίστει εὗρον τὸν ἀγαπώμενον καὶ οὐκέτι μεθήσω τῇ τῆς πίστεως τοῦ εὑρεθέντος ἀντεχομένη ...

Further still, Völker suggests that Gregory leaves to one side the question of the relationship between faith and knowledge and between faith and grace. This too seems open to question. In *De virginitate*, arguably his earliest work, Gregory considers David in ecstasy. Gregory says that David contemplated the intelligibles 'through the mind alone'.[91] Gregory uses the word *dianoia* for mind or faculty of (discursive) knowledge. But by the time Gregory composes the *Contra Eunomium* and speaks of a similar ascent, this time by Abraham, faith, not mind, is the means of approach—not the intelligibles as before but beyond them into the non-discursive realm. And in one of Gregory's latest works, *Commentarius in Canticum canticorum*,[92] the same experience is attained 'through faith alone'.[93] This is a noteworthy development on the part of Gregory. What at the beginning of his career took place only through mind, becomes, through the Eunomian controversy, something that takes place only through faith. In light of this is it likely that Gregory did not consider the relationship between faith and knowledge?

There is a paucity of texts which speak explicitly of faith and grace. On the other hand, however, it would be extraordinary indeed to assert that Gregory saw no relation whatever between the two. For Gregory the mind itself is the subject of grace, without which it could never embark upon its ascents. We see this clearly in *De vita Moysis*, for example, when the grace of baptism purifies mind and puts to death its 'grabbing' tendency,[94] or when sacred scripture (the grace of revelation) leads the mind (χειραγωγεῖ τὴν διάνοιαν).[95] For Gregory of Nyssa, then, the mind is immersed in and guided by grace.

When the bride in Homily 6 on the Song, for example, having let go of all concepts, finds the ever-elusive Beloved by means of faith, this happens at the height of the ascent of graced *dianoia*[96]. It would hardly seem likely that the grace which has purified mind and taken it by the hand at the beginning of the process would be somehow absent, as this ascent comes to fruition in the grasp of faith.

---

[91]   *De virg.*, SC, x. 2. 9: διὰ μόνης διανοίας.

[92]   On the chronology of Gregory's works see J. Daniélou, 'La chronologie des œuvres de Grégoire de Nysse', *Studia Patristica* 7 (Texte und Untersuchungen 92, Berlin, 1966), 159–69; G. May, 'Die Chronologie des Lebens und der Werke des Gregor von Nyssa,' in M. Harl (ed.), *Écriture et culture philosophique dans la pensée de Grégoire de Nysse* (Leiden, 1971), 51–67; see also J. Cahill, 'The Date and Setting of Gregory of Nyssa's "Commentary on the Song of Songs"', *Journal of Theological Studies* 32 (1981), 447–60.

[93]   *In Cant.* III, GNO VI. 87. 7.   [94]   *De vita Moysis*, SC, II. 125. 10.

[95]   Ibid., II. 152. 2: χειραγωγεῖ τὴν διάνοιαν.

[96]   *In Cant.* VI, GNO VI. 182. 5 f.

In drawing attention to the relationship between knowledge and faith and to the relationship between grace and faith, Völker has raised an important question. But his solution, that Gregory has simply left the question to one side, is untenable. Indeed to understand properly Gregory's concept of exalted faith, this relationship between mind and faith will need considerable examination.

(D) Amongst the scholars we have considered there is a general consensus that faith, in its exalted sense, operates in the realm of the apophatic. Like *gnophos*, faith is part of Gregory's apophatic vocabulary. But there is another aspect of Gregory's notion of exalted faith which stands in dialectical tension with its properly apophatic role. This characteristic has been hinted at, it seems to me, by Canévet (and to a certain extent by Dünzl). Canévet identifies an important characteristic of faith both when she says that it is a form of knowledge and especially when she observes that the intuitions of faith attempt to translate themselves into concepts.[97] This idea is not developed to any extent. But it can be seen often enough in the Cappadocian (with or without the explicit mention of faith) to merit investigation. I propose that it reveals another dimension of Gregory's thought which stands in tension with the more readily acknowledged apophatic dimension. I propose the neologism '*logophasis*' to designate that dynamic tendency of faith to express itself in concepts and language after it has reached the heights of apophatic ascent typified by the letting-go of such concepts and language. Logophatic discourse, then, is to be distinguished from kataphatic discourse. If *kataphasis* involves language that is searching for God, *logophasis*, as we shall see, involves language that is full of God. This would be yet another of the coincidences of opposites that is fairly typical of Gregory of Nyssa. One example among many can be seen in Homily 1 on the Song of Songs.

The bride wishes to touch the good.[98] By virtue of the kiss of the Beloved, the bride searched the depths of God within the innermost Sanctuary. Note that in this encounter with God there is no mention of faith. But because of what he has said elsewhere and more specifically about the dynamics of union, one may assume its presence in the bride. The thrust of this passage is interior and apophatic.[99] However, the

---

[97] Canévet, *Grégoire de Nysse et l'herméneutique biblique*, 63–4.

[98] *In Cant.* I, GNO VI. 40. 2 f. ψαύω and the language of touch in general is part of Gregory's vocabulary of union.

[99] For Gregory there is but imageless silence in the sanctuary.

tenor changes, and the bride, having stood face to face with the Word, has suddenly become a source of nourishment for others as she feeds those who are infants in Christ.[100]

This encounter with God is immediately followed by another encounter along similar lines. John places his heart like a sponge on the Lord's breast, the fountain of life, and is filled by an ineffable (ἄρρητος) transmission of the hidden mysteries in the heart of the Lord. The apophatic context, albeit subtle, is clearly present. But then John takes the breast of the Word, upon which he has lain, and offers us the good things he has received and he *proclaims* the Word who exists from all ages.[101] An encounter which started out as apophatic (ἄρρητος) has of its own dynamism become 'logophatic'.

Another example is seen in Homily 3 on the Song of Songs. Paul (or the soul) becomes a dwelling place through faith, a vessel of election,[102] and reveals Christ living and speaking in him.[103] Here faith mediates a process of union whose apophatic context has been established a little earlier.[104] But balancing, or standing in tension with, this apophatic thrust is a 'logophatic' one: Christ speaking within.[105]

Each of these examples, and there are many more, reveal a similar structure. In each case something happens and something follows. There is contact or union with God in an apophatic context; this union is either explicitly or implicitly mediated by faith. However, this apophatic dimension does not rest alone: the bride yet feeds the infants in Christ through the breast of the Word, with whom she is one; John turns round and offers us the teat of the Word and fills us with the good things he himself received; and Christ dwelling within Paul speaks. This second phase, following the apophatic phase, I term '*logophasis*'.

---

[100] *In Cant.* i, GNO vi. 41. 3–4.

[101] Ibid. 41. 6–13.

[102] This image of a vessel which can be filled will be of some importance for understanding Gregory's notion of divinization and virtue. Cf. the image of the crystal vase at *In Cant.* xv, GNO vi. 441. 12–15, where this motif is even stronger: the clear vase reveals on the outside what lies within: lilies of radiant virtue.

[103] *In Cant.* iii, GNO vi. 87. 15–88. 6.

[104] Ibid. 87. 5–8: τὴν οὖν διὰ τῶν τοιούτων νοημάτων χειραγωγουμένην ψυχὴν πρὸς τὴν τῶν ἀλήπτων περίνοιαν διὰ μόνης πίστεως εἰσοικίζειν ἐν ἑαυτῇ λέγει δεῖν τὴν πάντα νοῦν ὑπερέχουσαν φύσιν.

[105] Ibid. 88. 4–6: ἐν δὲ τῷ μηκέτι αὐτὸν ζῆν, ἀλλ᾽ ἐν ἑαυτῷ δεικνύειν ζῶντα ἐκεῖνον καὶ δοκιμὴν διδόναι τοῦ ἐν αὐτῷ λαλοῦντος Χριστοῦ οἶκος περιληπτικὸς τῆς ἀπεριλήπτου γενόμενος φύσεως.

These themes having been announced, this study will unfold in the following manner. Chapters 2 and 3 are to be taken more or less in tandem. Chapter 2 will have as its purpose to describe in some detail what Gregory has to say about the discursive and non-discursive capabilities of the mind in the context of grace. This will be helpful for establishing the backdrop against which the specific role of faith may be seen in bolder relief in Chapter 3. Chapter 3 will then examine the significant occurrences of exalted faith with a view to designating what Gregory means when he uses faith as a technical term. With this technical sense clearly established, Chapter 4 will attempt to situate this faculty of apophatic union in the more general history of the Hellenic concern for such a mediating faculty; whilst Gregorian faith is rather idiosyncratic, the designation of a mediating faculty of union has clear parallels in Gregory's cultural heritage.

While Chapters 3 and 4 clearly emphasize the apophatic context in which exalted faith operates, Chapter 5 will explore how Gregory yet values propositional, orthodox teaching and grounds this in the experience of God. Chapter 5 serves to prepare the ground for examining a largely unnoticed dimension of Gregory's apophaticism, which I have termed *logophasis*: the Word's tendency to express Itself through the deeds and discourse of those who experience apophatic communion with the Word. Finally, in Chapter 7 the question of Gregory's mysticism of darkness will be examined with a view to redressing the over-identification of Gregory with this theme.

2

The Flow of the Mind

Introduction

In order to understand the exalted epistemological sense which Gregory bestows on the term *pistis* it is necessary to view it in the context of what Gregory has to say about the mind itself. Gregory has no single term to designate the mind or intelligence, but *dianoia* and *nous* are among the most frequent. For our specific purpose of studying the significance of faith as a technical term as well as its role in his thought, the term *dianoia* is the more helpful for approaching the topic. Hence, we shall consider Gregory's understanding of the mind through the lens of *dianoia* as it occurs principally in three works: *De virginitate, De vita Moysis* and *Commentarius in Canticum canticorum*.[1] Lexical work in Gregory of Nyssa is being greatly facilitated by the appearance of the *Lexicon Gregorianum*.[2] The entry under *dianoia* reveals a fairly wide and indeed frequent usage relating to various functions and states of the discursive mind. A general term for thinking, thoughts, understanding, *dianoia* can also refer to decision-making, reflection, recognition, perception; it is subject to influence by the passions and also has limited access to God.[3] In looking at *dianoia* I will pay particular attention to different states of awareness

---

[1] I have decided for a number of reasons to focus upon these works in particular: *De virginitate* suggests itself for consideration because it manifests in a fairly sustained manner the awareness of the problem that the discursive mind poses for ascetic training. The other two works are important not only for the occurrence of πίστις in the technical sense in which I am interested, but also because of the opportunity they afford for attaining some understanding of the relationship between the mind and πίστις. An auxiliary reason for choosing these works is that, taken together, they span Gregory's career, which has the minor advantage of getting a sense of the broad sweep of things.

[2] F. Mann (ed.), *Lexicon Gregorianum: Wörterbuch zu den Schriften Gregors von Nyssa* (Leiden, 1999–).

[3] *Lexicon Gregorianum*, vol. ii, s.v. διάνοια, 341–55.

which the mind exhibits, i.e. involvement with the world of sensuality and passions, contemplation of the intelligibles, the mind in the presence of God, as well as the mind's need of assistance, particularly from scripture and baptism.

The Mind and Passions

The Thick Mind

What happens to the mind when it is involved in the world of sensuality or passions? Gregory has various ways of describing what happens to the mind in such cases. In chapter IV of *De virginitate* he describes as 'thick' that mind which looks down to the pleasures of the body as do cattle to their pasture, living only for their stomachs.[4] Plato uses a very similar image in *The Republic* to describe those people who, lacking wisdom and virtue and devoted to satisfying their hunger, are like grazing cattle, 'with eyes ever bent upon the earth and heads bowed down over their tables'.[5] In *The Nicomachean Ethics* Aristotle uses the same image to describe people who, enslaved to their senses, live like cattle.[6] But Gregory draws attention to the effect this bovine life has on the mind. Thus in *De virginitate* XI he claims that the majority of people live habitually in this same 'thickness of mind'.[7]

If Gregory does not describe as cows such people who are preoccupied with the life of physical pleasure, he likens them to pigs. With their minds (*dianoia*) turned towards the passions of flesh and blood, they are like pigs who have their eyes always looking down to the ground and never up towards heavenly beauty.[8]

What is the result of this thickening of *dianoia*? Gregory says it results in alienation from the life of God (Eph. 4: 18) and from the covenants of the promise (Eph. 2: 12).[9] Elsewhere Gregory says that this thickness of mind renders people incapable of distinguishing by means of reason; nor can they separate matter from the beauty perceived therein and from

---

[4] *De virg.*, SC, iv. 5. 1–4.   [5] *Rep.* ix. 586a: ἀλλὰ βοσκενημάτων.
[6] *Eth. Nic.* 1095ᵇ20: βοσκημάτων βίον.
[7] *De virg.*, SC, xi. 2. 2: παχύτητι τῆς διανοίας. According to Aubineau (318 n. 3) this thickness is due to involvement of the senses. See *Orat. cat.* viii. 6, GNO iii. iv. 31. 2). Gregory Nazianzen uses the term in a similar way; see for example *Orat.*, SC, xx. 19. 9; xxxi. 30. 7–8.
[8] Ibid., v. 1–15.   [9] Ibid., iv. 5. 5.

coming to know the nature of beauty itself.[10] It would seem, then, that knowledge of beauty is the proper function of *dianoia*, but its capacity to get entangled in the realm of the senses causes it to grow thick and obstruct its more natural tendency.

The Dispersed Mind

In *De virginitate* VI Gregory offers Elijah and John as models for those who seek union with God. They separated themselves from worldly concerns; their abstemious life in the desert freed them from becoming accustomed to the illusions which come through the senses and which cause them to become confused and fall into error in judging what is good.[11] Life in the desert freed them from disturbances to the senses (taste, hearing, sight). Thus Elijah and John were established in calm and stillness and consequently they were raised up by divine grace.[12] Gregory goes on to say that we can learn from these two biblical figures: anyone who desires to be united to God should not allow the mind to be concerned with worldly things, for this would seem to disperse the mind and prevent it from proceeding directly to the knowledge of God.[13]

This metaphor of the dispersed mind is set in yet bolder relief when Gregory compares the mind to a flowing stream. He says that if water were dispersed into different streams as it emerged from its source, it would be of no use for farming. But if someone could bring together these different streams and collect what had been dispersed, the collected water could be put to useful purpose.[14] This is rather like the mind (*nous*), says Gregory. If it flows in every direction, it becomes dispersed by following what brings pleasure to the senses and has no power for the journey to the good.[15] But if the mind were drawn together, it would move according to its own energy, and nothing would impede its being borne aloft and touching the truth of beings.[16] Gregory suggests that this flow of the mind towards the spiritual realm happens more or less of

---

[10] *De virg.*, SC, XI. 2. 3–4. Cf. *Enn.* I. 6. 3. 8.   [11] Ibid., VI. 1. 7–10.

[12] Ibid., VI. 1. 18–20.

[13] Ibid., VI. 1. 42–6: Τὸ καθ' ὁμοιότητα τῶν ἁγίων ἀνδρῶν μηδενὶ τῶν βιωτικῶν πραγμάτων προσασχολεῖν τὴν διάνοιαν τὸν ἐπιθυμοῦντα τῷ θεῷ συναφθῆναι. Οὐδὲ γάρ ἐστι δυνατὸν τὸν εἰς πολλὰ τῇ διανοίᾳ διαχεόμενον πρὸς θεοῦ κατανόησιν καὶ ἐπιθυμίαν εὐθυπορῆσαι.

[14] Ibid., VI. 2. 1–11.   [15] Ibid., VI. 2. 11–14.

[16] Ibid., VI. 2. 17–19: κατὰ φύσιν ἐνέργειαν κινοῖτο, οὐδὲν τὸ κωλύον αὐτὸν ἔσται πρὸς τὰ ἄνω φέρεσθαι καὶ τῆς ἀληθείας τῶν ὄντων ἐφάπτεσθαι. On the phrase ἀληθείας ἐφάπτηται, cf. Plato, *Sym.* 212a, and *Timaeus* 90c.

itself. Just as when water enclosed in a pipe goes up because it can flow nowhere else, so the mind (*nous*) constrained by a pipe of self-control will be raised up by a natural sort of movement to a desire for loftier things.[17]

While Gregory implies that the mind has a natural tendency to go down,[18] he also claims that the mind, with suitable ascetic support, will rise upwards and will be borne aloft. But note that if it is unaided by ascetic practice, as we saw in the case of Elijah and John, the mind has a tendency to flow down into sensible pleasures, to disperse, to become thick. We shall have more to say about this later in this chapter when we consider the relationship between the mind and grace, but for the present purpose what seems even more obvious than whether or not the mind can ascend unaided, or tends only to flow downwards when unaided, is the perpetually *dynamic* character of the mind implied by the fluid imagery of water and dispersion. Gregory says that the mind, because of the nature it received from its Creator, cannot stand still; it is in perpetual movement.[19] It is only a question of the direction of the mind's flow: will it flow downwards and become dispersed among what is pleasing to the senses or will it flow upwards to the spiritual realm? Ascetic practice, such as that exemplified by Elijah and John, would seem to render a person incapable of not ascending directly towards the spiritual realm.[20] Hence, after suitable ascetic training, the mind would appear to be in perpetual ascent.[21]

Though the theme of perpetual movement is something of a hallmark of Gregory's thought, it is well to note that it is not a concept unique to him. Indeed there are noteworthy adumbrations of Gregory's *leitmotif* in the Alexandrine tradition to which he was heir. Philo of Alexandria, for example, draws attention to the perpetual movement of the soul. 'The soul', he says, 'is perpetually in movement and can turn ten thousand

[17] Ibid., vi. 2. 19–26. Aubineau notes that the image of a pipe is used by Gregory of Nazianzus in a similar way in *Orat*. 37. 12.

[18] Ibid., vi. 2. 21–2: καὶ ταῦτα κατωφεροῦς αὐτῷ τῆς κατὰ φύσιν οὔσης κινήσεως,...

[19] Ibid., vi. 2. 26–8: Οὔτε γὰρ στῆναί ποτε δύναται τὸ ἀεικίνητον ὑπὸ τοῦ πεποιηκότος εἰληφὸς τὴν φύσιν....

[20] Ibid., vi. 2. 28–31: καὶ εἰς τὰ μάταια κεχρῆσθαι τῇ κινήσει κωλυόμενον ἀμήχανον μὴ πρὸς τὴν ἀλήθειαν πάντως εὐθυπορῆσαι, τῷ πανταχόθεν ἀπὸ τῶν ἀτόπων ἀπείργεσθαι.

[21] Ascetic practice, however, does not seem to involve exterminating the passions, so much as training them. We see this very clearly in the role of Solomon in Homily 1 on the Song of Songs, where Gregory exhorts one to be passionate about the search for God; see *In Cant.* i, GNO vi. 23. 8–9.

different ways.'[22] In another text Philo has Moses speak of 'the cities of
the Levites as "ransomed forever," because the worshipper of God has
reaped eternal freedom, and while in the continuous flux of the soul
change succeeds change, healing also succeeds healing in him'.[23] In a
very intriguing and largely pejorative analysis of the senses and emotions,
Philo presents a brief phenomenology of vision. He observes that 'whilst
the eyes when open are constant and unceasing in their activities; they
have always room for more, and in this way they shew their kinship with
the soul. But... the soul is always in motion and wakeful day and
night....'[24] While the theme of the mind's perpetual movement plays
a notably less obvious role in Philo than in Gregory of Nyssa, it is
nevertheless present. Perhaps closer to Gregory's notion of perpetual
movement, however, is Origen. Although Origen does not stress the
mind's perpetual movement as much as Gregory of Nyssa, he does
introduce the theme in much the same way as Gregory does in his
own classic doctrine on *epektasis*. Since we can never know enough of
God, says Origen in Homily 17 on Numbers, those who follow divine
wisdom are as those living in tents, 'with which they always walk and
always move on, and the farther they go, so much more does the road
still to walk grow long and stretch out endlessly.... For it never happens
that a mind, enkindled by the spark of knowledge, can come to quiet
repose; it is always called to move on, from the good to the better and
from the better to still higher things.'[25] Didymus the Blind, contempor-
ary of Gregory of Nyssa, commenting on Zech. 1: 11, says that 'the soul
has within itself its principle of activity and it is in constant perpetual
activity.'[26] Hence, when Gregory of Nyssa considers Phil. 3: 13 in Homily
6 on the Song of Songs, for example,[27] and establishes the metaphysical
foundations of his doctrine on perpetual progress, he is not inventing a

---

[22] *Leg. All.* III. 234 (trans. F. Colson and G. Whitaker, LCL, Philo vol. i, 459). Note
also how Philo highlights the negative influence the senses have on the soul: 'the mob
of the senses has introduced into it [sc. the soul] from outside an untold host of
mischiefs....'.

[23] *Sac.* 127 (trans. F. Colson and G. Whitaker, LCL, Philo vol. ii, 185–7).

[24] *Abr.* 154–5 (trans. F. Colson, LCL, Philo vol. vi, 79); see also ibid., 162: 'And the
understanding affected in like manner is not quiescent, but, unsleeping and constantly in
motion as it is,...'.

[25] *Hom. in Num.* 17. 4 (GCS 7, 160. 11–26), quoted in B. Daley, in *The Hope of the Early
Church: A Handbook of Patristic Eschatology* (Cambridge, 1991), 50.

[26] *In Zachariam*, SC, I. 43. 5–6: Τῆς λογικῆς ψυχῆς αὐτοκινήτου καὶ ἀεικινήτου
ὑπαρχούσης.

[27] *In Cant.* VI, GNO VI. 174. 15 ff. This of course is not to say that it is the first
occurrence in Gregory's writings of this rather ubiquitous theme.

theme so much as developing a line of thought already in existence and doing so in a way unique to him.

A dispersed mind renders it impossible for a person to fulfil the first and greatest commandment of the Lord: 'Love God with your whole heart and strength' (cf. Deut. 6: 5 and Matt. 22: 37).[28] One who has turned *dianoia* towards the world, worrying oneself over being pleasing to others,[29] would be suffering from a divided heart[30] and unable to love God with a whole heart. Love that is owed to God alone is squandered on human passions.[31] This divided heart, and hence a dispersed or thick *dianoia*, is apparently the risk which the married person runs.[32] In order for the heart to be whole the mind must in some way be recollected, withdrawn from the affairs of the world. Here it finds its wholeness and ability to ascend.

The Grasping, Wandering Mind

In *De vita Moysis* Gregory refers to the capacity of *dianoia* to wander aimlessly. Assistance comes from scripture, specifically from the figures of Abraham and Sarah, which guides those whose mind is without a pilot.[33] It is worth noting the implication that the mind can be without a pilot. This would seem to stand in contrast to Plato's *Phaedrus* which identifies mind itself as pilot.[34]

Speaking in the context of what takes place in baptism, Gregory sees *dianoia* on the same level as other things that must be converted. Not only do such things as unbridled desires and impulses need to be put to death in the waters of baptism but also the snatching, ravishing

---

[28] *De virg.*, SC, ix. 2. 13–14.   [29] Ibid., ix. 2. 9–11.   [30] Cf. ibid., ix. 2. 15.
[31] Ibid., ix. 2. 16–17.

[32] Ibid., ix. 2. 17–19. Cf. 1 Cor. 7: 32–3. This seems a rather disparaging view on marriage, and the context (a treatise on virginity) should be kept in mind. Gregory has previously stated rather emphatically in *De virg.* viii, that he in no way wishes to disparage marriage. The married person can indeed give priority to spiritual values, but it is difficult to do so and requires a certain strength to avoid giving the mind (νοῦς, viii. 3) completely over to passion and becoming a 'lover of pleasure rather than a lover of God' (viii. 35). But because of the weakness of nature, most do not have this strength or balance (συμμετρία, viii. 37). Gregory recommends that these latter ones pursue virginity. On this and other ironies in *De virg.*, see M. Hart, 'Reconciliation of Body and Soul: Gregory of Nyssa's Deeper Theology of Marriage', *Theological Studies* 51 (1990), 450–78; idem, 'Gregory of Nyssa's Ironic Praise of the Celibate Life', *Heythrop Journal* 33 (1992), 1–19.

[33] *De vita Moysis*, SC, i. 11. 3–12.   [34] *Phaedrus* 247c.

thought[35] that characterizes the evil movements of the mind (τὰ πονηρὰ τῆς διανοίας κινήματα).[36]

We have seen that Gregory likens the mind to a current of water that flows in all directions. The mind can disperse itself among the pleasures of the senses but it can also, like water in a pipe, unable to flow elsewhere, 'be taken up by the nature of the movement for higher things'.[37] It is worth noting that for Gregory the same mind which interacts with and disperses itself among base desires is the same mind which is taken up towards the spiritual order and higher desires. There is no 'disjunction of reason from passion' which would 'ignore the fact that concrete moral life is always a matter of intelligence interacting with impulse'.[38] Moreover, this appears to be a view Gregory holds from his early writings to the end of his career. In *Commentarius in Canticum canticorum* the bride is praised because her mind is guarded in purity and dispassion (ἀπαθείᾳ).[39] But Gregory reminds us that the fountain of *dianoia* can be either squandered on lower things (here things of the body) or turned towards higher things.[40] Having considered examples of texts which demonstrate the mind subject to various impulses and capable of growing thick, resembling a pig or cow, being dragged about, divided, squandered, and dispersed, let us consider *dianoia* operating at higher levels.

The Mind and the Intelligible World

Not only is *dianoia* capable of squandering itself in the world of sensibility and multiplicity but it also performs basic discursive processes. At the beginning of *De virginitate* x, Gregory asks what increase of *dianoia* is required to describe the indescribable.[41] While we shall have occasion to speak at greater length of the relationship between *dianoia* and the ineffable, it is sufficient for our present purposes to note the discursive

---

[35] *De vita Moysis*, SC, ii. 125. 10.   [36] Ibid., ii. 125. 13–15.

[37] *De virg.*, SC, vi. 2. 23–6: ὁ νοῦς ὁ ἀνθρώπινος... ἀναληφθήσεταί πως ὑπὸ τῆς τοῦ κινεῖσθαι φύσεως πρὸς τὴν τῶν ὑψηλῶν ἐπιθυμίαν,... Aubineau makes the interesting observation that ἀναλαμβάνω is the same verb used for the ascents of Elijah in 2 Kgs. 2: 9 and of Jesus in Mark 16: 19 and Acts 1: 2, 11.

[38] R. Williams, 'Macrina's Deathbed Revisited: Gregory of Nyssa on Mind and Passion', in L. Wickham and C. Bammel (eds.), *Christian Faith and Greek Philosophy in Late Antiquity* (Leiden, 1993), 229.

[39] *In Cant.* ix, GNO vi. 276. 12.   [40] Ibid., 277. 5–7.

[41] *De virg.*, SC, x. 1. 4–5.

function *dianoia* plays in attempts at verbal expression of any sort. Canévet would seem to refer to this discursive operation of *dianoia* when she highlights that aspect of intelligence which produces 'a discourse by which the soul attempts to express what it has grasped'.[42]

At the end of *De virginitate* XI it is once again *dianoia* which performs the function of discursive understanding: 'There is no one', Gregory says, 'whose intelligence is so blind as not to understand by oneself that the principal and the first and the only beautiful, good and pure is the God of all.'[43]

The mind, then, can adapt. It can be thick and dispersed amongst lower things or it can adapt itself to the higher processes of reason. In proportion to the greatness of what is desired, *dianoia* must be lifted up.[44] Precisely because the mind can be either dispersed and divided or elevated and recollected, Gregory recommends the unmarried state in *De virginitate*. The unmarried man bears more easily the misfortunes of life because his mind is not dragged about. Nor is *dianoia* divided by concerns for wife and children; rather it remains gathered.[45]

In Book II of *De vita Moysis* it is *dianoia* which performs tasks of ratiocination such as critical discernment and understanding. For example, Gregory leaves it to the critical *dianoia* of his readers to decide the deeper significance of the physical appointments of the tabernacle.[46]

When Moses was instructed in the theophany, he was able to know that none of the things considered by the mind truly existed, but only the transcendent essence.[47] This consideration or contemplation on the part of *dianoia* is a straightforward discursive process, just as we see, a little further on, when *dianoia* sees that things exist only by participation.[48]

We see another example of *dianoia* operating in a discursive sense when Gregory explains why irrational animals are driven from the mountain of the knowledge of God. Human contemplation of the intelligibles surpasses the knowledge which originates in the senses. But it is 'according to the nature of irrational animals that they guide themselves by sense perception alone apart from reason'.[49] By implica-

---

[42] Canévet, *Grégoire de Nysse et L'herméneutique biblique*, 63.
[43] *De virg.*, SC, XI. 6. 9–11: ὅτι γὰρ τὸ κυρίως καὶ πρώτως καὶ μόνως καλὸν καὶ ἀγαθὸν καὶ καθαρὸν ὁ τῶν ὅλων ἐστὶ θεός, οὐδεὶς οὕτω τυφλὸς τὴν διάνοιαν, ὡς μὴ καὶ ἀφ' ἑαυτοῦ συνιδεῖν.
[44] Ibid., x. 2. 33–4.   [45] Ibid., III. 9. 6–12. Cf. 1 Cor. 7: 32–3.
[46] *De vita Moysis*, SC, II. 173. 9–11.   [47] Ibid., II. 24. 3.
[48] Ibid., II. 25. 2–5.
[49] Ibid., II. 156. 6–8: Ἴδιον γὰρ τῆς τῶν ἀλόγων φύσεως τὸ κατ'αἴσθησιν μόνην δίχα διανοίας οἰκονομεῖσθαι.

tion human sense perception is not divorced from *dianoia*, and indeed we saw how it can thicken and disperse *dianoia*, but here we see that *dianoia* functions not only at this level of sensual involvement but also at the higher level of the intelligibles.

A final example of the ratiocination which *dianoia* performs is seen in an important text from the *Commentarius in Canticum canticorum*. In Homily 9 Gregory says that the life of virtue is like a garden, 'but the garden also has need of a fountain so that its grove might remain flourishing and always watered'.[50] It is precisely *dianoia* which serves this function. Gregory emphasizes its discursive role by referring to it as 'the reasoning faculty of our soul'.[51] This rational faculty swells up and overflows in thoughts (*dianoia*) which assist us in gaining possession of the good.[52] Not only does this passage show the discursive function of *dianoia* but it also shows knowledge in service of the life of virtue.[53]

It would seem then that when the mind is free from involvement in the senses it is free to contemplate the intelligibles. In Homily 10 on the Song, Gregory describes this freedom from the senses in the language of sleep. When the mind (*nous*) is no longer annoyed by the senses 'it is as though the nature of the body is overtaken by sleep and goes into a trance'.[54] Indeed the mind can look disdainfully on all these impressions of the senses, however marvellous, and 'through the contemplation of things truly good' the body's eye grows tired.[55] When this happens the mind is then free 'to gaze only at what transcends objects visible to the sense',[56] and 'reason looks above and remains untouched and unmuddied by the movement of the senses'.[57]

---

[50] *In Cant.* x, GNO vi. 275. 8–10: Ἀλλὰ τῷ κήπῳ τούτῳ καὶ πηγῆς ἐστι χρεία, ὡς ἂν εὐθαλὲς διαμένοι τὸ ἄλσος τῷ ὕδατι πρὸς τὸ διηνεκὲς πιαινό- μενον.

[51] Ibid., 275. 20–1: ἡ διανοητικὴ τῆς ψυχῆς ἡμῶν δύναμις....

[52] Ibid., 275. 21–276. 2.

[53] On the relationship between knowledge and virtue in Gregory of Nyssa see A. Meredith, 'Homily 1', in S. Hall (ed.), *Gregory of Nyssa: 'Homilies on Ecclesiastes'* (Berlin, 1993), 145–58, esp. 146–7; see also idem, *The Cappadocians* (London, 1995), 59 f.

[54] *In Cant.* x, GNO vi. 312. 11–12: ὡς ὕπνῳ τινὶ καὶ κώματι πάρετος ἡ τοῦ σώματος γίνεται φύσις.... Note that Gregory does not imply that the senses have been destroyed. For a general perspective on two fundamental ways of viewing the passions see J. Dillon, 'Rejecting the Body, Refining the Body: Some Remarks on the Development of Platonist Asceticism', in V. Wimbush and R. Valantasis (eds.), *Asceticism* (Oxford, 1995), 80–7.

[55] Ibid., 313. 1–3: διὰ τὴν τῶν ἀληθινῶν ἀγαθῶν θεωρίαν.

[56] Ibid., 313. 4–5: διὰ τὸ μόνα βλέπειν τῇ διανοίᾳ τὰ τῶν ὁρατῶν ὑπερκ- είμενα.

[57] Ibid., 313. 15–16: πρὸς τὸ ἄνω βλέπει ὁ λογισμὸς ἀπεριήχητος μένων ἐκ τῆς αἰσθητικῆς κινήσεως καὶ ἀθόλωτος.

We have seen in this section that the same *dianoia*, which can grow thick and dispersed and be squandered by involvement in senses, passions, and phantasms, also performs basic discursive processes of ratiocination such as critical thought, verbal expression, and contemplation of the intelligibles. If unclouded, untroubled, or unimpeded by the senses and passions, the same mind, and not a different compartment or level, will move upward towards the spiritual, intelligible world. Given appropriate ascetic training, there is in the mind an upward orientation, a dynamic capacity to ascend. Let us look more closely, then, at this capacity of *dianoia* to ascend.

The Mind's Ascent

When David ascends 'in that blessed ecstasy'[58] to a vision of incomprehensible beauty, it is none other than *dianoia* that is 'lifted up by the power of the Spirit'.[59] Having been raised up from the coverings of the flesh, David arrives at the contemplation of the incorporeal and intelligible, through *dianoia* alone.[60]

As to whether the mind is engaged discursively or non-discursively, this passage presents a certain ambiguity. David's ecstasy has a clearly apophatic element which might lead one to agree with Aubineau that the experience is non-discursive.[61] David glimpses beauty which is ἀμήχανον and ἀπερινόητον.[62] Gregory says it is an experience of ineffable light (ἀφράστου φωτός).[63] Moreover, the experience of archetypal beauty escapes all comprehension.[64] Indeed the abundance of alpha-privatives suggests the non-discursive.[65] However, the mind yet contemplates the intelligibles.[66] Hence, one is led to the conclusion that *dianoia* is engaged in contemplation of a discursive sort.

Not dissimilar to David is the bride, whose mind ascends to the intelligible realm. 'With her mind she arises and wanders about the intelligible and supramundane nature'.[67] This ascent would seem to

[58] *De virg.*, SC, x. 2. 6: ἐν τῇ μακαρίᾳ ἐκείνῃ ἐκστάσει.
[59] Ibid., x. 2. 4: τῇ δυνάμει τοῦ πνεύματος ὑψωθεὶς τὴν διάνοιαν....
[60] Ibid., x. 2. 8–9: καὶ εἰσελθὼν διὰ μόνης τῆς διανοίας εἰς τὴν τῶν ἀσωμάτων καὶ νοητῶν θεωρίαν.
[61] See Aubineau, 374 n. 4.   [62] *De virg.*, SC, x. 2. 5–6.   [63] Ibid., x. 2. 13.
[64] Ibid., x. 2. 22: διαφεύγει τὴν κατανόησιν,...
[65] See J. Pelikan, *Christianity and Classical Culture* (New Haven, 1993), 40–56.
[66] *De virg.*, SC, x. 2. 8–9: εἰσελθὼν... εἰς τὴν... νοητῶν θεωρίαν.
[67] *In Cant.* vi, GNO vi. 182. 5–6: ἀνίστησιν ἑαυτὴν καὶ περιπολεῖ τῇ διανοίᾳ τὴν νοητήν τε καὶ ὑπερκόσμιον φύσιν,...

reveal *dianoia* functioning at a discursive level, for she goes about naming the various heavenly realms and questioning continually the entire angelic order.[68]

Whilst the mind has this orientation towards the intelligible, towards which it ascends if it can free itself from the grip of the passions, it is capable of slipping back down, as it were, to this realm of phantasms and pleasures, or, as Gregory expresses it in Homily 11 on the Song, *dianoia* can become drowsy.[69] For this reason the Lord has given precepts in order to make *dianoia* desire the transcendent.[70] This leads to another aspect of *dianoia* worth highlighting. The mind can either ascend towards the intelligibles or remain thick, dispersed, and drowsy amongst the world of phantasms and pleasures. While the mind seems to have a native capacity to ascend, it does not seem to be able to do so unassisted.

We see this sense of exalted *dianoia* when Gregory speaks of Paul in *De vita Moysis*. Far from being thickened or dispersed by the passions, the 'divine Apostle' is characterized by his elevated *dianoia*.[71]

The Mind and Grace

Although *dianoia* functions best in an elevated mode free of the dispersing effects of the sensible and, moreover, has the capacity to ascend in a natural sort of way from the sensible towards the intelligible order, it does not seem to be able to do so unassisted. Dynamically oriented to ascend on high as it is, the mind yet seems equally unstable and can easily remain in or fall back into dispersion. Hence, *dianoia* is in need of assistance in order to negotiate this ascent. Gregory has a number of ways of addressing this issue: the metaphors of *paideia*, the effects of scripture on the mind, and the grace of baptism.

Training and Guidance

Gregory has already drawn attention to the fact that the mind can grow thick.[72] As we have noted, this thickness makes it difficult for the mind to make necessary distinctions and to come to know the nature of Beauty

[68] *In Cant.* vi, GNO vi. 182. 6–11.   [69] Ibid., xi. 315. 22.

[70] Ibid., 15–18.

[71] *De vita Moysis*, SC, i. 5. 8–11: ὁ γὰρ πολὺς ἐκεῖνος καὶ ὑψηλὸς τὴν διάνοιαν ὁ θεῖος Ἀπόστολος ἀεὶ διὰ τῆς ἀρετῆς τρέχων οὐδέποτε τοῖς ἔμπροσθεν ἐπεκτεινόμενος ἔληξεν.

[72] *De virg.*, SC, iv. 5. 1 and xi. 2. 2. Cf. *Orat. cat.* viii, GNO iii. iv. 6.

itself. The cause for this difficulty is that 'the sense faculties are not suitably trained for the discernment of what is beautiful and what is not'.[73] Although this passage does not specifically identify *dianoia* as standing in need of training, the appropriate exercise of the senses will presumably benefit *dianoia*.

When speaking of young people who embark on a life of virginity, Gregory advises them to seek a good guide and master (ἀγαθὸν καθηγεμόνα τε καὶ διδάσκαλον), for their minds are as yet unformed, and owing to their ignorance they are likely to wander off the right path.[74] Hence, *dianoia* is in need of guidance.[75]

We have seen that Gregory says the mind must practise vigilance in order to stave off drowsiness. He asserts that we have been given precepts from sacred scripture which assist this process by making the minds of the disciples desire the transcendent.[76] Hence, we see another way in which *dianoia* is assisted.

Scripture and the Mind

Indeed scripture would seem to exert an influence upon the mind. In *De vita Moysis* scripture leads *dianoia* in its ascent 'towards higher degrees of virtue'.[77] But it does more than simply lead; there is a real contact suggested by the verb χειραγωγέω: Scripture leads the mind by the hand.[78] The verb is particularly appropriate, for *dianoia* seems to like to have something to grasp, whether in the grasping, rapacious thought which characterizes *dianoia* when at the level of dispersion amongst the passions[79] or whether *dianoia* in a loftier moment tries (albeit in vain) to grasp the divine nature in an act of comprehension.[80]

---

[73] Ibid., XI. 2. 7–8: μὴ ἀκριβῶς. . .γεγυμνάσθαι τὰ αἰσθητήρια πρὸς τὴν τοῦ καλοῦ καὶ μὴ τοιούτου διάκρισιν.

[74] Ibid., xxiii. 3. 1–6

[75] On the importance of spiritual guidance in the ancient world see I. Hadot, 'The Spiritual Guide', in A.H. Armstrong (ed.), *Classical Mediterranean Spirituality* (New York, 1986), 436–59; R. Valantasis, *Spiritual Guides of the Third Century* (Minneapolis, 1991); see also M. Clarke, *Higher Education in the Ancient World* (London, 1971); H. I. Marrou, *Histoire de l'Education dans l'Antiquité* (Paris, 1948).

[76] *In Cant.* xi, GNO vi. 315. 15–22.

[77] *De vita Moysis*, SC, ii. 152. 1–2: Πάλιν ἡμῖν δι' ἀκολούθου τινὸς ἀναβάσεως πρὸς τὰ ὑψηλότερα τῆς ἀρετῆς ὁ λόγος χειραγωγεῖ τὴν διάνοιαν.

[78] See Liddel and Scott, s.v. χειραγωγέω.

[79] Ibid., 125,10: ἁρπακτικὴν διάνοιαν.

[80] *In Cant.* iii, GNO vi. 86. 13–14:. . .ἡ θεία φύσις πάσης ὑπέρκειται καταληπτικῆς διανοίας.

In *Commentarius in Canticum canticorum*, Gregory says that the spiritual interpretation (θεωρία) of the Song's prologue has a purifying effect upon *dianoia*.[81] In this instance *dianoia* is not so much the mind as a discursive content of the mind, an understanding. We can observe, then, two different ways in which scripture acts on the mind. It purifies the mind with the result that a more spiritual understanding is produced, and it moves the mind, taking it by the hand towards the non-discursive.

One scriptural image used by Gregory seems particularly illustrative of the assistance which scripture as a whole offers *dianoia*. Drawing upon the image of Elijah in the chariot of fire (2 Kgs. 2: 11), Gregory says that the mind, like Elijah, 'is taken into a fiery chariot and borne on high towards the heavenly beauty'.[82]

Gregory then says that this fire is understood to be the Holy Spirit.[83] We shall have occasion later to say more about the role of the Holy Spirit, but for our present purpose it is sufficient to observe that the ascent of *dianoia* to the heavenly realm is under the aegis of the Holy Spirit.[84]

Indeed scripture can lead *dianoia* into the non-discursive region of the sanctuary itself. In Homily 1 on the Song Gregory says that 'through the Song of Songs [Solomon] initiates the mind into the divine sanctuary' where no thought or image enters.[85] But scripture is not the only thing that assists the mind in its ascent, for this assistance is itself one of the effects of baptism.

The Grace of Baptism

What effects does baptism have on the mind? We have noted that there is an aspect of the mind which has a tendency to grab in a snatching, ravishing sort of way. Baptism, says Gregory, focuses on this aspect of *dianoia*, among other things, with the result that it is 'put to death'. For, as he says in *De vita Moysis*, 'those passing through the sacramental water of baptism must put to death in the water the entire army of evils such as

---

[81] *In Cant.* III, GNO VI. 71. 16–18:. . .ὅσον ἐκπλῦναι καὶ ἀποκλύσαι τοῦ ῥύπου τῆς σαρκὸς τὴν ἐν τοῖς λεγομένοις διάνοιαν.

[82] Ibid., X. 295. 11–12: καὶ ἀναληφθεῖσα τῷ πυρίνῳ ἅρματι ἡμῶν ἡ διάνοια μετάρσιος πρὸς τὰ οὐράνια κάλλη μετατεθείη . . . .

[83] Ibid., 295. 13–15.

[84] This seems entirely consistent with the largely purifying role played by the Holy Spirit in much of the *In Canticum*.

[85] Ibid. I, 22,16–17: διὰ τοῦ Ἄισματος τῶν Ἀισμάτων ἐντὸς τῶν θείων ἀδύτων μυσταγωγεῖ τὴν διάνοιαν.

avarice, undisciplined desire [and] rapacious thinking.... '[86] Indeed all the 'evil movements of the mind' must be put to death.[87]

Baptism, then, would seem to free the mind from the enslavement which undisciplined passion exerts on one's reason.[88] Indeed, undisciplined passion is like a tyrant, and Gregory would seem to imply that if one were to remain enslaved to passion, then, even though one might have passed through water, one has not in fact touched sacramental water.[89]

If the ransoming of the mind from the tyranny of undisciplined passion is one way of viewing the effects of baptism, the mind's purification is another. Gregory says that 'the one whose mind has been purified by crossing the water ... accedes to the contemplation of transcendent nature'.[90] The context of this passage suggests that this is discursive contemplation.[91] This is significant for it implies the role of grace even in the contemplation of the intelligibles. The effects of baptism on *dianoia*, however, do not stop here; this baptismal imagery of washing continues to purify *dianoia*.

Gregory says that the contemplation of God involves neither sight nor hearing (the realm of the senses); nor is the contemplation of God

---

[86] *De vita Moysis*, SC, II. 125. 7–14: τὸ δεῖν πάντας τοὺς διερχομένους τὸ μυστικὸν ὕδωρ ἐν τῷ βαπτίσματι πᾶσαν τὴν τῆς κακίας παρεμβολήν, οἷον τὴν πλεονεξίαν, τὴν ἀκόλαστον ἐπιθυμίαν, τὴν ἁρπακτικὴν διάνοιαν ... νεκρὰ ποιεῖν, ...

[87] Ibid., II. 125. 14–15: τὰ πονηρὰ τῆς διανοίας κινήματα....

[88] Ibid., II. 129. 1–4: Δεσπότης γάρ τίς ἐστιν ἄγριος καὶ λυσσώδης τὸ ἀκόλαστον πάθος τῷ ἀνδραποδώδει λογισμῷ, οἷόν τισι μάστιξι ταῖς ἡδοναῖς αἰκιζόμενος.

[89] Ibid., II. 129. 9–12: οἷς δουλεύων τις, κἂν διεξεληλυθὼς τύχῃ τὸ ὕδωρ, οὔπω κατά γε τὸν ἐμὸν λόγον τοῦ μυστικοῦ ὕδατος ἔθιγεν, οὗ ἔργον ἐστὶν ἡ τῶν πονηρῶν τυράννων ἀπωλεία. Gregory makes an interesting comment; does he mean to imply that there is a synergistic aspect to sacramental efficacy? See P. Fedwick, 'The Knowledge of Truth or the State of Prayer in Gregory of Nyssa', *Polyanethema: Studi di Letteratura Cristiana offerti a Salvatore Costanza. Studi Tardoantichi* 7 (1989), 349–71 at 361.

[90] Ibid., II. 153. 6–18: ... κεκαθαρμένος ἐν τῇ διαβάσει τοῦ ὕδατος...τότε προσάγεται τῇ τῆς ὑπερκειμένης φύσεως θεωρίᾳ.

[91] Cf. ibid., II. 154. 5–6: τῇ τῶν ὄντων θεωρίᾳ, which could lead one to think that Gregory intends non-discursive contemplation both here and above at II. 153. 18. But there is significant MS variation at II. 154. 5. Five of ten MSS read differently: four read νοητῶν for ὄντων and one reads νοημάτων for ὄντων. This, along with ἐν τῇ τῶν νοητῶν θεωρίᾳ at II. 156. 6, would support the view that in this context the activity of διάνοια is of a discursive nature. Daniélou claims (205 n. 1) that by ἡ τῶν ὄντων θεωρία Gregory normally intends the contemplation of creation as a stage towards the knowledge of God.

comprehended by our customary concepts.[92] To contemplate God is somehow to move beyond both the realm of the senses and the contemplation of intelligibles. We have seen that *dianoia* plays a role, however infelicitous, at the level of the senses as well as at the level of the intelligibles, but now we see that *dianoia* also plays a role in moving beyond the intelligibles into the presence of God. For Gregory says that the person who wants to ascend to the knowledge of higher things must wash *dianoia* of all opinion born of conceptions previously held and of commerce with the senses.[93] Only then is one ready to assault the mountain of divine knowledge.

With this baptismal imagery of washing Gregory describes how the mind comes to the knowledge of God. While this passage itself does not describe such an experience, it brings us to the threshold and reveals another capacity of *dianoia*. We have seen *dianoia* thick and dispersed among the senses and passions. We have seen *dianoia* ascend to the contemplation of the intelligibles by being taken by the hand by sacred scripture or by being washed in the waters of baptism. Now we see *dianoia* on the verge of entering the apophatic. We shall have abundant opportunity later in this study to see that one of Gregory's preferred ways of describing an apophatic ascent is through *aphairesis*: the letting go of sense perception, images, concepts, to enter the presence of God, the Holy of Holies, the darkness where God dwells.[94] In this passage we see, however tacitly, this *aphairesis*; for, as part of its purification, *dianoia* must shed all commerce with the senses, and this shedding of knowledge is begun with the washing away of opinion. Other levels of knowledge will be abandoned in the ascent of the mountain of divine knowledge and when the darkness of God is entered.[95] But what is particularly worthy of note in the present context is not simply the role of grace in assisting *dianoia* in its ascent but specifically the baptismal context in which the ascent is situated. The lofty ascent of the mind up the mountain of

---

[92] *De vita Moysis*, SC, II. 157. 1–3: Ἡ δὲ τοῦ Θεοῦ θεωρία οὔτε κατὰ τὸ φαινόμενον οὔτε κατὰ τὸ ἀκουόμενον ἐνεργεῖται, οὔτε τινὶ τῶν συνήθων νοημάτων καταλαμβάνεται.

[93] Ibid., II. 157. 5–10: Ἀλλὰ χρὴ τὸν μέλλοντα προσβαίνειν τῇ τῶν ὑψηλῶν κατανοήσει πάσης αἰσθητικῆς τε καὶ ἀλόγου κινήσεως προκαθᾶραι τὸν τρόπον καὶ πᾶσαν δόξαν τὴν ἐκ προκαταλήψεώς τινος γεγενημένην τῆς διανοίας ἐκπλύναντα τῆς τε συνήθους ὁμιλίας χωρισθέντα τῆς πρὸς τὴν ἰδίαν σύνοικον, τουτέστι τὴν αἴσθησιν, ...

[94] Another common motif is the stringing together of negatives such as we see at *In Eccl.*, SC, VII. 8. 100–1.

[95] *De vita Moysis*, SC, I. 163.

the knowledge of God into the darkness is at the same time grounded in the liturgical and sacramental life of the Christian community. While this is an observation more obviously characteristic of someone like Denys the Areopagite,[96] it is clearly present in Gregory of Nyssa, not simply as an adumbration, but as a consistent theological concern.

Now that we have seen in some detail how *dianoia* can undergo dispersion among the senses and be likened to a pig[97] and how, washed in the waters of baptism, taken by the hand by scripture, led up to the contemplation of the intelligibles and to threshold of non-discursive knowledge, let us see how the same *dianoia* can cross that threshold and enter the sanctuary.

The Presence of God

In *De vita Moysis* Gregory considers at some length the entrance of Moses into the darkness of God, and in this context we see an important example of the heights to which *dianoia* can rise. In Book I we see that Moses approached the darkness (γνόφος) and 'entered the Sanctuary of divine mystagogy. There, having disappeared from sight, he was one with the Invisible.'[98] Gregory nearly always uses 'darkness' to indicate divine incomprehensibility.[99] The fact that Moses has entered darkness indicates that he has entered the non-discursive. This is supported by Moses' entry into the sanctuary, and particularly by the oxymoronic formulation: Moses penetrates the impenetrable (παραδυείς τὸ ἄδυτον). Gregory often uses oxymoron and other paradoxes to designate a certain barrier beyond which discursive reason does not pass.[100] The language of invisibility also implies elevation beyond the intelligible, for in becoming invisible himself, Moses is becoming like God. This motif, namely, that only like knows like reaches far back into Greek

[96] A. Louth, *Denys the Areopagite* (London, 1989), 101–9 and more recently the comments of D. Turner, *The Darkness of God: Negativity in Christian Mysticism* (Cambridge, 1995), 258.

[97] *De virg.* v. 11.

[98] *De Vita Moysis*, SC, I. 46. 4–5: Πρὸς γὰρ τὸ ἄδυτον τῆς θείας μυσταγωγίας παραδυείς, ἐκεῖ τῷ ἀοράτῳ συνῆν μὴ ὁρώμενος....

[99] Cf. ibid., II. 162. 1 ff. See Simonetti, *Vita di Mosè*, 269–70, his comment on γνόφος. Later in this study we shall have more to say about Gregory's doctrine on darkness.

[100] See, for one example among very many, *In Cant.* v, GNO VI. 156. 18; see the treatment of Daniélou, *Platonisme et théologie mystique*, 274 ff.

philosophical tradition.[101] If Moses is to know God, Moses must become like God.

Having noted Moses' disappearance into the darkness of the sanctuary, Gregory speculates as to what this event must mean. Moses teaches, he says, that anyone who wants to be one with God must depart from all that is visible and do two things: stretch forth *dianoia* to the invisible and incomprehensible and believe that God is present where the understanding does not reach.[102]

It would seem by this, then, that Gregory believes the mind capable of entering in some sense into the sanctuary, that it can penetrate the impenetrable. However, it is important to note that *dianoia* is not capable of doing anything in the presence of God. It is not capable of understanding; no κατανόησις is performed. While Moses communes with God, Gregory does not say that it was specifically *dianoia* which came in contact with God. Indeed *dianoia* seems capable of nothing; the only activity taking place is believing.[103]

In Book II of *De vita Moysis*, we read of the approach to 'the mountain of divine knowledge'.[104] Scripture has led *dianoia* to higher levels of virtue.[105] This is necessary, says Gregory, for one who 'would undertake to ascend by means of intelligence to the mountain of divine knowledge and ... enter into the darkness where God is....'[106] Again we see that *dianoia* is *both* the means of approaching the knowledge of God *and* the means of entering the darkness of God. But Gregory mentions no knowing encounter after the mind has entered the darkness.

A few chapters further on Gregory says that the contemplation of God is not concerned with the ordinary activities of thought.[107] In order to approach such lofty things *dianoia* must be purified of all opinions born of sense perceptions. Then, with the mind purified, one may assault the mountain of knowledge.

---

[101] Plato, *Phaedo* 67b2; Aristotle, *De an.* I 404ᵇ 17–18; *Met.* B 1000ᵇ 5–6.

[102] Cf. *De vita Moysis*, SC, I. 46. 6–10: ὅτι δεῖ τὸν μέλλοντα συνεῖναι Θεῷ ἐξελθεῖν πᾶν τὸ φαινόμενον καὶ ἐπὶ τὸ ἀόρατόν τε καὶ ἀκατάληπτον τὴν ἑαυτοῦ διάνοιαν, οἷον ἐπί τινα ὄρους κορυφήν, ἀνατείναντα ἐκεῖ πιστεύειν εἶναι τὸ θεῖον ἐν ᾧ οὐκ ἐφικνεῖται ἡ κατανόησις.

[103] We shall withhold until the next chapter any discussion of the role of πίστις.

[104] Ibid., II. 152. 8.   [105] Ibid., II. 152. 1–2.

[106] Ibid., II. 152. 8–10: τολμήσῃ ποτὲ τῇ διανοίᾳ προσβῆναι τῷ τῆς θεογνωσίας ὄρει ... καὶ εἰσελθεῖν εἰς τὸν γνόφον οὗ ἔστιν ὁ Θεὸς....

[107] Ibid., II. 157. 1–3: Ἡ δὲ τοῦ Θεοῦ θεωρία ... οὔτε τινὶ τῶν συνήθων νοημάτων καταλαμβάνεται·

Gregory asks, 'But what does it mean that Moses entered the darkness and there saw God in it'?[108] His response to this question involves a description of the mind entering the presence of God. This entrance into the divine presence is a single movement with two aspects. One movement entails a letting go or a leaving behind of all appearances, 'not only what the senses grasp but also what the mind (*dianoia*) thinks it sees'.[109] The other movement reveals a certain dynamic quality of the mind to push ahead and penetrate deeper. This quality of the mind Gregory terms πολυπραγμοσύνη.[110] It is the mind's curiosity that 'goes deeper and deeper within until it penetrates into what is invisible and incomprehensible and there sees God'.[111] Gregory hastens to add, however, that this seeing is a non-seeing that is also the highest form of knowledge, 'surrounded on all sides by incomprehensibility as though by a kind of darkness'.[112] This darkness which the mind has entered is the 'luminous dark' in which the sublime John, who discovered that no intelligence can reach the divine essence, was immersed.[113]

Once again we may observe that, although the mind may enter the darkness of God, the mind is capable of nothing once in the darkness of

---

[108] Ibid., ii. 162. 1–2: Τί δὲ δὴ βούλεται τὸ ἐντὸς γενέσθαι τοῦ γνόφου τὸν Μωϋσέα καὶ οὕτως ἐν αὐτῷ τὸν Θεὸν ἰδεῖν;

[109] Ibid., ii. 163. 1–3: Καταλιπὼν γὰρ πᾶν τὸ φαινόμενον, οὐ μόνον ὅσα καταλαμβάνει ἡ αἴσθησις, ἀλλὰ καὶ ὅσα ἡ διάνοια δοκεῖ βλέπειν,...

[110] Gregory uses this term with some frequency but not always in the same sense. For example, it is used in a negative sense in *Contra Eunomium*, GNO ii. 253. 28 and *In Cant.* xi, GNO vi. 339. 17. But it is used positively here (*De vita Moysis*, SC, ii. 163. 4) and at *In Cant.* vi, GNO vi. 182. 18 to describe the means by which διάνοια moves into the non-discursive. See B. Brox, 'Zur Legitimität der Wissbegier (*curiositas*)', in H. Bungert (ed). *Das antike Rom in Europa: Die Kaiserzeit und ihre Nachwirkungen* (Regensburg, 1985), 33–52, esp. 40–9.

[111] Ibid., ii. 163. 3–5: ἀεὶ πρὸς τὸ ἐνδότερον ἵεται, ἕως ἂν διαδύῃ τῇ πολυπραγμοσύνῃ τῆς διανοίας πρὸς τὸ ἀθέατόν τε καὶ ἀκατάληπτον κἀκεῖ τὸν Θεὸν ἴδῃ.

[112] Ibid., ii. 163. 7–8: οἷόν τινι γνόφῳ τῇ ἀκαταληψίᾳ πανταχόθεν διειλημμένον.

[113] Ibid., ii. 163. 9–13. The 'luminous dark' is among Gregory's most well-known oxymorons which constitute a characteristic feature of his apophatic theology. Langerbeck argues forcefully that these oxymorons and other paradoxical expressions are not merely rhetorical features but an important component of his negative theology. However, Langerbeck speculates at no great length as to what role such oppositional phrases and images do play; see 'Zur Interpretation Gregors von Nyssa', *Theologische Literaturzeitung* 82 (1957), 83. For a fascinating general study of paradoxical language and other features of mystical literature see M. Sells, *Mystical Languages of Unsaying* (Chicago, 1994). While Sells, alas, does not include Gregory as one of his case studies, much of what Sells says is nonetheless useful for understanding Gregory's use of paradoxical language.

God's presence. It cannot grasp anything in an act of understanding; it performs no κατανόησις; nor does the mind *per se* attain union with God. What precise faculty actually finds God and unites to God we shall address in a subsequent chapter.

An important passage from Homily 7 on Ecclesiastes indicates clearly the inability of *dianoia* to grasp anything, which would constitute an act of comprehension, when it enters the non-discursive. Gregory likens the soul that has passed beyond what is accessible by concepts to someone standing on a cliff and who, when edging his foot over the side, realizes there is no foothold: he becomes dizzy, is thrown into confusion and soon returns to solid ground.[114] So the soul, 'having nothing it can grab, neither place nor time, neither space nor any other thing which offers our mind something to take hold of, but, slipping from all sides from what it fails to grasp, in dizziness and confusion, it returns again to what is natural to it'.[115] It seems that the nature of the mind is to try to catch hold of something in a discursive act, but when it moves beyond to what cannot be grasped, such as darkness, the divine sanctuary, and, here, an abyss, it cannot function properly and can even experience duress and disorientation, as we see in this text from *In Ecclesiasten*.

Another important example of the fact that *dianoia* can enter the realm of the non-discursive is seen in the figure of the bride. In Homily 6 on the Song of Songs we see the bride, like Moses, 'in the darkness where God is'.[116] She moves beyond the level of senses by forsaking sensual perceptions and then, she says, 'I am embraced by the divine night and search for him who is hidden in the darkness'.[117] The bride seeks the beloved so that she might know his essence (οὐσία), but the beloved escapes her desire to know him.[118] She then begins to ascend, by means of *dianoia*, and wanders about the intelligible and angelic realm searching for her beloved; but he is not there.[119] Finally, after the bride has gone through the incorporeal and intelligible realm 'with the curiosity of her

---

[114] See *In Eccl.*, SC, vii. 8. 88–106.

[115] Ibid., vii. 8. 100–4: Οὐκ ἔχουσά τι οὗ περιδράξηται, οὐ τόπον, οὐ χρόνον, οὐ μέτρον, οὐκ ἄλλο τι τοιοῦτον οὐδὲν ὃ δέχεται τῆς διανοίας ἡμῶν τὴν ἐπίβασιν, ἀλλὰ πανταχόθεν τῶν ἀλήπτων ἀπολισθαίνουσα ἰλιγγιᾷ τε καὶ ἀμηχανεῖ καὶ πάλιν πρὸς τὸ συγγενὲς ἐπιστρέφεται,... Plotinus speaks along strikingly similar lines of the mind's difficulty in reaching beyond space and time at *Enn.* VI. 9. 3.

[116] *In Cant.* VI, GNO. VI. 181. 6.

[117] Ibid., 181. 13–14: ὅτε περιεσχέθην τῇ θείᾳ νυκτὶ τὸν ἐν τῷ γνόφῳ κεκρυμμένον ἀναζητοῦσα,...

[118] Ibid., 181. 17–19.   [119] Ibid., 182. 4–14.

mind',[120] she begins to abandon everything: 'I abandoned the entire creation and went beyond every intelligible thing in creation and forsaking every means of grasping with the mind, I found my beloved by faith.'[121]

This passage demonstrates rather clearly that *dianoia* not only can operate at the level of the intelligibles but also can arrive at the non-discursive level of the divine night, the darkness where God is. Once again we see that this ascent is negotiated by a certain quality of mind which Gregory calls 'curiosity'. However, having been embraced by the 'divine night', having entered the darkness of God's presence, *dianoia* cannot grasp anything in an act of comprehension. Only after a process of *aphairesis*, with all conceptual understanding abandoned, does the bride encounter her beloved. However, this encounter, it is important to note, is achieved not by the mind (whether *nous* or *dianoia*) but by faith; the bride enters the divine darkness by means of *dianoia*, but attains union by means of faith.[122]

When the mind is in the divine sanctuary, in the darkness of God's presence or hanging over the abyss of unknowing, it cannot function properly; there is nothing for it to grasp in an act of understanding, and, as we saw in a powerful text from *In Ecclesiasten* VII, it can even experience the turmoil of dizziness and confusion. But, while it is generally true that *dianoia* cannot *actively* function, it does undergo something rather important.

In Homily 11 on the Song of Songs we find Gregory presenting one of his many résumés of what the bride has accomplished, and he reminds us that the bride has been embraced by the divine night.[123] Gregory immediately asks, how can what is invisible, the Bridegroom, appear at night?[124] Gregory's answer is well known: the Bridegroom 'gives the soul a perception of presence'.[125] He questions further, 'What happens

---

[120] Ibid., 182. 18: τῇ πολυπραγμοσύνῃ τῆς διανοίας.

[121] Ibid., 183. 6–8: ἀφεῖσα πᾶσαν τὴν κτίσιν καὶ παρελθοῦσα πᾶν τὸ ἐν τῇ κτίσει νοούμενον καὶ πᾶσαν καταληπτικὴν ἔφοδον καταλιποῦσα, τῇ πίστει εὗρον τὸν ἀγαπώμενον....

[122] We shall say more about the relationship between διάνοια and πίστις in a subsequent chapter.

[123] *In Cant.* XI, GNO VI. 324. 7–9.

[124] Ibid., 324. 9–10.

[125] Ibid., 324. 10–11: ἀλλ'αἴσθησιν μέν τινα δίδωσι τῇ ψυχῇ τῆς παρουσίας.... For a study of the significance of this phrase see M. Canévet, 'La Perception de la présence de Dieu. A propos d'une expression de la XIème homélie sur le Cantique des Cantiques', in J. Fontaine and C. Kannengieser (eds.), *Epektasis* (Paris, 1972), 443–54.

to the soul in the mystagogy of this night?' 'The Word touches the door'
(Song 5: 2), Gregory responds, and goes on to say that this door which
the Word touches is the mind itself, *dianoia* in its discursive search for
what is ineffable. Through this same *dianoia* the sought-after Beloved
comes to dwell.[126] Notice that the mind does not comprehend the
Beloved; nor is union described. Nevertheless *dianoia* somehow allows
the Beloved to enter and take up residence.[127]

With rather different imagery Gregory says something quite similar in
Homily 3 on the Song, where he likens the mind not to a door but to
fertile, cultivated earth, and here the vine of the Bridegroom is rooted.
Gregory is probably drawing this image from the description in Psalm
1 of the happy man, who 'is like a tree planted beside the watercourse,
which yields its fruit in due season and its leaf never withers: in all that he
does he prospers'.[128] Gregory develops this image from Psalm 1 in a way
that reflects his own concerns for the spiritual depths of the human. This
fertile earth in which the Bridegroom has taken root is, says Gregory,
'the deep mind which is watered by divine teaching.'[129]

This text merits consideration for at least two reasons. Not only does
it provide another example of *dianoia* as the subject of divine indwelling,
even though this divine presence is not grasped by *dianoia* in an act of
understanding, but it also shows that the mind is nonetheless given

---

[126] Ibid., 324. 13–15: ἅπτεται τῆς θύρας ὁ λόγος. θύραν δὲ νοοῦμεν τὴν
στοχαστικὴν τῶν ἀρρήτων διάνοιαν, δι'ἧς εἰσοικίζεται τὸ ζητούμενον.

[127] There are at least two other noteworthy passages which evince this capacity of
διάνοια to serve as a means of divine indwelling: *In Cant.* III. 87. 2–8 and VI. 182.
18–183. 13. However, these texts differ from the present one in an important way. Unlike
the present text διάνοια undergoes a process of *aphairesis*, and Gregory becomes more
precise as to what exactly facilitates divine indwelling. When Gregory is being
more precise it would seem that the mediation of divine indwelling is accomplished by
πίστις, especially at the non-discursive level. This invites speculation as to the relation of
διάνοια to πίστις, which I shall later take up. Suffice it to say for the moment that this
cluster of texts, among other things, leads me to take a position contrary to that proposed
by B. Pottier, who sees a 'rupture' between faith and knowledge in Gregory of Nyssa (*Dieu
et le Christ selon Grégoire de Nysse* (Namur, 1994), 207). While there is an important and
consistent discontinuity between διάνοια and πίστις, there is also an important and
consistent continuity between the two.

[128] Ps. 1. 3; translation from *The New English Bible* (Oxford and Cambridge, 1970).

[129] *In Cant.* III, GNO VI. 97. 18–98. 2: ἡ τοῦ νυμφίου ἄμπελος ἐν τῷ
Γαδί, τῷ πίονι τούτῳ τόπῳ ἐρριζωμένη (τουτέστιν ἐν βαθείᾳ τῇ διανοίᾳ
τῇ διὰ τῶν θείων διδαγμάτων καταρδουμένη)....Cf. Gregory's treatment of
Ps. 1: 3 in *In inscrip. Psalm.*, GNO V. 37. Gregory continues to supply the image
of being watered with divine teaching but no specification of the 'deep mind'
(ἐν βαθείᾳ τῇ διανοίᾳ) as the subject of this watering.

something worth knowing, namely, 'divine teaching', which the mind in its turn would be capable of grasping. This text, therefore, reveals something else of which the mind is capable as it encounters divine presence: not only is the mind the subject of divine indwelling, it also receives something as a result.

In Homily 11 on the Song of Songs Gregory comments briefly on the phrase 'the drops of the night' (Song 5: 2)[130] and says 'it is not possible for someone who has entered the sanctuary of the invisible to meet a shower of rain or a swollen torrent of knowledge'. There is nothing surprising in this, for we would not expect that there would be any discursive activity whatever in the sanctuary. But Gregory goes on to say that one who has entered the sanctuary, presumably by means of *dianoia*, 'must be content if truth bedew one's knowledge with delicate and indistinct insights'.[131] This passage is significant, for, while the mind does not actively accomplish anything in the sanctuary, it does receive something: it receives these insights. What stands out here is that there is an exchange of some sort that takes place between the non-discursive and the discursive. While the mind cannot grasp God, God yet moistens the mind, and from this moisture a certain discursive content, a *dianoia*, congeals. This 'moisture of thought'[132] can in turn nourish God's plants, which are the virtues.[133] Indeed *dianoia* can be rather like a fountain which teems and finally overflows, thus aiding in the possession of the good.[134]

The mind seems never capable of comprehension when it is in the darkness of divine presence or embraced by the divine night. But this is not to say it is capable of nothing whatever. It maintains a certain receptive capacity. By virtue of this capacity the Bridegroom can enter and dwell. Moreover, this divine indwelling has an effect upon the mind:

---

[130] *In Cant.* xi, GNO vi. 325. 20 f.

[131] Ibid., 325. 21–326. 5: οὐ γάρ ἐστι δυνατὸν τὸν ἐντὸς τῶν ἀδύτων τε καὶ ἀθεωρήτων γενόμενον ὄμβρῳ τινὶ τῆς γνώσεως εντυχεῖν ἢ χειμάρρῳ ἀλλ' ἀγαπητὸν εἰ λεπταῖς τισι καὶ ἀμυδραῖς διανοίαις ἐπιψεκάζοι τὴν γνῶσιν αὐτῶν ἡ ἀλήθεια διὰ τῶν ἁγίων τε καὶ θεοφορουμένων τῆς λογικῆς σταγόνος ἀπορρεούσης.

[132] *In Cant.* ix, GNO vi. 276. 6. Water, especially flowing water, in the *In Canticum canticorum* often indicates divine presence. See for example *In Cant.* i, GNO vi. 32. 12–15 and *In Cant.* ii, GNO vi. 62. 3–7, among many others. In a subsequent chapter we shall consider more deeply this imagery of flowing water and its epistemological implications.

[133] Ibid., 277. 7–9: ἀρετὰς δὲ εἶναι τὴν φυτείαν τοῦ θεοῦ μεμαθήκαμεν, περὶ ἃς ἡ διανοητικὴ τῆς ψυχῆς ἡμῶν δύναμις ἀσχολουμένη.... Note that virtue is not subordinated to knowledge in this text.

[134] See ibid., 275. 19–276. 2.

it 'waters it with divine teaching'; it 'moistens the mind'. The mind in turn
can distil this moisture into insight, discourse, and action.

Conclusion

As helpful as Mann's *Lexicon Gregorianum* is, with its multi-column list of
occurrences of *dianoia*, the advantage of the present examination has
been the opportunity to look closely at an abundant sampling of significant texts in which *dianoia* occurs, and it places us in a position to suggest
a working definition of *dianoia*: *dianoia* is a general term that refers to
that discursive state of mind characterized optimally by reason and
the performance of ratiocination, but which less optimally can also be
characterized by the domination of the passions. It can also refer to the
product of ratiocination such as a thought, reflection, or perception.[135]
It is responsive to grace, seen especially in the guidance of scripture and
baptism and under such assistance comes into the presence of God, but
without grasping God in an act of comprehension.

The following points serve as useful observations regarding the
portrait of the mind that has emerged from this survey.

(A) One observation which by now should seem rather obvious is that
Gregory uses a single lexical item to refer to several states of mind or
intelligence. In this regard he stands in bold contrast to Plato, whose
well-known Allegory of the Line ascribes a rather precise meaning to
epistemological terms such as *nous*, *dianoia* and *pistis*. The Allegory
suggests that *dianoia* is a technical term which refers to a faculty inferior
to *nous* and limited to discursive reason, whereas *nous* designates a non-
discursive, intuitive grasp of the first principle. However, this technical
meaning of *dianoia* is unique to Plato and arguably limited to the Allegory
of the Line. [136] For Gregory *nous* and *dianoia* do not seem to exhibit this

---

[135] This, however, does not prevent Gregory from using other terms such as
αἰσθήσις or νοῦς to express the same thing.
[136] *Rep.* vi. 511d–e. It is well to note that outside the specific context of the Allegory of
the Line διάνοια cannot be presumed to have the technical meaning seen at 511e. In the
nineteenth century Jowett and Campbell (*Plato's Republic*, 3 vols. (Oxford, 1895), 325)
observed that 'in the great majority of instances διάνοια . . . is used in the ordinary Greek
acceptations of (1) mental activity, (2) mind in act, (3) a particular thought or conception,
(4) meaning, (5) intention'. To refer to a faculty or state of mind between πίστις and
νοῦς, it is 'hardly to be found elsewhere in Plato'. J. Adam (*The Republic of Plato*, 2 vols., 2nd
edn. (Cambridge, 1963), 72) says that 'διάνοια is the most general word for a state (ἕξις)

technical difference; in fact they seem roughly synonymous. For example, in *De virginitate*, we saw that it was *dianoia* which looked down upon and became embroiled in the passions.[137] But a little further on in this treatise the same epistemological state was described of *nous*: scattered and dispersed among sensual pleasures.[138]

This interchangeability of terminology seems to continue into Gregory's maturity. In *De vita Moysis* he states that it was through *dianoia* that one approached the mountain of divine knowledge and entered the darkness where God was.[139] But this same exalted state of mind was likewise described of *nous*, which enters into the invisible and unknowable 'and there sees God'.[140] This is not to say, however, that whenever Gregory says *dianoia* he could just as easily have said νοῦς; he can and does make distinctions.[141] The point is simply that in general the two words are not technical terms which designate two separate states.[142] As Völker has observed of Philo and Clement, *nous* and *dianoia* are roughly synonymous terms denoting the mind or intelligence.[143]

(B) Whether Gregory speaks of the mind as *nous* or *dianoia*, we see it (1) involved in passionate struggle; (2) performing tasks of ratiocination and

---

of mind or mode of thought in Greek'. The technical sense which is accorded διάνοια in the Allegory of the Line (511e) 'is entirely Plato's own'. In his Loeb edition (*The Republic* (Cambridge, Mass., 1935)), Shorey observes that even in the context of the Allegory of the Line, e.g. 511c (line 8), διάνοια 'is general and not technical' (115 n. f). For more discussion on the Allegory of the Line see G.M.A. Grube, *Plato's Thought* (London, 1935), 1–50, esp. 26–8; D. Melling, *Understanding Plato* (Oxford, 1987), 103–13; for a helpful review of a variety of positions on the Allegory of the Line see R. C. Cross and A. Woozley, *Plato's Republic: A Philosophical Commentary* (London, 1964), 203–28.

[137] *De virg.*, SC, v. 3–5: ... καὶ ἀντὶ τοῦ μετεωροπορεῖν καὶ εἰς τὰ ἄνω βλέπειν τὴν διάνοιαν ἡμῶν πρὸς τὰ σαρκὸς καὶ αἵματος πάθη κατενεχθεῖσαν πεσεῖν.

[138] Ibid., vi. 2. 11–14: Οὕτω μοι δοκεῖ καὶ ὁ νοῦς ὁ ἀνθρώπινος, εἰ μὲν πανταχοῦ διαχέοιτο πρὸς τὸ ἀρέσκον ἀεὶ τοῖς αἰσθητηρίοις ῥέων καὶ σκεδαννύμενος, μηδεμίαν ἀξιόλογον δύναμιν σχεῖν πρὸς τὴν ἐπὶ τὸ ὄντος ἀγαθὸν πορείαν.

[139] *De vita Moysis*, SC, ii. 152. 7–10: ἵνα τολμήσῃ ποτὲ τῇ διανοίᾳ προσβῆναι τῷ τῆς θεογνωσίας ὄρει καὶ ... εἰσελθεῖν εἰς τὸν γνόφον οὗ ἔστιν ὁ Θεὸς....

[140] Ibid., ii. 163. 5: κἀκεῖ τὸν Θεὸν [ὁ νοῦς (162. 10)] ἴδη.

[141] The above passage, *De vita Moysis*, SC, ii. 162. 10–163. 5, provides a good example of how Gregory can distinguish between the two.

[142] I shall argue later in this study quite the opposite regarding the term πίστις. Πίστις, in certain contexts, has a technical meaning distinguishable, though ultimately not separable, from the *sensus vulgaris*.

[143] W. Völker, *Der wahre Gnostiker nach Clemens Alexandrinus* (Berlin, 1952), 366.

contemplation of the intelligibles; (3) ascending on high; (4) in the sanctuary or in the darkness of divine presence.

(1) We have seen Gregory spend much time describing the mind struggling with passion. This struggle seems to be of at least two sorts.

(a) A struggle as a result of being caught up with physical pleasures of the body. Gregory likens the mind in this state to a cow or a pig, which are constantly looking down, presumably to the concerns of the flesh.

(b) But this preoccupation with the concerns of the flesh is not the only problem *dianoia* undergoes, for the mind seems to undergo struggles that are rooted *not* in its involvement with the body—as though the human person were, in Stead's words, 'an animal with reason added on'[144]—but within the mind itself. For the mind can also be caught up with worrying about and being preoccupied with what others think of one.[145] Moreover, Gregory speaks of the importance of the mind being converted from ravishing, snatching thoughts and from the mind's own sordid movements.[146]

The capacity of *dianoia* to be preoccupied by these things leaves it in a state which Gregory describes varyingly as thick, dispersed, or grasping, and the effects of this are the same. The mind flows in every direction like gushing water, and the love due to God is dispersed among other things. One is alienated from God and unable to use reason properly, notably for distinguishing a beautiful thing from Beauty itself.[147] The mind must be converted from all this, which is precisely, according to Gregory, one of the implications of receiving baptism.

(2) The same mind which can grow thick or dispersed can assume a more noble state and perform basic discursive processes of ratiocination. In this state *dianoia* can also refer to the rational capacity of the soul[148] as well as to the product of discursive thought. Finally, it can also contemplate the intelligibles, which, says Gregory, is accomplished through *dianoia* alone.[149]

(3) The mind ascends to the contemplation of the intelligibles through the curiosity of the mind itself as well as through grace, which guides and trains the mind, and particularly when scripture leads *dianoia* not only to

---

[144] G. C. Stead, 'The Concept of the Mind and the Concept of God in the Christian Fathers', in B. Hebblethwaite and S. Sutherland (eds.), *The Philosophical Frontiers of Christian Theology* (Cambridge, 1982), 48.

[145] *De virg.*, SC, ix. 2. 9–11.   [146] *De vita Moysis*, SC, ii. 125. 10 and 13–15.

[147] *De virg.*, SC, xi. 2. 3–4.   [148] *In Cant.* ix, GNO vi. 275. 20–1.

[149] *De virg.*, SC, x. 2. 8–9; see also *De vita Moysis*, SC, ii. 24. 3.

the lofty heights of discursive contemplation but beyond the threshold
into the sanctuary, the darkness of divine presence.[150]

(4) At this most noble level of the mind there is no ratiocination. It
cannot see, for it is embraced by the divine night. It cannot understand,
for there is no object to grasp. Nevertheless, we have observed that the
mind in this darkness is particularly receptive to two important events.
Gregory says the mind is like a doorway through which the Bridegroom
enters and dwells. An aspect of this indwelling involves some sort of
knowing encounter. This is certainly not a torrent of knowledge, but, as
Gregory says, the mind that enters the sanctuary is 'bedewed' with
knowledge.[151]

(C) This portrait of a mind capable of assuming various states along a
single continuum places one in a position to respond to a remark made
by G.C. Stead concerning Gregory's *De anima et resurrectione*. Stead claims
that Macrina 'repeats Aristotle's mistake of regarding man simply as an
animal with reason added on as an extra capacity. . . .'[152] Hence, one is
left with an anthropology which effectively alienates human intelligence
from the impulsive world of senses and passions. To what extent Stead's
appraisal is a fair reading of Gregory of Nyssa's *De anima et resurrectione*
has been queried by Rowan Williams in an admirable essay devoted to
clarifying some important notions regarding the relationship between
the mind and the passions.[153] Our survey of mind, under the lens of
dianoia, supports Williams, who argues that impulses are part of the
mind, 'part of how mind realises itself' and that the human being does
not, according to Gregory, 'consist of a rational core with some embar-
rassing additions'.[154]

An important statement of Gregory's anthropology occurs in
Oratio catechetica VI. Gregory says that in the creation of humanity a
mixture or blending (μίγμα) of the intelligible and sensible is produced

---

[150] On χειραγωγία see I. Gargano, *La Teoria di Gregorio di Nissa sul Cantico dei Cantici*
(Rome, 1981), 93, 127, 230–1 *et passim*; see also A. Cortesi, *Le Omelie sul Cantico dei Cantici di
Gregorio di Nissa: Proposta di un itinerario di vita battesimale* (Rome, 2000), 54 and 224–5 *et
passim*.

[151] *In Cant.* XI, GNO VI. 325. 21–326. 5.

[152] Stead, 'The Concept of the Mind and the Concept of God', 48.

[153] Williams, 'Macrina's Deathbed Revisited,' 227–46. See also M. Barnes, 'The
Polemical Context and Content of Gregory of Nyssa's Psychology', *Medieval Philosophy
and Theology* 4 (1994), 1–24; and J. Behr, 'The Rational Animal: A Rereading of Gregory of
Nyssa's *De hominis opificio*', *Journal of Early Christian Studies* 7 (1999), 219–47.

[154] 'Macrina's Deathbed Revisited', 235 and 236.

by God.[155] The intention of this image of blending suggests a basic unity not allowed for by Stead's suggestion that Gregory sees the human being as 'an animal with reason added on'. Moreover, this unity is important for consolidating humanity as a microcosm. 'Man is essentially a microcosm, that man might be at the same time both a link being and also in the image of God.'[156] If Gregory's anthropology really envisaged the tenuous link between the world of animal passion and sensibility, on the one hand, and intelligence on the other, as Stead suggests, it seems unlikely that this mediating role of the human being as microcosm could obtain.

The anthropology set forth in the *Oratio catechetica* would imply that 'humanity cannot be thought of without reference to passion. The reasonable soul is the crown of the evolving history of animality, gradually blended with increasing degrees of self-moving capacity'.[157]

Any number of texts we have considered demonstrate that the problem of the passions is a problem *within* the mind itself and not something to which mind has been merely superadded. For example, desire (ἐπιθυμία) can be a problem for the soul by allowing it to be tripped up by sense perceptions and objections, or it can rise above these sense perceptions to spiritual beauty. In *De virginitate* we see that the power of desire can be wasted on objects that are distracting, or, by contrast, this same power of desire can be purified of its obsession with baser things and ascend 'to where perception does not reach'; thus the soul arrives 'at the intelligence of that magnificence beyond the heavens'.[158] The sense here is that desire is a power within the soul. While it can clearly present a problem for the soul, it can also enable intelligence to arrive at a loftier vision, provided desire is sufficiently purified. But the advance is through a purified desire, not an exterminated desire. The passionate desire that can inhibit the soul's ascent can also facilitate the soul's ascent.[159] Indeed the whole world of sense perception 'is joined to our nature as its proper companion'.[160]

[155] *Orat. cat.* VI, GNO III. iv. 22. 11.

[156] A. Meredith, *The Cappadocians* (London, 1995), 92.

[157] Williams, 'Macrina's Deathbed Revisited', 237. Williams's essay focuses mainly upon *De hominis opificio* and *De anima et resurrectione*, but the observation seems equally true of the *Oratio catechetica*.

[158] See *De virg.*, SC, XI. 3. 5–18.

[159] Perhaps there is no clearer example of this than *In Cant.* I, GNO VI. 23. 9: τὸ ἐράσθητι·

[160] *De vita Moysis*, SC, II. 157. 10–11: ... τουτέστι τὴν αἴσθησιν, ἢ σύζυγός πως ἐστὶ τῇ ἡμετέρᾳ φύσει καὶ σύνοικος, ... See also II. 122.

Another example of the passionate struggles of the mind having to do with the nature of the mind and not merely with its involvement with the body *per se* is seen in a particular trait with which Gregory characterizes the mind: πολυπραγμοσύνη. It can be used negatively of the mind to describe a certain meddlesomeness.[161] However, the same quality of the mind can at other times be quite positive; this same dynamic quality of the mind is used to penetrate into the incomprehensible, where God is seen.[162]

To suggest that the underlying anthropology in all this is nothing more than that of 'an animal with reason added on' or that intelligence were nothing but an adjunct to impulse would be far too simplistic.[163]

(D) By viewing Gregory's notion of the mind under the lens of *dianoia* we see that Gregory has a dynamic view of the mind. The mind can flow, as it were, from one state to another. What determines which state of awareness the mind assumes? Is it due to something within the mind itself, or is it due to the object which confronts the mind? Gregory himself does not seem to address the question directly. Nevertheless, one feels drawn to speculate that it is rather the object confronting the mind which determines the mind's response. At least this seems to be the case when the mind is faced with divine incomprehensibility. As we saw briefly in Homily 7 on Ecclesiastes, when the mind put its foot over the cliff, i.e. when it came into the presence of God, it lost control; it became disoriented and grew dizzy. This state of unknowing seems like a *response*, a result of placing its foot over the abyss of incomprehensibility, rather than a state into which the mind has somehow put itself.

The mind's dynamic quality is perhaps best seen in Gregory's likening the mind to flowing water.[164] Caught up in the world of obsession with physical pleasures and reputation, the mind gushes in dispersion. Ascetic practice serves as a pipe which constrains the water of the mind to protect it from dispersion. If so constrained, the dynamism of the mind, previously encouraging a downward flow into dispersion, pushes the water up to higher levels. With support the mind flows up; with no support the mind flows down. This is the passion of the mind; it will

---

[161] *Contra Eunom.*, GNO ii. 253. 28 and *In Cant.* xi, GNO vi. 339. 17.

[162] See *De vita Moysis*, SC, ii. 163. 3–5; see also *In Cant.* vi, GNO vi. 182. 18.

[163] Williams, 'Macrina's Deathbed Revisited', 229 n. 9. Cf. Daniélou, *Platonisme et Théologie Mystique*, 61–71, esp. 63.

[164] *De virg.*, SC, vi. 2; cf. xx. 1.

move. It is a question of training this mind so that it moves in the right direction.

(E) The same mind which flows into the thick, dispersed state of a pig or cow is also taken up, flows up, to the contemplation of the intelligibles and even into the darkness of the sanctuary. While it does so according to the dynamism proper to its own nature, it does not flow unassisted. The mind is graced and ascends with the aid of scripture and liturgy. Scripture takes the mind by the hand and leads it to more profound contemplation, and through the conversion associated with baptism it is purified of base passions so that it might proceed to the contemplation of the intelligibles.

However, we also observe that even though the mind flows into the sanctuary, it does not, to change metaphors, grasp in comprehension the Beloved whom it seeks. The function of grasping the Beloved in union, that is to say, the faculty which bridges the gap between intelligence and God, is reserved by Gregory of Nyssa for faith. To an examination of this exalted and highly nuanced role of faith we shall now turn.

3

The Grasp of Faith

Introduction

In the preceding chapter we saw how the mind can enter the presence of God. Indeed *dianoia* can flow from states embroiled with concerns of the flesh or for reputation, which merit comparison with a pig or a cow, to the contemplation of the intelligibles and even beyond this discursive activity to the point of entering, and indeed entering through the mind's own curiosity, the sanctuary, the darkness wherein God dwells. However, we also saw that in this exalted state of awareness the mind was not capable of grasping in an act of comprehension the divine essence, whom the soul seeks above all: 'For I sought him at night upon my bed in order to know his essence....'[1] However, this search for the incomprehensible divine essence is frustrated: 'But I did not find him.'[2] In this text the bride's frustration is softened by her plangency, but elsewhere Gregory expresses this same frustration in rather more dire, even shocking, imagery such as we saw in Homily 7 on Ecclesiastes. Here the soul, in the presence of the Incomprehensible, has nothing to grasp, no foothold whatever, and becomes dizzy and confused: 'Having nothing it can grab, neither place nor time, neither space nor any other thing which offers our mind something to take hold of, but, slipping from all sides from what it fails to grasp, in dizziness and confusion, it returns again to what is natural to it....'[3] With autobiographical nuance Gregory had already pursued this same line of thought in *De beatitudinibus*. Gazing into the ineffable, Gregory says his mind is like one who gazes from atop a rocky precipice. He has been borne to such heights by scripture and he becomes dizzy looking down into the unfathomable depths of the divine abyss, for the steep rock allows no basis for one's

---

[1] *In Cant.* vi, GNO vi. 181. 16–18.   [2] Ibid., 181. 19.
[3] *In Eccl.*, SC, vii. 8. 100–4.

thoughts; the mind can in no way approach.[4] Indeed Gregory can give the impression that God is completely unapproachable, being cut off on all sides by the darkness of incomprehensibility.[5] What, then, of the desire for the very essence of God? Does Gregory lead us down a path of scepticism? Must one despair of attaining all contact with the incomprehensible God?[6] Is this desire perpetually frustrated?[7] Is there at our disposal no means of approaching the ineffable God, of bridging the gap between the mind and God? Gregory clearly gives the impression that there is, for he insists that the beloved disciple can penetrate into the 'luminous dark',[8] can place his head like a sponge on the breast of the Lord and receive from there that flow of ineffable mystery hidden in the heart of the Lord.[9] The contact is real. However, in this passage Gregory does not tell us precisely what means we have at our disposal for establishing contact with the Incomprehensible. But in the bride we see it clearly: 'Having let go of all manner of comprehension, I found the Beloved by faith and never will I let him go once found by the grasp of faith.'[10] For Gregory of Nyssa this grasp of faith is the sole means of approaching, indeed uniting with, the Incomprehensible: faith bridges the gap between the mind and God. This chapter proposes, then, to examine important texts which demonstrate this exalted view of faith.

In inscriptiones Psalmorum

In what is generally considered a very early work, *In inscriptiones Psalmorum*, Gregory already entertains the notion that faith is the principal means by which one approaches what is beyond all manner of comprehension.[11] Towards the beginning of Part II of his commentary Gregory says that while God is hidden from understanding, is hidden from sight,

---

[4] See *De beat.* vi, GNO vii. ii. 137. 16–22. See M. Girardi, 'Annotazioni al *De beatitudinibus*', *Augustinianum* 35 (1995), 161–82; R. Leys, *L'image de Dieu chez Saint Grégoire de Nysse* (Paris, 1951), 39–55.

[5] *De vita Moysis*, SC, ii. 163. 8.   [6] Canévet, 'Grégoire de Nysse', col. 994.

[7] This is, in part, von Balthasar's dissatisfaction with Gregory; see *Présence et pensée*, 76. See the response of C. Desalvo to von Balthasar, in *L' 'oltre' nel presente*, 242 n. 36.

[8] *De vita Moysis*, SC, ii. 163. 9.   [9] *In Cant.* i, GNO vi. 41. 6–10.

[10] *In Cant.* vi, GNO vi. 183. 7–9.

[11] On dating and background of this work see, Daniélou, 'Chronologie des œuvres de Grégoire de Nysse'; M.-J. Rondeau, 'Exégèse du Psautier et anabase spirituelle chez Grégoire de Nysse', in J. Fontaine and C. Kannengiesser (eds), *Epektasis: Mélanges patristiques offerts au Cardinal Jean Daniélou* (Paris, 1972), 517–31; idem, 'D'où vient la technique exégétique utilisée par Grégoire de Nysse dans son traité "Sur les titres des

and transcends every thought, faith somehow has an access which comprehension does not have: 'For how truly is that hidden which is incomprehensible, invisible, and which transcends every thought which conveys direct apprehension, although he who draws near through faith achieves the goal of victory.'[12]

Therefore we see from very early on in his career that Gregory can speak of faith in a way that goes beyond mere notional assent or conviction. Moreover, this particular, if not technical, use of faith occurs in an apophatic context. Although in this specific passage the apophatic context is somewhat muted, and we see none of the *aphairesis* that will characterize other texts which we shall presently consider, the alpha-privatives stand out nonetheless: ἀκατανόητος, ἀόρατος. Indeed this location of faith within clusters of apophatic terminology and motifs will remain a consistent indicator of the technical meaning this exalted faith acquires and its role in the apophatic dimension of his thought.

Contra Eunomium I

About midway through Book I of his massive refutation of Eunomius, Gregory contrasts divine eternity with the temporality of creatures, and this in a more general context of the relationship between divine οὐσία and ἐνέργεια.[13] Gregory argues forcefully that since God is beyond all time and measurement, the discursive mind, being bound to the created world of space and time, cannot pass beyond the border of finitude and arrive at the infinite. 'Where no shape is perceived, no place, no extent, no measure of time or other comprehensible feature, the comprehending power of mind, seeking to take hold of something like time and what

---

psaumes"?', in *Mélanges d'histoire des religions offerts à Henri-Charles Puech* (Paris, 1974), 263–87; R. Heine, *Gregory of Nyssa's Treatise on the Inscriptions on the Psalms* (Oxford, 1995), 8–11.

[12] *In inscrip. Psalm.*, GNO v. 82. 25–83. 2: κρύφιον γὰρ ὡς ἀληθῶς ἐκεῖνό ἐστιν τὸ ἀκατανόητόν τε καὶ ἀόρατον καὶ πάσης ὑπερκείμενον καταληπτικῆς ἐπινοίας, ᾧπερ ὁ προσεγγίσας διὰ τῆς πίστεως εἰς τὸ τῆς νίκης ἔφθασε τέλος. Translation by Heine, 135.

[13] On points of literary structure of Book I see Pottier, *Dieu et le Christ*, 31–5 and 413–24. Pottier (p. 208) wishes to counter Mühlenberg's claim (*Die Unendlichkeit Gottes bei Gregor von Nyssa* (Göttingen, 1966), 98–100) that, at least regarding literary structure, the *Contra Eunomium* is something of a ' "patchwork" '.

is created in it, settles upon what is congenial and related to itself, slipping off every side of the inapprehensible nature.'[14]

He continues this section in much the same way, but here the apophatic character of his discourse is more pronounced. God is not in space or in time but before these and above these in an ineffable way. God is self-contained, 'immeasurable by ages; without the accompaniment of time; seated and resting in himself without associations with past or future, since there is nothing beside God and nothing beyond God'.[15]

It is difficult to overlook the apophatic terminology: 'ineffable', 'immeasurable', 'without time', 'nothing beside', 'nothing beyond'. As Françoise Vinel has indicated, this stringing together of negative terms, with or without an alpha privative, is typical of Gregory's apophatic language.[16]

Homily 3 on the Beatitudes provides another example of this same sort of stringing together of alpha privatives. Admitting the incapacity of thought to grasp the nature of God, Gregory asks: 'How shall I name the invisible (ἀθέατον)? How shall I describe the immaterial (ἄϋγον)? How am I to show what cannot be seen (ἀειδές)? How am I to lay hold of what is without size (ἀμεγεθές) without quantity (ἄποσον), without attribute (ἄποιον) or form (ἀσχημάτιστον)? How shall I discover what is neither in place nor in time (μήτε τόπῳ μήτε χρόνῳ), which escapes all limitation and every form of definition?'[17]

Striking examples of this same type of apophatic discourse are seen in both Philo and Clement of Alexandria. In *De posteritate Caini* Philo says the Cause of all things is not in space and time but above them both and not surrounded by anything.[18] In Clement of Alexandria's commentary on Exodus 33: 13, God 'is not in space at all. He is beyond space and time and anything belonging to created beings. Similarly, he is not found in any section. He contains nothing. He is contained by nothing. He is not subject to limit or division.... He has nothing to do with space.... He

---

[14] *Contra Eunom.* 1. 369, GNO 1. 136. 1–7 Trans. Stuart G. Hall in L. Mateo-Seco and J. Bastero (eds), *El 'Contra Eunomium I' en la producción literaria de Gregorio de Nisa* (Pamplona, 1988), 89. Once again we see this imagery of falling back or slipping away as a result of attempting to grasp what is beyond intellect and finding comfort on a lower and more secure level. The same imagery in even more graphic and perhaps autobiographical terms is seen at *In Eccl.*, SC, vii. 8. 100–4 and *De beat.* vi, GNO vii. ii. 136. 25–137. 26. Cf. Plotinus, *Enn.* vi. 9. 3.

[15] Ibid., 371, GNO 1. 136. 14–16.

[16] See *In Eccl.*, SC, 388 n. 2 for Vinel's observation.

[17] *De beat.* iii, GNO v. 104. 15–19.   [18] *De post.* v. 14.

simply rests in the enjoyment of his handiwork.'[19] However, while Philo, Clement, and Gregory speak of God as beyond space and time, contained or limited by nothing, and enjoying a certain rest in this, Gregory inserts something which Philo and Clement do not.

In this apophatic context, whose entire orientation is towards the unknowability of God, Gregory states in what way God can be known: 'contemplated through faith alone'.[20] We have previously seen Gregory employ in *De virginitate* quite similar phraseology in order to describe David in 'that blessed ecstasy'.[21] As we have already observed David is borne aloft by the Spirit to the discursive contemplation of the intelligibles (νοητῶν θεωρίαν); this contemplation, by contrast, was achieved through the mind alone.[22]

It is well to indicate that the specific context of this passage from the *Contra Eunomium* is more clearly non-discursive than the similar phrasing of the earlier *De virginitate*. God, being beyond space and time, and, hence, beyond concepts, cannot be approached through that aspect of the mind which contemplates the intelligibles. Therefore, the mind, which, as we have shown in the previous chapter, cannot function properly in the realm of the non-discursive (even though it can apparently arrive there), would not likely be suggested by Gregory as the means by which one approaches God beyond all discursive activity. Instead Gregory suggests something much along the same lines as *In inscriptiones Psalmorum*: one draws near the invisible, incomprehensible God not by means of mind but by means of faith.[23]

How then to interpret the paradoxical statement that follows? Gregory has just said that God is known by faith alone (διὰ μόνης τῆς πίστεως). However, he says just a few lines further on that God is known only in the impossibility of knowing.[24] This coincidence of knowing and not knowing, or as von Balthasar has put it, '*une mystérieuse et parallèle croissance de l'ignorance et du savoir*',[25] is a motif which Gregory will

---

[19] *Strom.* 11. 2. 6 (1–3). Trans. J. Ferguson, *Clement of Alexandria, Stromateis*, Fathers of the Church 85 (Washington, DC, 1991) 160–1.

[20] *Contra Eunom.* 1. 371, GNO 1. 136. 17: διὰ μόνης τῆς πίστεως θεωρεῖται. This is not to suggest that Clement would be averse to such an exalted view of faith, for this is very much his concern in his *Stromateis*. On πίστις in Clement see Moingt, 'La Gnose de Clément d'Alexandrie'; (1950), Lilla, *Clement of Alexandria*, 118–42; Osborn, *The Philosophy of Clement of Alexandria*, 127–45; Mortley, *Connaissance religieuse et herméneutique*, 109–25; Berchman, *From Philo to Origen*, 176–9.

[21] *De virg.*, SC, x. 2. 6.   [22] Ibid., x. 2. 8–9: διὰ μόνης τῆς διανοίας.

[23] The relationship between διάνοια and πίστις will be explored in Chapter 4.

[24] *Contra Eunom.* 1. 373, GNO 1. 137. 5–6.   [25] von Balthasar, *Présence et pensée*, 79.

employ again.[26] Though characteristic of Gregory, it goes back at least to
Philo, in fact to the same passage which we just considered and which he
likely has in mind. Philo says, 'when, therefore the soul that loves God
seeks to know what the one living God is according to his essence, it is
entering upon an obscure and dark subject of investigation, from which
the greatest benefit that arises to it is to comprehend that God, as to his
essence, is utterly incomprehensible to any being, and also to be aware
that he is invisible'.[27]

Is Gregory contradicting himself in the space of a few lines? He has
just said that God is known through faith alone and then a few lines later
says that God is known in not knowing. Or is he establishing a connection between faith, in the exalted apophatic sense in which he has just
used it, and this coincidence of knowing and unknowing, what Augustine has termed *docta ignorantia*,[28] that has played such an important role in
Neoplatonic mystical theory, both Christian and non-Christian?[29] That
is to say, is faith another way of expressing this ignorance of the mind, an
unknowing higher than knowing that has abandoned all concepts and
images, in the face of incomprehensible mystery, in a way which ultimately allows Gregory to say much more?

Contra Eunomium II

The Migration of Abraham

As dense as Book II of the *Contra Eunomium* may be, Pottier discerns
a rather well-defined structure that has two overriding aims which
Gregory wishes to accomplish: (1) he wants to argue that no human

---

[26] e.g. *De vita Moysis*, SC, II. 163. 6–7 and *In Cant.* VI, GNO VI. 183. 2–5. While many
authors before Gregory, both Christian and non-Christian, have spoken of the coincidence of knowledge and ignorance, no other author before Gregory resolves this paradox
through πίστις. See Philo, *De post.* v. 15; Plotinus, *Enn.* VI. 9 (38); Basil, *Ep.* 234. 2;
Gregory of Nazianzus, *Orat.* 38. 7; Denys the Areopagite, *Ep.* 1; *De Myst. Theol.* II.

[27] *De post.* v. 15: ὅταν οὖν φιλόθεος ψυχὴ τὸ τί ἐστιν τὸ ὂν κατὰ τὴν οὐσίαν
ζητῇ, εἰς ἀειδῆ καὶ ἀόρατον ἔρχεται ζήτησιν, ἐξ ἧς αὐτῇ περιγίνεται μέγ-
ιστον ἀγαθόν, καταλαβεῖν ὅτι ἀκατάληπτος ὁ κατὰ τὸ εἶναι θεὸς παντὶ καὶ
αὐτὸ τοῦτο ἰδεῖν ὅτι ἐστὶν ἀόρατος. Trans. F. Colson and G. Whitaker, LCL, Philo
vol. ii (Cambridge, Mass., 1950), 337.

[28] See Augustine, *Ep.* 130. 15. 28. Gandillac, 'Docte Ignorance', s.v., *Dictionnaire de
Spiritualité*, gives the impression that Nicholas of Cusa introduces this term.

[29] A point very well demonstrated by S. Lilla, 'La teologia negativa dal pensiero greco
classico a quello patristico e bizantino', *Helikon* 22–7 (1982–7), 235 n. 59; and idem,
'Diogini', in *La Mistica: fenomenologia e riflessione teologica*, 2 vols., ed. E. Ancilli and
M. Paparozzi (Rome, 1984), 381–7, esp. 385–6.

faculty can comprehend the divine essence; and (2) he wants to refute the theses of Eunomius.[30]

Gregory offers three proofs, metaphysical, mystical, and epistemological,[31] in support of his first argument that human nature has no capacity to comprehend the divine essence.[32] The metaphysical proof concerns the distance between created and uncreated being,[33] The mystical proof focuses on the faith of Abraham,[34] while the epistemological proof develops views on the nature of human knowledge[35] and the nature of the divine names.[36] Pottier has described this entire section of Book II as a 'systematic', 'personal' and 'small *chef-d'œuvre*' of Gregory's theology,[37] and it is here, specifically in the so-called 'mystical proof' of the migration of Abraham, that we find the most revealing occurrence of faith in the *Contra Eunomium*.

When Gregory comments upon the great patriarchs of the Old Testament he usually follows the typological or moral exegesis of the Alexandrian tradition to which he was heir.[38] However, the figure of Abraham is an exception to this. The patriarch constitutes 'one of Gregory's most personal interpretations because the figure of Abraham illustrates and establishes his doctrine of the incomprehensibility of the divine nature'.[39] Hence, while Gregory's treatment of Abraham shares some things in common with both Philo's and Origen's treatment of the patriarch,[40] he adapts the traditional exegesis of Abraham to the exigencies of anti-Arian polemic.[41]

[30] Pottier, *Dieu et le Christ*, 35–9, describes the organization of Book II.
[31] Ibid., 36.   [32] *Contra Eunom.* II. 67, GNO I. 245.
[33] Ibid., 68–83, GNO I. 245–51.   [34] Ibid., 84–96, GNO I. 251–4.
[35] Ibid., 97–124, GNO I. 255–62.   [36] Ibid., 125–47, GNO I. 262–8.
[37] Pottier, *Dieu et le Christ*, 36.
[38] Canévet, *Grégoire de Nysse et l'herméneutique biblique*, 94–5.
[39] Ibid., 95: 'La figure d'Abraham, en revanche, se prête à l'une des interprétations les plus personelles de Grégoire, puisqu'elle illustre et fonde sa doctrine de l'incompréhensibilité de la nature divine.'
[40] Philo, *De mig. Abr.*, LCL, Philo vol. iv (Cambridge, Mass., 1932); *Abr.*, LCL, Philo vol. vi (Cambridge, Mass., 1935); Origen, *Hom. in Gen.* III, SC. An interesting passage from Philo suggests a possible source for Gregory's notion of πίστις as a faculty of union. Philo says at *De mig. Abr.* 132: 'What then is the cementing substance? Do you ask, what? Piety, surely, and faith: for these virtues adjust and unite (ἐνοῦσιν) the intent of the heart to the incorruptible Being: as Abraham when he believed is said to "come near to God"' (Gen. 18: 23). LCL, trans. F. Colson and G. Whitaker. I am grateful to M. Canévet for pointing out to me this quotation from Philo. For a concise summary of how Gregory follows his Alexandrian predecessors see Canévet, *Grégoire de Nysse et l'herméneutique biblique*, 95–6; see also, Gargano, *La teoria di Gregorio di Nissa*, 45–95, and M. Simonetti, *Lettera e/o Allegoria: Un Contributo alla Storia dell' Esegesi Patristica* (Rome, 1985), 145–56; see also M. Simonetti, *Biblical Interpretation in the Early Church*, trans. J. Hughes, ed. A. Bergquist and M. Bockmuehl (Edinburgh, 1994), 65–7.
[41] Canévet, *Grégoire de Nysse et l'herméneutique biblique*, 96.

If we turn, then, to Gregory's interpretation of the migration of Abraham, it should come as no surprise that it reveals important characteristics of Gregory's exalted notion of faith, for at the outset of his treatment of Abraham's journey, Gregory refers to him as 'father of the faith'.[42]

Indeed the figure of Abraham, at least as he appears here in the *Contra Eunomium*, is something of a composite. More than simply the patriarch of Genesis 12: 1–5 f., we have a reading of this story through the lens of Hebrews 11: 8.[43] It is the version of the story in the Letter to the Hebrews which turns the discussion in the direction of faith and sets the stage for Gregory's claim that the problem of attaining to God who is unknowable is resolved in faith. For in the Letter to the Hebrews we read that Abraham sets out on his journey, structured by Gregory along the lines of a Neoplatonic ascent, by means of faith; and by means of faith he journeys without knowledge.[44]

With a Hebrews 11 reading of Genesis 12 as an exegetical base, we see Abraham begin his journey, at divine behest, by leaving his land and people.[45] But Gregory immediately translates the story into an epistemological key by saying that Abraham 'went out by Divine command from his own country and kindred on a journey taken by a prophet eager for knowledge of God'.[46] And instead of leaving his land Abraham leaves himself and the realm of base and earthly thoughts:

For going out from himself and from his own country, by which I understand his earthly and carnal mind, and raising his thoughts as far as possible ... and forsaking the soul's kinship with the senses, ... 'walking', as the Apostle said, 'by

---

[42] *Contra Eunom.* II. 84, GNO I. 251. 21.

[43] Gregory implies he is reading Gen. 12: 1–4 (ἱστορία) through Heb. 11: 8 (ἀλληγορία) at *Contra Eunom.* II. 85, GNO I. 251. 22–5: ἐκεῖνος, εἰ δεῖ κατὰ τὴν τοῦ ἀποστόλου μεγαλοφυΐαν ἀλλάξαντα τὴν φωνὴν ἀλληγορικῶς τὸν νοῦν τῆς ἱστορίας κατανοῆσαι, μενούσης δηλαδὴ καὶ τῆς ἱστορικῆς ἀληθείας,... By 'apostle' Gregory intends Paul; conforming to oriental tradition, Gregory did not contest Paul's authorship of the letter (Canévet, *Grégoire de Nysse et l'herméneutique biblique*, 202).

[44] See Heb. 11: 8–9; the entire chapter is an exaltation of faith which provides the various *loci* of great deeds accomplished by means of πίστις. One cannot overlook the fact that πίστις appears as an instrumental dative. An instrumental sense of πίστις appears with great emphasis some 20 times in the course of a single chapter: 18 of these occur as an instrumental dative, the largest proportions being attributed to Abraham and Moses (3 each), and 2 occur as the object of the preposition διά. It is precisely these biblical forms which, as we shall see, Gregory transfers to an epistemological sense according to the Neoplatonic *esprit du temps* and incorporates them as technical terms of his apophatic vocabulary.

[45] *Contra Eunom.* II. 85, GNO I. 251. 25–6.

[46] Ibid., 251. 26–8 (trans. LNPF, 259).

faith, not by sight' (2 Cor. 5: 7), he was raised so high by the sublimity of his knowledge that he came to be regarded as the acme of human perfection, knowing as much of God as it was possible for finite human capacity at its full stretch to attain.[47]

This first part of Abraham's journey is characterized by a twofold movement of *anabasis* and *aphairesis*, but, it is important to note, it remains firmly grounded in scripture. We see the *anabasis* in the ascensional imagery of going out, of being raised up to knowledge of God. The other side of this coin of ascent is seen in the aphairetic imagery of letting go of sense-knowledge as Abraham leaves behind all commerce with the senses. Gregory emphasizes with clearly apophatic language that this ascent involves *not* the workings of the senses, *not* seeing and *not* hearing.[48] Gregory, however, grounds this ascent in 2 Corinthians 5: 7.

Having described the ascent of the mind and its movement away from what can be grasped through the senses to a certain knowledge of God, Gregory equates this inner journey with the meaning of 2 Cor. 5: 7: 'we walk by faith (διὰ πίστεως) and not by sight'. Quoting this Pauline text as he does, Gregory seems to be saying that this ascent to knowledge of God is tantamount to moving out in faith, much as Abraham does in the Hebrews version of the story,[49] indeed tantamount to an ascent in faith. At least at this phase in Abraham's ascent, knowledge does not supplant faith, rather knowledge and faith coincide.[50] By reading Heb. 11: 8 and 2 Cor. 5: 7 together, Gregory leads us into a paradox.

While on the one hand, this ascent, this setting out by means of faith (Heb. 11: 8a), this walking by faith and not by sight (2 Cor. 5: 7) leads to a knowledge of God in creation,[51] a knowledge which does not supplant faith but coincides with it; on the other hand, however, this faith is at the same time an unknowing. Gregory cites the Letter to the Hebrews and reminds us that this walking by faith is a walking in unknowing: 'He [sc. Abraham] did not know where he was going.'[52] Moreover, this

---

[47] Ibid., 86, GNO i. 252. 1–14 (trans. LNPF, 259—translation altered).

[48] See ibid., 86, GNO i. 252. 6–7: μηδενὶ...αἰσθησιν...ἀοράτων,...μήτε ἀκοῆς περιηχούσης...

[49] Heb. 11: 8a: Πίστει καλούμενος Ἀβραὰμ ὑπήκουσεν ἐξελθεῖν εἰς τόπον....

[50] Here Gregory departs from the traditional Alexandrian view which tends to supplant πίστις by γνῶσις. See Völker, *Gregor von Nyssa als Mystiker*, 141 n. 7, and Dünzl, *Braut und Bräutigam*, 295–6. For a list of various texts concerning γνῶσις and πίστις see F. Mann, *Lexicon Gregorianum*, vol. ii, s.v. γνῶσις at 221.

[51] *Contra Eunom.* ii. 87, GNO ii. 252. 14–16.

[52] Ibid., 252. 16–17: ἀλλ' ὅμως τί θησι περὶ ἐκείνου ὁ λόγος; ὅτι ἐξῆλθεν οὐκ ἐπιστάμενος ποῦ ἀπέρχεται... Cf. Heb. 11: 8b: καὶ ἐξῆλθεν μὴ ἐπιστάμενος ποῦ ἔρχεται.

unknowing is thought to be favourable, for Abraham 'went out not knowing whither he went, no, nor even being capable of learning the name of him whom he loved, yet he was not impatient or ashamed on account of such ignorance'.[53] Hence this moving out in faith is also a moving out in unknowing. Once again we see in Gregory the coincidence of knowledge and ignorance. As we noted above in our discussion of the text from *Contra Eunomium* I, Gregory draws a connection between faith and the well-established tradition of 'learned ignorance': faith is that unknowing which, on a purely rational plane, coincides with knowledge but which, at the non-discursive level, is higher than all discursive knowing. In order to see this more clearly, as well as what other role faith serves, let us return to Abraham's ascent.

The father of the faith, by setting out in faith and walking by faith, has come to a knowledge of God in creation. But this knowledge has not supplanted faith; he continues his journey; the mind moves towards what lies beyond all knowing.[54] So Abraham moves beyond the Chaldaean philosophy, which is built on appearances, and beyond what can be known by the senses; and from the beauty of the things he contemplated and the harmony of celestial wonders, Abraham desired to see the prototype of beauty.[55] The patriarch has been growing in discursive knowledge and understanding as he ascends in faith. By reason he grasped all qualities attributed to the divine nature: power, goodness, that God is without beginning, that God is not circumscribed by any limit.[56] Abraham uses all these as steps on his heavenly ascent but realizes that they fall short of what he seeks. At this point in the text an aphairetic process of letting go and of purification ensues, and Abraham begins to leave behind the knowledge he has acquired.[57] He renounces all concepts and images that represent God.[58] Having done this Abraham acquires a faith that is unmixed and purified of all concepts.[59]

Is faith capable of anything in this state that is purified of all images and concepts? Abraham says, with apophatic emphasis, that, after arriv-

---

[53] *Contra Eunom.* II. 252. 16–19 (trans. LNPF, 259—translation altered).
[54] Ibid., 252. 23–4: . . .τὴν διάνοιαν στῆναι τῆς εἰς τὸ ἐπέκεινα τῶν γινωσκομένον πορείας.
[55] Ibid., 252. 24–253. 1.   [56] Ibid., 253. 1–5.   [57] Ibid., 253. 11.
[58] Canévet, *Grégoire de Nysse et l'herméneutique biblique*, 96.
[59] *Contra Eunom.* II. 89, GNO I. 253. 12–14: ἐκκαθήρας τὸν λογισμὸν τῶν τοιούτων ὑπονοιῶν ἀμιγῆ τε καὶ καθαρὰν πάσης ἐννοίας τὴν πίστιν ἀναλαβών,. . .

ing at this purified faith, he is speechless (ἄφωνος) and incapable (ἀνενέργητος) of explaining rationally what his mind has seen.[60] Within this context of epistemological ascent, which has brought the mind through knowledge to silence, we see the specific function of faith: Gregory says that faith 'unites the searching mind to the incomprehensible God'.[61] Faith, then, is Gregory's term for that faculty of union between mind and God.[62]

Union, however, is not the only function which faith performs; faith also mediates.[63] Just as faith performs the function of union between mind and God, so faith mediates between mind and God. Faith mediates to the mind knowledge of a discursive sort: namely, that God is greater than any symbol by which he can be known.[64] Hence, while we are in the context of an apophatic ascent of the mind, and faith is the zenith of this ascent, grasping in union the divine essence, the mind is not left with nothing. Faith gives the discursive mind something of what it 'knows'; it is obliged, as Canévet has stated, to translate itself into discursive thoughts.[65] The discursive mind receives 'the likeness of gold', that is, the knowledge that God is greater than any symbol that can be known, but this is not 'gold itself' (the divine nature),[66] that is, the non-discursive experience of, indeed union with, the divine nature by faith alone.

Gregory concludes his discussion of the migration of Abraham as he began it, by returning to Paul as his exegetical base. He recapitulates Abraham's journey by saying that the patriarch left behind meddlesome knowledge (πολυπραγμοσύνη) and arrived at a stance of faith. It is important to keep in mind the context in which Gregory makes this claim. This is not faith in opposition to knowledge; that is to say, it is not

---

[60] Ibid., 253. 21–2.

[61] Ibid., 253. 25–8: οὐκ ἔστιν ἄλλως προσεγγίσαι θεῷ, μὴ πίστεως μεσιτευούσης καὶ συναπτούσης δι' ἑαυτῆς τὸν ἐπιζητοῦντα νοῦν πρὸς τὴν ἀκατάληπτον φύσιν.

[62] The designation of a faculty that bridges the gap between *intellectus* and God is certainly not new, but the designation of πίστις as the faculty which performs this noblest of deeds is quite novel. We shall have occasion in Chapter 4 to examine briefly the history of this notion in order to see more clearly Gregory of Nyssa's specific contribution to the history of this idea.

[63] *Contra Eunom.* 11. 89, GNO 1. 253. 25–8.

[64] *Contra Eunom.* 11. 89, GNO 1. 253. 14–17.

[65] Canévet, *Grégoire de Nysse et l'herméneutique biblique*, 63: '. . . cette connaissance [sc. de la foi] essaie cependent de se traduire en pensées, bien que l'infinité de l'essence divine soit incompatible avec le caractère défini de nos concepts'.

[66] *In Cant.* 111, GNO vi. 85. 18–19.

the irrational faith of, for example, Porphyry's anti-Christian derision.[67] It is exalted faith, higher than knowledge, the apex of apophatic ascent, that which rests solidly and surely after *aphairesis* has shed all images, concepts, and movement. It is this exalted state of mind which Gregory then says is tantamount to that of Paul's claim that faith renders one just before God: 'leaving behind the meddlesomeness of knowledge, "Abraham believed in God and this was reckoned to him as justice (Rom. 4: 3/ Exod. 15: 6)"'.[68] That Paul aligns faith and justification is something of a hallmark of the Pauline tradition and beyond. The Letter to the Galatians recalls the same Abraham justified by putting faith in God (Gal. 3: 6), and the catholic Epistle to James repeats this, adding that this justification made Abraham a friend of God (Jas. 2: 23). But that this justification by faith is aligned with the apophatic ascent of the mind to God, bridging the gap between the mind and God, attaining union with God, is something of an innovation on the part of Gregory of Nyssa and allows him to conclude his presentation of the migration of Abraham, by giving a provocative, albeit brief, reading of Hebrews 11: 1.

Extolling faith over knowledge, Gregory says that knowledge is concerned with only what is known; 'But the faith of Christians acts otherwise. For it is the substance, not of things known, but of things hoped for.'[69] This statement is more than simply an occasion to quote Hebrews 11: 1.[70] For the Hebrews text enables Gregory to say why faith is exalted over knowledge and that it provides a certainty that knowledge cannot provide; faith is able to do something knowledge cannot do: 'faith makes our own that which we see not, assuring us by its own certainty of that which does not appear'.[71] Faith is the 'substance of things hoped for' in that it somehow puts one in possession of, 'makes our own', that which is beyond the realm in which the mind, with its concern for knowledge, operates. Again we see faith play a mediational role. What precisely it mediates we shall have occasion to see more clearly when we consider other texts which feature divine indwelling and

---

[67] See Eusebius, *Praep. evang.*, SC, I. 1. 11. 4–5; I. 2. 4. 2–3; I. 3. 1. 5–6.

[68] *Contra Eunom.* II. 92, GNO II. 253. 28–30: καταλιπὼν γὰρ τὴν ἐκ τῆς γνώσεως πολυπραγμοσύνην Ἐπίστευσε, φησίν, Ἀβραὰμ τῷ θεῷ, καὶ ἐλογίσθη αὐτῷ εἰς δικαιοσύνη.

[69] *Contra Eunom.* II. 93, GNO I. 254. 4–6 (trans. LNPF, 259).

[70] Heb. 11: 1: Ἔστιν δὲ πίστις ἐλπιζομένων ὑπόστασις, . . .

[71] *Contra Eunom.* II. 93, GNO I. 254. 8–10 (trans. LNPF, 259). Gregory precedes this statement with another Pauline text, Rom. 8, 24, but it does not contribute to his present line of argument in the way that the Hebrews text does.

union.[72] For the moment, suffice it to observe that whilst ratiocination and its resulting knowledge can provide certainty with respect to what 'appears', to what can be circumscribed and grasped by the mind, this is not possible when the divine essence is the object in question, for it cannot be circumscribed by an act of understanding. 'Vain, therefore', Gregory warns, 'is he who maintains that it is possible to take knowledge of the divine essence . . .'[73] Faith, however, can put one in contact with this essence. Returning to the authority of Paul in the Letter to the Hebrews Gregory says, 'For so speaks the Apostle of the believer, that "he endured as seeing him who is invisible" (Heb. 11: 27).'[74] Once again Gregory uses scripture to lead us into paradox: faith sees what cannot be seen. Whatever 'making our own' of the 'substance of things hoped for' there is, whatever possessing of the divine essence is accomplished by faith, the certainty of faith is achieved without the grasp of comprehension. In contrast to knowledge which thrives on seeing what becomes visible to the mind, faith negotiates the paradox of seeing the invisible.[75] Indeed Gregory's treatment of the migration of Abraham is an early and rich example of Gregory's exaltation of faith that reveals a nuanced epistemology grounded in scripture.

Canévet has observed that although Gregory's treatment of the migration of Abraham begins in the traditional Alexandrian manner, he adapts this to the philosophical exigencies of anti-Arian polemic.[76] In light of the role played by the theme of divine incomprehensibility in the anti-Eunomian phase of this polemic, the point is understandable. However, the question of divine comprehensibility has been developing in one way or another at least since Protagoras.[77] Whether or not God can be grasped by the intellect, if so, how? if not, why not?—is it due to

---

[72] Why faith can do this will become clearer after we have looked at *De vita Moysis* and *Commentarius in Canticum canticorum* and have considered faith in the light of what Neoplatonism has to say generally about faculties of union (the subject of Chapter 4).

[73] *Contra Eunom.* II. 93, GNO I. 254. 11–13 (trans. LNPF, 260).

[74] Ibid., 254. 10–11 (trans. LNPF, 259).

[75] On paradox see Canévet, *Grégoire de Nysse et l'herméneutique biblique*, 339, who notes Gregory's use of paradox; it serves to move beyond the principle of non-contradiction in order to penetrate to the interior of the Transcendent.

[76] Ibid., 95–6.

[77] See H. Diels, *Die Fragmente der Vorsokratiker*, vol. ii (Berlin 1951–2), 80. B. 4. The history of this theme in ancient authors both Christian and non-Christian has recently been presented in an admirable way by D. Carabine, *The Unknown God: Negative Theology in the Platonic Tradition: Plato to Eriugena* (Louvain, 1995); see also Lilla, 'Teologia negativa'; W. Jaeger's Gifford Lectures are still a helpful orientation to the background, *The Theology of the Early Greek Philosophers* (Oxford, 1947).

divine greatness or human deficiency or both?—constitute a cluster of questions that have been in circulation quite irrespective of Eunomius. Moreover, apart from an element of specifically anti-Eunomian polemic in Gregory's exegesis of the migration of Abraham, there is at issue the more general encounter between Neoplatonism and Christianity and especially the role played in this encounter by Christian exegesis of scripture.[78]

While indeed Gregory's apophatic language and ascensional motif are evocative of the Neoplatonic style in general, and not entirely dissimilar to the inspiring ascent to Beauty described by Plotinus at *Ennead* I. 6. 8, Gregory is not simply placing the words of Diotima in the mouth of Abraham or attaching the wings of *Phaedrus* to the patriarch's back.[79] For Gregory is not interpreting Plato but the Bible.[80] This is not an ascent to the One, but that of Abraham to the God of Jesus Christ. In this ascent, we see not the exaltation of the Platonic faith of *Republic* 511e1, or of *Timaeus* 29c4. Nor do we see the somewhat more positive view taken of Platonic faith by Plotinus.[81] Rather in the migration of Abraham we

---

[78] For a general orientation see B. Studer, 'Eruditio Veterum' and 'Sapientia Veterum', in A. di Berardino and B. Studer (eds.), *Storia della Teologia*, vol. i: *Epoca Patristica* (Casale Monferrato, 1993), 333–71 and 373–411.

[79] It is not our purpose here to assess the influence of Plotinus on Gregory. For an orientation to this rather complex question see J. Daniélou, 'Grégoire de Nysse et Plotin', *Congrès de Tours, Association Guillaume Budé* (1954), 259–62; idem, 'Grégoire de Nysse et le néo-Platonisme de l'école d'Athènes', *Revue des études grecques* 80 (1967), 395–401; P. Courcelle, 'Grégoire de Nysse lecteur de Porphyre', *Revue des études grecques* 80 (1967), 402–6; A. Meredith, 'Gregory of Nyssa and Plotinus', *Studia Patristica* 17 (1982), 1120–6; idem, 'The Good and the Beautiful in Gregory of Nyssa', in *EPMHNEYMATA: Festschrift für Hadwig Hörner zum sechzigsten Geburtstag*, ed. H. Eisenberger (Heidelberg, 1990), 133–45; J. Rist, 'Basil's "Neoplatonism": Its Background and Nature', in *Basil of Caesarea: Christian, Humanist, Ascetic. A Sixteen Hundreth Anniversary Symposium*, ed. P. Fedwick (Toronto, 1981), 137–220; idem, 'Plotinus and Christian Philosophy', in *The Cambridge Companion to Plotinus*, ed. L. Gerson (Cambridge, 1996), 386–413; for a study which emphasizes similarities between Plotinus and Gregory see S. Lilla, s. v. Platonism and the Fathers, *Encyclopedia of the Early Church*, ed. A. Di Berardino, trans. A. Walford (Cambridge, 1992), 689–98, at 694–5; for a clear statement of important and enduring contrasts see K. Corrigan, ' "Solitary" Mysticism in Plotinus, Proclus, Gregory of Nyssa, and Pseudo-Dionysius', *Journal of Religion* 76 (1996), 28–42, at 38–40.

[80] The connection between metaphysics and exegesis is fairly ubiquitous in Gregory, for he discerns in the Bible itself the structure of being and knowing. A clear example of this is seen in the prologue to Homily 6 on the Song of Songs. There Gregory finds verified in Phil. 3: 13 the relationship between created and uncreated being (*In Cant.* VI, GNO VI. 174. 13–16); moreover, the bride models throughout the homily everything she has taught 'lovers of transcendent beauty concerning God' (ibid., 172. 22–173. 1).

[81] See *Enn.* IV. 7. 15 and VI. 9. 10, a text we shall consider in greater detail in the following chapter. On Neoplatonic faith see Rist, *Plotinus: The Road to Reality*, 231–46.

see the exaltation of Christian faith. With his characteristic blending of metaphysics and exegesis Gregory draws out the epistemological implications of faith in the language and motifs which characterize the Neoplatonic *esprit du temps*.

The Archers of Benjamin

A final text in Book III is worth considering before drawing to a close this examination of faith in the *Contra Eunomium*. While we find no ascent with Neoplatonic resonances of *apophasis* and *aphairesis*, there is, nevertheless, a clear exaltation of faith over discursive knowledge.

In this section of the *Contra Eunomium* Gregory is well occupied with the task of refuting the seven arguments of Eunomius, and in particular the contention on the part of Eunomius that since the Lord was named a door, it follows that the divine essence may be comprehended.[82] In order to demonstrate the 'vanity of the "technology" of Eunomius',[83] Gregory likens the tactics of Eunomian 'theo-technology' to the situation of the Benjamites (Judg. 20).

Eunomius is quite sure that he not only can see him whom no one has seen but can also measure God. Gregory laments that Eunomius does not see that faith is higher than any product of ratiocination. Eunomius is like the archers of Benjamin who had no time for law but could take aim and shoot their arrows within a hair's breadth of anything (Judg. 20: 16). They are brilliant at taking aim at things of little consequence and altogether without substance, but regarding things of real import, they are, alas, ignorant.[84] Of what precisely are they, or Eunomius, ignorant? They think that God can be grasped through comprehension, approached through ratiocination. Rather faith is the doorway;[85] faith, not the grasp of comprehension, is the recommended approach to the incomprehensible nature. Hence, Gregory advises young archers not to be bothered with shooting within a hair's breadth, that is, thinking they can grasp with reason the incomprehensible. Rather they are to have eyes for the door of faith. Faith opens to God. They are to drop their useless concerns about the incomprehensible and not lose the profit that is at hand, which is found 'through faith alone'.[86]

---

[82] See *Contra Eunom.* III. 8, GNO II. 241. 18. Cf. John 10: 9. For an overview of the general structure of *Contra Eunomium* III see Pottier, *Dieu et le Christ*, 47–57.

[83] M. Canévet, *Grégoire de Nysse et l'herméneutique biblique*, 110; see also B. Pottier, *Dieu et le Christ*, 208.

[84] *Contra Eunom.* III. 8. 12, GNO II. 242. 25–243. 9–11.   [85] Ibid., 243. 9.

[86] Ibid., 242. 11: διὰ μόνης τῆς πίστεως.

Gregory's recommendation of faith to the archers of Benjamin is not the clear exaltation of faith as the apex of apophatic ascent that we saw in the migration of Abraham, yet faith is valued, nevertheless, over discursive knowledge. While the nature of God cannot be grasped by the mind in an act of understanding, God can nevertheless be found by means of faith. Gregory formulates this finding 'by faith alone' in a manner which gives the term 'faith' a technical meaning in these apophatic contexts: that which supersedes discursive knowledge, bridging the gap between the mind and God, and establishing contact, indeed union with God who yet remains ever incomprehensible (ἀκατάληπτος) to the mind.

De vita Moysis

In the previous chapter's description of the role of the mind, especially that of *dianoia* in certain texts of *De vita Moysis*, we observed that *dianoia* can enter the presence of God. Whether this be the darkness of the sanctuary or the darkness wherein God dwells, the mind could somehow penetrate the impenetrable (παραδυεὶς τὸ ἄδυτον).[87] However, even though mind could enter this non-discursive realm beyond images and concepts, it was capable of doing nothing. Let us return to some of these texts concerning the patriarch Moses, considered by Gregory a pillar of faith[88] and consider especially the role played by faith after mind has entered (1) the sanctuary and (2) the darkness where God dwells.

The Inner Sanctuary

Let us first turn to *De vita Moysis* I. 46. At this point in the biography of Moses we find ourselves in two contexts which Gregory has fused into one: mystery religions and priesthood. Moses is guide for the people in a secret initiation,[89] but he is no less a priest who mediates on behalf of the people and helps the people bear their own weakness.

---

[87] *De vita Moysis* SC, I, 46, 4–5.

[88] *De beat.* VI, GNO VII, ii, 137, 23–24. See M. Girardi, 'Annotazioni al *De beatitudinibus,*' *Augustinianum* 35 (1995): 161–182; see also J. Daniélou 'Moïse exemple et figure chez Grégoire de Nysse,' *Cahiers sioniens* 2–4 (1955), 386–400.

[89] *De vita Moysis,* SC, I. 42. 1–2: Ἐν τούτῳ δὲ καί τινος αὐτοῖς ἀπορρητοτέρας μνήσεως ὁ Μωυσῆς καθηγεῖτο,... In presenting Moses as one who initiates into the mysteries Gregory follows Philo; see Philo's *De vita Moysis* II. 71–5 and *De dec.* 10. 41, where Philo employs mystery terminology to describe Moses' reception of the Law. On the use of mystery terminology see Daniélou, *Platonisme et théologie mystique,* 181 ff., and idem in *Moïse: L'homme de l'alliance,* ed. H. Cazelles *et al.* (Paris, 1955), 274 f.; see also

During the tremendous theophany on Mount Sinai 'the entire people were unable to bear what they saw and heard', so they asked that Moses mediate (μεσιτευθῆναι) on their behalf.[90] Not only does Moses mediate, he also helps them bear their weakness. At 11. 43 we read that as Moses led the people towards the fire he himself grew frightened; indeed so frightened that he trembled. However, when the people left Moses alone and returned to the foot of the mountain, having asked him to act as their mediator, Gregory says that Moses was no longer afraid and that the great fear he had previously shown was not in fact his own. He felt this out of compassion for those who were truly frightened.[91]

As both guide and priest, then, Moses stands alone. No longer afraid,

> he faced the darkness and entered the invisible realities and was no longer seen by the onlookers. Having penetrated into the sanctuary of divine mystagogy, Moses encountered the Invisible, teaching by this, I think, that he who wants to encounter God must leave behind all appearances and, stretching forth the mind towards the invisible and incomprehensible, as though to a mountain summit, believe God is present there where the understanding does not reach.[92]

This passage merits consideration for it shows faith in an exalted mode and is situated in a context of ascent and apophasis that reveals a rather characteristic blending of Platonic and biblical concerns.

The opening lines of 1. 46 are significant for their conflation of biblical and philosophical elements: Moses faces the darkness, enters the invisible realities and is seen no more. The theme of 'divine darkness' is something of a hallmark of the Judaeo-Christian tradition of negative

A. Nock, *Early Gentile Christianity and its Hellenistic Background* (New York, 1964), 132–43 *et passim*.

[90] Ibid., 1. 45. 1–3. Gregory uses the same verb μεσιτεύω at *Contra Eunom.* 11. 91, GNO 11. 26, to describe the function of πίστις mediating and uniting the soul to God. It is well to note that as a symbol of πίστις Moses performs a similar role of mediation. M. Simonetti (*Vita di Mosè*, 269) indicates that in emphasizing the mediational role of Moses, Gregory is forcing somewhat Exod. 19; 16: the people do not actually ask Moses to mediate on their behalf. It serves to highlight the importance of this theme to Gregory. Cf. *De vita Moysis*, SC, 11. 130 and 160; see also *In inscrip. Psalm.* 1, GNO v. 45. 9.

[91] Ibid., esp. 45. 12–13: ἀλλὰ διὰ τὴν πρὸς τοὺς κατεπτηχότας συμπάθειαν ταῦτα παθεῖν.

[92] Ibid., 46. 2–10: . . . τότε καὶ αὐτοῦ κατατολμᾷ τοῦ γνόφου καὶ ἐντὸς τῶν ἀοράτων γίνεται μήκετι τοῖς ὁρῶσι φαινόμενος. Πρὸς γὰρ τὸ ἄδυτον τῆς θείας μυσταγωγίας παραδυείς, ἐκεῖ τῷ ἀοράτῳ συνῆν μὴ ὁρώμενος, διδάσκων, οἶμαι, δι' ὧν ἐποίησεν, ὅτι δεῖ τὸν μέλλοντα συνεῖναι τῷ Θεῷ ἐξελθεῖν πᾶν τὸ φαινόμενον καὶ ἐπὶ τὸ ἀόρατόν τε καὶ ἀκατάληπτον τὴν ἑαυτοῦ διάνοιαν, οἷον ἐπί τινα ὄρους κορυφήν, ἀνατείναντα ἐκεῖ πιστεύειν εἶναι τὸ θεῖον ἐν ᾧ οὐκ ἐπικνεῖται ἡ κατανόησις.

theology.[93] But Gregory combines this biblical metaphor (e.g. Exod. 20: 21) with the Aristotelian principle that only like knows like.

In *De anima* Aristotle says that 'like is known in fact by like'[94] and in the *Metaphysics* the same idea is expressed: 'the knowledge of like takes place by means of what is like'.[95] However, it is an idea which goes back at least to Plato. In *De anima* Aristotle seems to be referring to the *Timaeus*, and we see the same idea expressed with but the slightest change in the *Phaedo*, when Socrates says in the course of dialogue that 'it cannot be that one who is impure can touch what is pure'.[96] Therefore, because Moses is drawing near the Invisible, he himself becomes invisible, he disappears from view; for only like can know like.[97] However, Gregory does not seem to absorb uncritically this Platonic patrimony, for, as we shall see, he incorporates this into his own apophatic and Christian concerns, especially regarding knowledge of God.

Approaching darkness and entering the invisible realities are tantamount to entering the inner sanctuary of divine mystagogy.[98] In this context of the darkness of the Holy of Holies Moses encounters the Invisible. Gregory then explains what Moses is teaching in this. It is in his interpretation of Moses' entry into the darkness of the sanctuary that we see Gregory press into the service of his Christian apophatic concerns the Aristotelian motif mentioned above.

While entering the darkness of the sanctuary and becoming invisible implies a becoming like God, as Plato and Aristotle suggest, it does not involve the positive comprehension which Plato and Aristotle would imply. Gregory overturns such a position by means of an apophatic ascent which culminates in faith. He says that the one who wants

---

[93] However, as Carabine has pointed out (*The Unknown God*, 65), it is not an exclusively Judaeo-Christian concern, for Celsus speaks of the darkness that besets one if the knowledge of God comes too suddenly; see Origen, *Contra Celsum* VI. 36 (*sic*). Cf. her statement with that of B. McGinn in *The Foundations of Mysticism* (London, 1992), 175, who says that the theme of divine darkness is not found amongst the non-Christians. We shall have occasion to say more in a subsequent chapter about the theme of darkness in Gregory of Nyssa.

[94] *De an.* I 404^b 17–18: γιγνώοσκεσθαι γὰρ τῷ ὁμοίῳ τὸ ὅμοιον.

[95] *Met.* B 1000^{b}5–6: ἡ δὲ γνῶσις τοῦ ὁμοίου τῷ ὁμοίῳ.

[96] *Phaedo* 67b2: μὴ καθαρῷ γὰρ καθαροῦ ἐφάπτεσθαι μὴ οὐ θεμιτὸν ᾖ.

[97] Philo aligns divine darkness and invisibility at *De post.* V. 14, but Moses himself does not become invisible.

[98] The sanctuary is also a largely (though not exclusively) biblical theme which had been interiorized by Philo and it is taken up by Gregory with some frequency; see Daniélou, *Platonisme et théologie mystique*, 182–9. See also Simonetti, *Vita di Mosè*, 270. Cf. *Enn.* V. 1. 6 and VI. 9. 11.

communion with God must lift up the mind to the invisible and incomprehensible, and there, at a level where the understanding does not reach, one believes God is present.

That faith crowns an apophatic ascent and mediates union with God is not as clear in this passage as in the migration of Abraham. Nevertheless we can discern its exalted status. In the darkness of the sanctuary, beyond comprehension, there is no κατανόησις. Faith, however, is capable of functioning in this darkness. Moreover, Gregory connects it with divine presence: one believes God to be present. Finally, although he does not say explicitly that faith unites one to God as he did in the *Contra Eunomium*, there is a noteworthy parallel between encountering (σύνειμι) God in the darkness of the sanctuary and believing God to be present at the mountain top where understanding does not reach. Indeed on this mountain summit, in the darkness of the sanctuary, three elements obtain: encountering (σύνειμι), belief (πίστις) and divine presence (ἐκεῖ...εἶναιτὸ θεῖον). The philosophical principle that like knows like has been subtly changed to like *believes (in)* Like.

A very similar use of faith occurs in II. 188. Once again we find ourselves in the Holy of Holies and we see faith in an apophatic context and favoured above comprehension. Gregory says, 'the truth of being is ungraspable (ἄληπτον) and unapproachable (ἀπρόσιτον) to the multitude'; 'since it resides in the impenetrable and forbidden regions of the tabernacle of mystery, we should not concern ourselves with the knowledge of realities that transcend our understanding'.[99] Rather than engage in an act of comprehension in this realm which is dark to the mind, faith is required: Gregory says we should believe that the desired one is present in the hidden and inaccessible regions of the mind.[100] While we do not see faith, as we have seen it elsewhere, marking the zenith of an apophatic ascent or bridging the gap between the mind and God, we do see it once again exalted over comprehension. We have seen this exalted status in each of the texts we have considered so far and perhaps stated nowhere more clearly than in the *Contra Eunomium*. 'God reckons faith over knowledge.'[101] Moreover, faith is once again

---

[99] *De vita Moysis*, SC, II. 188. 4–8.

[100] Ibid., 188. 8–10:... πιστεύοντας εἶναι μὲν τὸ ζητούμενον, οὐ μὴν τοῖς ὀφθαλμοῖς πάντων προκεῖσθαι, ἀλλ᾽ἐν τοῖς ἀδύτοις τῆς διανοίας μένειν ἀπόρρητον.

[101] *Contra Eunom.* II. 92–3, GNO I. 254. 1–3: ὁ ἀπόστολος λέγει, ἀλλὰ δι᾽ ἡμας, ὅτι τὴν πίστιν, οὐχὶ τὴν γνῶσιν ὁ θεὸς εἰς δικαιοσύνην τοῖς ἀνθρώποις λογίζεται.

situated in a clearly apophatic context: ἄληπτος, ἀπρόσιτος, ἄδυτος, ἀπόρρητος. Faith is closely associated with divine presence, very similarly to what we saw at I. 46.

The question suggests itself: Does Gregory simply intend by faith, in this specific case, nothing other than firm Platonic conviction such as we see in the celebrated Allegory of the Line? However, Platonic faith is rather associated with sensibility. Such conviction would, in Plato's understanding, have to be based on the experience of the senses, and that is certainly not the case here, given the apophatic character of the text. Nor is faith lower than mind, which would be the case if we were dealing with faith as Platonic conviction. In this text Gregory suggests that faith is in the deepest depths of mind and certainly not subordinated to it; on the contrary, faith is not only exalted over comprehension, a characteristic function of mind, it has some appropriate association with divine presence that comprehension cannot enjoy.

Finally we see Gregory use this biblical image of the Holy of Holies to shape epistemological positions. The mind itself is the temple;[102] comprehension is the multitude which cannot enter the sanctuary. As we saw in the previous chapter, one has the impression not so much that mind/comprehension is denied all access to the divine presence, but rather that it does not perform its characteristic function; for there is nothing to grasp. In this text it seems that comprehension is denied all entry to the hidden, inaccessible regions (even though it presumably could find nothing to grasp were it admitted). Is Gregory being inconsistent, or imprecise? In this particular context I suggest that it is simply due to the biblical image of the Holy of Holies which is shaping the direction of his thought. Because the metaphor of the temple involves strict boundaries of admission and access, Gregory's epistemological scheme reflects these same concerns. Hence, the categories are slightly less fluid. However, the point remains the same. Regarding the presence of God, it is faith not knowledge that is the preferred method of approach.

Darkness

Having considered faith in the context of the metaphor of the sanctuary, let us turn to another important metaphor in *De vita Moysis* in which faith plays an important role.[103]

---

[102] See also *De orat. dom.* III, GNO VII. ii. 31–3 Cf. *Enn.* VI. 9. 11.

[103] Gregory is often considered a representative of the 'mysticism of darkness', and this *in contrast* to Origen's 'mysticism of light'. We shall have occasion later in this study to examine in greater detail the appropriateness of this claim.

Let us consider first an occurrence of faith towards the end of *De vita Moysis*. It is in fact the only text in *De vita Moysis* II which explicitly links faith and darkness. However, it is an important text for our purposes of establishing both the technical meaning of faith as well as the connection between faith and darkness, for *De vita Moysis* II. 315 is Gregory's own summary of perhaps the most important occurrence of darkness in *De vita Moysis*.

A summary of various events and stages already traversed opens II. 315. Amongst these Gregory mentions entering darkness, 'unfathomable darkness'.[104] While he does not use the term 'unfathomable' to describe this darkness at II. 163,[105] an event which Gregory has in mind at II. 325, darkness is nevertheless situated in a context of apophatic ascent.

Having been purified, Moses begins to ascend the 'mountain of the knowledge of God';[106] he begins, not unlike Abraham, to let go of knowledge previously acquired:

Letting go of all appearances, not only what the senses grasp but also what the mind thinks it sees, [the mind] goes deeper and deeper within until, by the mind's own curiosity, it penetrates into what is invisible and incomprehensible and there sees God. In this is the true knowledge of what is sought and in this is the seeing that is a not seeing, because the one who is sought transcends all knowledge, being separated on every side, as though by a kind of incomprehensible darkness. That is why the sublime John, who was in the luminous dark, said 'No one has ever seen God (John 1:18)', making it clear by this denial that the knowledge of the divine essence is altogether beyond the grasp not only of humans but of every intellectual nature.[107]

---

[104] *De vita Moysis*, SC, II. 315. 10: δυσθεωρήτῳ γνόφῳ.

[105] The language of impenetrability, as we have seen, is more characteristic of the sanctuary.

[106] On the symbolism of the mountain in Gregory of Nyssa see Canévet, *Grégoire de Nysse et l'herméneutique biblique*, 312–13.

[107] *De vita Moysis*, SC, II. 163. 1–164. 1: Καταλιπὼν γὰρ πᾶν τὸ φαινόμενον, οὐ μόνον ὅσα καταλαμβάνει ἡ αἴσθησις, ἀλλὰ καὶ ὅσα ἡ διάνοια δοκεῖ βλέπειν, ἀεὶ πρὸς τὸ ἐνδότερον ἵεται, ἕως ἂν διαδύῃ τῇ πολυπραγμοσύνῃ τῆς διανοίας πρὸς τὸ ἀθέατόν τε καὶ ἀκατάληπτον κἀκεῖ τὸν Θεὸν ἴδῃ. Ἐν τούτῳ γὰρ ἡ ἀληθής ἐστιν εἴδησις τοῦ ζητουμένου καὶ ἐν τούτῳ τὸ ἰδεῖν ἐν τῷ μὴ ἰδεῖν, ὅτι ὑπέρκειται πάσης εἰδήσεως τὸ ζητούμενον, οἷόν τινι γνόφῳ τῇ ἀκαταληψίᾳ πανταχόθεν διειλημμένον. Διό φησι καὶ ὁ ὑψηλός Ἰωάννης, ὁ ἐν τῷ λαμπρῷ γνόφῳ τούτῳ γενόμενος, ὅτι· Θεὸν οὐδεὶς ἑώρακε πώποτε, οὐ μόνον τοῖς ἀνθρώποις, ἀλλὰ καὶ πάσῃ νοητῇ φύσει τῆς θείας οὐσίας τὴν γνῶσιν ἀνέφικτον εἶναι τῇ ἀποφάσει ταύτῃ διοριζόμενος. I have taken the subject of the first sentence still to be ὁ νοῦς at 162. 10.

This text is important not least for its apophatic concerns and its use of paradox. The passage begins in a manner reminiscent of the ascent of Abraham, who, after having moved through various levels of knowledge, begins to leave behind the knowledge he has acquired.[108] Likewise Moses, having assaulted the mountain of divine knowledge, begins to leave behind levels of knowledge previously acquired and gains access to the incomprehensible. Notice the apophatic discourse that begins when the mind enters this realm: invisible (ἀθέατον), incomprehensible (ἀκατάληπτον), not seeing (μὴ ἰδεῖν), incomprehensible dark (γνόφῳ τῇ ἀκαταληψίᾳ), unattainable (ἀνέφικτον), denial (ἀποφάσει). Moreover, this apophatic language is situated amidst a series of paradoxes: the ascent of the mountain of knowledge is at the same time an inward movement; entering the incomprehensible realm, the mind's vision of God is described as a seeing which is a not seeing, a knowing which is a not knowing; John's penetration into the luminous dark. Once again we have the coincidence of knowledge and ignorance.[109]

It is specifically by means of *dianoia* that Moses has entered 'into the darkness where God is'.[110] Indeed there is a sense of divine presence into which mind has penetrated, but the overriding sense of this divine darkness is one of separation: 'being separated on all sides as though by a kind of darkness'. There is no mention of union of any sort. This is significant.

Based on our consideration of other texts which featured a strongly apophatic ascent motif, one would expect Gregory to mention the role of faith. However, he tends to reserve this term for emphasizing access, proximity, encounter, indeed communion. Because he emphasizes in this text the ungraspability of the divine essence, Gregory has not mentioned faith. However, when he summarizes this very passage at II. 315, the sense of separation is much less to the fore. Indeed Gregory emphasizes that having entered darkness, one draws close, even communes with God: 'in the unfathomable darkness you approach God'. While Gregory clearly has in mind II. 164, he has not simply reduplicated its content; he has introduced a subtle change. The emphasis at II. 164 is on gaining access to the incomprehensible darkness at the zenith of an epistemological ascent. Here it is by means of mind, specifically the curiosity of the

---

[108] *Contra Eunom.* II, GNO II. 253. 11.

[109] On Gregory's paradoxical language in general see Daniélou, *Platonisme et théologie mystique*, 274–84, but esp. Canévet, *Grégoire de Nysse et l'herméneutique biblique*, 340–2.

[110] *De vita Moysis*, SC, II. 152. 10.

mind, that Moses gains access to the darkness. Since, as we have shown in the previous chapter, mind is capable of nothing in this realm (whether it is the sanctuary or the darkness where God is), the accent, however understated, is rather on separation. But in II. 315, Gregory, as it were, presumes the mind's entry into darkness and focuses rather on drawing close or communing with God. In this case, mind is unsuitable. Hence, he says that 'in the unfathomable darkness one draws near God through faith'. The apophatic ascent at II. 164 is completed really at II. 315. The mind enters the darkness where God is and sees in not seeing, but by means of faith one nevertheless draws near God. It would seem then that Gregory establishes a certain parallel between this seeing that consists in not seeing and faith. The paradoxical expression presents a block to reason,[111] but faith can move beyond this obstacle and approach God. Faith, it would seem, resolves this coincidence of opposites.

Commentarius in Canticum canticorum

The Grasp of Faith

Once again we see faith in an exalted role in Homily 3 on the Song. In the course of his commentary on Song 1: 11–12 ('we shall make for you likenesses of gold with studs of silver while the king is on his couch'),[112] Gregory says that 'every teaching concerning the ineffable nature [sc. of God] ... is the likeness of gold and not gold itself';[113] for 'the divine nature transcends every grasp of the mind'.[114] While our conceptions bear a resemblance to what is sought, they fall short of comprehension; they fall short of grasping God.[115] In bold contrast, however, to the inability of mind to grasp the divine nature we see what faith is capable of. Gregory says that 'the soul, guided by such conceptions towards the knowledge of incomprehensible things, must establish in itself through faith alone the nature that transcends every intelligence'.[116] Immediately

---

[111] Canévet, Grégoire de Nysse et l'herméneutique biblique, 339, maintains that pardoxical expressions serve to move beyond the logical principle of non-contradiction in order to penetrate to the interior of the Transcendent.

[112] In Cant. III, GNO VI. 83. 1 ff.   [113] Ibid., 85. 16–19.

[114] Ibid., 86. 13–14: ἡ θεία φύσις πάσης ὑπέρκειται καταληπτικῆς διανοίας.

[115] Ibid., 86. 14–87. 3.

[116] Ibid., 87. 5–8: τὴν οὖν διὰ τῶν τοιούτων νοημάτων χειραγωγουμένην ψυχὴν πρὸς τὴν τῶν ἀλήπτων περίνοιαν διὰ μόνης πίστεως εἰσοικίζειν ἐν ἑαυτῇ λέγει δεῖν τὴν πάντα νοῦν ὑπερέχουσαν φύσιν. See F. Dünzl, Braut und Bräutigam (Tübingen, 1993), 79–81.

the friends of the bridegroom address the soul, and the language of indwelling is taken up again: 'through faith, you will be put under the yoke and become a dwelling place for the one who, by dwelling within you, is going to recline in you. For you will be his throne and will become his abode.'[117] Paul, a symbol of faith,[118] then embodies this indwelling through faith; he has become a vessel of election and 'a house containing the nature which nothing can contain'.[119]

The texts we have heretofore considered tended to present faith as the epistemological apex of an apophatic ascent, the means by which union with God is attained. In the present text faith is the means by which divine presence enters and dwells within the soul. The ascensional and apophatic motifs, albeit muted, are certainly not altogether absent. Gregory accomplishes this not through the language of *aphairesis* and *apophasis*, but through paradoxical statements.

Through faith the bride becomes a house in which Christ dwells. Paul is likewise a house, a house that 'contains what cannot be contained'. According to Canévet's study of Gregory's use of symbol, this sequence of images would connote intimacy, ascent, and penetration into the non-discursive realm. The idea of ascent is subtly present in the image of the soul being taken by the hand and led through thoughts to the knowledge of what cannot be grasped.[120] This notion of ascent is reinforced by the soul's becoming a house or dwelling place, which, Canévet argues, is part of Gregory's imagery of verticality and associated with the idea of ascension. Moreover, the image of the house is likewise tied to notions of interiority and intimacy.[121] Hence, the idea of union is certainly not far away; we have the *res* if not the word.

In *De beatitudinibus*, Gregory identifies Paul as pillar of faith, which is again an image of verticality.[122] Hence, it is not surprising to see Gregory conflate the image of Paul with the image of becoming a dwelling place through faith. Paul is a house that contains what cannot be contained. Canévet has observed that such a '*double négation*', has a 'precise symbolic function' in Gregory of Nyssa: to move beyond the principle of non-contradiction in order to penetrate within the Transcendent.[123]

---

[117] *In Cant.* III, GNO 87. 14–17: σὺ δὲ ταῦτα δεξαμένη ὑποζύγιόν τε καὶ οἰκητήριον γενήσῃ διὰ πίστεως τοῦ σοι ἐνανακλίνεσθαι μέλλοντος διὰ τῆς ἐν σοὶ κατοικήσεως· τοῦ γὰρ αὐτοῦ καὶ θρόνος ἔσῃ καὶ οἶκος γενήσῃ.

[118] *De beat.* VI, GNO VII. ii. 137. 23–4.　　　[119] *In Cant.* III, GNO VI. 88. 6.

[120] Ibid., 87. 5–6.

[121] Canévet, *Grégoire de Nysse et l'herméneutique biblique*, 309–11.

[122] *De beat.* VI, GNO VII. ii. 137. 23–4.

[123] Canévet, *Grégoire de Nysse et l'herméneutique biblique*, 337–42, esp. 339.

The sense of paradox is heightened by the adjectives περιληπτικός and its apophatic correlate ἀπερίληπτός.[124] While the present contexts of dwelling places and abodes favour their translation as 'containable' and 'not containable', the words also have clearly epistemological overtones: understanding, comprehension.[125] This image of Paul, then, lends itself to considerable nuance. As a house Paul (the bride as well[126]) contains the incomprehensible nature, who through faith indwells the soul. However, one can also read this along more epistemological lines. Paul, especially Paul as an embodiment of faith, comprehends what cannot be comprehended. This is paradox, not contradiction; it is language which points beyond the realm of discursive reason, an elevation which is at once a deeper penetration into the depths of the soul as well as the depths of God,[127] and designates faith as capable of grasping without grasping, knowing without comprehending.

As an apophatic faculty of unknowing (as Daniélou has termed it[128]) faith moves beyond the hindrance to reason which the paradox or the coincidence of opposites imposes on the mind's understanding. Faith can do what mind could never do, even if the latter managed to enter into the divine presence: grasp the ungraspable. This language of the grasp of faith, subtly present here in Homily 3, is more obviously present in a very important text in Homily 6.

Having presented his well-known metaphysical paradigm in the Prologue to Homily 6, Gregory comments on Song 3: 1 'on my bed at night I sought him whom my soul loved' and we find the bride, like Moses, 'in the darkness where God was' (Exod. 20: 21).[129] The bride's entry into this darkness marks an apophatic ascent in which the bride moves through the marketplace of various levels of knowledge in order to find her Beloved by means of faith.

The search for her Beloved forces the bride to forsake sense perception, and, having done this, she is embraced by the divine night and seeks him hidden in the darkness.[130] 'Then', she says, 'I felt love for the one whom I desired, but my Beloved escaped the grasp of my thoughts';[131] yet she clearly seeks him 'in order to know his substance'.[132] So the bride

---

[124] *In Cant.* III, GNO VI. 88. 6.

[125] Plato, *Timaeus* 28a, c; for other examples see Lampe as well as Liddell & Scott, s.v.

[126] In fact Paul becomes the bride a few lines later at *In Cant.* III, GNO VI. 91. 4.

[127] See Canévet, *Grégoire de Nysse et l'herméneutique biblique*, 342.

[128] Daniélou, *Platonisme et théologie mystique*, 146.

[129] *In Cant.* VI, GNO VI. 181. 6.   [130] Ibid., 181. 13–14.

[131] Ibid., 181. 15–16.   [132] Ibid., 181. 17–18: ὥστε γνῶναι τίς ἡ οὐσία.

continues her ascent; 'she arises and in her mind traverses the intellectual and celestial nature'.[133] These levels of knowledge are the city, market-place and street (Song 3: 2) through which the bride goes in search of her Beloved, but she does not find him at these higher levels of knowledge. She even asks the angelic rank, 'have you perhaps seen him whom my soul loves?'[134] The angels keep silent, and the bride construes their silence as meaning that the one whom she seeks cannot be grasped (ἄληπτον) by the mind.[135]

Until now the bride has focused on acquiring knowledge of the intelligibles, having abandoned sensual perception, with the hope of finding the Beloved there; but after this encounter with the silence of the angels and having searched the entire city through the curiosity of her mind, the bride's ascent moves to a new level. The bride realizes that the one whom she seeks is known in not knowing.[136] We have already seen Gregory use this *coincidentia oppositorum*. This movement to a higher level of ascent is characterized by the motifs of *aphairesis*. Earlier we saw the bride abandon knowledge gained through sensual perception and move upwards to the higher level of the intelligibles. Now, however, she begins to forsake this as well. 'She abandons everything she has found.'[137] And just further on she says, 'I left behind every creature and passed by every intelligible thing in creation, and leaving behind all comprehension, I found the Beloved by faith.'[138]

This ascent of the bride began as a search for knowledge, knowledge of the Beloved's essence, and it is her desire for knowledge which characterizes this ascent from beginning to end: the bride felt love for her desired one even though he escaped her thoughts; the one who is sought is known by not knowing; the bride sets forth with the curiosity of the mind and searches the city for the Beloved. Indeed all the language of grasping serves to underscore the intensity of her desire for know-ledge. However, at the summit of this ascent we find not knowledge but faith. Has the bride's desire for knowledge ended in frustration? Is faith, then, merely a 'consolation prize'?[139] By placing faith at the zenith of an

---

[133] *In Cant.* vi, GNO vi. 182. 5–6.   [134] Ibid., 182. 14–15.
[135] Ibid., 182. 15–17.
[136] Ibid., 183. 2–3: τὸ ἐν μόνῳ τῷ μὴ καταλαμβάνεσθαι τί ἐστιν ὅτι ἔστι γινωσκόμενον,...
[137] Ibid., 183. 1–2.
[138] Ibid., 183. 6–8:...ἀφεῖσα πᾶσαν τὴν κτίσιν καὶ παρελθοῦσα πᾶν τὸ ἐν τῇ κτίσει νοούμενον καὶ πᾶσαν καταληπτικὴν ἔφοδον καταλιποῦσα, τῇ πίστει εὗρον τὸν ἀγαπώμενον....
[139] Harrison, *Grace and Human Freedom*, 67.

epistemological ascent Gregory clearly intends us not to think this but rather that faith is itself a form of knowledge that resolves the *coincidentia oppositorum* of knowing and unknowing.

In her recent study of the early history of negative theology Deirdre Carabine says that for Gregory of Nyssa, 'the knowledge obtained in this darkness is simply the knowledge that God cannot be known'.[140] While one feels a certain sympathy with her overall reading of Gregory, one gets the impression she does not appreciate sufficiently the role of faith in the matter of God's knowability. Her statement is not false but it runs the risk of missing a deeper point which Gregory himself pursues.

To know that God cannot be known is positive knowledge about God. Is this all Gregory is saying in this finding of God by means of faith? The bride has been desiring knowledge of the Beloved throughout her many ascents. Can this knowing be reduced to knowledge about God? Or is there a type of knowing which encounters but does not grasp, a knowing which is an unknowing? This, I believe, comes much closer to what finding by means of faith intends. Faith is a form of knowing found in what A.C. Lloyd has called 'the non-discursive intellect' which is ungrasping.[141] Faith unites with the Beloved without laying hold of or seizing the Beloved, or—to cast this into the language of paradox—the grasp of faith is the grasp of an open palm.

This knowledge by means of faith, moreover, is not unconnected to knowledge of a more discursive type, and Gregory is not encouraging the disparagement of one for the sake of the other. For the soul has had to grasp or recognize in a rational way the unknowable character of the divine, previous to God's self-manifestation beyond the grasp of such thoughts. But it is part of a single dynamic ascent into knowledge of God by faith alone.[142]

---

[140] Carabine, *The Unknown God*, 254; this view was voiced earlier in her 'Gregory of Nyssa on the Incomprehensibility of God,' in *The Relationship between Neoplatonism and Christianity*, ed. T. Finan and V. Twomey (Dublin, 1992), 97.

[141] A. C. Lloyd, *The Anatomy of Neoplatonism* (Oxford, 1990), 164; see also idem, 'Non-Discursive Thought: An Enigma of Greek Philosophy', *Proceedings of the Aristotelian Society* 70 (1969–70), 261–74. Lloyd has not gone uncontested on this topic; see R. Sorabji, 'Myths about Non-Propositional Thought', in *Language and Logos*, ed. M. Schofield and M. Nussbaum (Cambridge, 1982), 295–314. However, the application of this term to πίστις in Gregory of Nyssa is my own and suggests what is the relationship between mind and πίστις, a question which I shall address in the following chapter.

[142] M. Canévet would seem to agree that the grasp of πίστις is not on the order of thought but is nonetheless related to propositional, discursive knowledge; see *Grégoire de Nysse et l'herméneutique biblique*, 63: 'La saisie de la foi n'est donc pas de l'ordre de la pensée:.... Du même coup, cette saisie devient réellement une connaissance, car c'est

With this finding of the Beloved by means of faith[143] the process of *aphairesis* stops.[144] The bride says that once found 'by the grasp of faith' she will never let him go until he comes into her chamber.[145] This is a significant change of language on the part of Gregory. Previous to this grasp of faith the Beloved was consistently ἄληπτος—not capable of being grasped by the mind,[146] but after the bride has abandoned all knowledge the Beloved is paradoxically λῆπτος. Gregory suggests, then, two opposed characteristics that are simultaneously present. The Beloved is ungraspable on the level of mind but is clearly graspable on the level of faith.

What is the result of this grasp of faith? Through the bride's grasp of faith the Beloved enters into her chamber. Gregory identifies this chamber as the bride's heart.[147] Hence, through this union of bride and Beloved in the grasp of faith, the bride herself becomes God's dwelling place, thus returning to the original state for which she was created.[148]

We may conclude this section by observing that Gregory began his commentary on Song 3: 1–4 with the image of a chamber[149] and with this same image he draws it to a close. However, although both images relate to divine presence, there is a significant difference. As Gregory began to comment on Song 3: 1–4, the chamber was implicitly present as the environment in which the soul was united with God at night on the bed of participation.[150] The chamber was, as it were, external to the

---

la foi qui sert de médiation dans la quête apparemment vaine de l'essence divine: à travers les mots, les pensées, l'âme se tend vers Dieu: c'est la foi qui l'unit à Lui.' F. Dünzl, *Braut und Bräutigam*, 296, would seem to agree with M. Canévet: 'Andererseits plädiert Gregor hier auch keineswegs für einen "einfachen Glauben" als Alternative oder Korrektive der Theologie'. While indeed πίστις transcends both thought and speech, 'in diesem Prozeß wird die Theologie nicht verabsolutiert, aber auch nicht negiert....'

[143] Once again we observe the use of the instrumental dative (πίστῃ) to express the technical sense which Gregory accords the term.

[144] This final phase of the bride's ascent is rife with aphairetic language: καταλείπω (*In Cant.* vi. GNO vi. 183. 1), ἀφίημι (183. 6), παρέρχομαι (183. 6), μεθίημι (183. 9).

[145] *In Cant.* vi, GNO vi. 183. 8–10: τῇ πίστει εὗρον τὸν ἀγαπώμενον καὶ οὐκέτι μεθήσω τῇ τῆς πίστεως λαβῇ τοῦ εὑρεθέντος ἀντεχομένη, ἕως ἂν ἐντὸς γένηται τοῦ ἐμοῦ ταμιείου.

[146] Ibid., 182. 17.   [147] Ibid., 183. 10–12.   [148] Ibid., 183. 12–15.

[149] Ibid., 180. 9.

[150] Ibid., 181. 10–16. The bride herself understands 'bed' as meaning participation (μετουσία, 181. 3); cf. Prologue, GNO vi. 174. 6. See D. Balás, *ΜΕΤΟΥΣΙΑ ΘΕΟΥ: Man's Participation in God's Perfections according to Saint Gregory of Nyssa* (Rome, 1966), 72–5; on bed as symbol of union see Cortesi, *Le 'Omelie sul Cantico dei Cantici'*, 95–6.

bride. However, as Gregory concludes this section, the situation is exactly the opposite: the chamber is interior to the bride; it has become her heart, an 'acceptable dwelling place of God'.[151] The symbol of divine presence has been interiorized.

The chamber of divine presence is not only something which the bride enters but also something which the bride has become through the grasp of faith: a dwelling place of God. This interiorization of a divine characteristic appears again through the mediation of faith in the image of the arrow with which the archer deals the bride a great wound.

The Wound of Love and the Arrow of Faith

We saw in Homily 3 how faith was the means by which God came to dwell within the soul. While the primary thrust of this text was in the direction of divine indwelling, there were also important auxiliary themes with nuances of ascent and knowledge, even though there was no explicit apophatic ascent crowned by faith. Homily 4 continues on very similar lines but with completely different imagery and is more concerned with ascent and union, the concern for knowledge being for the moment effaced.

Near the end of Homily 4 Gregory turns his attention to Song 2: 5b: 'I am wounded by love.' In a fascinating interpretation of this *lemma* Gregory begins with the image of the bride as target of the wounding arrow and ends by shifting the imagery to that of nuptial union, thus conflating the two images so that we see the bride become this very arrow and herself being taken up, aimed and shot. In all of this the role of faith is central.

In response to having been penetrated by the arrow to the depths of the heart, the bride proclaims: 'I am wounded by love.' These are not words of despair but of praise for the archer's fine marksmanship.[152] Gregory tells us that the archer is love (ἀγάπη), which he will identify a few lines on as God (1 John 4: 8);[153] the arrow is the only-begotten Son.[154] The archer penetrates the heart along with the arrow.[155] Gregory implies that the bride's words are not only words of praise for the

---

[151] Ibid., 183. 10–11.

[152] See *In Cant.* IV, GNO VI. 127. 7–10. Dünzl, *Braut und Bräutigam*, 95, sees behind this image that of Eros with his bow. While the story of the birth of Eros is recounted perhaps most notably in the *Symposium* 203b ff., the arrows are missing from Plato's account; see C. Osborne, *Eros Unveiled: Plato and the God of Love* (Oxford, 1994), 71 n. 35.

[153] Ibid., 127. 10–11.   [154] Ibid., 127. 12–13: τὸν μονογενῆ θεόν.

[155] Ibid., 127. 15–16.

archer's marksmanship but actual words of boast for the wound she now bears: 'Therefore, having been elevated through these divine ascents, the soul sees within herself the sweet arrow of love by which she was wounded and she boasts of this blow, saying "I have been wounded by love".'[156]

However, to understand the role of faith one must consider more closely this arrow which Gregory has already identified as the only-begotten Son. Having identified the arrow, he then describes the three-pointed tip of the arrow. 'The tip of the arrow is faith,' Gregory says.[157] Moreover, this tip, which is faith, has been moistened by the spirit of life.[158] Hence, while this 'sweet arrow of love' is the Only-begotten, the tip of this arrow is faith, and by means of faith the arrow as well as the archer (God) are introduced into the heart.[159] This is the reason for the bride's boastful oxymorons: 'O beautiful wound and sweet blow', for by means of faith, a doorway has been opened up to allow divine life to enter and dwell within.[160]

In previous observations of this technical sense of faith we noted a real sense of instrumentality. Often this sense has been reflected morphologically, i.e. faith appeared either as an instrumental dative or was governed by the preposition διά. Although there is no question here of the instrumental dative, the sense of instrumentality remains by virtue of the imagery: as the pointed tip of this arrow, faith allows the divine indwelling by creating a doorway by which to enter.

As instrumental as faith is, however, it should not be viewed in isolation from the element of grace which Gregory suggests: faith has been moistened with the spirit of life (Rom. 8: 2).[161] Moreover, faith does not penetrate the heart under its own power, but only through the prowess and fine marksmanship of the archer.

---

[156] See In Cant. IV, GNO VI. 127. 18–128. 3: ὁρᾷ τοίνυν ἡ διὰ τῶν θείων ἀναβάσεων ὑψωθεῖσα ψυχὴ τὸ γλυκὺ τῆς ἀγάπης βέλος ἐν ἑαυτῇ, ᾧ ἐτρώθη, καὶ καύχημα ποιεῖται τὴν τοιαύτην πληγὴν λέγουσα ὅτι Τετρωμένη ἀγάπης ἐγώ.

[157] Ibid., 127. 14–15: ἀκὶς δὲ ἡ πίστις ἐστίν.

[158] Ibid., 127. 13–14.

[159] Ibid., 127. 14–17: (ἀκὶς δὲ ἡ πίστις ἐστίν), ἵνα, ᾧ ἂν γένηται, συνεισαγάγῃ μετὰ τοῦ βέλους καὶ τὸν τοξότην, ὥς φησιν ὁ κύριος ὅτι ἐγὼ καὶ ὁ πατὴρ Ἐλευσόμεθα καὶ μονὴν παρ' αὐτῷ ποιησόμεθα.

[160] Ibid., 128. 3–5.

[161] This would counter Völker's suggestion in Gregor von Nyssa als Mystiker, 141, that Gregory leaves to one side the question of grace and πίστις.

When we considered faith in the respective accounts of the migration of Abraham and the entrance of Moses into the sanctuary or darkness, we observed an explicit ascensional motif in which faith figured preeminently: faith was the apex of a more or less explicitly apophatic ascent by means of which union with God occurred. In the present text, however, the direction of the imagery is reversed, even while the role of instrumentality remains. Here the movement is inward and the goal is not expressed in the language of union but in the imagery of indwelling: an arrow penetrates into the depths of the heart and introduces there divine indwelling.

Whether in the imagery of ascent or that of interiority the instrumentality of faith remains. In fact, the two, ascent and interiority, should not be separated in Gregory. Indeed, as he continues his commentary on this very *lemma* (by way of transition to the following *lemma* (Song 2: 6)), the imagery shifts from predominantly that of introversion to predominantly that of ascent as, in his own words, the imagery changes 'from archery into marital joy' when the bride was wounded by the arrow of love.[162]

In mid-paragraph the bride is no longer the target at which the archer takes aim. She has become the arrow.[163] By virtue of the indwelling presence of the arrow within her she has herself become an arrow.[164] Thus we see how closely Gregory aligns indwelling presence (mediated by faith) and union. He describes how she is placed like an arrow in the bow of the archer. But he says that the significance of this is described in marital imagery, not that of archery.

By now it is obvious that Gregory is trying to move from one *lemma* to another, from Song 2: 5, 'I am wounded by love' (which he has chosen to interpret, following Origen, in the tradition of the archer[165]), to Song 2: 6,

---

[162] Ibid., 128. 5–7.

[163] Ibid., 128. 13–14.

[164] The theme of purification is introduced at 129. 5. For Plato the purpose of the purification was to become like God, as the bride does here in becoming an arrow. See for example *Phaedo* 67b2.

[165] See Origen, *Comm. in Cant.* III. 8, GCS 195, 28 ff; see also *Hom. in Cant.* II, SC 37 *bis*, 134. There are, however, significant differences between Origen's and Gregory's commentary on Song 2: 5b. For example, while Origen designates the arrow as cause of the wound and God as the archer, he does not mention the tip of the arrow, which Gregory has identified as πίστις. Origen mentions the shield of faith which protects the soul from the darts of the evil one. But this faith does not faciliate divine indwelling and union as in Gregory. For a discussion of this theme of arrows, particularly in Origen, see 'Arrows, Eros, Agape', in Osborne, *Eros Unveiled*, 52–85, esp. 71–4.

'His left hand is under my head, and his right hand shall embrace me.' It is the marital image of this *lemma* which precipitates the need to change from the archer to the bridegroom; it is an exegetical move, however, that allows him to express his own theological conviction that indwelling presence, ascent, and union are all different facets of the same encounter between finite and Infinite, an encounter mediated by faith. Hence, instead of the archer holding the tip of the bride's head in the bow, it is the bridegroom holding her head with his left hand and the rest of her body he embraces with his right.[166]

Gregory has conflated perfectly these two images: the bride's head is the tip of the arrow held in the bow by the archer's left hand. Her body is the shaft of the arrow held at the notched end by his right hand.[167] At the same time, however, she is the bride embraced by the bridegroom. Her head is held by his left hand and her body embraced by his right. God is the archer as well as the bridegroom.[168] This identification affords Gregory the opportunity to lead us into another coincidence of opposites. The bride is at once in movement and at rest: 'I am at once shot forth like an arrow and am at rest in the hands of the archer.'[169]

Union does not stand at the end-point of a linear ascent but is the context of such ascent. The interior ground of ascent is the union of finite creature and infinite Creator, and the exterior ground of union is continual ascent.

In this image of the bride wounded by the arrow who is the bridegroom and then embraced by the same bridegroom, faith has played an important role. The bride can boast, 'O beautiful wound and sweet blow' because of what faith has allowed to happen: faith has created a doorway that allows the divine to enter and dwell within.[170] Gregory situates this exalted role of faith in a trinitarian context. The tip of the arrow, which opens up the way for divine indwelling, has been 'moistened' by the Spirit which is evocative both of the Holy Spirit and baptism,[171] and he

---

[166] *In Cant.* iv, GNO vi. 128. 20–129. 1.   [167] See ibid., 128. 11–15.

[168] Ibid., 129. 3–4.

[169] Ibid., 129. 15–16: ὡς ὁμοῦ τε φέρεσθαι διὰ τῆς βολῆς καὶ ταῖς χερσὶ τοῦ τοξότου ἐναναπαύεσθαι. Brian Daley has noted this transformation of the bride but overlooks both the conflation of images and the role of πίστις in her transformation; see B. Daley, ' "Bright Darkness" and Christian Transformation' in M. Himes and S. Pope (eds), *Finding God in All Things: Essays in Honor of Michael J. Buckley, S. J.* (New York, 1996), 215–30, esp. 225.

[170] We saw this image of πίστις as doorway at *Contra Eunom.* iii. 8. 12, GNO ii. 243. 9.

[171] See Dünzl, *Braut und Bräutigam*, 375.

has identified the shaft of the arrow as the Son and the archer as God. Therefore, while the importance of the function of faith for divine indwelling is undeniable for Gregory, faith is yet suffused in grace from the beginning.

Once again we see faith functioning within a coincidence of opposites: the indwelling by means of faith is also union with the bridegroom (arrow), and hence the bride becomes an arrow and is shot forth, yet she is at the same time in repose, for the bridegroom has embraced her, and she rests in his hands. Such language points beyond the realm of discursive reason where, as we have seen, *dianoia* does not function but where faith unites with God who is beyond reason.[172]

Gregory returns to this catechesis of archery when he comments on Song 5: 7 at the end of Homily 12. In this text we see faith serve both a mediational role and as an opportunity to agree and disagree with Origen.

The arrow which Gregory mentions at the close of Homily 12 comes at the end of a sequence of images of wounding. These images are all part of Gregory's commentary on Song 5: 7: 'They found me, the sentinels who make their rounds in the city, they smote me; they wounded me. . . . ' The instrument used to wound the bride is a divine rod, which he identifies with the Spirit.[173] As with the wound dealt her in Homily 4, the bride boasts of this wound, and Gregory calls it a beautiful wound.[174]

He says that this wounding with the rod can be likened to Isaiah's vision (Isa. 6: 1 ff.), but instead of a wound-dealing rod there is a burning coal. Gregory hastens to add, however, that the result is the same: purification (a work often associated with the Holy Spirit). Therefore, Isaiah does not reel from the pain, nor the bride from the fierce blow.[175]

Having considered this wounding first through the instrumentality of a rod, then by likening it to a coal, Gregory says there is yet another way of understanding this wounding and so introduces once again the image of the arrow.[176] In Homily 4 we saw that the wounding arrow had two

---

[172] M. Canévet has identified paradox as pertaining to the structure of symbolic mystical language in Gregory; see *Grégoire de Nysse et l'herméneutique biblique*, 340–2; see also Daniélou, *Platonisme et théologie mystique*, 274–84; and Dünzl, *Braut und Bräutigam*, 390.

[173] *In Cant.* xii, GNO vi. 365. 17–18. In the *De vita Moysis*, SC, ii. 136. 8, the rod used to strike the rock (Christ) to draw forth water is identified as the 'rod of faith'. It does not stretch things too much to see the mediation of πίστις implied here, especially in light of the symbolic equivalence in the context of the present Homily between the rod and the arrow whose tip is πίστις.

[174] Ibid., 366. 6.   [175] Ibid., 369. 8–12.

[176] This movement from image to image is characteristic of Gregory and is discussed by Canévet, *Grégoire de Nysse et l'herméneutique biblique*, 314–16.

effects which caused her to boast in her wound: union and divine indwelling. Because he explicitly identified the tip of the piercing arrow as faith we can say that faith mediated both of these. In Homily 12 the bride's heart is again struck by the arrow tip of faith,[177] but we see a different effect of this mediation by faith. Not only does the arrow tip of faith mediate union with and the indwelling presence of the bridegroom, it also causes the bride's desire for the Beloved to expand.[178] Far from the divine encounter exhausting the desire of the bride, it makes it expand even more.[179]

This unceasing expansion of desire would seem to be something of a critique of Origen's notion of κόρος.[180] When Origen comments on the arrows of divine love, he gives them precisely the same meaning which we find here in Homily 12: the arrow increases the bride's desire for the bridegroom:

---

[177] *In Cant.* XII, GNO VI. 370. 9–10.

[178] Ibid., 370. 6–7: ἐν σφοδροτέρῳ τείνεται πόθῳ ....

[179] Von Balthasar laments this aspect of Gregory's thought that gives dissatisfaction too important a role. See *Présence et pensée*, 18–19 and 76. Von Balthasar is well aware that such is the logical outcome of the relationship between finite creature and infinite being (clearly set forth e.g. in the Prologue to *In Cant.* VI). However, one has the impression that von Balthasar has too linear a view of unceasing desire. To view the matter as constant frustration is to view the search for God along too linear a line, as though Gregory were a theological anticipation of Gödel's theory, and God were playing metaphysical *cache-cache*: the more one moves from point A to point B, the more point B recedes. Gregory's image of infinite expansion, as seen here in Homily 12 and underlying his doctrine on *epektasis* in general, precludes such a linear view. See Desalvo, *L' 'oltre' nel presente*, 242 n. 36.

[180] On this theme in Origen see M. Harl, 'Recherches sur l'origénisme d'Origène: la satiété (koros) de la contemplation comme motif de la chute des âmes', *Studia Patristica* 8 (1966), 374–405. In his introduction to the life and thought of Origen, H. Crouzel warns against a too facile identification of *satietas* with the idea that 'God can in some way surfeit a creature'; see his *Origen*, trans. A. Worrall (New York, 1989), 210. It is indeed tempting to suggest, as R. Heine has done, that Gregory's doctrine on ἐπέκτασις is a counterpoint to Origen's κόρος. See Heine, *Perfection in the Virtuous Life*, 5–10 and 76 ff. See also Mühlenberg, *Unendlichkeit Gottes* 27. But one must proceed with caution. M. Simonetti (*Vita di Mosè*, xx and esp. xxx–xxxvi) has criticized Heine on this very point, noting that Origen himself would seem to anticipate the theme of ἐπέκτασις in *Hom. Num.* 17. 4, GCS 7. 160. 11–26. Moreover, Simonetti says: 'per formulare la dottrina del progresso senza fine non è indispensabile ammettere l'infinità di Dio: infatti anche Origene, che non l'ammette, ammette però la sua abissale trascendenza rispetto alla finitezza del uomo, e su tale base può proporre anche lui quella dottrina' (xxxvi). Finally Simonetti claims that even the inclination to overcome κόρος with ἐπέκτασις comes from Origen. B. Daley, apparently independent of both Heine and Simonetti, cites the same text from *Hom. Num.* and suggests that Gregory developed rather than invented this theme: 'here Origen sketches out a picture of the eschatological contemplation of God as constant spiritual movement and growth, a view which Gregory of Nyssa will later develop into his own theory of beatitude as eternal self-transcendence or ἐπέκτασις'; see *Hope of the Early Church*, 50.

If there is anyone who has received the sweet wound of Him who is the chosen dart,... so that he yearns and longs for Him by day and night, can speak of nought but him, would hear of nought but Him, can think of nothing else and is disposed to no desire nor longing nor yet hope, except for Him alone—if such there be, that soul then says in truth: I have been wounded by charity.[181]

On this Gregory agrees with his master Origen, but he adds an important nuance, a nuance which at once characterizes Gregory as a theological thinker in his own right and distances him from Origen.[182] 'Origen's view of the divine nature is that it is limited, and, because limited, incapable of giving lasting satisfaction to the created spirit.'[183] For Gregory, by contrast, God is infinite and we are finite; therefore, the search is never-ending and always expanding.[184] This fundamental distinction is evident in this passage from Homily 12 even as it evinces Origen's influence. Gregory says of the bride:

But the garment of her grief is taken away through learning that eternal progress in searching and never ceasing to ascend is the true enjoyment of the Beloved, for whenever her desire is fulfilled, it produces further desire for the transcendent.[185]

---

[181] *Comm. in Cant.* III. 8, GCS 195, trans. R.P. Lawson, *The Song of Songs Commentary and Homilies*, Ancient Christian Writers 26 (New York, 1957), 198.

[182] For a discussion of convergences and divergences of Origen and Gregory on fundamental issues see A. Meredith, 'Origen's *De Principiis* and Gregory of Nyssa's *Oratio Catechetica*', *Heythrop Journal* 36 (1995), 1–14. See also idem, *The Cappadocians*, 54–62 *et passim*; E. Pietrella, 'L'antiorigenismo di Gregorio di Nissa', *Augustinianum* 26 (1986), 143–76. For a general orientation to the problem of Origenism see H. Crouzel and M. Simonetti (eds. and trans.), Origène, *Traité des Principes*, vol. i, SC 252 (Paris, 1978), 33–45; H. Crouzel, 'Origene e l'origenismo: le condanne di Origene', *Augustinianum* 26 (1986), 295–303, where the author argues for a strict distinction between Origen and origenism (whether that of the origenists or that of the anti-origenists); see also idem, 'Origenism', in *Encyclopedia of the Early Church*, ed. A Di Berardino and trans. A. Walford (Cambridge, 1992), s. v.; for a more in-depth study see E. Clark, *The Origenist Controversy: The Cultural Construction of an Early Christian Debate* (Princeton, 1992); NB the perceptive review of Clark's study by M. Sheridan in *Collectanea Cisterciensia* 58 (1996), 38–42. See also R. Placida, 'La presenza di Origene nelle *Omelie sul Cantico dei cantici* di Gregorio di Nissa', *Vetera Christianorum* 34 (1997), 33–49.

[183] Meredith, *The Cappadocians*, 77.   [184] See *In Cant.* vi, GNO vi. 172–4.

[185] *In Cant.* xii, GNO vi. 369. 22–370. 3: ἀλλὰ περιαιρεῖται τὸ τῆς λύπης θέριστρον διὰ τοῦ μαθεῖν ὅτι τὸ ἀεὶ προκόπτειν ἐν τῷ ζητεῖν καὶ τὸ μηδέποτε τῆς ἀνόδου παύεσθαι τοῦτό ἐστιν ἡ ἀληθὴς τοῦ ποθουμένου ἀπόλαυσις τῆς πάντοτε πληρουμένης ἐπιθυμίας ἑτέραν ἐπιθυμίαν τοῦ ὑπερκειμένου γεννώσης.

Hence, while both Origen and Gregory would view the experience of wounding along similar lines (though for Gregory the themes of union and divine indwelling are more pronounced), Gregory emphasizes this coincidence of opposites: fulfilment and non-fulfilment, satisfaction and eternal progress. Therefore, when the bride is wounded by the arrow, her desire to experience the Beloved is, from one perspective, fulfilled. The effect of the arrow, however, does not quench this desire but serves to expand it. The bride's enjoyment of and her search for the Beloved are one, and for Gregory this is mediated by faith which allows the arrow of the Word to enter and dwell, causing the bride's desire to expand unceasingly even as she delights in the Beloved.

A final image of the arrow-tip of faith occurs in Homily 13. Gregory comments on Song 5: 8: 'I am wounded by love.' The treatment of the wound of love is briefer in this Homily than in the previous two. Nevertheless, Gregory mentions all the important themes which we saw in Homilies 4 and 12. The bride shows the arrow of love deeply embedded in her heart. This image of the arrow deep in the heart of the bride represents union with God, who is love.[186] Divine love entered the heart, Gregory claims, through the arrow-tip of faith. Finally, he says that this dynamic of union and indwelling is nothing other than Paul's description of 'faith working through love' (Gal. 5: 6). This statement is worthy of note, for once again we see that it is Gregory's reading of Paul that has motivated him to exalt faith as the mediator of union and divine indwelling.

The Flowing Water of Divine Nature

The last occurrence of faith which I would like to present before concluding this chapter suggests that through faith one has access to the divine nature. In Homily 9 Gregory links faith with flowing water. Subtle and provocative as this occurrence is, it nonetheless harmonizes well with what we have seen so far regarding faith. Towards the end of Homily 9 Gregory is drawing to a close his commentary on Song 4: 15: 'Fountain of the garden, well of living water flowing down from Lebanon.' The image speaks of the bride herself. She is a well which contains the inflow of water from the fountain of God.[187] It is an image of participation and divinization: 'We become partakers who possess that

---

[186] *In Cant.* xiii, GNO vi. 378. 16–17: τουτέστι τὴν τῆς θεότητος αὐτοῦ κοινωνίαν.

[187] *In Cant.* ix, GNO vi. 293. 13–18.

well.'[188] Indeed Gregory has just identified this flowing water with the divine nature itself. He does this through a reading of John 7: 37–9: ' "Let anyone who is thirsty come to me! Let anyone who believes in me come and drink! As scripture says, 'From his belly will flow living water' " '.' Then he says that this living water which flows out of the believer is 'the divine nature'.[189] Even though the use of faith in this passage is a citation from John, in light of what we have seen of Gregory's at times highly exalted understanding of the term, we can see that Gregory has elevated John's use of faith. John does not specify the nature of the living water, but Gregory does. Hence faith is viewed as having access to the divine nature itself. Moreover, this access implies real contact with the divine nature, for the believer doesn't simply drink from this well but *becomes* a well flowing from the belly of the believer. That this use of faith is Gregory's exalted sense of the term is further suggested by the paradox that immediately ensues, a paradox which he himself notices.[190] Having drunk from the living, flowing, water, she is not simply a well that contains still water, she is also a source of flowing water. Hence, having come into contact with the divine nature through faith, she embodies a *coincidentia oppositorum*: the bride is both still and moving. Another paradox is implied as the Homily comes to a close. The bride contains the water of divine nature, which by definition cannot be contained. Though Gregory does not state the paradox explicitly in this text, we see him state it quite clearly in Homily 3 when speaking of Paul who became a house containing what cannot be contained.[191]

However brief, this passage is yet another testimony to the fact that while Gregory does not allow comprehension of the divine nature, the soul has yet access to the divine nature by means of faith, which unites the soul to God, allowing God to make of the soul a dwelling place.

Conclusion

In this examination of various texts from the writings of Gregory of Nyssa, we have had ample opportunity to see the exalted role which Gregory can, in certain instances, bestow upon faith.

---

[188] Ibid., 293. 18–19.   [189] Ibid., 292. 20: τῆς θείας φύσεως.
[190] Ibid., 293. 3. On paradox see Canévet, *Grégoire de Nysse et l'herméneutique biblique*, 339.
[191] *In Cant.* III, GNO VI. 88. 6.

Faith, Divine Indwelling, Union

We have seen that the soul or the bride desires nothing but to know the divine essence,[192] but, when such an attempt was made, the mind was 'cut off on all sides as by a kind of darkness'.[193] What of this desire, then, to know the Beloved? Is it given in frustration? Is there no means of approaching and attaining union with the Beloved? Indeed there is: for Gregory of Nyssa faith is the sole means of such approach and union.

Even in an early work, such as *In inscriptiones Psalmorum*, we saw that already Gregory could speak of faith in this exalted sense as the means of apophatic approach to God. He continued to speak along these same lines as he entered the Eunomian debate. In the *Contra Eunomium* we proposed that Gregory spoke of faith as *docta ignorantia*, an unknowing higher than knowledge that has abandoned all concepts and images in the face of the Incomprehensible. In Gregory's account of the migration of Abraham the problem of attaining to and uniting with the unknowable God was resolved by faith. And the archers of Benjamin are counselled to put away their attempts to grasp by reason the Incomprehensible and to have eyes for the door of faith which opens to God.

This exalted notion of faith continues in his mature years with *De vita Moysis* and *In Canticum canticorum*. We saw that in the contexts of the Holy of Holies and especially while in the darkness where God dwells, the darkness was both a context of separation from God and union with God. The darkness brought to the mind a sense of separation, but for faith it brought presence and union.

In the *In Canticum canticorum* Gregory weaves these same themes, along with one or two others, into his interpretation of the bride grasping the bridegroom by means of faith, the bride being wounded by love, and through the image of flowing water.

We saw that the bride grasps the Beloved in Homilies 3 and 6 on the Song. However, Gregory is careful to show that this grasping of the Beloved was not done by means of mind, which would constitute an act of comprehension, but by means of faith. This grasping by faith yielded several results: union with God, divine indwelling, and the passing on to the discursive mind something of what faith had grasped in the darkness.

In Homilies 4, 12, and 13 faith was the tip of the arrow that wounded the bride and expanded her desire for the Beloved, even as she enjoyed

---

[192] *In Cant.* VI, GNO VI. 181. 16–19.

[193] See *In Eccl.*, SC, VII. 8. 100–4; *De beat.* VI, GNO VII. ii. 137. 16–22; *De vita Moysis*, SC, II. 163. 8.

union and became a vessel of divine indwelling. While faith clearly mediates this union and divine indwelling, Gregory makes it clear that this exalted function of faith is yet suffused in grace. As the tip of the arrow, which is the only-begotten Son, shot by the archer who is God, faith is moistened by the Spirit and therefore comes as gift in the form of that sweet wound in which the bride finds occasion to make her eloquent boast. Finally, in Homily 9, we see faith able to approach the divine nature itself, which Gregory presents in the fluid imagery of fountains and wells.

The prominence of the theme of union in our discussion, and especially of faith as the mediating faculty, leads inevitably to the thesis of Ekkehard Mühlenburg.[194] The overriding concern of his important study is the concept of God's infinity, which, according to Mühlenberg, is Gregory's contribution to 'philosophical and Christian thought'.[195] While we agree with not a few aspects of his thesis and with several of the conclusions he draws on the basis of this (for example, that God cannot be grasped by concepts),[196] we cannot accept all his conclusions. In light of the present discussion, the theme which presents itself for immediate consideration is precisely this notion of divine union.

Despite the fact that Gregory states explicitly at the outset of the *Commentarius in Canticum canticorum* that union with God is the purpose of the Song,[197] Mühlenberg would deny that Gregory allows for the possibility of union with God, and in his well-known review of Mühlenberg's study, Charles Kannengieser has pointed out a caveat in this regard.[198] On the basis of our study of the role which exalted faith has played in any number of texts, we would have to agree with the critique of Kannengieser, for the primary concern of faith, as we have seen time and again, is union, with divinization as one of the most consistent and

---

[194] Mühlenburg, *Unendlichkeit Gottes*.

[195] Ibid., 26: 'Bei Gregor von Nyssa findet sich dieses Gottesprädikat [sc. das Unendliche] zum ersten Mal in der Geschichte des philosophischen und christlichen Denkens.'

[196] Ibid., 28 *et passim*.

[197] *In Cant.* I, GNO VI. 15. 13–15: διὰ γὰρ τῶν ἐνταῦθα γεγραμμένων νυμφοστολεῖται τρόπον τινὰ ἡ ψυχὴ πρὸς τὴν ἀσώματόν τε καὶ πνευματικὴν καὶ ἀμόλυντον τοῦ θεοῦ συζυγίαν.

[198] C. Kannengieser, 'L'Infinité divine chez Grégoire de Nysse', *Recherches de Science Religieuse* 55 (1967), 55–65 at 64: 'Mais doit-on pour autant nier avec lui [sc. Mühlenberg] que Grégoire ait envisagé une union de l'âme avec la divinité infinie et une divinisation de l'homme'? See also the observations of Pottier, *Dieu et le Christ*, 217–19.

noteworthy results of this union mediated by faith.[199] Mühlenberg
would argue that union with God would imply a knowledge tantamount
to enclosing God in the grasp of comprehension. We have seen, however, that this is precisely what union with God through the grasp of
faith does *not* involve. For it is not knowledge of a conceptual order but
rather an unknowing which is higher than the conceptual grasp of the
mind. This union by the grasp of faith safeguards the distinction between
finite creature and infinite Creator, for it is a union beyond knowledge.

Mühlenberg is aware that Gregory has parted company with his
master Origen on the question of divine infinity[200] but seems less
aware that Gregory has also parted company with the general Alexandrian notion that faith is overcome in knowledge. For Gregory of Nyssa,
on the basis of what we have seen in the migration of Abraham, Moses'
ascent of the mountain of divine knowledge and the bride's union with
the Beloved by faith alone, it is knowledge that is overcome in faith.

Even if Daniélou's threefold division of the ascent of the mind is
questionable,[201] presuming, that is, that Daniélou intends it as more than
a merely heuristic device, union with God is an explicit concern of
Gregory of Nyssa, a concern which takes account in a fairly consistent
manner of his overarching concern for protecting both the infinity and
the incomprehensibility of the divine nature.

Both Dünzl and Desalvo have observed that Mühlenberg does not
consider in any detail the role of faith in Gregory's thought.[202] This
oversight prevents Mühlenberg from seeing the epistemological function which faith plays. A strict boundary between finite creature and
infinite Creator runs the risk of preventing any access to the Infinite
without the loss of one's status as a creature.[203] While Gregory is
consistent in maintaining that the divine nature cannot be grasped by
the mind, and the boundary is never blurred, he does, nevertheless, know
'the language of grasping'.[204] It is the grasp of faith. This is the special

---

[199] Perhaps the reason why Mühlenberg does not allow for union is simply as Dünzl
has observed: Mühlenberg gives πίστις no consideration. See Dünzl, *Braut und Bräutigam*,
326 n. 119: 'Die Sonderstellung der πίστις und ihre Bedeutung für die Einwohnung
Gottes im Menschen hier [sc. Hom III] und in Hom VI (s.o. S. 295–298) findet bei
Mühlenberg keine Beachtung.'

[200] See Origen, *De princ.* II. 9.

[201] Mühlenberg, *Unendlichkeit Gottes*, 25; cf. Daniélou, *Platonisme et théologie mystique*,
146 ff.

[202] Dünzl, *Braut und Bräutigam*, 326 n. 119; Desalvo, *L' 'oltre' nel presente*, 220.

[203] See Desalvo, *L' 'oltre' nel presente*, 221.

[204] Canévet, *Grégoire de Nysse et l'herméneutique biblique*, 62.

epistemological role of faith: it allows union between finite and Infinite without compromising the distinction between finite and Infinite. Gregorian faith, therefore, serves closely related epistemological functions which Mühlenberg has not taken into account. Because union by the grasp of faith is beyond the grasp of concepts, it does not constitute the knowledge which Mühlenberg fears would enclose the divine nature in the grasp of comprehension. Nor does it compromise the ontological gulf between finite and Infinite.

The Vocabulary of Union

Gregory has a wide vocabulary of union. Words such as ἀνάκρασις, ἕνωσις, κοινωνία, προσεγγίσας, συνάπτω, σύνειμι, συζυγία are all used to express in one way or another the mystery of the encounter with the divine. But equally important are certain images Gregory uses to express the idea of union: bed, kiss, scent of perfume, finding by the grasp of faith, resting in the arms of the Beloved yet shot forth like an arrow, are likewise images that express this transforming encounter. But whether a precise word or an evocative image to express the idea of union, Gregory intends something very different from a Plotinian union with the One. As Bouchet argued long ago, and Cortesi more recently, Gregory's understanding of union between humanity and God is grounded in his understanding of the union of humanity and divinity in the incarnation of the Word.[205] 'In the light of the union between divinity and humanity that is accomplished in Christ Gregory reads the union between the human and God that constitutes the profound message of the *Commentarius in Canticum canticorum...*'.[206] For Gregory, union expresses the idea that, without bringing about a change in divinity, humanity is transformed and changed for the better.[207]

Faith as a Technical Term

One can agree with Völker that when Gregory speaks of faith in this exalted manner, he departs from his Alexandrian patrimony which saw faith ultimately supplanted by knowledge.[208] However, there are indeed

---

[205] J. Bouchet, 'Le Vocabulaire de l'union et du rapport des natures chez saint Grégoire de Nysse', *Revue Thomiste* 68 (1968), 533–82; Cortesi, *Le Omelie sul Cantico dei Cantici*, 85–7, 177–80 *et passim*. See also Dünzl, *Braut und Bräutigam*, 340–5.
[206] Cortesi, *Le Omelie sul Cantico dei Cantici*, 87.   [207] Ibid., 85.
[208] Völker, *Gregor von Nyssa als Mystiker*, 143.

other positions taken by Völker which, on the basis of our examination, cannot be accepted.

Völker states somewhat cavalierly that Gregory accords the term no technical meaning but has instead a wide range of meaning.[209] Simonetti, by contrast, lists among technical terms in his edition of *De vita Moysis* the term faith.[210] One of the contentions of the present chapter has been that it is *precisely* as a technical term that faith stands out from its various other meanings noted at the end of Chapter 1.[211] Hence, on the basis of our examination we are led to agree with Simonetti.

When used in certain apophatic contexts, whether or not there be an explicit epistemological ascent in which faith is always the summit, such as we saw in the migration of Abraham or in the case of the bride in Homily 6 on the Song of Songs, faith takes on a technical meaning which designates the means by which the soul attains to divine union. Such union, as we have seen, yields any number of results: faith renders the soul a dwelling place of God; faith expands the soul's desire for God even as the soul delights in God; faith does what mind can never do: grasp the incomprehensible nature of God; faith, nevertheless, passes on to the mind something of what it has grasped of the Ungraspable. These are the principal functions of faith when seen in its technical sense of bridging the gap between *intellectus* and God.

Moreover, the technical meaning of faith is often rendered by a particular grammatical morphology. The mediational sense which technical faith serves is often expressed conveniently either as an instrumental dative (πίστῃ) or with the preposition διά (διὰ [μόνης] τῆς πίστεως). Hence, when faith is used in these conditions, it can rightly be said to have a technical meaning in the writings of Gregory of Nyssa.

In speaking of faith in such a lofty manner, however, has Gregory forgotten the *sensus vulgaris* of the term? Harrison has observed that faith comes not at the beginning of, for example, Abraham's journey but at the conclusion of various stages of increasing knowledge.[212] Harrison's point is well-taken, and one is tempted to argue that in speaking of this lofty faith the *sensus vulgaris* of the term has been eclipsed and ultimately superseded. But this would be misleading. For as certainly as Abraham arrives at a pure faith after traversing many levels of knowledge, he also embarked upon his journey in faith (Heb. 11: 8). Indeed it is not the case that faith functions for the first time when we see it operating at the

---

[209] Völker, *Gregor von Nyssa als Mystiker*, 140.   [210] Simonetti, *Vita di Mosè*, 351.
[211] See p. 22, nn. 86–8.   [212] Harrison, *Grace and Human Freedom*, 64.

summit of Abraham's (or for that matter the bride's) epistemological ascent and mediating union. It has been present from the beginning. A more attentive reading of these texts suggests that, having left behind images, concepts, etc., there is nothing left *but* faith, and this unites one to God.

Faith and Grace

Völker contends that Gregory leaves to one side the relationship between faith and grace. In Chapter 2 we saw that the mind itself was subject to grace and without it could never embark on its ascents. This was clearly the case in *De vita Moysis*, where we saw that the grace of baptism purified the mind, putting to death its 'grabbing' tendency[213] or when scripture led the mind (χειραγωγεῖ).[214] If the mind is immersed in and guided by grace, is it likely that faith, which crowns the ascents of the mind, would not also be immersed in grace? Indeed we saw that the image of faith as the tip of the arrow precludes all ambiguity in the matter of grace. For while faith has a distinct role, it comes as gift. It is moistened in the Spirit, comes with the arrow of the Word that was shot by the archer (God).

Exegesis and Epistemology

Throughout this examination of Gregory's exalted understanding of faith we have seen frequent examples of the way in which Gregory grounds his thought in the exegesis of Scripture.[215] Perhaps the most provocative among these was seen in the image of the bride being shot forth like an arrow while in the arms of her Beloved.[216] This blending of the imagery of archery with the imagery of marriage allows Gregory to express his own theological conviction that indwelling presence, ascent in faith, and union are all bound up with each other, different facets of the same encounter with God. However, at the same time this blending of archery and nuptial imagery has an exegetical base. The text Gregory is commenting upon itself moves directly from the imagery of archery to the imagery of marriage: 'I am wounded by love. His left hand is under my head, and his right hand shall embrace me' (Song 2: 5b-6). Hence, Gregory's theological conviction has a strong exegetical grounding.

---

[213] *De vita Moysis*, SC, II. 125. 10.   [214] Ibid., II. 152. 2.

[215] B. Studer, 'Una teologia biblica', in Di Berardino and Studer, *Storia della Teologia*.

[216] In Cant. IV, GNO VI. 128. 5–14.

Another example of this sort of thing, though along more explicitly epistemological lines, was seen in Gregory's use of the biblical image of the Holy of Holies in the *De vita Moysis*. Gregory took the mind to be the temple and comprehension to be the multitude.[217] Just as the multitude is denied access to the sanctuary, so comprehension is denied access to the divine substance; this is an epistemological position based on Gregory's exegesis of the biblical image of the Holy of Holies. But perhaps the clearest example of an epistemological position grounded in exegesis is provided by Abraham.

Gregory had Abraham, the Father of faith, unite with God by means of faith. As will be shown in the following chapter, the means of union is reserved in Neoplatonic culture to a faculty located in the further reaches of intellect. Gregory's ascription of this function to faith, as well as his treatment of the Abraham material from Genesis, is largely due to his reading of Paul. For it was Paul who looked at Abraham and highlighted faith, and Gregory quoted these texts (Gal. 3: 6; Rom. 4: 3; see also Jas. 2: 23) in his own treatment of the Abraham material. Moreover, Gregory read the Genesis account of Abraham through the lens of the Letter to the Hebrews (considered by Gregory to be Pauline): Leaving his homeland, Abraham went out by means of faith (Heb. 11: 8). Not only did Gregory read Gen. 12: 1–5 ff. and Heb. 11: 8 together, but he also read Heb. 11: 8 and 2 Cor. 5: 7 together (we walk by faith and not by sight). The point of highlighting this quilt of Pauline texts is that the exalted epistemological status which Gregory accords faith is to a large extent grounded in his reading of Paul. In the context of a Neoplatonic, religious-philosophic milieu, Paul's justification by faith has become Gregory of Nyssa's union by faith.

As we move to the next chapter, let us keep in mind Gregory's words at the beginning of Homily 1 on the Song. He says that through the words of the Song the soul is 'escorted to an incorporeal, spiritual, and pure union (συζυγίαν) with God'.[218] Indeed divine union is a theme of capital importance in Gregory's writings and especially in the *In Canticum canticorum*. As important as this theme is, however, Gregory does not always specify what there is in the human being that enables union to take place. However, when he does specify we see that it is faith that unites the soul to God.[219] But Gregory is not always specific; for

---

[217] *De Vita Moysis*, SC, ii. 188.   [218] *In Cant.* i, GNO vi. 15. 13–15.

[219] In her recent study of the concept of union in Denys the Areopagite, *Henosis: L'Union à Dieu chez Denys l'Areopagite* (Leiden, 1996), Y. De Andia makes frequent and perceptive reference to Gregory. She says, however (p. 17), that for Gregory union is

example, in Homily 13 on the Song of Songs Gregory simply says that it is the pure mind which draws near (προσοικειοῦντα) to God.[220] Is union implied in this statement? If so, is the role of faith also implied? These questions suggest a more fundamental question to which we shall now turn our attention: What is the relationship between the mind and faith? Is there a radical discontinuity? Is faith nothing but the mind illumined by grace, or is there both continuity and discontinuity between the mind and faith?

---

mediated by the Holy Spirit. While I do not wish to contest the role of the Holy Spirit in the transformation of the soul, the role of the Holy Spirit seems more explicitly linked by Gregory to purification, illumination, divinization, etc. See e.g. *In Cant.* I, GNO VI. 40; *In Cant.* II, GNO VI. 45; *In Cant.* IV, GNO VI. 105–6, 115. One text which would speak in favour of De Andia's position is found at *In Cant.* XV, GNO VI. 466. 18–21. But with respect to union itself, the texts we have considered suggest that union is more often mediated διὰ μόνης τῆς πίστεως.

[220] *In Cant.* XIII, GNO VI. 376. 8–13.

4

The Grasp of Faith
and Supranoetic Union

Introduction

In Chapter 2 we saw how the mind was characterized by flow. This flow was perhaps most vividly depicted in *De virginitate*, where we saw Gregory clothe the mind in the metaphor of irrigation. He likened the mind to a flowing stream. If water were allowed to disperse into different streams as it emerged from the ground, it would be of little use to farmers. But if these different streams were drawn together by a pipe, the collected water could be put to a useful purpose.

Given the enclosure of the pipe, the water's own dynamism would cause it to flow upwards. This is rather like the mind, according to Gregory. If the mind is allowed to flow in every direction, it becomes dispersed by following what brings pleasure to the senses, or by following ambition, and thus the power of its flow would not be able to serve the ascent to the good. However, if the mind were drawn together, its own energy would impel it upwards, and nothing would impede its being borne aloft and touching the truth of beings.[1]

But this ascent to 'touching the truth of beings' does not exhaust the heights to which the mind can rise. In *De vita Moysis* we saw how Moses disappeared into the darkness of the sanctuary. Gregory says this event teaches us something: anyone who wants to commune with God must stretch forth the mind towards the Invisible and the Ungraspable.[2] Assisted by scripture, the mind is a means of ascending the mountain of divine knowledge and 'entering the darkness where God is'.[3] In

---

[1] See *De virg.*, SC, vi. 2. 1–26.   [2] See *De vita Moysis*, SC, i. 46. 6–10.
[3] Ibid., ii. 162. 1–2.

In Canticum canticorum VI we saw the bride ascend by the curiosity of her mind. Having been embraced by the divine night, she moves ever deeper into the divine presence.[4]

The mind, then, can enter the presence of God, can penetrate the impenetrable and enter the darkness where God dwells. However, it is also important to take note both of what the mind is capable of doing in the divine presence and what it is not capable of doing.

What is the capability of the mind during the night by which it is embraced? Gregory mentions two aspects of the mind's movement into divine presence. One aspect features the dynamic of *aphairesis* which ensues. The mind begins 'to let go not only of what the senses grasp but also of what the mind thinks it sees'.[5] After the bride had ascended and wandered about the entire intelligible and angelic realm, she began to abandon everything: she abandoned every creature and went beyond every intelligible creature and forsook every means of grasping with the mind.[6] There is yet another aspect of this dynamic which accompanies the process of *aphairesis*: the mind penetrates yet deeper. Through mind's own curiosity it penetrates deeper and deeper until it penetrates into what is invisible and incomprehensible and there sees God—a seeing which is a not seeing.[7] However, while it is important to acknowledge that Gregory allows the mind to enter the unfathomable presence of God, where it is 'surrounded on all sides by incomprehensibility as though by a kind of darkness',[8] it is likewise important to observe that the mind does not seem capable of doing anything in this presence. It cannot grasp anything in an act of understanding. Nor does the mind *per se* attain union with God. The inability of the mind to grasp in an act of comprehension when confronted with the darkness of divine presence is powerfully described in *In Ecclesiasten* VII, where Gregory likens the soul that has passed beyond what is accessible by concepts to someone standing on the edge of a cliff, who, when edging a foot over the side, realizes that there is no foothold: one becomes dizzy and is thrown into confusion and soon returns to solid ground.[9] Likewise the soul, 'having nothing it can grab, neither place nor time, neither space nor any other thing which offers our mind something of which to take hold, but, slipping from all sides from what it fails to

[4] See *In Cant.* VI, GNO VI. 182–3.   [5] *De vita Moysis*, SC, II. 163. 1–3.

[6] See *In Cant.* VI, GNO VI. 183. 6–8.

[7] See *De vita Moysis*, SC, II, 163. 3–7. The phrase also occurs at *In Cant.* VI, GNO VI. 182. 18. Cf. νοῦς ἐρῶν at *Enn.* VI. 7. 35. 24.

[8] Ibid., II. 163. 8.   [9] See *In Eccl.*, SC, VII. 8. 88–106.

grasp, in dizziness and confusion, it returns again to what is natural to it. . . . '[10]

Indeed the mind that enters the darkness of divine presence is not capable of grasping this divine presence in an act of comprehension. But if this is so, and it would appear to be, how, then, does the soul attain union? This is precisely what we saw as the specific role of faith in its technical sense, and Gregory places the two, i.e. the mind and faith, in very close proximity.

One of the clearest examples of this proximity is depicted by the figure of the bride in *In Canticum canticorum* VI. As noted just above, the bride has set out in ascent by the curiosity of her mind and traversed the entire intelligible and angelic realms in search of her Beloved. Not finding the Beloved, she abandons all means of grasping with the mind. Having done this, she finds her Beloved by means of faith.[11] Through this grasp of faith, not the grasp of the mind, the soul attains union with God.

This example of the bride's ascent is similar to that of Abraham in the *Contra Eunomium*. Abraham moved through various levels of knowledge and then began to leave behind all he had learnt and thus arrived at a faith purified of all concepts.[12] Moreover, we saw the specific function of this faith which came into play after the mind had assumed a posture of *aphairesis*: faith unites the searching mind to the nature of God.[13]

Again we saw that faith went beyond mind in *De vita Moysis*. Describing mind immersed in the darkness of the sanctuary, Gregory says that whoever wishes to commune with God must lift up the mind to the invisible and incomprehensible and there, at a level where understanding does not reach, one believes God is present.[14] At this exalted epistemological level, where understanding cannot reach but faith can, what exactly takes place 'there'? Gregory makes this more explicit in Book II of the same work. In much the same context of epistemological darkness Gregory says: 'in the unfathomable darkness one communes with God through faith'.[15] With the mind immersed in the darkness of divine presence, to believe is to commune and faith mediates this union.

These texts reveal a rather intriguing relationship between the mind and faith. The mind ascends through various levels of truth which it can

---

[10] Ibid., 100–4. Cf. *Enn.* VI. 9. 3.   [11] See *In Cant.* VI, GNO VI. 182. 18–183. 10.
[12] See *Contra Eunom.* II. 89, GNO I. 253. 12–14.   [13] See ibid., 25–8.
[14] See *De vita Moysis*, SC, I. 46. 4–10.
[15] Ibid., II. 315. 10: ἐν τῷ δυσθεωρήτῳ γνόφῳ διὰ πίστεως τῷ Θεῷ προσεγγίσῃς. . . . Cf. ibid., II. 164.

grasp in an act of understanding until it arrives at and *enters* the sanctuary or darkness of God's presence, which it cannot grasp. But then faith seems to come into play, continuing the yearning to grasp which the mind can no longer perform; and faith can indeed grasp God, as we have seen. The grasp of faith is not an act of comprehension but a union beyond understanding.

While Gregory's notion of faith in this exalted technical sense is, as Anthony Meredith has said, 'sui generis',[16] this notion of something continuous-yet-discontinuous with the mind that unites the soul to God is by no means idiosyncratic on Gregory's part; it is something of a commonplace in Middle and Neoplatonic epistemology. The purpose of this chapter will be to present the main lines of this tradition up to and including Plotinus and to suggest that this tradition situates Gregory's notion of exalted faith in a general (Neo)platonic cultural milieu. Thus situated, his notion of faith as a faculty of union stands in bolder relief. I will maintain that the relationship between mind and faith is roughly that which we see between the mind and the 'flower of the mind' or 'crest of intellect' found in other ancient authors.

The fact that we shall see some noteworthy parallels among such disparate figures as Celsus, the author of the *Chaldaean Oracles*, Plotinus, and Gregory of Nyssa on this topic of a faculty of union that unites the mind to God is not so much to suggest direct dependence or influence of one on the other (which would be singularly difficult to substantiate and indeed is not the line of approach taken here) as to indicate how diffuse was this notion of a faculty of union that crowns *nous*, part of the general Neoplatonic *esprit du temps*.

Celsus

While the greater weight of our attention will focus on that faculty that unites the mind to God in *The Chaldaean Oracles* and in Plotinus, we find a noteworthy adumbration of this theme in the second-century philosopher Celsus.[17] Celsus is significant in this regard for distinguishing

---

[16] A. Meredith, review of *Dieu et le Christ selon Grégoire de Nysse* by Bernard Pottier, *Vigiliae Christianae* 49 (1995), 408–11, at 411.

[17] On the identity, dates and theology of Celsus, see. H. Chadwick (trans), *Origen: Contra Celsum* (Cambridge, 1953), xvi–xxii and xxiv–xxix; A.-J. Festugière, *La Révélation d'Hermès Trismégiste*, vol. iv (Paris, 1954), 115–23; Wilken, *Christians as the Romans Saw Them*, 94–125; M. Fédou, *Christianisme et religions païennes dans le Contre Celse d'Origène* (Paris, 1988);

himself from other pre-Plotinian Platonists by positing 'a God who transcends both *ousia* and *nous*'.[18] If God is beyond being and mind, how can God be known? To answer this Celsus suggests in his Ἀληθὴς λόγος, conserved in part by Origen, an idea which will attain increasing importance in Neoplatonism: 'since he [sc. God] transcends all things and is intelligible by a certain indescribable power'.[19] Celsus, then, identifies a certain power or faculty by means of which God can be encountered. It is, moreover, significant that Celsus says that this faculty has an ineffable quality. For Celsus, God is also ineffable since God is not 'attainable by reason'.[20] There is, then, a certain similarity between this faculty and God, namely ineffability (once again the ancient principle that only like knows like). Celsus would appear to prefigure what will become quite explicit by the time we see this same faculty described by Plotinus as being the presence of the One in *nous*, something in *nous* which is not *nous*.

The Chaldaean Oracles

Presumably ' "handed down by the gods" to a certain Julian the Chaldaean and/or his son, Julian the Theurgist', this somewhat cryptic late second-century collection of what E.R. Dodds has called 'bad hexameter verse'[21] came to exert notable influence on Neoplatonists such as Porphyry, Iamblichus, and Damascius, who considered it revelation, and even on such 'Platonizing Christians' as Arnobius of Sicca, Marius Victorinus, and Synesius of Cyrene.[22]

Lilla, 'Teologia Negativa' (1982–1987), 270–3; idem, *Introduzione al Medio Platonismo* (Rome, 1992), 79–86; Carabine, *The Unknown God*, 62–6; J. Dillon, *Middle Platonism* (London, 1977); R.E. Witt, *Albinus and the History of Middle Platonism* (Cambridge, 1937).

[18]   Carabine, *The Unknown God*, 65; J. Whittaker, 'Ἐπέκεινα νοῦ καὶ οὐσίας' *Vigiliae Christianae* 23 (1969), 91–104, esp. 101–2. Cf. *Rep.* 509b.

[19]   *Contra Celsum* VII. 45: ἀρρήτῳ τινὶ δυνάμει νοητός. Trans. Chadwick, 433.

[20]   Ibid., VI. 65: οὐδὲ λόγῳ ἐφικτός ἐστιν ὁ θεός. Trans. Chadwick, 380; see Carabine, *The Unknown God*, 63.

[21]   E.R. Dodds, 'New Light on the "Chaldaean Oracles" ', in H. Lewy, *Chaldean Oracles and Theurgy*, new edition by M. Tardieu (Paris, 1978), 693.

[22]   R. Majercik, *The Chaldean Oracles: Text, Translation, and Commentary* (Leiden 1989), 1–3. On problems of authorship see P. Hadot, 'Bilan et Perspective sur les Oracles Chaldaïques', in Lewy, *Chaldean Oracles and Theurgy*, 703–7; see also Lewy, *Chaldean Oracles and Theurgy*, 3–7; W. Theiler, *Die Chaldäischen Orakel* (Halle, 1942), 1–2. J. Dillon does not wish to rule out the influence of the *Chaldaean Oracles* on Plotinus; see 'Plotinus and the Chaldaean Oracles', in S. Gersh and C. Kannengiesser (eds), *Platonism in Late Antiquity* (Notre Dame, 1992), 131–40.

The possible relevance of *The Chaldaean Oracles* to this study on Gregory of Nyssa is as limited as it is remote. The purpose of turning to this work is not to consider what it has to say about faith[23] but to see how this rather esoteric work of Middle Platonic provenance conceives of and expresses how the mind attains union with God.

In this respect Fragment 1 suggests itself for consideration, for it names this faculty the 'flower of the mind':

For there exists a certain Intelligible which you must perceive by the flower of the mind (νόου ἄνθει). For if you should incline your mind toward it and perceive (νοήσεις) it as perceiving a specific thing, you would not perceive (νοήσῃς) it. For it is the power of strength, visible all around, flashing with intellectual divisions. Therefore, you must not perceive (νοεῖν) that Intelligible violently but with the flame of mind completely extended (νόου ταναοῦ ταναῇ φλογὶ) which measures all things except that Intelligible. You must not perceive it intently, but keeping the pure eye of your soul turned away, you should extend an empty mind (τεῖναι κενεὸν νόον) towards the Intelligible in order to comprehend it, since it exists outside of (your) mind.[24]

In so far as this Intelligible can be thought, it cannot be thought by *nous*. Since the Intelligible is not circumscribable, it cannot be conceived. Hence, the *Chaldaean Oracles* envisions two ways of knowing and two corresponding states of mind. One mode of knowing is a 'violent' perception oriented towards defined objects. Its proper state of mind is characterized by vehement and intense conceptualization. The other mode of knowledge is receptive; its state of mind is the flower of the mind, subtle flame of mind, the eye of the soul kept pure and 'turned away', the mind empty of thought.[25]

Scholars have discussed whether this passage is fundamentally theurgic in scope and character, or whether it suggests a contemplative experience such as we see in Plotinus (e.g. *Enn.* VI. 9. 8–11). In his study of the *Chaldaean Oracles* H. Lewy sees in this text nothing which would prefigure any such contemplative experience as found in Plotinus. For Lewy, the *Oracles* quite simply use Platonic visionary language 'in order to represent the illumination of their initiate'.[26] Following

---

[23] πίστις is mentioned only once at 46. 2 as part of that 'praiseworthy triad' (Faith, Truth, and Love) which purifies and leads back to God. Cf. Porphyry, *Ad Marcel.* 24 and Proclus, *Theo. plat.* I. 25. 5, for a likewise exalted notion of πίστις.

[24] Trans. Majercik, *The Chaldean Oracles*, 49.   [25] De Andia, *Henosis*, 212.

[26] Lewy, *Chaldean Oracles and Theurgy*, 176. See the reconciling position (between theurgic purification and contemplative purification) of Hadot in 'Bilan et perspective', esp. 718–19. Cf. Majercik, *The Chaldean Oracles*, 34–5.

Lewy, F. Cremer argues that this text describes merely that state of mental passivity cultivated by the theurgist so that he might embark upon his theurgic endeavours.[27] Majercik, however, disagrees with both Lewy and Cremer.

While acknowledging that the majority of the fragments evince clear theurgic concerns, Majercik maintains that Fragment 1 (as well as Fragment 9a) is an exception and indeed suggests 'some form of con-templative experience'.[28] The 'flower of the mind', the 'flame of mind' and 'eye of the soul' are all expressions which describe 'that discreet, fiery organ or faculty (the highest power of the soul and akin to the fiery essence of the First God) which permits apprehension and/or union with the Highest God'.[29] The extension of an empty mind 'is a movement away from concrete, sensible images . . . towards an intuitive grasp of Highest Reality . . . achieved by the "flower/flame of mind" '.[30] The language of Fragment 1 is, she argues, similar to a Plotinian ascent with its ' "stripping away" of multiplicity, . . . "going forth from the self", . . . "extension towards contact" '.[31] This language of ascetic effort is expressed in Fragment 1 by the phrase 'keeping the pure eye of your soul turned away'. For Plotinus the experience of union with the One is achieved through ' "that element in *nous* which is not *nous*" '.[32] In Frag-ment 1 the experience is achieved through the flower of the mind. 'Thus, in both instances, the ultimate experience is that of a supra-rational state of unified intuition at the very highest levels of ascent.'[33]

What is the relationship between the flower of the mind and the mind itself and between the flower of the mind and the Highest Reality which it would grasp? The presence of the subjective genitive itself would suggest a certain continuity between *nous* and 'flower' just as there is a certain continuity between an apple tree and its blossom. On the one hand 'flower' is part of the human epistemological structure; the flowering of *nous* is consonant with *nous* in full extension. On the other hand, however, there is something which is not simply *nous*. This leads us to consider the relationship between the flower of the mind and the

---

[27] See F. Cremer, *Die Chaldäischen Orakel und Jamblich de mysteriis*, (Meisenheim am Glan, 1969), 11–13. Cf. Majercik, *The Chaldean Oracles*, 33–4, who disagrees with Cremer.

[28] Majercik, *The Chaldean Oracles*, 33.

[29] Ibid., 138. See her comments on lines 3, 8, and 10, 138–40.   [30] Ibid., 33.

[31] Ibid. See *Enn.* VI. 9. 8–11.

[32] *Enn.* V. 5. 8. 22–3 cited in Majercik, *The Chaldean Oracles*. Plotinus has various formulations for this, which we shall consider in due course.

[33] Majercik, *The Chaldean Oracles*, 33; she goes on to present her position on the relationship between theurgy and contemplation on 36 ff.

Highest Reality which it would grasp. In his study of the *Chaldaean Oracles*, H. Lewy reminds us that there is, nevertheless, a constitutive element of the flower of the mind that is not the mind itself; it is rather an 'offshoot of that which is to be cognized. This homogeneity appears', he continues,

> to be consequent upon the conception that a portion of the Paternal Intellect is commingled with the human soul, endowing it with the faculties of this Intellect from whom it descends. The intellectual substance subsisting in the human soul cognizes the primordial noetic substance because of its organic affinity with it. The cognition of the noetic being is an apprehension of like by like, or, more accurately, of the whole by one of its parts.[34]

Hence, whatever continuity there may be between the human mind and its flowering, Lewy would not let one lose sight of a constitutive discontinuity as well: the flower of *nous* indicates that there is something in *nous* which is not *nous* that enables contact with the Highest Reality.[35] That 'something' is the presence of the Highest Reality in *nous*. It is a knowing by like. This would seem to be a clear adumbration of what later becomes standard Neoplatonic doctrine on union, to which we shall now turn.

The questions of theurgy aside, and in light of our present purpose of considering that faculty of the mind which attains divine union, I would simply like to point out certain parallels, however remote, between Fragment 1 and the role which exalted faith plays in Gregory of Nyssa, for while the Plotinian parallels observed by Majercik are indeed worthy of note, parallels with Gregory's faith are also worth considering.

Fragment 1 is not cast in the form of an explicit ascent but it does reveal that fundamental dynamic often expressed in ascensional motifs: the movement of *nous* beyond discursive concerns of ratiocination which cannot grasp the Intelligible through understanding. The Intelligible is not grasped by *nous* but by the flower of *nous*, which obtains presumably as a result of the extension of an empty mind towards the Intelligible (τεῖναι κενεὸν νόον εἰς τὸ νοητόν).

---

[34] Lewy, *Chaldean Oracles and Theurgy*, 168.

[35] The allusion to *Enn.* v. 5. 8. 22–3, about which we shall have more to say, is purposive and is noted by Majercik, 33. Extreme caution, however, regarding the probability of Plotinus' knowledge of the *Chaldaean Oracles* is counselled by E.R. Dodds, 'Theurgy and its Relationship to Neoplatonism', *Journal of Roman Studies* 37 (1947), 55. Hadot, 'Bilan et perspectives', 709–11.

Though formulated rather differently, these elements feature in some of Gregory's more important ascents. In the migration of Abraham, for example,[36] we saw that the father of faith likewise moves through various levels of discursive knowledge, from knowledge derived from the senses to the contemplation of celestial wonders and the qualities attributed to the divine nature. At this point a process of *aphairesis* ensues, and Abraham begins to abandon all the knowledge previously acquired and arrives at a state purified of all concepts.[37] This is roughly the same concern voiced by the *Oracles*, though without Gregory's more elaborate *aphairesis*, when Fragment 1 speaks of the need 'to extend an empty mind' towards the Intelligible. This state of being purified of all concepts roughly parallels this empty mind, encouraged by the *Oracles*, in its 'awareness, ready to apprehend or intuit the unified simplicity of the Highest God'.[38]

The notion of the mind in extension is absent from this story of the migration of Abraham, but it is present in an important ascent in *De vita Moysis*. Reflecting on the meaning of Moses' disappearance into the darkness of the sanctuary, Gregory speculates on its significance and says that anyone who wants to be one with God must depart from all that is visible and do two things: extend the mind towards the invisible and incomprehensible, and believe God is present where the understanding does not reach.[39] Here the lexical parallel implies parallel thought: the mind's extending movement towards that which thought cannot grasp.

Finally, with Abraham's mind purified of all concepts, of all knowledge previously acquired, Gregory introduces the notion of faith and says it 'unites the searching mind to the nature of God'.[40] This union is accomplished in Fragment 1 of *The Oracles* by the flower of the mind.

What one might say of the parallel between the role of faith in the migration of Abraham and the role of the flower of the mind in Fragment 1 one might also say of the bride in the *Commentarius in Canticum canticorum*. In Homily 6 on the Song the bride embarks upon one of her many ascents in search of the Beloved. Her journey is characterized by the acquisition of knowledge as 'she traverses intellec-

---

[36] *Contra Eunom.* II. 84–96, GNO I. 251–4.   [37] Ibid., 89, GNO I. 253. 12–14.

[38] Majercik, *The Chaldean Oracles*, 140.

[39] *De vita Moysis*, SC, I. 46. 6–10: ὅτι δεῖ τὸν μέλλοντα συνεῖναι τῷ Θεῷ ἐξελθεῖν πᾶν τὸ φαινόμενον καὶ ἐπὶ τὸ ἀόρατόν τε καὶ ἀκατάληπτον τὴν ἑαυτοῦ διάνοιαν, οἷον ἐπί τινα ὄρους κορυφήν, ἀνατείναντα ἐκεῖ πιστεύειν εἶναι τὸ θεῖον ἐν ᾧ οὐκ ἐφικνεῖται ἡ κατανόησις.

[40] *Contra Eunom.* II. 91, GNO I. 253. 25–8.

tual and celestial nature'.[41] But after her encounter with the silence of the angels she realizes her Beloved is found in not knowing, and she begins to abandon all comprehension.[42] This ascent attains its zenith when the bride finds the Beloved not through an act of comprehension but through the grasp of faith.[43]

The parallel between this particular ascent of the bride and Fragment 1 seems obvious enough. Both are characterized by a general extending movement towards what is beyond the grasp of the mind. At the further reaches of this movement towards what the mind cannot grasp there is a certain sense of unknowing. With the bride this is due to the aphairetic gesture of letting go of what she has previously understood. In the case of Fragment 1 it is the 'empty mind'. In this state of unknowing a faculty is introduced to mediate the encounter with the desired object: in the case of the bride it is the grasp of faith; in Fragment 1 it is the flower of the mind.

Certainly Gregory's notion of exalted faith, as seen in the grasp of faith, contrasts sharply with the flower of the mind. As we have seen elsewhere in this study, Gregory's notion of exalted faith is inseparable from notions of grace, sacrament, scripture, and desire. Nevertheless, an important parallel remains not simply in the epistemological structure underlying the mind's movement towards and ultimately union with what lies beyond the mind and its ability to grasp in an act of understanding, but especially in the role played by a particular faculty in that union. The role which the flower of the mind plays in the *Chaldaean Oracles*, exalted faith plays in the ascents of Gregory of Nyssa: that faculty of union which unites the soul to God.[44]

Plotinus

It is generally admitted that Plotinus had no knowledge of the *Chaldaean Oracles*, or, if in fact he did, he showed no interest in them.[45] However,

---

[41] *In Cant.* VI, GNO VI. 182. 5–6.   [42] Ibid., 183. 2–8.   [43] Ibid., 183. 8–10.

[44] The converse, however, would not seem to be true; for while exalted πίστις does what the flower of the mind does, the flower of the mind cannot do everything exalted πίστις can do. For example, the grasp of πίστις also involves divinization and the handing on to the mind something of what it has grasped of the Ungraspable. See e.g. *Contra Eunom.* II. 89, GNO I. 253. 14–17, where πίστις mediates to the mind knowledge of a discursive sort, namely, that God is greater than any symbol by which he can be known, and *In Cant.* III, GNO VI. 87–8, which brings more to the fore the theme of divinization.

[45] Dodds, 'Theurgy and its Relationship to Neoplatonism', 55. Hadot, 'Bilan et perspectives', 709–11 and idem, 'Fragments d'un commentaire de Porphyre sur le

there are elements in Plotinus' doctrine on the union of *nous* with the One which influenced the development of the doctrine of the flower of the mind by later Neoplatonists, who were quite probably familiar with the *Chaldaean Oracles*. Moreover, these same elements help situate what Gregory of Nyssa has to say about exalted faith in the general Platonic tradition of what mediates union or contact between the mind and God.

While the doctrine of Plotinus on union goes beyond his concerns for the contact of *nous* with the One,[46] this doctrine will nevertheless be the exclusive focus of the remarks which follow. For despite Hadot's criticism of this very thing,[47] it is precisely the way in which the union of *nous* with the One comes about that relates to the matter in question, both with respect to what we saw in Celsus and in the *Chaldaean Oracles* and what we have seen to be the capabilites of exalted faith in Gregory of Nyssa.

How does Plotinus describe union with the One? What faculty is involved in such contact, however fleeting it may be? To answer this it is necessary to look at a cluster of terms which Plotinus uses to suggest an important distinction within *nous* itself. Not least among these is an important distinction between Intellect knowing and Intellect loving:

Intellectual-Principle, thus, has two powers, first that of grasping intellectively its own content, the second that of an advancing and receiving whereby to know its transcendent; at first it sees, later by that seeing it takes possession of Intellectual-Principle, becoming one only thing [*sic*] with that: the first seeing is that of Intellect knowing (ἡ θέα νοῦ ἔμφρονος), the second that of Intellect loving (νοῦς ἐρῶν); stripped of its wisdom in the intoxication of the nectar, it comes to love; by this excess it is made simplex and is happy; and to be drunken is better for it than to be too staid for these revels.[48]

Parménide', *Revue des Études Grecques* 74 (1961), 426. J. Dillon, however, finds this view untenable; see 'Plotinus and the Chaldaean Oracles', 131–40.

[46] On the experience of union with the divine Intellect see P. Hadot, 'L'union de l'âme avec l'Intellect divin dans l'expérience mystique plotinienne', in G. Boss and B. Seel (eds), *Proclus et son Influence*, Actes du Colloque de Neuchâtel, juin 1985 (Zurich, 1987), 3–27; idem, 'Neoplatonist Spirituality: Plotinus and Porphyry', in A. Armstrong (ed.), *Classical Mediterranean Spirituality* (New York, 1986), 230–49, esp. 239–41; J. Bussanich, 'Mystical Elements in the Thought of Plotinus', in W. Haase (ed.), *ANRW* ii. 36/7 (Berlin, 1994), 5300–30, esp. 5305.

[47] P. Hadot, 'Les Niveaux de Conscience dans les états mystiques selon Plotin', *Journal de Psychologie* 77 (1980), 243–66 at 245.

[48] *Enn.* vi. 7. 35. 20–5. Unless otherwise noted all translations are from the MacKenna translation, recently abridged, with notes and introduction by J. Dillon for Penguin Books: Plotinus, *The Enneads* (Harmondsworth, 1991). Greek references are to the edition of A. H. Armstrong, *Enneads*, 7 vols., LCL (Cambridge, Mass., 1966–88). In his note on

We see by this that Plotinus intends two levels within *nous*, each with its own proper characteristics and activity. 'Intellect knowing' (ἡ θέα νοῦ ἔμφρονος or as Plotinus states more succinctly at v. 5. 10. 9: νοῦς νοῶν) is concerned with contemplation of the intelligibles; comprehension would be suggested by the language of grasping. But 'Intellect loving' (νοῦς ἐρῶν) is somewhat different. This higher level of *nous* is not characterized by grasping but by movement towards what transcends it, i.e. the One, and by the capacity to receive the One.[49] This receptivity is described by Plotinus as a type of possession, but a possession not arrived at through the grasping that characterizes the lower level of *nous*, rather a possession through receptivity. This dimension of receptivity is heightened by the sense of *aphairesis* that is rendered by 'stripping' (ἄφρων—letting go of reason). This receptive, intellect loving is stripped of the wisdom that it had gained in intellect knowing. It is, then, by rising from the 'discursivity of reasoning' to this higher *nous* that 'the soul is already entering into "mystical" union, through an experience that transcends reason'.[50] This 'non-thinking',[51] as Hadot calls it, is higher than thinking, higher than intellect knowing.

While Plotinus seems clear on the distinction he makes within *nous*, it is important to note the continuity: the two levels are within the same *nous* and both levels are in rapport with the Good. As Hadot expresses it: 'The Intellect thus has a double rapport with the Good: a mediated rapport when it contemplates the refraction of the power of the Good in the system of Ideas; an unmediated rapport when it tries to remain in contact with the Good from which it emanates, by trying not to be caught up in the multiplicity of Ideas.'[52]

---

this passage Armstrong draws attention to the paradox in the allusion to *Symposium* 203b5; its application 'to Intellect's eternal self-transcendence in vision of and union with the One is strikingly powerful and paradoxical. Intellect must be eternally out of its mind with drink or love to be the Divine Mind.'

[49] See G. O'Daly, 'The Presence of the One in Plotinus', in *Problemi Attuali di Scienza e Cultura* 198, Atti del Convegno Internazionale sul tema: Plotino e il Neoplatonismo in Oriente e in Occidente, Roma, 5–9 ottobre, 1970 (Rome, 1974), 160; see also J. Rist, 'Mysticism and Transcendence in Later Neoplatonism', *Hermes* 92 (1964), 213–25; Hadot, 'Neoplatonist Spirituality: Plotinus and Porphyry'; idem, 'Structures et thèmes du Traité 38 (vi. 7) de Plotin', in W. Haase (ed.), *ANRW* ii. 36/2 (Berlin, 1987), 624–76; J. Bussanich, *The One and its Relation to Intellect in Plotinus: A Commentary on Selected Texts* (Leiden, 1988), 46, 174–5, *et passim*; idem, 'Mystical Elements in the Thought of Plotinus'.

[50] Hadot, 'Neoplatonist Spirituality', 244; Hadot expresses his concerns regarding the anachronistic term 'mystical' in 'L'Union de l'âme avec l'intellect divin', 3–6.

[51] Hadot, 'Neoplatonist Spirituality', 244.

[52] Ibid., 243.

While *Ennead* vi. 9. 35 would seem to suggest an underlying unity of *nous*, despite whatever discontinuity between intellect knowing and intellect loving it might support, Plotinus can also speak in such a way that a sense of discontinuity comes to the fore:

> It is Intellect which comes, and again Intellect which goes away, because it does not know where to stay and where he stays, that is in nothing. And if it was possible for Intellect to abide in that nowhere . . . it would always behold him, or rather not behold him, but be one with him not two. But as it is because it is Intellect, it sees him, when it does see him, with that of it which is not Intellect.[53]

Compared with the previous passage, this text states more clearly that the vision which Intellect has of the One is tantamount to union with the One. Moreover, whereas in the previous passage the continuity between *nous* and that faculty which unites with the One is, on the continuity—discontinuity continuum, rather more emphasized—the faculty in question being itself a higher aspect of *nous*—in this passage, by contrast, the discontinuity is emphasized; that faculty is not so much a higher level of *nous* (*Enn.* vi. 7. 35), as something within *nous* that is not *nous*. This change of emphasis, or perhaps inconsistency, on the part of Plotinus, causes one to pay close attention indeed to other texts in which Plotinus speaks of this faculty.

In an important passage concerning contact with the Good, Plotinus says that before approaching the Good which is beyond all knowledge, one must first attain some knowledge of it.[54] This acquisition of knowledge constitutes an ascent: We come to this knowledge, says Plotinus, 'of all that is derived from the good, by the upward steps towards it.'[55] This is 'ascent within intellect'.[56] As important as this acquisition of knowledge is, however, having ascended to the heights of *nous* one must nevertheless abandon this: 'Here, we put aside all learning.'[57] Plotinus then describes contact with the One: 'suddenly, swept beyond it all by

---

[53] *Enn.* v. 5. 8. 16–23. Trans. Armstrong. In his note on this passage Armstrong reminds us of the difficulty this passage presents because elsewhere Plotinus speaks of the changelessness of νοῦς (e.g. *Enn.* iii. 7). Armstrong explains this by suggesting that Plotinus is speaking from his own experience without considering the metaphysical implications.

[54] *Enn.* vi. 7. 36. 4–5. On gaining this primary knowledge of the One Plotinus advocates a threefold path of analogy, abstraction, and 'knowledge of its subsequents'. In this he simply follows Maximus of Tyre, Celsus, and Alcinous. But Plotinus goes beyond them in his emphasis on the importance of ultimately letting go of this knowledge in order to attain union with the One; see Carabine, *The Unknown God*, 139.

[55] *Enn.* vi. 7. 36. 8.   [56] *Enn.* vi. 7. 36. 9.   [57] *Enn.* vi. 7. 36. 15–16.

the very crest of the wave of Intellect surging beneath, he is lifted and sees, never knowing how;... no longer is there thing seen and light to show it, no longer Intellect and object of Intellection; this is the very radiance that brought both Intellect and Intellectual object into being.... With this he himself becomes identical....'[58]

The contact made with the One clearly involves *nous* and yet not only *nous*; *nous* alone is not sufficient. Only by a sudden swell is *nous* lifted up, and between this swelling and lifting a crest forms on the wave of *nous* and union with the One obtains.[59]

It is difficult to know precisely what Plotinus means. Is the crest of *nous* continuous or discontinuous with *nous*? I propose that, following the sense of the metaphors employed by Plotinus, there is both continuity and discontinuity. The element of discontinuity is rendered by the sense that it is obviously not under the aegis of *nous* alone that it arises and is identical with the One. This sense is achieved by a number of factors. Plotinus seems keen to emphasize the suddenness of the experience, as though not precipitated by whatever power Intellect would produce. Moreover, there is a sense of not knowing.[60] Finally, these two elements, combined with the fact that elsewhere in the *Enneads* Plotinus seems clear in his insistence that *nous* can but wait in silent preparation for the

---

[58] *Enn.* VI. 7. 36. 18–24 f. Numenius, Fragment 2. 7–12, compares the vision of God to a ship on the wave of the ocean. See Bussanich, *The One and its Relation to Intellect*, 137.

[59] The language of identification has been the occasion of considerable discussion; see J. Rist, *Plotinus*, 213–30; idem, 'Back to the Mysticism of Plotinus: Some More Specifics', *Journal of the History of Philosophy* 27 (1989), 183–97, esp. 184–90; J. Bussanich, 'Mystical Elements in the Thought of Plotinus', 5325–8; P. Mamo, 'Is Plotinian Mysticism Monistic?' in R. Harris (ed.), *The Significance of Neoplatonism* (Norfolk, Va., 1976), 199–215; and W. Beierwaltes, 'Reflexion und Einung: Zur Mystik Plotins', in *Grundfragen der Mystik* (Einsiedeln, 1974), 7–36, esp. 9.

[60] This element which Christians call 'grace' is underscored by Rist, *Plotinus*, 225; Carabine, *The Unknown God*, 142; Armstrong, 'Tradition, Reason and Experience in the Thought of Plotinus', in *Plotino e il Neoplatonismo in Oriente e in Occidente*, Atti del Convegno Internazionale dell' Accademia Nazionale dei Lincei (Rome, 1970), 171–94 at 186 and 191. However, one should be cautious when applying the Christian notion of grace to Plotinus, who operates out of a quite different anthropology. As Armstrong has noted, the soul for Plotinus is naturally divine. The Christian notion of grace accompanies an altogether different anthropology, particularly regarding the natural divinity of the soul. On this see B. McGinn's relevant observation in *The Foundations of Mysticism*, 54–5. On the suddenness (ἐξαίφνης) of the experience cf. Diotima's speech in *Symp.* 210e and *Ep.* VII. 341c; see also W. Beierwaltes, 'Exaiphnes oder: Die Paradoxie des Augenblicks', *Philosophisches Jahrbuch* 74 (1966–7), 271–83 as well as the sane remarks of J. Dillon, ' "A Kind of Warmth": Some Reflections on the Concept of "Grace" in the Neoplatonic Tradition', in L. Ayres (ed.), *The Passionate Intellect: Essays on the Transformation of Classical Traditions Presented to Professor I.G. Kidd* (New Brunswick, 1995), 323–32.

One to reveal itself,[61] highlight the discontinuity between *nous* and the faculty that brings it to union with the One: that in *nous* which unites it to the One is not quite *nous* (*Enn.* v. 5. 8. 23). Not the wave of *nous* as it heads towards the sands of the One, but the crest of this wave. Nevertheless, this discontinuity between *nous* and its receptive capacity/faculty for union with the One need not be affirmed at the price of denying any continuity whatever, for it is the same Intellect knowing, which the presence of the One has swelled into a crest.

The crest of the Intellect is not the only metaphor which Plotinus employs to describe the event of union by means of a mediating faculty. Some of these metaphors emphasize more the continuity between *nous* and its faculty of union, while others emphasize the contrast between the two. For example, in *Ennead* vi. 9. 3 we read not of the crest of Intellect but the 'summit of Intellect', an image which suggests a drawing together and focusing of all that precedes it. Plotinus says: 'We are in search of unity; we are to come to know the principle of all, the Good, the First;... and with the summit of intellect (τοῦ νοῦ τῷ πρώτῳ), we are to see the All-Pure.'[62] This search for the One-Good is characterized by a movement from multiplicity towards unity, a movement which involves going from *psyche* to *nous*, and then, becoming firmly established in *nous*, the One is glimpsed, not simply with *nous* but with the summit of *nous*. The image clearly evokes a sense of continuity between *nous* and its summit which mediates contact with the One. However, this quickly changes.

In *Ennead* vi. 9. 4, Plotinus takes up again the question of access to or awareness of the One. This awareness, Plotinus tells us, 'is not by way of reasoned knowledge or of intellectual perception'.[63] I take Plotinus to be referring to lower Intellect, intellect knowing (*Enn.* v. 5. 10. 9), in contrast to intellect loving (vi. 7. 35. 19–24). But then, instead of speaking of the crest of intellect or the summit of intellect as the means or faculty by which one enjoys union or becomes aware of the One, Plotinus simply says it is achieved not by the crest or summit of *nous* but 'by way of a presence superior to knowledge'.[64] This way of speaking of the means of approaching the One emphasizes its discontinuity with *nous*. This shift, moreover, is effected in the space of a few lines. Is

---

[61] *Enn.* v. 5. 8. 3–6: 'So one must not chase after it, but wait quietly till it appears, preparing oneself to contemplate it, as the eye awaits the rising of the sun'; see also v. 3. 17.

[62] *Enn.* vi. 9. 3. 27.   [63] *Enn.* vi. 9. 4. 1–2. Trans. Armstrong.

[64] *Enn.* vi. 9. 4. 3–4. Trans. Armstrong.

Plotinus contradicting himself? Is he 'unsaying' what he said at vi. 9. 3?[65] Is Plotinus simply exemplifying what A.C. Lloyd has described as the 'habitual vexation on the part of Neoplatonic writers to leave it at first sight unclear not so much what they mean as what they are referring to'?[66] Or is this an example of Plotinus' language 'hovering', as he seeks to describe an experience of his own?[67] While each of these questions is in itself intriguing, what I wish to emphasize here is the fact that, with respect to that faculty of union with the One, Plotinus can land at various points on a continuum of continuity–discontinuity; the same faculty from one perspective is summit of *nous*, crest of *nous*, but seen from another perspective is Presence, a trace of the One in *nous*, hence not *nous*.

Having stressed the continuity between *nous* and this faculty or means of union with the One at vi. 7. 35. 19–24; vi. 7. 36. 15–24; vi. 9. 3. 27, and in turn the discontinuity at vi. 9. 4. 1–2, Plotinus evokes at vi. 9. 10 a sense of both continuity and discontinuity. Plotinus is speaking of the vision of the One and how the soul loses its ground. He admits that he should not speak of this vision at all, 'but', he says, 'we cannot help talking in dualities, seen and seer, instead of, boldly, the achievement of unity. In this seeing ... there is no two.'[68] We fall from this unity when 'we withdraw from vision and take to knowing by proof, by evidence, by the reasoning processes of the mental habit. Such logic is not to be confounded with that act of ours in the vision.' Plotinus does not say exactly what he means by 'this act of ours', but he does seem clear that it is not the result of discursive reason: 'it is not our reason that has seen; it is something greater than reason, reason's Prior'.[69]

We have seen numerous passages which clearly designate the capacity of *nous* to unite with the One, a union which, however, *nous* does not seem capable of achieving on its own; but this faculty is not simply *nous* on its own. From one perspective it is the further reaches of *nous*, but from another perspective it is something in *nous* that is not *nous*, a trace of the One in *nous*. On the one hand Plotinus would seem to envisage a clearly distinct faculty, for it can do what intellect loving cannot do, but on the other hand, this faculty is never separate from *nous*, it is its noblest aspect, its summit, its crest.

---

[65] On this see M. Sells, 'Apophasis in Plotinus: A Critical Approach', *Harvard Theological Review* 78 (1985), 47–65; see also idem, *Mystical Languages of Unsaying*, 14–33.

[66] A.C. Lloyd, 'Review of *Proclus' Commentary on Plato's "Parmenides"*, translated by Glenn R. Morrow and John M. Dillon', *Journal of the History of Philosophy* 27 (1989), 299.

[67] See *Enn.* vi. 9. 3. 53–5.   [68] *Enn.* vi. 9. 10. 11–15.

[69] *Enn.* vi. 9. 10. 5–8.

Plotinus' distinction between *nous* and its summit or crest is in turn taken up by subsequent Neoplatonic writers. Porphyry likewise distinguishes two states of *nous*. According to Proclus, Porphyry taught that *nous*, while being eternal, possessed something pre-eternal, which united *nous* to the One.[70] Having just seen several texts in which Plotinus speaks along rather similar lines, one is inclined to agree with Hadot that Plotinus could be at the origin of this doctrine often associated with the later Neoplatonists.[71] However, Porphyry's Plotinus was modified by his reading of the *Chaldaean Oracles*.[72] It is this convergence of Plotinus' distinction within *nous* and the *Chaldaean Oracles* which will enable Proclus to develop a 'formal theory that just as by soul we attain likeness to Soul and by *nous* to the Intelligible World, so it is by the flower of *nous*, by our ἕνωσις, our unity, that we attain union with the One'.[73] It is Proclus who in turn hands on this tradition to Denys the Areopagite and Damascius.[74]

Parallels between Plotinus and Gregory of Nyssa

The difficulties in speaking of the relationship between Plotinus and Gregory of Nyssa 'should not at the outset be underestimated'.[75] Nevertheless, drawing attention to certain parallels between the two writers serves our purpose of situating Gregory's exalted faith or the grasp of faith in the breadth of a tradition which speaks of a faculty that bridges the gap between the mind and God.

---

[70] Proclus, *Theol. plat.* i. 11.

[71] Hadot, 'Fragments d'un Commentaire', 424–5.

[72] Rist, 'Mysticism and Transcendence', 223–4 and Carabine, *The Unknown God*, 157.

[73] Rist, 'Mysticism and Transcendence', 217. Because of changes made by Proclus to Plotinus' system, Proclus designates another faculty, ἄνθος τῆς ψύχης, that is needed to reach the One-Good; ἄνθος τοῦ νοῦ is retained for a lower stage of union, πρώτη νοητὴ τρίας, still beyond intelligence. See *Ecl. chald.* iv. 194; *In Timaeum*, ii. 203. 30–204. 13; *De providentia* v. 31–2; *In Alcibiadem* 247. 7–248. 4; *Theol. plat.* i. 3. For comments on these and other texts see De Andia, *Henosis*, 216–24; see also Rist, 'Mysticism and Transcendence', 215–20; Rosán, *Philosophy of Proclus*, 212–17; Siorvanes, *Proclus*, 196–8.

[74] Denys the Areopagite, *De div. nom.* i. 4; see De Andia, *Henosis*, 211–24 *et passim*. For Damascius see *De prim. princ.* 25 (65. 4–7).

[75] Meredith, 'The Good and the Beautiful', 133. J. Rist is also very cautious in acknowledging direct influence of Plotinus on Gregory, in 'Plotinus and Christian Philosophy', 399–401.

If Merlan can suggest that Plotinus' mysticism is a mysticism of *nous*, I would propose that Gregory's is a mysticism of faith.[76] In light of the present discussion the most obvious parallels focus on these respective roles of *nous* and faith or more specifically the crest or summit of *nous* and the grasp of faith, for what this crest or summit would accomplish in Plotinus, exalted faith accomplishes in Gregory.

Both authors draw from the wellspring of a generally Platonic tradition concerning the eros of the mind. We see this in Plotinus in his famous distinction between Intellect knowing and Intellect loving. In Gregory we see this in several places. Abraham leaves behind all that he has learnt and moves out in a 'searching mind'.[77] In the figure of Moses we see the mind stretching forth towards the Ungraspable.[78] Later we see that it is through the curiosity of the mind that access (not comprehension) to the Incomprehensible is gained.[79] Not unexpectedly the bride exhibits the same characteristic as she ascends by the curiosity of her mind.[80] In this context of the mind's ascent through eros, common to both Plotinus and Gregory, other noteworthy parallels emerge.

For both authors *nous* performs the act of comprehension (one must include *dianoia* as well for Gregory), and both authors have a similar way of describing what happens when the mind in search of comprehension comes into the presence of the Incomprehensible.

At *Ennead* vi. 9. 3. 1–11 Plotinus describes powerfully that level of mind he calls *psyche* in the presence of what it cannot grasp.

> The soul or mind reaching towards the formless finds itself incompetent to grasp where nothing bounds it or to take impression where the impinging reality is diffuse; in sheer dread of holding to nothingness, it slips away. The state is painful; often it seeks relief by retreating from all this vagueness to the region of sense, there to rest as on solid ground. . . .

Images of slipping and loss of stability are likewise employed by Gregory in at least two texts which we have already considered. In Homily 7 on Ecclesiastes we read that in the presence of the Incomprehensible, the mind,[81] as in the text from Plotinus, has nothing it can grasp; hence, it becomes dizzy and disorientated:

---

[76] P. Merlan, *Monopsychism, Mysticism, Metaconsciousness* (The Hague, 1963), 2. Regarding Gregory, B. Pottier has already identified πίστις as the core of his mystical theory in *Dieu et le Christ*, 215.

[77] *Contra Eunom.* ii. 91, GNO i. 253. 27.   [78] *De vita Moysis*, SC, i. 46. 9.

[79] Ibid., ii. 163. 4.   [80] *In Cant.* vi, GNO vi. 182. 18.

[81] However, as we have shown in Chapter 2, Gregory does not draw the sharp distinctions which Plotinus does between the levels of the mind; for Gregory such

Having nothing it can grab, neither place nor time, neither space nor any other thing which offers our mind something to take hold of, but, slipping from all sides from what it fails to grasp, in dizziness and confusion, it returns again to what is natural to it . . . [82]

Similar imagery is taken up again by Gregory in *De beatitudinibus*. Gazing into the Ineffable, Gregory says his mind is like one who gazes from a rocky precipice. He has been borne to such heights by scripture that he becomes dizzy from looking down into the unfathomable depths of the divine abyss, for the steep rock allows no basis for one's thoughts; the mind can in no way approach.[83]

Whether Gregory has Plotinus' description directly in mind (or *Phaedrus* 246c remotely in mind) or whether he is more directly inspired by the steep, lunar landscape of his native Cappadocia, both authors paint a similar picture of the grasping mind in the presence of the Ungraspable. Moreover, both authors overcome the dilemma by placing a faculty of union with the Ungraspable at a higher level in each respective (and different) epistemological structure. And they do this in similar ways. As we saw in Plotinus, in the context of intellect loving, he spoke of the summit or crest of Intellect, of reason's Prior, which served as metaphors of this faculty of union. In Gregory of Nyssa, as we have had occasion to see on any number of occasions in previous discussions, this faculty of union is called faith, and both Abraham and the bride were important examples of this. Abraham ascended through various stages of knowing but ultimately was purified of all such concepts. Here, at the apex of an epistemological ascent, having left behind the curiosity of knowledge,[84] Abraham arrives at a pure faith. This, says Gregory, is the only way of drawing near God: faith alone unites the searching mind to the incomprehensible nature.[85] In the *Commentarius in Canticum canticorum*, we saw the bride ascend through *dianoia*, ultimately forsaking everything she had found in her search to know the Beloved. Finally she was united to the Beloved by the 'grasp of faith'.[86]

Both authors employ the Platonic motif of the mind's ascent to the Incomprehensible and both place a distinct faculty of union at the apex of this apophatic ascent. Plotinus has termed this faculty the crest or

---

terms as ψυχή, διάνοια and νοῦς are roughly synomous. See A. Meredith, 'The Concept of Mind in Gregory of Nyssa', *Studia Patristica* 22 (1989), 35–51 at 35.

[82] *In Eccl.*, SC, VII. 8. 100–4.   [83] See *De beat.* VI, GNO VII. ii. 137. 16–22.
[84] *Contra Eunom.* II. 92, GNO I. 253. 28–9.   [85] Ibid., 91, GNO I. 253. 25–8.
[86] *In Cant.* VI, GNO VI. 182. 18–183. 10.

summit of *nous*, Gregory has termed it faith. Distinct as this faculty is, however, it would not appear to be altogether separate, as though it operated irrespective of lower levels of the mind. For we have only seen this faculty operate, in both authors, when the mind has moved through various and exalted epistemological forms as an intrinsic part of its search only to assume, as the next step in this search for knowledge, a posture of *aphairesis*: 'we put aside all learning',[87] says Plotinus; the bride 'abandons every form of comprehension', says Gregory.[88] Then and only then does the crest of *nous* or the grasp of faith perform its role.

In the Introduction we pointed out that Proclus had another way of speaking of union. Now that we have seen how Gregory describes faith as a faculty of apophatic union, it is worth looking again briefly at the *Platonic Theology* to see Proclus, writing well after Gregory, describe faith as a means of union with the Good: 'What will unite us with the Good? What will still all activity and movement? . . . In a word, it is the Faith of the gods which, by means beyond description, brings all ranks of gods and *daemons*, and the blessed among souls, into union with the Good. For the Good must be sought not by knowledge and its imperfection, but only by surrender to the divine radiance.'[89] Both Gregory and Proclus ground what they have to say about faith in a revealed text; Gregory draws inspiration from biblical models of faith (Abraham, Moses, the bride) and Proclus from the *Chaldaean Oracles*, which sees faith as part of a divine triad (faith, truth, and love). For both Gregory and Proclus, God is beyond *nous*; hence, some non-noetic means of approaching God is necessary. We have seen that for Gregory faith can move into and commune with God, while the discursive faculty could not. For Proclus too, 'the Good must not be sought by knowledge and its imperfections';[90] Proclus likewise designates faith, which 'is above the level of *nous*'.[91]

However, whatever parallels there may be between the crest of the wave of *nous*, the faith of Proclus, and Gregory's exalted faith, significant differences remain. Regarding late Neoplatonic faith, there is a clear difference from what Gregory has in mind. While both can regard faith as a means of union, Gregory views faith in the context of a relationship: Abraham and Moses in search of God; the bride searching

---

[87] *Enn.* VI. 7. 36. 15–16.   [88] *In Cant.* VI. GNO VI. 7–8.

[89] Proclus, *Platonic Theology* I. 25, ed. H. Saffrey and L. Westerink, *Théologie Platonicienne* (Paris, 1968), p. 110, 1–10; trans. Gregory, *The Neoplatonists*, 170.

[90] Ibid.   [91] Rist, *Plotinus*, 243.

the marketplaces for the Beloved (Song 3: 2); the bride with her mouth on the Bridegroom's (Song 1: 2); Paul saying 'I live now not I but Christ lives in me' (Gal. 2: 19–20); the Beloved Disciple reclined on the breast of the Lord (John 13: 25). These models of faith for Gregory betoken a relationship that finds no parallel in 'Platonic firm rational confidence' or late Neoplatonism's 'reliance on the *Chaldaean Oracles*'.[92]

Moreover, Gregory emphasizes the sacramental origin and development of faith as well as the transforming character of divine union.[93] A clear example of this was seen in the figure of the bride in Homilies 4, 12, and 13, where she was wounded by the arrow of divine love. This wounding revealed two important elements. As the tip of the arrow which wounded the bride, faith mediated the indwelling presence of God. In his description of this union Gregory wished to emphasize the dynamic, developmental character of this union. The effect of the arrow wounding the bride was the expansion of her desire for union, even as she enjoyed union and became a vessel of divine indwelling; faith, in its role of mediating union, likewise expanded with the bride's desire for union. Moreover, the transformational character of this dynamic union is seen in the provocative image which Gregory created to express the divinizing union enjoyed by the bride. In Homily 4 the bride was suddenly no longer the target at which the arrow of divine love was aimed, but had herself become this arrow and was placed in the bow of the archer and shot forth.[94] But at the same time the image of union was not lost as Gregory conflated this image of the archer holding the arrow with an image of the Bridegroom holding the bride. We have already pointed out how the change in the scriptural text itself encouraged this blending of images, but at the same time it allowed Gregory to express his own theological conviction that ascent, indwelling presence, and union are all different facets of the same encounter between finite and Infinite, a dynamic encounter mediated by faith that expands and develops. Indeed Gregory's concerns for development and transformation as a result of union, in which the soul could never become

---

[92] Rist, *Plotinus*, 245.

[93] On the developmental character of the mind in Gregory see M. Canévet, 'L'Humanité de l'embryon selon Grégoire de Nysse', *Nouvelle Revue Théologique* 114 (1992), 678–95.

[94] *In Cant.* iv, GNO vi. 128. 13 ff.

identical with the One, distinguish him definitively from the non-Christian Neoplatonist.

Conclusion

The purpose of this chapter has been to situate Gregory's view of exalted faith. While indeed it is somewhat idiosyncratic, the role played by this grasp of faith is far from idiosyncratic, but a fairly common concern for what mediates between the mind and the Incomprehensible. The fact that we have looked at authors who are not generally taken as exercising enormous influence upon one another serves to indicate just how ubiquitous was this concern; authors concerned with union with an incomprehensible God tend to speak of a mediating faculty at the apex of an epistemological ascent.

Moreover, while authors have called this faculty by different names and with varying epistemological presuppositions,[95] they have tended to speak of this faculty in a similar way.

Two modes of intellect are normally designated. One mode is concerned with images, discursive processes of ratiocination, and even contemplation of the intelligibles. The *Chaldaean Oracles* had, not surprisingly, a rather cryptic way of speaking of this mode as 'perceiving that Intelligible violently' or 'intently.'[96] This corresponded in Plotinus with intellect loving[97] and was negotiated by *dianoia* or *nous* in Gregory of Nyssa.

But we saw that another mode was called for when turning towards or ascending to a higher intuitive, non-discursive awareness of Highest Reality. The *Chaldaean Oracles* described this as 'extending completely

---

[95] Celsus called it an 'ineffable power'; the *Chaldaean Oracles* termed it 'the flower of the mind'; for Plotinus, the summit or crest of νοῦς, reason's Prior, etc.; for Gregory of Nyssa, πίστις; for Proclus, the flower of the soul. Origen has been left out of this survey because, according to John Dillon, who would claim the support of Henri Crouzel, Origen admitted no supranoetic contact with God; see J. Dillon, 'Looking on the Light: Some Remarks on the Imagery of Light in the First Chapter of the *Peri Archon*', in C. Kannengieser and W. Petersen (eds.), *Origen of Alexandria: His World and His Legacy* (Notre Dame, 1988), 227–9; see H. Crouzel, *Origène et la 'connaissance mystique'* (Paris, 1961), 496–508.

[96] Fragment 1. 7: σφοδρότητι νοεῖν τὸ νοητόν; Fragment 1. 9–10 (trans. Majercik, 49).

[97] *Enn.* v. 5. 10. 9.

the flame of the mind'.[98] Harking back to the *Symposium* and *Phaedrus*, Plotinus spoke of intellect loving[99] and Gregory spoke very similarly of a desiring or searching mind.[100]

In all the writers we have considered, this 'second' or 'higher' intellect assumed importance when the question of union was at issue. Moreover, as the ascent, implicit or explicit, reaches its apogee, an element of *aphairesis* appears. It is rather subtly present in the *Chaldaean Oracles* in which we are counselled 'to extend an empty mind toward the Intelligible'.[101] Plotinus is more straightforwardly aphairetic when he speaks of putting aside all learning[102] or being 'stripped of wisdom' as intellect loving 'comes to love'.[103] And the bride 'letting go of all manner of comprehension'[104] is but one among many aphairetic images; for we have noted previously how Gregory's ascents are filled with such terms and images.

This summary of parallels amongst the various authors, which serves to situate Gregory's exalted notion of faith in a relatively broad tradition regarding the mediating faculty of union with God, has obviously not focused upon important differences amongst the various authors. Gregory, in fact, would stand out in this regard, even in comparison with Plotinus. Gregory's different manner of conceiving of God, his 'new sense' of the soul's transformation, and notably, as we have seen in Chapters 2 and 3, the role played in that transformation, by baptism, liturgy, and scripture, amongst others,[105] would caution prudence regarding any over-hasty conclusions to be drawn from general parallels in patterns of thought. Nevertheless, these parallels serve their purpose.

While virtually no writer before Gregory of Nyssa spoke of faith in the way he did, a number of diverse authors spoke of a mediating faculty of union. Gregory is no innovator in this regard; his novelty is that he called it faith.

---

[98] Fragment 1. 8: νόου ταναοῦ ταναῇ φλογὶ (trans. Majercik, 49).

[99] *Enn.* vi. 7. 35. 20–5.

[100] *Contra Eunom.* ii. 91, GNO i. 253. 27: συναπτούσης δι' ἑαυτῆς τὸν ἐπιζητοῦντα νοῦν πρὸς τὴν ἀκατάληπτον φύσιν. *In Cant.* vi, GNO vi. 182. 18: τῇ πολυπραγμοσύνῃ τῆς διανοίας. As noted in Chaper 2, n. 106, it should be remembered that the term πολυπραγμοσύνη can also have a pejorative sense such as we see at *Contra. Eunom.* ii. 92, GNO i. 253. 29.

[101] Fragment 1. 11: τεῖναι κενεὸν νόον εἰς τὸ νοητόν (trans. Majercik, 49).

[102] *Enn.* vi. 7. 36. 15–16.

[103] *Enn.* vi. 7. 35. 24.

[104] *In Cant.* vi, GNO vi. 183. 7–8.

[105] Corrigan, ' "Solitary" Mysticism', esp. 38.

5

Fountain of Presence, Breasts of Wine:

The Flow of Knowledge in the *In Canticum canticorum*

Introduction

In order to understand more fully the technical meaning which Gregory accords the term faith in the various texts we have examined, it is not sufficient to isolate its primary function of union without also examining something of the effects of this union. In this chapter we shall have occasion to observe that, while arriving at the grasp of faith involves radical and consistent *aphairesis*, faith also gives something to the mind.

R. Brightman, among others, claims that any study of Gregory's thought which does not take sufficiently into account the centrality of the apophatic is *ipso facto* incomplete.[1] The apophatic dimension of Gregory's thought is widely acknowledged indeed, and the preceding chapters have consistently pointed out that when faith crowns an apophatic ascent, which is characterized by the letting go of all concepts and images, Gregorian faith assumes its rather idiosyncratic usage and technical function. Time and again we have seen Gregory's epistemological ascents move through the acquisition of knowledge but then begin to flower in *aphairesis*, abandonment of all knowledge previously acquired. This is Abraham who, as he approaches God, begins to leave

---

[1] R. Brightman, 'Apophatic Theology and Divine Infinity in St. Gregory of Nyssa', *Greek Orthodox Theology Review* 18 (1973), 97–114, at 102 and 111. See also e.g. Daniélou, Louth, McGinn, Carabine, *inter alii*.

behind the levels of knowledge previously enjoyed.[2] This is the bride who, in Homily 6 on the Song of Songs, lets go of everything she has understood of the Beloved in her epistemological ascent, only then to find her Beloved by the grasp of faith beyond all concepts.[3] We see the same in the figure of Moses who enters the sanctuary or the darkness where God dwells. In this darkness there is no image, no concept, no act of comprehension. Hence, one can only agree with the many scholars who note the apophatic character of his thought whether or not they appreciate the role of faith in Gregory's apophaticism.[4]

But is this flowering of epistemological abandonment that accompanies union the end of the process? Is Gregory the relentless apophaticist that Brightman and others would have him? He is and he is not, and in what way he is *not* the relentless apophaticist seems largely overlooked by scholars of Gregory's apophaticism. Indeed for all Gregory's apophaticism he values at the same time positive knowledge of God. For whilst the mind does not grasp God in comprehension, God 'puts down roots in the depths of the mind' and waters it with teaching; beyond the grasp of comprehension though the divine nature is, something of God has the capacity to make itself cognitively useful.

In order to see something of the rather subtle relationship between the mind and God I will focus on the metaphor of gold and the imagery of flow. The imagery of flow suggests itself especially for consideration, for it holds together a constellation of concerns which might otherwise seem not quite so tightly interconnected as they are: divine presence, nourishment, sacramental life and divinization, divine instruction, thought. All these themes are organized by the more general metaphor of flow. The flow which characterizes divine presence is mirrored in the flow of thought, reflected in its structure of outward flow and streaming forth. By examining this imagery of flow we can more easily see the non-apophatic, epistemological concerns that are at issue in the encounter between the mind and God.

The Gold of Knowledge

Amongst the things which the Song of Songs would have us learn, according to Gregory, is that we can indeed know something of God

---

[2] *Contra Eunom.* II, 89–91, GNO I, 253.   [3] *In Cant.* VI, GNO VI. 183. 5–10.

[4] For example, D. Carabine's helpful presentation of Gregory's apophaticism in her *The Unknown God*, overlooks the role of πίστις.

even if it is not the divine nature itself.[5] One of the clearest statements of this occurs rather early on in the *In Canticum* when Gregory uses the metaphor of gold to describe knowledge of God.

In Homily 3 on the Song Gregory sets out to interpret the following *lemma* (Song 1: 11): 'we shall make for you likenesses of gold with silver studs'.[6] The likenesses of gold and silver will be used to beautify the horse which the king will mount. It is significant to Gregory that the text says 'likenesses of gold' and not simply gold.[7] He understands this distinction to refer to the difference between what we understand about the nature of God and the divine nature itself. No matter if our understanding of God is the 'best and the highest understanding', this understanding, this knowledge of God is the 'likeness of gold and not gold itself'.[8] For the divine nature itself is 'inexpressible', 'ineffable'.[9] Any good thoughts which a person may offer refer to the likeness of gold and not the gold, for the divine nature itself cannot be captured by words. Gregory admits, however, that it is possible to think that these understandings are gold, but 'for those who are capable of gazing on the truth, they are likenesses of gold and not gold'.[10]

However, so as not to overemphasize the difference between our understanding of God and the divine nature, Gregory states quite clearly that there is a similarity. The likeness of gold is just that, a likeness of gold; our understanding of the divine nature bears a resemblance to what we seek.[11] So Gregory thinks we can indeed have positive, accurate knowledge of God; the divine nature simply transcends the grasp of concepts.[12] While the knowledge is accurate, it falls short of comprehension,[13] of closing its grasp around God. Only faith can grasp God.[14]

Gold serves Gregory's epistemological purposes again in Homily 7 on the Song of Songs. Here he leaves to one side his distinction between gold and the likeness of gold (for indeed the scriptural text he comments on, Song 3: 10: 'He fashioned its pillars silver, its back gold', itself parts with the distinction), but continues his interpretation of gold along nevertheless similarly cognitive lines. Gold is 'the gold of knowledge of God'[15] and 'the gold of pure teachings'.[16]

[5] Harrison, *Grace and Human Freedom*, 24–60, esp. 47 and 59.

[6] *In Cant.* III, GNO vi. 83. 1–2.   [7] See ibid., 85. 6–15.

[8] Ibid., 85. 17–19.   [9] Ibid., 86. 1.   [10] Ibid., 86. 8–9.

[11] Ibid., 86. 14–15: τὸ δὲ περὶ αὐτῆς ἡμῖν ἐγγινόμενον νόημα ὁμοίωμά ἐστι τοῦ ζητουμένου·

[12] Ibid., 86. 13–14: ἡ θεία φύσις πάσης ὑπέρκειται καταληπτικῆς διανοίας.

[13] Ibid., 87. 2–5.   [14] Ibid., 87. 6–7.

[15] *In Cant.* VII, GNO vi. 205. 18: τὸ τῆς θεογνωσίας χρυσίον....

[16] Ibid., 211. 2–3: τὸ τῶν καθαρῶν δογμάτων χρυσίον ἐστίν,...

Another text which demonstrates Gregory's belief that we do have positive knowledge about God is found in his interpretation not of gold but of the Bridegroom's hands (Song 5: 4) in Homily 11. At the end of this Homily he says that we can know something of the divine nature through God's works: the incomprehensible, unattainable divine nature is made known through these works alone.[17] It would seem to be Paul, in Rom. 1: 20, who prompts Gregory to take this position and claim further that we know something of God from creation.[18] While he does not back away from his position that the divine nature cannot be comprehended, there is yet something of God that can be known through his operations.[19]

But to know something of God is not to grasp God in comprehension. While the positive knowledge we can have of God is real and in theory accurate, this does not exhaust God. No amount of knowledge, however true a likeness to gold it may seem, can measure our comprehension of what we desire.[20] Gregory says that the mind should realize that all perfection of knowledge is but the beginning of a higher desire.[21] At the opening of Homily 8 on the Song, he says that Paul alone knew what was beyond the third heaven, but even knowing this he did not cease to ascend.[22] Though the pure of heart see God, this seeing does not exhaust God.[23]

While this knowledge is partial, the likeness of gold and not the gold itself, it is valued by Gregory, especially insofar as it takes the form of orthodox teaching, for this teaching about God captures something of what it represents. We see this in Homily 3's description of divine indwelling through a vinicultural metaphor. The mind is likened to fertile earth and the Bridegroom to a vine which is rooted in the earth of the mind. The depths of the mind, Gregory says, are watered with divine lessons.[24] The interaction of the root (Bridegroom), the fertile earth (the depths of the mind), and irrigation (divine lessons) causes

---

[17] *In Cant.* XI, GNO VI. 339. 6–8: ὧν ἡ μὲν ὑποτίθεται τὴν θείαν φύσιν ἀκατάληπτον οὖσαν παντελῶς καὶ ἀνείκαστον διὰ μόνης τῆς ἐνεργείας γινώσκεσθαι,...

[18] Ibid., 339. 14–16: ἐκ μὲν γὰρ τοῦ γνῶναι, ὅτι τοῦ θεοῦ τὸ γνωστὸν κατὰ τὴν τοῦ Παύλου φωνὴν διὰ τῆς τοῦ κόσμου κτίσεως νοούμενον καθορᾶται,...

[19] A point well illustrated by Harrison, *Grace and Human Freedom*, 47.

[20] *In Cant.* VI, GNO VI. 180. 1–3.   [21] Ibid., 180. 4–7.

[22] *In Cant.* VIII, GNO VI. 245. 17–22.   [23] Ibid., 246. 5–10.

[24] *In Cant.* III, GNO VI. 97. 18–98. 2: ἡ τοῦ νυμφίου ἄμπελος ἐν τῷ Γαδί, τῷ πίονι τούτῳ τόπῳ ἐρριζωμένη (τουτέστιν ἐν βαθέᾳ τῇ διανοίᾳ τῇ διὰ τῶν θείων διδαγμάτων καταρδομένῃ)....

the vine to blossom and bear fruit in which the vinedresser (God) can be seen.[25] Gregory goes on to relate this to his doctrine on virtues, but what I wish to observe here (which will be of use in the following section) is simply that the vital element of water serves as an epistemological, indeed pedagogical, metaphor. Divine presence as water is described as a teaching or lesson, a divine lesson. The point is that as incomprehensible and apophatic as the divine nature is, something of it has the capacity to make itself cognitively useful, capable of being rendered into discourse, and this to the enormous benefit of the life of virtue which, as we see if we read further on, reveals divine beauty.[26]

Not only is positive knowledge favourable, but orthodox notions of God are a prerequisite for drawing close to God. This is clearly stated in Homily 13, where Gregory says that correct notions concerning reality are necessary for associating with God.[27] Although this knowledge 'does not make known the greatness of the divine nature',[28] and will be abandoned in the later stages of ascent as one arrives at that level where there is only faith, Gregory nevertheless values the importance of the limited knowledge which our notions of God constitute. No matter how apophatic Gregory becomes, positive knowledge is and remains important.

The Flow of Water

In Chapter 2 we saw how for Gregory the mind was characterized by flow. In fact, as early as *De virginitate* the metaphor of irrigation was used successfully and consistently by Gregory to describe the basic dynamism of the mind.[29] In what follows I should like to return to some of this imagery, this time in the *In Canticum*, and show not only that it does continue to have epistemological overtones but that it is also linked to Gregory's vast and intricate symbolism of divine presence and transformative union.

A Fountain of Presence and Source of Nourishment

Gregory draws upon the biblical image of a water source, a fountain, to describe the presence of God to the soul.[30] In Homily 13 on the Song he

[25] Ibid., 98. 3–5.   [26] Ibid., 98. 5–99. 2.

[27] *In Cant.* XIII, GNO VI. 376. 8–11.

[28] *In Cant.* XII, GNO VI. 357. 4–5: οὐκ...τὸ μέγεθος τῆς θείας γνωρίζηται φύσεως....

[29] *De virg.*, SC, VI. 2. 1–19.   [30] Gen. 2; 6: πηγὴ δὲ ἀνέβαινεν ἐκ τῆς γῆς...

describes this fountain as a 'fountain of wisdom whose emanation established the nature of beings'.[31] And in Homily 8 this fountain of wisdom is a fountain of beauty which 'renders all things extremely beautiful as they pour forth from the fountain of beauty'.[32] But this fountain that sustains all things in being is more obviously seen as divine presence. In Homily 11 Gregory uses the image to clarify the fact that, although the soul knows something of the Beloved, what she does not know is infinitely greater than what she has comprehended. 'Because of this the Bridegroom appears often to the soul.'[33] To explain the fact that the Bridegroom's appearance can never be fully appreciated by the soul, Gregory likens this presence of the Bridegroom to the fountain mentioned in Gen. 2: 6. If one were to look at this fountain one would marvel at the endless flow of water pouring forth and gushing out and yet never see all the water which is under the earth. The water would always seem new.[34] And so it is for the one who looks upon divine, invisible beauty; it is inexhaustible.[35] Divine presence for Gregory is not difficult to fathom because of distance or immensity,[36] but rather because of its very nature (infinite) which he clothes in a metaphor of intense, creative, and superabundant presence: a fountain gushing up from the earth.

If through the image of the fountain God is creative presence, this flowing presence is also a source of nourishment. For this fountain of beauty is at the same time a 'fountain of goodness drawing to itself those who are thirsting'.[37] In Homily 5 Gregory says that when human nature was in Paradise it thrived and was nourished by those fountains of water.[38] The nourishment of water enables the blossoming of virtues, which are the flowers of our life.[39] If being close to the source of nourishment in Paradise is expressed by the metaphor of moisture, the fall from Paradise is expressed as dryness, hence the 'bud of immortality' falls to the ground, and the 'grass of virtues is dried up' while the love of God grows cold.

---

[31] *In Cant.* XIII, GNO VI. 386. 3–4.

[32] *In Cant.* VIII, GNO VI. 255. 16–17: (... ποιεῖν τὰ πάντα καλὰ λίαν τὰ ἀπὸ τῆς τοῦ καλοῦ πηγῆς ἀναβρύοντα),...

[33] *In Cant.* XI, GNO VI. 320. 20–321. 4.   [34] See ibid., 321. 10–16.

[35] Ibid., 321. 17.

[36] As for Origen, who expresses a Middle Platonic view of the matter.

[37] *In Cant.* VIII, GNO VIII. 248. 5–6.   [38] *In Cant.* V, GNO VI. 152. 18–153. 1.

[39] Ibid., 153. 14–15.

Sacramental Life and Divinizing Union

The soul returns to the nourishment of this fountain of divine presence through the sacramental life in which the soul is divinized. In describing the sacramental life of baptism and eucharist, Gregory uses the same imagery of flowing water to describe the soul's partaking of divine life. This transformation, moreover, is mediated by faith, which, as we shall see, allows the fountain of divine presence to burst forth in the baptized.

Water imagery of divine presence frequently flows into sacramental imagery throughout the *In Canticum*. In Homily 2, the Word is a bath which washes clean the 'dirt of shameful thoughts'. This cleansing by the Word prepares one to enter the Holy of Holies and gaze upon the marvels there.[40] But further on in the same Homily Gregory changes from the imagery of cleansing with water to the imagery of light in order to describe the effects of this 'bath of regeneration'.[41] Not only does this bath wash away the dark form of those whom Christ has called but it makes them 'shine like luminaries'.[42] Hence, we see Gregory combine themes of water and light to describe divine presence in baptismal contexts.

An important text in Homily 8 reveals the mediating role of faith. Baptismal imagery is implicit in Gregory's mentioning of the Jordan River in his interpretation of the meaning of Song 4: 8: 'You will come and pass from the summit of faith (ἀπὸ ἀρχῆς πίστεως), the top of Sanir and Hermon.'[43] From this summit of faith, says Gregory, pour forth the fountains of the Jordan River, and 'the stream from these fountains has become the beginning of our transformation towards divinity'.[44] The summit of these mountains, which is faith according to Gregory's Septuagint text, is the source of these 'fountains of mystery'.[45] To come into contact with these waters is to be divinized, indeed to become oneself such a fountain of flowing streams, as we see in Homily 14, where again faith mediates this divinizing flow. Alluding to John 7: 38, Gregory says of someone who believes in Christ, that 'out of his belly will stream forth rivers of living water'.[46] The belly, Gregory says, is a

---

[40] *In Cant.* II, GNO VI. 45, 5–11.   [41] Ibid., 49. 2–3.   [42] See ibid., 49. 1–4.

[43] *In Cant.* VIII, GNO VI. 250. 8–9.

[44] Ibid., 250. 13–15: ... τὸ ἐκ τῶν πηγῶν τούτων ῥεῖθρον ἀρχὴ γέγονεν ἡμῖν τῆς πρὸς τὸ θεῖον μεταποιήσεως, ...

[45] Ibid., 250. 18. The connection between the Jordan River and the theme of divinization is perhaps more obvious at *In Cant.* XV, GNO VI. 468. 10–13, where the presence of the Holy Spirit is mentioned.

[46] *In Cant.* XIV, GNO VI. 414. 11–12: Ὁ πιστεύων εἰς ἐμέ, καθὼς εἶπεν ἡ γραφή, ποταμοὶ ἐκ τῆς κοιλίας αὐτοῦ ῥεύσουσιν ὕδατος ζῶντος.

pure heart which is 'smooth and gleaming', written upon by the Spirit of the living God.[47]

Hence, we see once again that the themes of divinization and light are associated with flowing water. What is important to notice, and we shall see this again when we look at texts with more obviously epistemological implications, is that this water of divine presence can penetrate the soul and flow within it, transforming the soul into a fountain of divine presence. The fountain comes out of the belly, and this flow is mediated by faith.

This sacramental flow of baptism can also manifest a eucharistic form in several of the homilies. In Homily 10, for example, Gregory comments on Song 4: 16: 'Let my Beloved descend into his garden and let him eat the fruit of his fruit trees.' It is the bride who speaks and she invites the Bridegroom, who descends 'as bread from heaven and gives life to the world'.[48] To this paraphrase of John 6: 33 Gregory adds that the Bridegroom who has descended as bread lets water stream from his own fountain of life.[49] Why he considers it appropriate to align these two images, bread and a flowing fountain, seems obvious enough from his allusion to John 6: 33. For the Evangelist himself describes this bread as preventing both hunger and thirst (John 6: 35). Since the bread can also slake thirst, it is not surprising to see the fountain imagery.

We see a powerful image of divine presence as a fountain, when Gregory comments on Song 1: 2: 'Let him kiss me with the kisses of his mouth.' The Bridegroom's mouth is a fountain which draws the bride to put her mouth to the fountain of his mouth.[50] A similar image, but with a eucharistic inflection, is seen in Homily 4, where Gregory comments on Song 2: 4: 'Lead me into the house of wine.'[51] It is the bride who desires to enter the house of wine in order to quench her thirst, and just as she drew her mouth to the mouth of the fountain (Bridegroom) in Homily 1, so she puts 'her mouth to the wine-vats which are overflowing with their sweet wine'.[52]

Gregory continues the imagery of fountains when he describes divinization, irrespective of an explicitly sacramental context. An important

---

[47] *In Cant.* xiv, GNO vi. 414. 17–415. 1.   [48] *In Cant.* x, GNO vi. 303. 12–13.
[49] Ibid., 303. 13–14: ... τὸν πᾶσι τοῖς οὖσι τὴν ζωὴν ἐκ τῆς ἰδίας πηγῆς ἐπιρρέοντα·
[50] *In Cant.* i, GNO vi. 32. 12–33. 2.   [51] *In Cant.* iv, GNO vi. 119. 12 ff.
[52] Ibid., 120. 3–4: ... καὶ αὐταῖς ταῖς ληνοῖς ὑποσχεῖν τὸ στόμα, αἳ τὸν οἶνον τὸν ἡδὺν ὑπερβλύζουσι, ... For more on the eucharistic significance of this portion of Homily 4 see Cortesi, *Le 'Omelie sul Cantico dei Cantici'*, 214–16.

example is seen in his interpretation of Song 1: 2 in Homily 1: 'Let him kiss me with the kisses of his mouth.' Having recalled the image of Moses conversing with God 'face to face', and how this encounter did not exhaust Moses' desire for God but enkindled an even greater desire after the theophanies,[53] Gregory likens this to the soul united to God: 'the more it lavishly takes its fill of beauty, the more the desire for it abounds'.[54] He then describes this inexhaustible divine presence as a fountain. 'The fountain is the mouth of the Bridegroom from which words of eternal life pour forth, filling the mouth drawn to it.'[55] Cortesi has observed that this kiss is for Gregory a 'spiritual communication',[56] but more than just this, it exemplifies how Gregory subtly incorporates this into a theme that pervades the *In Canticum*: divinization. That this text concerns divinization is made more clear if we note that just above, Gregory has subtly identified the words of the Bridegroom with the Holy Spirit: '... the words of the Bridegroom are spirit and life, and the one who is joined together with the Spirit becomes spirit ... '.[57] The kiss which the bride enjoys, her approaching the fountain (Bridegroom) 'mouth to mouth',[58] and being filled with the Bridegroom's words pouring forth, is an image of divinization. In this Homily, however, Gregory does not state the effects upon the soul (bride) of this drinking from the fountain of the Bridegroom's words. But in Homily 2 Gregory takes up the image once again, and the effects of this union are more clearly seen.

Once again the Bridegroom is a fountain, and the bride is running towards it to drink of this 'divine draught'.[59] The bride herself explains what follows when one makes contact with this fountain: 'the one tasting of it becomes a fountain of water welling up into eternal life'.[60] Hence, we see in these two texts concerning divinization that the Bridegroom is present to the bride as water, and when contact is made she takes on the

---

[53] *In Cant.* I, GNO VI. 31. 10–32. 1.   [54] Ibid., 32. 6–8.

[55] Ibid., 32. 12–14: ἡ δὲ πηγή ἐστι τοῦ νυμφίου τὸ στόμα, ὅθεν τὰ ῥήματα τῆς αἰωνίου ζωῆς ἀναβρύοντα πληροῖ τὸ στόμα τὸ ἐφελκόμενον,...

[56] Cortesi, *Le 'Omelie sul Cantico dei Cantici'*, 177: 'Al di là della lettera, il bacio è una communicazione spirituale referentesi all' ascolto della parola.'

[57] Ibid., 32. 8–10: ... τὰ ῥήματα τοῦ νυμφίου πνεῦμά ἐστι καὶ ζωή ἐστι, πᾶς δὲ ὁ τῷ πνεύματι κολλώμενος πνεῦμα γίνεται. ...

[58] Ibid., 32. 16.

[59] *In Cant.* II, GNO VI. 62. 4–5.

[60] Ibid., 62. 6–7. Gregory has conflated the image of water pouring forth from a fountain with water streaming from the side of Christ on the Cross.

qualities of water; she herself becomes a fountain. We see that for Gregory water is a symbol of transforming presence.

The imagery of water appears again in a context of divinization in Homily 5, where Gregory explains why, when the bride approaches the divine Fountain mouth-to-mouth and drinks from it, she herself becomes a fountain (we have already seen in Chapter 3 how Homily 4 depicts the bride, having been wounded by the divine arrow, becoming herself an arrow[61]). He says that 'those who gaze upon the real divinity receive in themselves the characteristics of divine nature'.[62] Gregory says that something similar happens if we look at idols; we are turned to stone, and this is precisely what has happened to human nature as a result of the worship of idols. Gregory describes recovery from this stony state in the language of light, warmth, and water. Light and warmth are associated with the effect on human nature of the Word and the Holy Spirit, which had become cold and stony.[63] The result of this warming is transformation into water: 'humanity... once again became water springing up into eternal life'.[64]

The Fountain of Divine Teaching

But Gregory can also adapt the image of the fountain as a symbol of sacramental, transformative, divine presence to serve other purposes of a more epistemological nature. In Homily 15, for example, the fountain of presence is not clothed in sacramental imagery as above, but is rather a divine fountain of teaching. In an incarnational metaphor we read that the Word is present as a source of irrigation for the virtues planted by God in the soul. By means of the Word, God waters these plants with the 'pure and divine fountain of teaching'.[65] A similar image is found in Homily 13, but instead of a 'fountain of teaching' Gregory speaks of the 'rain of teaching' that waters God's fields and makes them fertile.[66]

---

[61] *In Cant.* IV, GNO VI. 128. 13–15.

[62] *In Cant.* V, GNO VI. 147. 11–12: ὥσπερ γὰρ οἱ πρὸς τὴν ἀληθινὴν θεότητα βλέποντες ἐφ᾽ ἑαυτῶν δέχονται τὰ τῆς θείας φύσεως ἰδιώματα,... Gregory continues to say how it works both ways. Cf. *Phaedrus*, 253a.

[63] Ibid., 147. 21–2.

[64] Ibid., 147. 22–148. 1: ὁ...ἄνθρωπος...πάλιν γένηται ὕδωρ ἁλλόμενον εἰς ζωὴν αἰώνιον. (cf John 4: 14).

[65] *In Cant.* XV, GNO VI. 437. 4–8:...καὶ λυμηναμένου τὸ θεῖον γεώργιον κατέβη τοῦ πάλιν ποιῆσαι κῆπον τὴν ἔρημον τῇ τῶν ἀρετῶν φυτείᾳ καλλωπιζόμενον τὴν καθαρὰν καὶ θείαν τῆς διδασκαλίας πηγὴν ἐπὶ τὴν τῶν τοιούτων φυτῶν ἐπιμέλειαν ὀχετηγήσας τῷ λόγῳ.

[66] *In Cant.* XIII, GNO VI. 392. 5–7.

In Homily 15, it is the field of virtue that is watered by the fountain of teaching, but in Homily 3, it is the mind that is watered.[67] The mind is likened to Gadi and described as a deep and rich place watered by divine teaching. The vine of the Bridegroom is rooted here, and the water of divine teaching causes the vine to blossom.[68]

Gregory's imagery is often polysemous. For the present purpose, however, it is enough to emphasize the epistemological, indeed pedagogical, nuance in which Gregory depicts divine presence. God is present to the soul as teaching, another example of his concern for knowledge of God, and this teaching flows with the abundance of an overflowing fountain.

The question suggests itself: if God is present in the mind as a fountain of divine teaching, that water of which teaching presumably can be learnt or absorbed by the mind, is Gregory not suggesting, then, that we can know God in some sense? It seems to me that this is exactly what he is suggesting. Not that the divine essence is comprehended, but something of God is known by virtue of the presence of this fountain, by virtue of communion, mediated by faith, with this fountain of presence (*In Cant.* xiv. 414. 11–12: of the one believing Him it is said, 'out of his belly will stream forth rivers of living water'), by virtue of the bride putting her mouth to the fountain of presence which is the Bridegroom's mouth. Gregory's concern for what overflows into knowledge is perhaps best seen in his interpretation of the 'drops of the night', an image drawn from Song 5: 2.

While Gregory is rather consistent in his description of divine presence as a fountain, and even a fountain that instructs, he is likewise consistent in holding that whatever knowledge might actually result from such instruction is not comprehension of the divine essence. To know something of God is not to comprehend God; nevertheless it is knowledge. This is perhaps most clearly stated in Homily 11 where Gregory comments on Song 5: 2: 'Open to me, my sister, my consort, my dove, my perfect one, for my head is filled with dew, and my locks with drops of the night.'[69] In the course of commenting on this lemma Gregory has the Bridegroom instruct the bride. Having identified as the

---

[67] *In Cant.* iii, GNO vi. 98. 1–2.

[68] Ibid., 97. 18–98. 5: ἡ τοῦ νυμφίου ἄμπελος ἐν τῷ Γαδί, τῷ πίονι τούτῳ τόπῳ ἐρριζωμένη (τουτέστιν ἐν βαθείᾳ τῇ διανοίᾳ τῇ διὰ τῶν θείων διδαγμάτων καταρδομένῃ)....

[69] *In Cant.* xi, GNO vi. 322. 6–8.

mind the door which the bride shall open,[70] Gregory has the Bride-groom tell the bride that she must draw near to the truth and become its consort lest she be cut off from it. Her reward for thus taking him into her and letting him dwell within her is 'dew from my head, of which I am full, and the drops of the night running off my locks'. The dew of presence moistens the mind with knowledge, however obscure.

We notice once again the language of flow in an epistemological context (the door being opened to the Bridegroom is *dianoia*), but this time the flow is rather more subdued than a gushing fountain of divine teaching. The flow is merely that of 'drops of the night', for, as Gregory says, 'it is not possible for someone entering the interior of the sanctuary of the invisible to encounter inundating rainstorms of knowledge, but one must be content if truth bedew one's knowledge with delicate and faint insights'.[71] That the bride is not flooded with knowledge certainly does not imply in this case that she is in any way distant from the Bridegroom. For indeed this passage bespeaks an encounter of great intimacy: the Bridegroom has entered the doorway of her mind; she has received him and there he dwells. But what is important to observe is the epistemological dimension which Gregory lends this description of divine indwelling. The bride receives a certain knowledge, not an over-flowing fountain of knowledge which would parallel the gushing foun-tain of divine presence or divine teaching, but simply moisture from this fountain; a few drops of insight condense, not as a result of the grasp of comprehension of the divine essence, but by being in its presence and communing with it.

This is dew from the Beloved's head. While it is not full comprehen-sion of the divine essence, it is nonetheless knowledge, however obscure. A certain similarity, it seems, could be drawn between this passage and Gregory's treatment in Homily 3 of the difference between gold and the likeness of gold. While the divine nature transcends any concept, the concept resembles the divine nature that is sought.[72] Like-wise, in this image of the drops of the night that bedew one's knowledge:

---

[70] *In Cant.* xi, GNO vi, 324. 13–15: ἅπτεται τῆς θύρας ὁ λόγος. θύραν δὲ νοοῦμεν τὴν στοχαστικὴν τῶν ἀρρήτων διάνοιαν,…

[71] Ibid., 325. 21–326. 3: οὐ γάρ ἐστι δυνατὸν τὸν ἐντὸς τῶν ἀδύτον τε καὶ ἀθεωρήτων γενόμενον ὄμβρῳ τινὶ τῆς γνώσεως ἐντυχεῖν ἢ χειμάρρῳ, ἀλλ' ἀγαπητὸν εἰ λεπταῖς τισι καὶ ἀμυδραῖς διανοίαις ἐπιψεκάζοι τὴν γνῶσιν αὐτῶν ἡ ἀλήθεια….

[72] *In Cant.* iii, GNO vi. 86. 9–15.

the knowledge is partial, dilute, if you will, but nevertheless accurate, grounded in an experience of divine indwelling, and bespeaks presence.

That this knowledge is not only valid but efficacious is seen in Homily 13, where Gregory takes up again the same image from Song 5: 2: 'My locks are filled with drops of the night.'[73] Whereas in Homily 11 Gregory seemed rather restrained in his description of knowledge of God (the mind indwelled by the Bridegroom was not overwhelmed with knowledge, but received mere drops of knowledge), he is less restrained in Homily 13 when he depicts the epistemological character of these drops of the night. For in Homily 13 the moisture from the locks of the Beloved are not mere drops which bedew the mind, but are described as 'rain of teaching watering the living lands so that the fields of God bear fruit'.[74]

The Flow of Thought

We have considered several texts in which Gregory employs the imagery of flowing water to describe divine presence, but it is worth pointing out that the working of the mind is also depicted in the language of flow. We have already indicated in Chapter 2 a clear example of this in *De virginitate*,[75] which suggests, along with any number of other texts, that the mind is characterized by a certain flow; like divine presence, the mind flows like a fountain. Even thoughts themselves are described in this water imagery. We already saw in Homily 11 what is perhaps the clearest example of this. In the apophatic setting of the sanctuary, truth bedews knowledge with thoughts, albeit indistinct.[76] Moreover, these drops do not simply rest in the sanctuary. They continue to flow outwards; they stream forth through the holy ones and the bearers of God.[77]

In Homily 9 the discursive mind is described as a fountain that teems and overflows, and thoughts which it produces assist in acquiring the good. While the energy of these thoughts can be squandered, the 'moisture of thoughts' provides nourishment for the roots of our lives.[78] Hence, Gregory recalls the counsel of Proverbs not to let 'the source of mind (τὴν πηγήν τῆς διανοίας)' be squandered.[79]

---

[73] *In Cant.* XIII, GNO VI. 392. 3–4.   [74] Ibid., 392. 5–7.
[75] e.g. *De virg.*, SC, VI. 2. 1–19.   [76] *In Cant.* XI, GNO VI. 325. 21–326. 3.
[77] Ibid., 326. 3–5:... διὰ τῶν ἁγίων τε καὶ θεοφορουμένων τῆς λογικῆς σταγόνος ἀπορρεούσης.
[78] See *In Cant.* IX, GNO VI. 275. 19–276. 7.   [79] Ibid., 277. 5–6.

A final example of thoughts expressed in the imagery of water is seen at the opening of Homily 12 where Gregory develops an extended metaphor of a sea-voyage. With respect to the present argument it is worth pointing out that what Gregory says about the generation of thoughts comes into play as he develops this extended metaphor. He describes thoughts as waves upon the sea. These waves of thought are put into motion by the breath of the Holy Spirit.[80] Hence, by focusing on the imagery of water we see the coincidence of two concerns: divine presence and epistemology. The positive treatment of thoughts stands in contrast to their apophatic treatment which would require their being forsaken before approaching the divine. That this apophatic treatment of thoughts plays an important role in Gregory's mystical theory has been well noted in previous chapters of the present study, as well as by any number of scholars. There is nevertheless the paradoxical counterpart to the apophatic dimension; for thoughts or concepts also emerge from some divine contact or initiative. While all thoughts are at some point abandoned in order to enter the divine sanctuary or to grasp the Beloved in union by faith alone, the result of this contact is that truth bedews the mind with obscure insights; the Holy Spirit breathes on the mind and causes waves of thought to move upwards. This connection between divine presence and the moisture of thought bears closely on that aspect of Gregory's thought which I am concerned to designate by the term 'logophasis'. For all his concern for letting go of thoughts and concepts in poetic gestures of *aphairesis* in order to enable union by the grasp of faith, concepts are also the paradoxical result of such letting go and union. For in the grasp of faith the soul places her mouth on the fountain of the Bridegroom, and her mind is bedewed with knowledge, however indistinct and tentative. Her mouth is filled with words of eternal life.

But in order to see the epistemological framework within which Gregory conceives and expresses this flow that is grounded in the flow of divine presence and precipitated by contact or union with God (mediated by faith), let us consider another cluster of metaphors: the breast, both the Lord's and the bride's.

'Your Breasts are Better than Wine'

Another symbol which shows the epistemological flow with which we are concerned in this chapter is that of the breast, either the Lord's or the

---

[80] *In Cant.* XII, GNO VI. 342. 1–8.

bride's. It is an image which Gregory takes up at several points in the *In Canticum* and first occurs in Homily 1 as he interprets the second half of Song 1: 2.

In Gregory's exegesis of Song 1: 2a, 'Let him kiss me with the kisses of his mouth', we saw him liken the bride's kissing the Bridegroom, approaching him mouth to mouth, to the placing of her mouth on a fountain. This fountain in turn fills her mouth with 'words of eternal life'.[81] Although the imagery changes, this dynamic of flow and being filled continues as Gregory turns to Song 1: 2b: 'for your breasts are better than wine'. These breasts, says Gregory, are filled with 'divine milk', supplied from the treasure of the heart.[82] The breasts are divine powers by which God nourishes us,[83] and the milk flowing into these breasts is the milk of divine instruction.[84] While milk is normally associated with food for infants, this is divine milk, and therefore higher than the wine of human learning: 'Hence, better are the divine breasts than human wine.'[85]

For our purposes what is worthy of note is the language of flow and the epistemological nuance, subtle as it is, that Gregory accords this flow: out of the treasure of the divine heart, milk flows into the breasts of the divine energies, and this milk is teaching which presumably can be understood.

Guided by the image of the Bridegroom's breast, Gregory turns to the Beloved Disciple reclining on the Lord's breast. Again we see this motif of epistemological flow. Just as the bride drew close to the Bridegroom, placing her mouth on the fountain of his mouth, and was filled with words of eternal life, something similar happens to John when he reclines on the Lord's breasts, which Gregory identifies as the fountain of life.[86] As John places his heart 'like a sponge' on the heart of the Lord, a flow between these two hearts ensues. The flow is in one direction: from the Lord's heart to John's, and he is filled, as the bride was filled, with an 'ineffable communication of the mysteries lying hidden in the heart of the Lord'.[87] What is the effect of heart adhering to heart and

[81] See *In Cant.* I, GNO VI. 32. 11–15.   [82] Ibid., 33. 12–14.

[83] Ibid., 33. 18–21: μαζοὺς δὲ τὰς ἀγαθὰς τῆς θείας δυνάμεως ὑπὲρ ἡμῶν ἐνεργείας εἰκότως ἄν τις ὑπονοήσειε, δι᾽ ὧν τιθηνεῖται τὴν ἑκάστου ζωὴν ὁ θεὸς κατάλληλον ἑκάστῳ τῶν δεχομένων τὴν τροφὴν χαριζόμενος.

[84] Ibid., 35. 9.   [85] Ibid., 35. 13–14.

[86] Ibid., 41. 6–7: ἠγάπησε τοὺς μαζοὺς τοῦ λόγου ὁ ἐπὶ τὸ στῆθος τοῦ κυρίου ἀναπεσὼν Ἰωάννης....

[87] Ibid., 41. 7–10:... καὶ οἷόν τινα σπογγιὰν τὴν ἑαυτοῦ καρδίαν παραθεὶς τῇ πηγῇ τῆς ζωῆς καὶ πλήρης ἔκ τινος ἀρρήτου διαδόσεως τῶν ἐγκειμένων τῇ τοῦ κυρίου καρδίᾳ μυστηρίων γενόμενος....

receiving this flow of ineffable communication? John continues to mediate this flow as he turns round to offer us this 'teat filled by the Word'[88] and offers us the things he himself received from the fountain of this breast, as he 'proclaims loudly the eternal Word'.[89] Gregory concludes with an exhortation: 'Let us love, therefore, the flow of your teaching.'[90]

Cortesi has noted Gregory's use of a technical term for Christian proclamation,[91] but more provocatively indicates how in this beautiful passage the Beloved Disciple exemplifies, like the bride, a type of 'communication of the mysteries of the Word' that has the characteristics of a 'spiritual union with the fountain of life'.[92] In this context of union John performs the role which we have seen faith perform in contexts of divine union as it passed on to the mind something of what it had grasped of the Ungraspable. The Word continues its dynamic tendency to express itself, and in the case of John we see this tendency in the metaphor of a flowing exchange between John's heart and the heart of the Lord. This flow is described as teaching, albeit ineffable and mysterious. Moreover, this experience of contact with the Word has an effect on John. He becomes a vehicle of the Word and continues the dynamic tendency of the Word to express itself as he offers us this breast filled with good things.

In Homily 1 the breast is that of the Lord or Bridegroom identified in Song 1, 2, and 4. In Homily 7 Gregory returns to the image of the breast, but now that of the bride in Song 4: 5: 'Your breasts are as the two twin fawns of the roe.' Gregory says that the one who has an eye which can discern between what brings salvation and what causes destruction becomes a breast like the great Paul, nourishing with milk the Church's

---

[88] Ibid., 41. 10–11: καὶ ἡμῖν ἐπέχει τὴν πληρωθεῖσαν ὑπὸ τοῦ λόγου θηλ-ὴν....

[89] Ibid., 41. 11–13: καὶ πλήρεις ποιεῖ τῶν ἐντεθέντων αὐτῷ παρὰ τῆς πηγῆς ἀγαθῶν κηρύσσων ἐν μεγαλοφωνίᾳ τὸν ἀεὶ ὄντα λόγον.

[90] Ibid., 41, 18–42, 1: διὰ τοῦτω δὲ ἀγαπῶμεν τὴν τῶν σῶν διδαγμάτων ἐπιρροήν,....

[91] Cortesi, Le 'Omelie sul Cantico dei Cantici', 207–8; Cortesi cites, for example, Matt. 3: 1; 4: 17; Mark 1: 4; Luke 3: 3; 1 Cor. 1: 23; Gal. 2: 2 among others.

[92] Ibid., 297: 'La communicazione dei misteri del Logos è infatti un' operazione divina che si compie incontrando un desiderio della Sposa ed ha le caratteristiche di un' unione immateriale con la fonte della vita. Tipo di tale communicazione è l'apostolo Giovanni che si accostò al petto del Signore, al suo cuore, tesoro delle cose buone dal quale proviene alle mammelle il dono del latte divino.'

newly born.[93] Though this breast in Homily 7 is that of the bride, it has the distinguishing characteristic of the Bridegroom's breast which we saw in Homily 1: it is a source of nourishment. Moreover, Gregory gives it the same characteristics as the Lord's breast on which in Homily 1 John had lain, where John took this breast and offered to others 'the teat filled by the Word'.[94] In Homily 7 the breast has the same role: 'it does not keep grace enclosed within itself, but offers the teat of the Word to those who need it'.[95]

Once again we see this tendency of the one who adheres by faith to the Lord, whether the bride or John, or, as we shall see later, Paul, to become a vehicle of the Word's divine flow. The breasts, like 'the twin fawns of the roe' are the 'breasts better than wine'. For though the bride's, she nourishes with this breast those in need—with the 'teat of the Word' itself. The epistemological character of this nourishment comes to the fore once again in Homily 9. Not unlike the description of the Bridegroom's breasts as flowing with divine teachings,[96] the breasts of the bride in Homily 9 are likewise 'fountains of teaching'.[97]

Whereas in Homily 1 the milk of divine instruction was exalted over the wine of human learning, Gregory parts with this symbolism in Homily 9 and follows instead Paul's understanding of milk as food for infants (1 Cor. 3: 1–6).[98] In Homily 9 the bride's breasts flow not with milk but with wine suitable for the more perfect. How is it that her breasts come to flow with fountains of teachings, normally a divine characteristic? Gregory tells us that it is because she has become 'sister of the Lord' that her breasts have become fountains of doctrine.[99] 'The one who named her his sister and bride says her breasts change to what is better and more perfect, no longer swelling with milk, the food of infants, but gushing forth unmixed wine for the sheer delight of the more perfect.'[100] Hence, this wine gushing forth from the breasts of the bride are fountains of doctrine. But what is important to realize is the

---

[93] *In Cant.* vii, GNO vi. 241. 13–242. 2.   [94] *In Cant.* i, GNO vi. 41. 10–11.

[95] *In Cant.* vii, GNO vi. 242. 10–11:... οὐκ ἐν ἑαυτῷ κατακλείει τὴν χάριν, ἀλλ' ἐπέχει τοῖς δεομένοις τοῦ λόγου τὴν θηλήν,... The Bridegroom's breasts are also described as flowing with grace instead of milk at *In Cant.* ii, GNO vi. 46. 4.

[96] *In Cant.* i, GNO vi. 41. 18–42. 1.   [97] *In Cant.* ix, GNO vi. 263. 13.

[98] As he seems to do at *In Cant.* ii, GNO vi. 46. 4.

[99] *In Cant.* ix, GNO vi. 263. 14–15.

[100] Ibid., 263. 17–264. 2: ὁ τοίνυν ἀδελφὴν ἑαυτοῦ καὶ νύμφην αὐτὴν κατονομάσας τὴν αἰτίαν λέγει τῆς πρὸς τὸ κρεῖττόν τε καὶ τελειότερον τῶν μαζῶν αὐτῆς ἀλλοιώσεως, οἳ οὐκέτι γάλα βρύουσι τὴν τῶν νηπίων τροφήν, ἀλλὰ τὸν ἀκήρατον οἶνον ἐπὶ εὐφροσύνῃ τῶν τελειοτέρων πηγάζουσιν,...

fact that her breasts flow with the wine of doctrines rather than with milk for infants, as a result of union with the Bridegroom, which the metaphors 'sister' and 'bride' imply. Gregory says that the bride's breasts could not become fountains of good doctrine unless she first has made herself sister of the Lord through good works, is renewed in virginity through birth from above, and becomes espoused and bride of her betrothed. [101] He then goes on to state that these terms 'sister' and 'bride' join the soul of the bride to the Bridegroom.[102] As a result of this contact with the Bridegroom, the Word indwells her, and she takes on characteristics of the Word. Like Paul, who was a house containing what cannot be contained,[103] her breasts contain the Word and they flow with the wine of good teaching. While there is no question of comprehending the divine οὐσία in this union, there is nevertheless an epistemological dimension of this flow; teaching fills her breasts, which have been fed by the *hegemonikon*, the directing faculty, of her heart that is one with the Bridegroom.[104] Like the Beloved Disciple on the breast of the Lord, the sponge of his heart resting on the Lord's, she likewise performs the role which we see faith performing at the apex of apophatic ascents: union and mediation to the mind something of what has been grasped of the Ungraspable.

A Schema of the Flow of Knowledge

Having moved through an abundance of images, a synthetic statement of this epistemological flow suggests itself.

Gregory has mentioned in a number of Homilies the epistemological significance of the heart, which grounds and guides the flow of teaching (either as milk or as wine, depending on the Homily) and is identified as the *hegemonikon*.[105] The clearest statement of this is seen in Homily 3,

---

[101] Ibid., 263. 12–17.

[102] Ibid., 279. 9–12: οἷον ἀδελφὴ καὶ νύμφη τοῦ λόγου κατονομάζεται, ἀλλὰ συνάπτει τῶν ὀνομάτων τούτων ἑκάτερον τὴν ψυχὴν τῷ νυμφίῳ τῆς μὲν κατὰ τὴν νύμφην σημασίας σύσσωμον αὐτήν,...

[103] *In Cant.* III, GNO VI. 88. 6.

[104] The heart is a symbol of this directing faculty; see *In Cant.* VII, GNO VI. 242. 8–9 and *In Cant.* III. 94. 19. See also, *In Cant.* I, GNO VI. 33. 12–13.

[105] In identifying the heart with the directing part of the soul, Gregory would appear to be following Origen in this Christian development of a Stoic term (Liddell and Scott, s.v. ἡγεμονικός). C. Desalvo concurs with the Stoic provenance and suggests that Gregory's immediate source regarding the location of the ἡγεμονικόν in the heart is Galen, *De placitis Hippocratis et Platonis*; see Desalvo, *L' "oltre" nel presente*, 53–7, esp. n. 38.

where Gregory speaks of the relationship between the heart and the breast and designates both its physiological and epistemological role. Adopting an Aristotelian view of the calorific function of the heart, Gregory says that the heart is a source of heat which is distributed throughout the body by means of the arteries.[106] The heart's role, therefore, is to receive and to distribute warmth.

Parallel to this physiological function is an epistemological function; for the heart is also the *hegemonikon*, the directing rational faculty, or as Lampe has suggested, intellect. This governing faculty of intellect, which is the heart, operates in the same way as the physiological function of the heart: it receives and distributes. In Homily 3 we read that the *hegemonikon* receives not heat but the 'sweet fragrance of the Lord'. Hence, Gregory likens the *hegemonikon* to a sweet-smelling sachet that distributes its fragrance, pervading all her actions: 'Therefore, the bride received the sweet fragrance of the Lord in the intellect and made her own heart a sachet of such incense. She makes all the pursuits of her life come alive like the parts of the body with the breath pervading her heart.'[107] Just as the heart as physical organ receives and distributes warmth throughout the body, so the heart as *hegemonikon* receives and distributes the fragrant presence of Christ.

We see this intellectual faculty once again identified with the heart in Homily 7, and the same dynamic flow from within to without is revealed. In Homily 7 the *hegemonikon* is not distributing the fragrance of the Lord to the bride's actions as in Homily 3, but is incorporated into Gregory's interpretation of 'Your breasts are like two twin fawns of the roe that feed amongst the lilies' (Song 4: 5). But the dynamic is the same. The

---

[106] *In Cant.* III, GNO VI. 94. 15–17. Liddell and Scott (s.v. ἀρτηρία) suggests that if a distinction was made between arteries and veins, 'no use was made of such distinction'. See Aristotle, *De vita et mort.* 469^{b}10 ff.; *De part. anim.* 665^{b}18; *De spir.* 5. 11. See also Galen's discription of the role of the heart in respiration and heat in *De usu partium* VI. 7. 436; VI. 17. 499; *et passim*.

[107] Ibid., 94. 19–21: ἡ τοίνυν ἐν τῷ ἡγεμονικῷ παραδεξαμένη τοῦ κυρίου τὴν εὐωδίαν καὶ τὴν καρδίαν ἑαυτῆς ἔνδεσμον τοῦ τοιούτου ποιήσασα θυμιάματος πάντα τὰ καθ' ἕκαστον τοῦ βίου ἐπιτηδεύματα οἷόν τινος σώματος μέλη ζέειν παρασκευάζει τῷ ἐκ τῆς καρδίας διήκοντι πνεύματι....
The fact that her actions as well as what she might know or say are also controlled by the heart (ἡγεμονικόν) is an example of how Gregory keeps virtue and knowledge on an even par. See *In Cant.* IX, GNO VI. 277. 7–9, where the virtues are described as God's plants, with which the intellectual faculty of the soul is engaged (ἀρετάς δὲ εἶναι τὴν φυτείαν τοῦ θεοῦ μεμαθήκαμεν, περὶ ἃς ἡ διανοητικὴ τῆς ψυχῆς ἡμῶν δύναμις ἀσχολουμένη). On virtue and knowledge see Meredith, 'Homily 1', esp. 146–7; see also Meredith, *The Cappadocians*, 59 f.

breast 'does not keep grace enclosed in itself but gives the teat of the Word to those who need it'.[108]

The idea is not as complete as that in Homily 3, but Gregory obviously envisages the same epistemological flow. In Homily 3 the *hegemonikon* received and distributed the 'sweet fragrance of the Lord'; in Homily 7 we read that the breast distributed the 'teat of the Word'. One can presume that the breast received the milk of the Word in the same way as the bride's actions received the Lord's fragrances in Homily 3: through the *hegemonikon*. Receiving the Word from the heart, the breast turns it into milk and gives it in turn to those in need.[109] With this interior to exterior flow of epistemology seen in Homily 3 and Homily 9 one can appreciate more easily something of the meaning that lies beneath the first occasion in the *In Canticum* in which Gregory mentions the heart in this sense.

In the course of commenting in Homily 1 on the lines, 'Let him kiss me with the kisses of his mouth, for your breasts are better than wine' (Song 1: 2), Gregory paraphrases the Lord's reproach of Simon, 'You gave me no kiss.' Simon would have been cleansed had he received a purifying kiss. Such a soul 'looks at the treasure house of good things'.[110] Gregory then identifies this treasure house as 'the heart, from which there comes to the breasts an abundance of divine milk by which the soul is nourished'.[111] Reading this earlier text with the knowledge of what we come to know from Homilies 3 and 7 on the identity of heart and *hegemonikon*, we can see that indeed it is the *hegimonikon* that received a kiss. The effect of this kiss is passed on from the heart to the breasts as divine milk.

While it is difficult to read this text without the help of Homilies 3 and 7, the text does mention the role of the kiss, which the other texts do not mention, and this symbol of the kiss provides an important clue to the encounter between the divine presence (the Word or Bridegroom) and

---

[108] *In Cant.* vii, GNO vi. 242. 10–11.

[109] If the process of the Word becoming the milk of teaching requires any special faculty we can presume that Gregory has this in mind at *In Cant.* vii, GNO vi. 224. 3–7, when he speaks of a faculty (δύναμις) of the soul which refines teachings (διδάγματα) in such a way that makes them capable of being received. One can presume that this is the work of the ἡγεμονικόν, or under its dominion. See also *In Cant.* vii, GNO vi. 226. 18–227. 6, where this function is set in ecclesiological relief through the metaphor of teeth.

[110] See *In Cant.* i, GNO vi. 33. 5–11. Gregory seems to conflate Simon the Pharisee (Luke 7: 45) and Simon the Leper (Matt. 26: 6).

[111] Ibid., 33. 12–13.

the heart (*hegemonikon*). The divine kiss is generally associated with purification, and indeed this appears to be what it accomplishes in the *In Canticum*;[112] but it also has implications for union, which Gregory brings out in Homily 1 by associating the kiss with the sense of touch.

'A kiss', says Gregory, 'is accomplished through the sense of touch',[113] and there is likewise a corresponding spiritual sense of touch which has the specific purpose of 'grasping the Word'.[114] Hence a kiss unites with the Word in a partial, yet nevertheless real, contact between the Word and the bride.[115] This grasping of the Word in a kiss is rather similar, then, to the grasp of faith, both being faculties that unite and mediate.

In drawing this section to a conclusion, it is well to recall what we observed in Chapter 2 regarding the capacity of the mind (including this aspect of mind called *hegemonikon*) to penetrate into the ineffable divine presence, the Holy of Holies beyond images, thoughts, and concepts.[116] While the mind could penetrate there, it was not capable of comprehension, but there yet remained the possibility of union by the grasp of faith, or, stated in a different way, union through this kiss which grasps (of) the Word. The union achieved by this grasping, whether by faith or by a kiss, initiates the epistemological flow which this chapter has been concerned to reveal. This union has an effect upon the mind, or more specifically on the *hegemonikon*. It is 'bedewed with faint insights by the drops on the locks of the Beloved'; 'receives a transmission of mysteries hidden in the heart of the Lord'; 'receives the sweet fragrance of the Lord'. What is received is passed on to the breasts as 'milk of divine instruction', 'the wine of divine teaching'. As the Word cannot be contained but must express itself, so John cannot contain the Word which he has absorbed in the sponge of his heart, and so he offers the teat of the Word, his breast deified, for the nourishment of others. Neither the thoughts of John nor those of the bride have grasped the Word in comprehension, but in grasping the Word through faith, through a kiss, through placing one's head on the breast of the Lord, one's thoughts, words, and deeds

[112] *In Cant.* I, GNO VI. 33. 4–5: καθάρσιον γάρ ἐστι ῥύπου παντός τοῦτο τὸ φίλημα. See also *In Cant.* I, GNO VI. 40. 8–9 and *In Cant.* XI, GNO VI. 323. 18–324. 2.

[113] *In Cant.* I, GNO VI. 34. 9–10.

[114] Ibid., 34. 12: . . . ἡ ἁπτομένη τοῦ λόγου. . . .

[115] See Cortesi, *Le 'Omelie sul Cantico dei Cantici'*, 177–9; Cortesi subordinates the union mediated by the spiritual sense of touch (a kiss) to that mediated by the spiritual sense of smell.

[116] e.g. *In Cant.* I, GNO VI. 40. 6–7.

are moistened by this union with the Fountain of teaching, the Fountain of presence. Hence the bride's exhortations excite her maidens, and Paul, containing what cannot be contained, manifests 'Christ speaking himself'.[117]

Conclusion

By now it should be obvious why this chapter has focused on the imagery of flow: fountains, rivers, streams, waves, drops of dew and rain, breasts flowing with milk and wine are all part of an interconnected constellation of images which constitutes the metaphorical framework within which Gregory conceives and expresses some of his views on the transforming presence of God in the soul and something of the epistemological character of the effects of this union which are mediated to the mind: rain of teaching, fountain of teaching, fountain of thought, wave of thought, moisture of thought, milk of divine instruction, wine of divine teaching. These were some of the metaphors we saw used and grounded in an experience of divine presence and expressed in similarly flowing imagery as Fountain of presence, Fountain of beauty, Fountain of goodness, Fountain of mystery, filling the mouth of the bride with words of eternal life. Her mouth being filled, her breasts overflow.

While the role of faith was lexically less dominant in this constellation of metaphors, it did appear significantly in those texts concerning the sacramental birth of our access to divine life: baptism. Speaking of the summit of faith (which ironically is the epistemological level at which faith performs its role of union), Gregory says that from it pour forth fountains, and the streams from these fountains are the beginning of our transformation towards divinity.[118] Through the uniting function faith (which Chapter 3 explored), the Divine Fountain becomes present in the soul where it flows into the actions and words of the believer, and out of the belly of this believer, Gregory says, will stream forth rivers of living water.[119] Faith, then, mediates this union with the Fountain, and in so doing mediates the flow of 'words of eternal life' in the words and deeds of the believer. This function of faith is embodied by John and the bride.

In the preceding chapters, our focus was on the role of faith as the faculty of union between the soul and God at the summit of an

---

[117] *In Cant.* III, GNO VI. 88. 5–6.   [118] *In Cant.* VIII, GNO VI. 250. 13–15.
[119] *In Cant.* XIV, GNO VI. 414. 11–12.

apophatic ascent; in this reserved and exalted sense, and in this sense only, faith in Gregory of Nyssa takes on the role of a technical term. In the present chapter our emphasis has been slightly different. We see this exalted, technical sense of faith as it mediates and initiates this epistemological flow, the moisture of thought.

The grasp of faith, therefore, mediates in two directions. Along a fairly rigorously maintained apophatic trajectory, faith mediates union with God beyond all concepts (in the *In Canticum* it is most often the Word that is the object of union). However, this union with the Word by faith alone initiates another trajectory, the tendency of the Word to fill the mouth of John or the bride with discourse.

With faith's twofold mediation as a foundation the following chapter will explore the logophatic dimension of this encounter with the Word, that is, we will examine the Word's tendency to express itself in the discourse and deeds of those who attain apophatic union with the Word. While indeed the apophatic element is central to Gregory's thought, as many scholars have pointed out, this logophatic dimension will be seen to be no less central; for it is the other side of the coin of union 'by faith alone'. But without a sufficient appreciation of the mediating role of faith and epistemological flow that characterizes many of the encounters with the Word, this complementary dimension of *logophasis* will likely be overlooked.[120]

---

[120] For example, a recent and in many ways satisfactory treatment of Gregory's apophaticism is D. Carabine's chapter on Gregory in her *The Unknown God*. But although she is interested in faculties of union, she does not appreciate the role of πίστις in Gregory in this specific regard. Someone who does appreciate the role of πίστις is B. Pottier, in *Dieu et le Christ selon Grégoire de Nysse*, 215 *et passim*, but he only sees the apophatic side. Perhaps this is due to the fact that he emphasizes the 'rupture' between πίστις and γνῶσις, whereas this study, while clearly acknowledging a certain discontinuity between the two, emphasizes the continuity as well as the discontinuity. As we have said before: πίστις hands on to διάνοια (now we might say more specifically the ἡγεμονικόν) something of what it has grasped of the Ungraspable. M. Canévet, *Grégoire de Nysse et l'herméneutique biblique*, 63, would seem to agree when she observes that the *'intuition de la foi'* attempts to translate itself into concepts.

6

Christ Speaking Himself:
The Logophatic Discourse of Paul and the Bride

Introduction

In Chapter 2 we illustrated that while the mind can enter the presence of God, the darkness wherein God dwells, it cannot perform an act of understanding on the divine *ousia*. However, the mind does undergo something important. The Word touches the door of the mind and comes to dwell there.[1] The mind is fertile earth in which the Bridegroom takes root, and is watered by divine teaching.[2] Although the mind does not grasp in comprehension what it seeks in darkness (i.e. God), God yet acts upon the mind, or as Gregory says, moistens or bedews the mind with insight. This moisture is distilled by the mind, and this distillation can be reflected upon, understood, and expressed. It is not 'gold but the likeness of gold'. This is how the mind, hanging over the abyss of incomprehensibility in Homily 7 on Ecclesiastes, manages to arrive at its comprehension—its grasp—that the transcendent cannot be grasped beyond the knowledge that the transcendent is other than what can be known.[3] This is discursive knowledge grounded in the non-discursive. Hence, while the mind does not grasp the divine essence, this is not to

---

[1] *In Cant.* xi, GNO vi. 324. 13–15. Gregory goes on to explain (324. 20–325. 2 f.) that the key to the door of the mind is the 'beautiful words' of scripture; through spiritual interpretation of such words as 'sister', 'companion', 'dove', 'perfect one', the doors open up. See Canévet, *Grégoire de Nysse et l'herméneutique biblique*, 60; Dünzl, *Braut und Bräutigam*, 166; see also R. Norris, 'The Soul Takes Flight: Gregory of Nyssa and the Song of Songs', *Anglican Theological Review* 80 (1998), 517–32.

[2] *In Cant.* iii, GNO vi. 97. 18–98. 2.   [3] *In Eccl.*, SC, vii. 8. 104–6.

say that the mind is capable of nothing whatever. It maintains a certain receptive capacity.

That the mind does not grasp the Beloved in comprehension, however, is not to say that the Beloved is not grasped in any manner whatever. In Chapter 3 we demonstrated that the faculty which grasps the Beloved in union, the faculty which bridges the gap between the mind and God, is faith: faith allows the Beloved to enter and dwell within as a result of this union. By means of faith this soul is awash with divine presence, and faith gives to the mind something of what it has grasped of the Beloved, not overflowing torrents, but drops of knowledge, however faint, from the locks of the Beloved. The union is apophatic, but the effect is logophatic; for the Word fills the mouth of the bride 'with words of eternal life'.

Chapter 5 examined the epistemological framework which is grounded in union. God is a fountain of presence, and through baptism the soul becomes a flowing fountain. Faith mediates this transforming flow: from this summit of faith pour forth the fountains of the Jordan and 'the stream from these fountains has become the beginning of our transformation into divinity'.[4] The union achieved by faith initiates this flow of the 'fountains of the River Jordan', 'the fountain of mysteries'. This union has an effect upon the mind, specifically the heart as directing faculty (*hegemonikon*), which in turn distributes it to where it is needed.

Keeping in mind this idea of epistemological flow established in Chapter 5, the present chapter proposes to examine in greater detail what I have come to call *logophasis*: as a fruit of apophatic union with the Word (*logos*), the Word expresses (*phasis*) itself through the deeds and discourse of the one whom the Word indwells.

Paul and Logophasis

The *In Canticum* does not use spousal imagery exclusively of the bride. In Homily 2 Paul is the 'bride of Christ made radiant from darkness'.[5] In Homily 3 Paul is the 'bride who imitates the Bridegroom through his virtues'.[6] Indeed the experiences of Paul in the *In Canticum* merit consideration, for his experiences of indwelling union reveal some important characteristics of *logophasis*. More than once during the course of this study we have had occasion to examine the well-known passage from

---

[4] *In Cant.* VIII, GNO VI. 250. 13–15.   [5] *In Cant.* II, GNO VI. 48. 15–16.
[6] *In Cant.* III, GNO VI. 91. 4–5.

Homily 3 on 'gold and the likeness of gold'. Let us return once again to this Homily and consider the experience of Paul.

In the course of Homily 3 Gregory comments on Song 1: 11–12: 'we shall make for you likenesses of gold with studs of silver while the king is on his couch'. In the midst of commenting on this passage Gregory asks the question, 'why likenesses of gold and not gold?'[7] He sees in this distinction between the likeness of gold and the gold itself something analogous to our understanding of the nature of God: 'every teaching concerning the ineffable nature [sc. of God] . . . is the likeness of gold and not gold itself';[8] for 'the divine nature transcends every grasp of the mind'.[9] Gregory then draws on the example of Paul to prove his contention that every teaching concerning the divine *ousia* falls short of understanding the divine *ousia*, even if it is the most exalted understanding conceivable.

Gregory emphasizes the apophatic context in which Paul finds himself (2 Cor. 12:4). Paul has been initiated into the ineffable (ἀπόρρητα) where paradoxically he heard words that could not be pronounced (ἀλαλήτων ῥημάτων). If this is true of Paul, then any understanding of God remains unutterable (ἀνέκφραστα).[10]

In characteristic fashion Gregory subordinates *kataphasis* to *apophasis*. He says that 'good thoughts' about God, such as thoughts about his splendour, or the stamp of his nature (Heb. 1: 3) are not untrue; but that such kataphatic speech does not capture the divine nature, which is apophatic, inexpressible.[11]

In contrast to the inability of the mind to grasp the divine nature, however, we see faith's ability to do precisely that. Though Gregory does not employ in this Homily the language of grasping as he does, for example, in Homily 6,[12] we see faith in its technical role: in an apophatic context it is mediating divine indwelling. 'The soul . . . must make dwell within itself through faith alone the nature that transcends every intelligence.'[13] To emphasize this indwelling through the mediation of faith,

---

[7] *In Cant.* III, GNO VI. 85. 10–15.   [8] Ibid., 85. 16–19.
[9] Ibid., 86. 13–14: ἡ θεία φύσις πάσης ὑπέρκειται καταληπτικῆς διανοίας.
[10] Ibid., 85. 20–86. 1. On the importance of 2 Cor. 12: 4 in Gregory's works see Canévet, *Grégoire de Nysse et l'herméneutique biblique*, 200–1 and 368.
[11] Ibid., 86. 2–6.
[12] *In Cant.* VI, GNO VI. 183. 9: λαβὴ τῆς πίστεως as opposed to λαβὴ τῶν λογισμῶν at 181. 16.
[13] *In Cant.* III, GNO VI. 87. 5–8: τὴν οὖν διὰ τῶν τοιούτων νοημάτων χειραγωγουμένην ψυχὴν πρὸς τὴν τῶν ἀλήπτων περίνοιαν διὰ μόνης πίστεως εἰσοικίζειν ἐν ἑαυτῇ λέγει δεῖν τὴν πάντα νοῦν ὑπερέχουσαν φύσιν.

Gregory immediately has the Bridegroom's friends address the soul: 'through faith, you will be put under a yoke and become a dwelling place for the one who, by dwelling within you, is going to recline in you. For you will be his throne and will become his abode.'[14] Paul is for Gregory of Nyssa a symbol of faith[15] and Paul embodies this indwelling through faith. He has become a vessel of election and 'a house containing what cannot be contained'.[16] Through faith Paul has become an abode of divine indwelling, containing the uncontainable. However, as we pointed out in Chapter 3, the terms περιληπτικός and its apophatic correlate ἀπερίληπτός also have epistemological resonances of understanding and comprehension.[17] Hence, Paul not only contains the incomprehensible nature, who, through faith, indwells the soul, but Paul, and especially Paul as an embodiment of faith, also comprehends the incomprehensible. This is paradox, not contradiction, and points beyond the realm of discursive reason where, as we have seen on a number of occasions, faith plays its apophatic role of union, grasping with the open palm of *aphairesis*, knowing without comprehending.[18] This is the indwelling union by faith alone.

What are the results of this union? Obviously one important result is divine indwelling. But in light of what we established in the previous chapter, we might expect more to be taking place. In Chapter 5 we saw that any number of texts revealed a tendency on the part of the faculty of union (faith—whether explicitly mentioned or not), to give to the mind, the heart, the *hegemonikon*, something of what it has grasped in union with the Word. This was often expressed in the language of flow: dew, rain of divine teaching, milk of divine instruction, wine of instruction, etc. The heart then distributed this as it was needed, to the virtues or to speech. In the texts we shall now consider the same dynamic is revealed, but the imagery will shift from the flow of water to the effusion of scent. As Paul inhales divine fragrance he is transformed through indwelling union into a vehicle of the Word itself; his deeds and discourse become vehicles of divine presence.

---

[14] Ibid., 87. 14–17: σὺ δὲ ταῦτα δεξαμένη ὑποζύγιόν τε καὶ οἰκητήριον γενήσῃ διὰ πίστεως τοῦ σοι ἐνανακλίνεσθαι μέλλοντος διὰ τῆς ἐν σοὶ κατ-οικήσεως· τοῦ γὰρ αὐτοῦ καὶ θρόνος ἔσῃ καὶ οἶκος γενήσῃ.

[15] *De beat.* vi, GNO vii. ii. 137. 23–4.

[16] *In Cant.* iii, GNO vi. 88. 6. For the imagery of the house as part of Gregory's ascensional symbolism, see Canévet, *Grégoire de Nysse et l'herméneutique biblique*, 309–11.

[17] See Lampe as well as Liddell & Scott, s. v.

[18] On this language of paradox see Canévet, *Grégoire de Nysse et l'herméneutique biblique*, 337–42, esp. 339.

The Good Odour of Christ

In his recent study of the *In Canticum*, Alessandro Cortesi observes that
for Gregory of Nyssa Paul exemplifies 'one who announces and bears
witness to the gospel in the context of community. Paul... exemplifies
the bride, who above all lives the experience of encounter with the
Word, and who, in the transformation generated by this union, transmits
with her very presence to all to whom she is sent the gift of communion
in which she participates.'[19] Cortesi's observation is worthy of note for
the present argument; according to Cortesi Gregory sees Paul's proclamation of the Word grounded, like the bride, in an experience of
union. Moreover, this union reveals a dynamic that extends beyond
Paul and the bride themselves: they transmit to others the communion
with the Word that they themselves enjoy. The transforming dynamic of
the indwelling Word indwells and transforms others through Paul and
the bride. Paul's announcement of the gospel is also a vehicle of indwelling communion with the Word. Through Paul the Word brings itself,
expresses itself. This dynamic characterizes Gregory's treatment of
the effusion of scent and undergirds Paul's participation in *logophasis*:
the Word's self-expression through Paul.

In Homily 1 Gregory uses an olfactory metaphor to speak of a
particular capacity which the soul has to establish communion with
God: 'the scent of the divine perfume is not fragrance in the nostrils,
but relates to a certain intellectual and spiritual power that inhales the
good odour of Christ (2 Cor. 2: 15) by breathing in the Spirit'.[20] In
designating a spiritual sense Gregory voices an already established
tradition.[21] For our purpose it is sufficient to note that Gregory, drawing
inspiration from 2 Cor. 2: 15, envisages real contact obtained through
the spiritual sense of smell, contact which results in indwelling of the
Word present in the divine perfume. This capacity of the sense of smell
to establish union with the Word present in the fragrance is taken up
again in Homily 3 when Gregory, this time speaking of the bride, says:

---

[19] Cortesi, *Le 'Omelie sul Cantico dei Cantici'*, 228–9: 'Paolo rappresenta per Gregorio il
tipo esemplare di colui che annuncia e testimonia il vangelo in un ambito comunitario.
Paolo... è quindi esemplare della Sposa che vive innanzitutto l'esperienza dell' incontro
con il Logos, e nella trasformazione generata da questa unione trasmette con la sua stessa
presenza, a tutti coloro cui è inviata, il dono di communione di cui è fatta partecipe.'

[20] *In Cant.* i, GNO vi. 34. 15–18.

[21] See Canévet, 'Sens Spirituel', *Dictionnaire de Spiritualité*, vol. xiv, s. v. (Paris, 1990),
cols. 598–617; Meloni, *Il profumo dell' immortalità: L'interpretazione patristica di Cantico 1,3*
(Rome, 1975).

'Drawing close to the one whom she desires, before his beauty appears to her eyes, she touches the one whom she seeks through her sense of smell . . . '[22] The capacity of the spiritual sense of smell to establish union with the Word present in the scent of perfume has been well observed by Cortesi: 'the mystery of the union between the soul and the Word, mystery of communication of the life of the Word to the soul, and of transformation in the divine life reveals itself, even if only partially, by means of perfume. Precisely to describe this spiritual union Gregory avails himself of the multiple nuances inferred by the sensible element of perfume given off by ointment.'[23] The soul, then, is transmitted something in this union: the life of the Word and transformation in divine life. When Paul (or the bride) breathes in the 'good odour of Christ', Gregory intends an indwelling union by means of the spiritual sense of smell. But the union does not stop here; Cortesi has also suggested that there is a transmission of this gift of communion to others.[24]

Paul becomes the vehicle of this fragrant presence to others. In Homily 10 Gregory likens the perfume of Christ to rivers streaming from Paul. 'The great Paul is such a river of fragrance streaming from the garden of the Church by the Spirit, and his stream was the good odour of Christ.'[25] The fragrance of Christ inhaled by Paul is not simply about indwelling union. Through inhaling the Word present in the fragrance, Paul himself becomes fragrant, a fragrant transmission of the Word in the Church. Intimate and abiding as the indwelling presence of the Word is, it has at the same time a universal destination through Paul.[26] Paul's evangelical mission grounded in union with the Word is *logophatic*: the Word speaks in Paul.

Nor does Gregory limit this to Paul alone; for the same can be said of 'John, Luke, Matthew, Mark and all the others; all are noble plants of the bride's garden. When they were breathed through by that bright southerly wind at midday, they became fountains of fragrance that gave off the good odour of the Gospels.'[27] Indeed there is a certain identification between the perfume of Christ and the perfume generated in the life of Paul and the evangelists.[28]

---

[22] *In Cant.* III, GNO VI. 88. 11–13 f.
[23] Cortesi, *Le 'Omelie sul Cantico dei Cantici'*, 177. Chapter 5 of Cortesi's study (pp. 171–203) is devoted entirely to this theme of perfume; see also Canévet, *Grégoire de Nysse et l'herméneutique biblique*, 327–8.
[24] Ibid., 228–9.   [25] *In Cant.* X, GNO VI. 302. 13–16.
[26] Cortesi, *Le 'Omelie sul Cantico dei Cantici'*, 197.
[27] *In Cant.* X, GNO VI. 302. 16–303. 2.
[28] Cortesi, *Le 'Omelie sul Cantico dei Cantici'*, 183.

Gregory's way of treating the presence of Christ in the perfume of incense is carried over into his treatment of myrrh. In Homily 14 he comments on Song 5: 13: 'His jaws are like bowls of spice pouring forth perfumes, his lips are lilies that exude abundant myrrh.'[29] The Bridegroom's lips are described as dripping with myrrh. This myrrh has a transforming effect on those who receive it. 'Therefore, the perfect and pure eye, which makes of the jaw a bowl that pours and perfumes out of itself, blossoms with lilies in the form of words that proceed from the mouth of those who have been beautified by the divine radiance.'[30] The organ of speech has been transformed and now gushes forth perfume, lilies of scented words. While the theme of divine indwelling is not as obvious in this text as it is in others, given the way divine perfume works in Gregory, it is fair to infer that the scent of these words is gathered from the Word itself and therefore bears the presence of the Word. However, this scent of presence not only manifests itself in the discourse of those who receive in their mouths the myrrh dripping from the Word (Bridegroom), but also in deeds. 'For the text names those who are pure and who breathe out the sweet smell of virtue, from drops unceasingly the myrrh that fills the mind of those who receive it.'[31] Having identified this transforming process of taking in this divine presence and then giving it out again in transformed discourse and virtue, Gregory identifies Paul as one who has become this bowl of spice, this mouth dripping with myrrh. Paul has taken on the characteristics previously ascribed to the Word and manifests the same transforming effects of the Word.

Paul is a bowl of spice. Gregory says that this '"bowl" signifies the truth manifesting itself in simplicity, with no deceptive hollowness, and that the material it is made of is spice, and its function is to pour forth perfumes'.[32] Paul's conversion amounts to his becoming a vessel of the Lord and a great teacher. Gregory now draws out the implications of this in terms of the indwelling presence of Christ clothed in the language of knowledge and perfume.

After he had become a 'vessel of election' through this fashioning and had become a bowl for pouring out the wine of the Word, he no longer needed a human being to infuse into him a knowledge of the mysteries. . . . Rather he

---

[29] Myrrh and incense have similar functions; both are associated with divine presence and mortification.

[30] *In Cant.* xiv, GNO vi. 404. 15–19.   [31] Ibid., 404. 19–22.

[32] *In Cant.* xiv, GNO vi. 402. 2–5.

himself poured forth the divine drink from within himself and through the sweet fragrance of Christ poured it out, like a maker of perfume who blends for those who listened the various blossoms of the virtues. Thus the word was found to be spice adapted to the need of the one who sought it, in accord with the different characters and peculiarities of its recipients.[33]

The source of what Paul knows comes from the indwelling presence of the fragrant Christ. Just as the indwelling presence of the Word is scented, so the teaching that pours out from within Paul is likewise scented, scented with the presence of the Word. Paul teaches to the nations, and the *scent* of the teaching is the presence of Christ.

The same transforming presence of the fragrant Word is carried on as Gregory turns to the rest of the *lemma*: 'his lips are lilies that exude abundant myrrh' (Song 5: 13b). Once again Gregory introduces Paul and says that Paul is a mouth dripping with myrrh. Paul has taken on the qualities previously ascribed to the Bridegroom (Word). While Gregory has muted explicit reference to divine indwelling, the context of fragrance implies it. Just as the myrrh does not remain contained within the Word but pours into those receptive, so Paul, indwelled by the Word, pours forth myrrh into Thekla. 'Now Paul pours this myrrh from his mouth, myrrh mixed with the pure lily of temperance, into the ears of the holy virgin (her name was Thekla). She received within herself the flowing drops. She put to death the outer self and quenched every carnal thought and craving. After she received the good teaching, her youthful folly was dead, as well as her outward show of beauty and all her corporeal senses. The Word alone lived in her . . . '[34]

In this moving passage Gregory obviously draws on biblical material. The death of the outer self is clearly Pauline inspiration (Rom. 6: 3–11; 7: 22–3), and obviously Gregory is familiar with the second-century romance featuring Thekla.[35] However, Gregory is not simply making reference to widely known inherited material, whether biblical or apocryphal; rather, he presses these not only into the service of his commentary on the *lemma* in question, but also into the service of his own theological concerns regarding the incarnational dynamic of the Word

---

[33] Ibid., 403. 5–13.   [34] *In Cant.* xiv, GNO vi. 405. 1–9.

[35] See the second-century romance, *The Acts of Paul and Thecla*, in *New Testament Apocrypha*, vol. ii, ed. W. Schneemelcher, trans. R. Wilson (London, 1965), 353–64. For a recent study of Thekla in historical context, see S. Davis, *The Cult of Saint Thecla: A tradition of Women's Piety in Late Antiquity* (Oxford, 2001); see also A. Jensen, *Thekla: Die Apostolin. Ein apokrypher Text neu entdeckt* (Gütersloh, 1999); Gregory also mentions Thekla in *Vita Macrinae*, GNO viii. i. 372. 22.

that indwells Paul and indwells others through Paul. Paul's speech is myrrh, and because the myrrh contains the presence of the Word, Paul's words to Thekla have the same effect on her that the Word had on Paul: death to the outer self, dying and rising in Christ, indwelling presence of the Word. Paul speaks to Thekla, but it is the Word who is heard and enters her: and now 'the Word alone lived in her'. Moreover, as we saw above, Paul is not unique among the apostles to participate in this *logophasis*.

Gregory likewise sees Peter's preaching mission in the house of Cornelius along the same fragrant and transforming lines we have been exploring. Still commenting on the *lemma*, 'his lips are lilies that exude abundant myrrh' (Song 5: 13), Gregory recalls Peter's address to pagans about Jesus, during which Peter witnesses the descent of the Holy Spirit upon them and after which he gives instruction that they be baptized in the name of Jesus (Acts 10: 32–48). Interpreting this passage through the lenses of Song 5: 13 and Rom. 6: 3–11, Gregory says: 'In the same way the great Peter poured fourth the shining lilies of the Word when he was at the house of Cornelius, and filled the souls of his listeners with myrrh. As soon as they received the Word they were buried with Christ and were dead to the world.'[36] One could read this passage as simply a reworking of the Acts material, guided by the imagery of myrrh that dominates this section of Homily 14. In this case Gregory would simply be saying that when the people in Cornelius' house heard Peter preach, they found him convincing and were thus brought into the faith. But Gregory is saying more than just this. In light of what we have seen regarding the presence of Christ in the scent of perfume, incense, and myrrh,[37] it is fair to suggest that when Peter's audience receive the Christ-bearing myrrh of his discourse, they receive the Word that subsequently indwells them in the souls of his audience. Peter's discourse, like Paul's, the bride's, and the evangelists', is also about real presence of the Word in his own fragrant speech. Nor does this stop with the apostles' mission. Gregory claims that countless examples of the same dynamic can be seen in the lives of the saints, 'who, blossoming with the lilies of the word, became a mouth for the body of the church, and filled their listeners with the myrrh that mortifies the passions'.[38] The perfumed life and preaching of the apostles and all the holy ones

---

[36] *In Cant.* xiv, GNO vi. 405. 11–15.

[37] To say nothing of Gregory's understanding of what actually takes place in baptism, on which see Cortesi, *Le 'Omelie sul Cantico dei Cantici'*, 113–69.

[38] *In Cant.* xiv, GNO vi. 405. 16–19.

exude the presence of the Word that is preached by fragrant deeds and discourse.

The Perfume of Presence and the Directing Faculty

Because of Gregory of Nyssa's understanding of the presence of Christ in the scent of perfume, incense, myrrh, and the consequent perfumed quality of Paul's speech we can see more clearly what is at issue when in Homily 3 Gregory says that Paul revealed Christ speaking in him: 'When Paul became a "vessel of election" (Acts 9: 15), he no longer lived his own life, but revealed Christ living in him and gave proof of Christ speaking in himself.'[39] The divine nature which cannot be spoken by Paul, can itself speak through Paul. By virtue of Paul's union with the Word by faith alone, the scent of the Word dwelling within Paul, the Word's dynamic tendency to express itself, expresses itself in the actions and words of Paul.

In light of the relationship we saw in Chapter 5 between faith and the mind (or the heart or the *hegemonikon*) it is not surprising to see faith pass on to the mind something of what it has grasped of the ungraspable and then to see this rendered as speech.[40] But the mind also distributes this to the virtues. For, as Gregory says in Homily 9, the intellectual faculty is also occupied with the virtues.[41] Hence, while the intellectual faculty is bedewed with drops of knowledge, drops of the night from the locks of the Beloved (and this moisture of presence in turn distributed to and expressed in Paul's speech in such a way that when Paul speaks, it is 'Christ speaking himself') the bedewing of the intellectual faculty can also be passed on to the virtues; and likewise with the perfume of the Word's presence, for Gregory claims that 'the bride has received the good odour of Christ in the directing part of her soul and has made of her heart a sachet of such incense, and she makes all her actions, like the limbs of the body, seethe with the Spirit which spreads from her heart so that no iniquity cools her love of God in any part of her body.'[42] The ruling part of the soul receives the divine scent and

---

[39] *In Cant.* III, GNO VI. 88. 4–5:...ἐν ἑαυτῷ δεικνύειν ζῶντα ἐκεῖνον καὶ δοκιμὴν διδόναι τοῦ ἐν αὐτῷ λαλοῦντος Χριστοῦ....

[40] On the priority of thought over speech see Pottier, *Dieu et le Christ*, 193–206.

[41] *In Cant.* IX, GNO VI. 277. 7–9: ἀρετὰς δὲ εἶναι τὴν φυτείαν τοῦ θεοῦ μεμαθήκαμεν, περὶ ἃς ἡ διανοητικὴ τῆς ψυχῆς ἡμῶν δύναμις ἀσχολουμένη.

[42] *In Cant.* III, GNO VI. 94. 19–95. 3.

distributes it to all activity.[43] This is how Paul can inhale 'the good odour of Christ' (2 Cor. 2: 15) and find his actions perfumed with virtue, the presence of Christ. 'Thus Paul the bride imitated the Bridegroom by his virtues and inscribed in himself that unapproachable Beauty by means of their fragrance. From the fruits of the Spirit, love, joy and peace, he made his nard and said he was the "good odour of Christ" (2 Cor. 2: 15). Paul breathed in that transcendent, unapproachable grace and gave himself to others as incense to receive according to their ability.'[44] This text illustrates Gregory's understanding of virtue not simply as the performance of a good deed, but as outward manifestation of interior union with Christ who dwells within. Whether in his speech or in his actions, by virtue of union by the grasp of faith, Paul manifests Christ dwelling within (cf. Gal. 2: 19–20).[45] That is why Paul has a transforming effect on those around him. He has become a fragrance bringing either life or death, and those who inhale Paul's scent (Christ) are transformed accordingly: Titus, Silvanus, Timothy, Thekla partake of this perfume and advance in perfection. Paul is their example, but it is because of Christ's presence in Paul's fragrance that it is transforming.[46]

The Bride and the Daughters of Jerusalem

The bride is an example of *logophasis* par excellence. As we examine this in a number of significant places in the *In Canticum* we shall necessarily consider texts which we have already looked at whilst discussing apophatic union and its mediation by faith. It remains, however, to highlight the logophatic dimension of these apophatic texts.

---

[43] As Cortesi has well observed, virtue is not simply a question of the imitation of Christ as an exterior model; such imitation is sustained interiorly by the indwelling presence of Christ. See Cortesi, *Le 'Omelie sul Cantico dei Cantici'*, 184 *et passim*.

[44] *In Cant.* III, GNO VI. 91. 4–11.

[45] The theme is repeated at *In Cant.* VII, GNO VI. 207. 7–11, where Gregory seems to speak interchangeably of God indwelling the soul and Christ indwelling the soul: ὅτι μὲν οὖν ὁ τὸν θεὸν ἐν ἑαυτῷ φέρων φορεῖόν ἐστι τοῦ ἐν αὐτῷ καθιδρυμέ-νου, δῆλον καὶ πρὸ τῶν ἡμετέρων λόγων ἂν εἴη· ὁ γὰρ κατὰ τὸν ἅγιον Παῦλον μηκέτι αὐτὸς ζῶν ἀλλὰ ζῶντα ἔχων ἐν ἑαυτῷ τὸν Χριστὸν καὶ δοκι-μὴν διδοὺς τοῦ ἐν αὐτῷ λαλοῦντος Χριστοῦ....

[46] *In Cant.* III, GNO VI. 91. 17–92. 4. Gregory says the smell of this incense can bring either life or death depending on whether one is a dove or a beetle.

Arise Daughters of Jerusalem

A central text in this study has been Gregory's commentary on Song 3: 4 in Homily 6, where the bride grasps the Beloved by faith. It is a text which shows both apophatic and logophatic elements mediated by faith. Since we have discussed earlier the apophatic elements in this text, it is sufficient simply to summarize them now.

The bride embarks upon an apophatic ascent in search of the Beloved. Embraced by the divine night and seeking him in darkness, she abandons all knowledge gained from sense perception. There, in the divine night on the bed which symbolizes union, she loved the Beloved though he escaped the grasp of her thought.[47] But she wants to know his substance (*ousia*), so she sets out again in higher ascent, through higher realms of knowledge, searching but not finding. She then begins to abandon all she has learnt, realizing that her Beloved is known only in not comprehending. And so, forsaking all manner of comprehension, she found her Beloved by faith. The bride finds the Beloved not by the grasp of thought but by the grasp of faith, and once found by this grasp of faith she will not let him go.[48]

This well-known passage from Homily 6 features union by the faculty of *pistis*: the 'grasp of faith' rather than the 'grasp of thought'[49] crowns an apophatic ascent, an ascent that features a strong aphairetic motif of persistent release or letting go of images, concepts, and knowledge. While the text's major thrust is clearly this ascent to apophatic union by the grasp of faith, it ends in *logophasis*.

Although the logophatic element is more muted here than in other texts, we see it nevertheless just after Gregory draws to a close his commentary on Song 3: 1–4 with a full citation of the *lemma*. Having been embraced by the divine night, and searching in darkness for the Beloved, and letting go of all manner of comprehension only to arrive at that unknowing higher than knowing, where she is united to the Beloved by the grasp of faith, the bride then turns around and begins to speak to her maiden companions: 'after this the bride speaks lovingly to the daughters of Jerusalem'.[50] The apophatic silence of deep interiority, in which union by faith takes place, flows into speech. They are of a piece. It is important to note the exegetical base of this movement from apophatic union to speech: Gregory has moved from commenting on Song 3:4 which features the bride's finding and beholding the Beloved to

---

[47] *In Cant.* vi, GNO vi. 181. 12–16.   [48] Ibid., 183. 7–10.
[49] Cf. ibid., 181. 16 and 183. 9.   [50] Ibid., 184. 10–11.

the next *lemma*, which features the bride directly addressing her companions: 'I have charged you, O daughters of Jerusalem, by the powers and
by the virtues of the field neither to arouse nor awaken love until it
desires' (Song 3: 5). This movement is dictated by the scriptural text
itself. The logophatic element, exegetically grounded in the change of
perspective in the text of scripture itself, is seen in the *effect* which her
words have on the daughters of Jerusalem. The bride's words make the
daughters of Jerusalem 'rise up to an equal measure of love so that also in
them the will of the Bridegroom might be accomplished'.[51] The discourse of the bride provokes the same response in the daughters of
Jerusalem that the Word provoked in the bride: ascending desire 'to
know his substance and in what he consists'.[52] By virtue of her union
with the Beloved, the bride's discourse, like Paul's, manifests the Word
and bears witness to her union by faith.

The bride's union with the Beloved at night in the chamber of her
heart, is tantamount to Homily 3's description of the Bridegroom
dwelling in her heart as a sachet of incense between her breasts. These
are both images of union. But with the image of the sachet between her
breasts we read that the divine presence is somehow received by
the *hegemonikon*, which then distributes this (we suggested that this
reception was mediated by faith, since faith is the faculty of union).[53]
Hence, the bride's actions 'seethe with breath from her heart', that is,
with divine presence. And so with the bride's discourse.

In her apophatic union, faith has passed on to the mind (specifically
the *hegemonikon*) something of what it has grasped of the Beloved, not an
overflowing torrent of knowledge, but mere drops from the locks of the
Beloved. And so her discourse has taken on the quality of the Word by
which it has been moistened: the incarnational dynamism to express and
to excite desire for union. The bride herself has sought the Word and by
virtue of having grasped it by faith she has become an icon of this.

We see, then, the paradoxical double-face of union. The apophatic
face features the journey of desire elicited by the Word acting upon the
bride, a journey to union with the Word by the grasp of faith. Its defining
feature is the shedding of language, concept, and image in bold gestures
of *aphairesis*, and the resulting union renders the bride a vehicle of the
Word. *Logophasis*, by contrast, features the taking on of concept and
language in an ever deeper participation in the incarnational dynamic of

[51] *In Cant.* VI, GNO VI. 184. 14–15.   [52] See ibid., 181. 17–19.
[53] *In Cant.* III, GNO VI. 94. 19–95. 3.

the Word by virtue of her union with the Word. Its fundamental dynamism is incarnation and manifestation. Within the context of the incarnational dynamism is situated, parallel and harmonious, the characteristic of faith, noted by Canévet, to translate into concepts, and hence discourse, something of what it has grasped of the Infinite.[54] Faith mediates this *coincidentia oppositorum* of *apophasis* and *logophasis*, of silence and speech, of the abandonment of knowledge and the blossoming of virtue and discourse.

Honeycomb Full of Instruction

Taking the reference to the virgin soul in Homily 1 to be compatible with what can be said generally of the bride, we see another representative example of *logophasis*. In the course of interpreting Song 1: 2, 'Let him kiss me with the kisses of his mouth,' Gregory has the bride approach the Bridegroom, whose mouth is a fountain of words of eternal life.

> The virgin soul desires to approach the fountain of spiritual life. The fountain is the mouth of the Bridegroom, from which pour forth words of eternal life, filling the mouth drawn to it, just as the Prophet did when he drew in spirit through his mouth. Because it is necessary for someone drawing water from the fountain to attach mouth to mouth, ... so the thirsting soul desires to bring her own mouth to his mouth that pours out life and says, 'Let him kiss me with the kisses of his mouth.'[55]

The kissing of this fountain who is the Bridegroom is a metaphor of union. The result of this union is that the bride's mouth is filled with words of eternal life flowing from the fountain of the Word.[56]

Because the bride (the soul) communes with the fountain of the Word she herself becomes a fountain of words. In Homily 9, for example, her breasts are fountains of good teachings,[57] and the Bridegroom turns round to look at the bride and remarks: 'your heart has become a honeycomb full of every kind of instruction'.[58] The bride's heart is full of instruction because she adheres by faith to the fountain of teaching, who has moistened her heart with this instruction. Gregory then blends the imagery of the heart as fountain of good teaching with the heart as honeycomb by saying that this heart-become-honeycomb drips with

---

[54] Canévet, *Grégoire de Nysse et l'herméneutique biblique*, 63.

[55] *In Cant.* I, GNO VI. 32. 9–33. 2.

[56] On the kiss as a symbol of union in Gregory see Cortesi, *Le 'Omelie sul Cantico dei Cantici'*, 177–9; see also Canévet, *Grégoire de Nysse et l'herméneutique biblique*, 342–7, esp. 344.

[57] *In Cant.* IX, GNO VI. 263. 13.   [58] Ibid., 270. 7–8.

these words of teaching: 'Your heart has become a honeycomb full of every kind of instruction. From your heart's treasure come your words. They are honeyed drops that the Word might be blended with milk and honey.'[59]

Gregory observes how admirable are the words of the bride as they drip from the honeycomb of her mouth. 'They are not simply words', he says, 'but power.'[60] For the bride 'is guided by the Word'. The power of the bride's discourse is the fruitful productivity of the Word itself. Hence, Gregory says there is a 'garden blossoming from her mouth'; such is the fruitful discourse of one united to the Word.

The bride's union with the Word is the 'power' in her discourse, and we have described in the previous chapter the epistemological framework which guides and grounds this flow of words: faith hands on to the directing faculty of the heart something of what it has received from the incense of presence, something of what it has grasped of the Beloved, which in turn is distributed as needed: discourse that moves, excites, and transforms; actions that manifest the fragrant presence of the Word.

Those who receive the words that issue from the garden of her mouth receive, as it were, seeds into their hearts, and these 'words of faith become a garden planted in their hearts'.[61] The discourse of the bride, then, reveals the power, fruitfulness, and productivity of the Word, who, in a kiss of union, has filled her mouth with words of eternal life.

Shot Forth like an Arrow and at Rest with the Archer

This tendency of the bride to exhort with words of power is a dimension of her experience of union with the Word and is seen also in Homily 4, in a text which we considered in some detail in Chapter 3. The bride is wounded by an arrow. The arrow is the Son; the archer is love, later identified as God, and the arrow's tip is faith that has been moistened by the spirit of life.[62] As demonstrated previously, faith performs its technical role of mediating divine union, which Gregory expresses in the image of an arrow penetrating the heart of the bride. There is no need to represent that discussion here; what remains to be highlighted, however, is the logophatic dimension of, the Word's self-expression in, this union.

---

[59] *In Cant.* IX, GNO VI. 270. 7–11.
[60] Ibid., 280. 3: καὶ ταῦτα δύναμίς ἐστιν οὐ ῥήματα.
[61] Ibid., 282. 4–7.   [62] *In Cant.* IV, GNO VI. 127. 10–16.

Having been penetrated by the divine arrow, the bride herself becomes an arrow with which the archer takes aim and fires into the air. Gregory describes in the language of marital embrace the archer's embrace of the arrow-bride. The effect of this conflation of imagery allows Gregory to state his theological view that ascent and interiority, ascent and rest, are a single movement. Hence, the bride says, 'I am at once shot forth like an arrow and am at rest in the hands of the archer.'[63] Yet in the context of this divine union, the bride 'exhorts the daughters of Jerusalem'.[64] She instructs them and leads them to a life of virtue.[65]

Again we see what appears to be a characteristic of Gregory's apophaticism, i.e., a logophatic dimension. By virtue of her (apophatic) union, the bride yet speaks. Indeed she must speak, for in this union she takes on the incarnational dynamic of the Word. The Word penetrated her heart like an arrow, and her desire was enflamed. She herself becomes this arrow, and as a characteristic of this arrow is to elicit desire, so the words of exhortation of this bride-become-arrow instruct, guide, and elicit from those around her a burning desire for the Beloved.

Just as ascent and interiority are two aspects of one movement, so *logophasis* and *apophasis* are not movements in opposite directions, but different aspects of her union with the Word. That the bride is at once an arrow being shot and a spouse embraced reinforces this. The power of her words of exhortation to her maiden companions is the same power which has sent the bride aloft.

Conclusion

To conclude this examination of *logophasis* in Paul and the bride, we can observe that it should come as no particular surprise to see why Gregory refers to Paul as bride.[66] Both figures reveal the dialectic of *apophasis–logophasis*, this movement towards and procession from union mediated by faith, and both are paradigms of that exalted faith which has led Pottier, among others, to identify the central role of faith in Gregory's

---

[63] Ibid., 129. 15–16.   [64] Ibid., 129. 20–1.

[65] Ibid., 131. 4–10. Once again we note the exegetical base that guides Gregory's apophatic–logophatic thought: the scriptural text itself moves from the image of embrace (union) to one of exhoration: 'His left hand is under my head, and his right hand will embrace me. I have charged you daughters of Jerusalem ... ' (Song 2: 6–7).

[66] *In Cant.* II, GNO VI. 48. 15; *In Cant.* III. 91. 4–5; see also *In Cant.* I. 40. 9–12 and *In Cant.* IX. 279. 12–13.

understanding of divine union.[67] However, while both figures reveal the apophatic–logophatic union mediated by the grasp of faith, one is not the complete replica of the other, and differences between Paul and the bride are worth observing.

Logophasis is seen on the part of both Paul and the bride within the general context of *theosis*. However, it is elaborated with respect to each within the exegetical parameters delineated by the scriptural texts upon which Gregory is commenting. Hence, the bride's *logophasis* tends to be linked to explicit experiences of union with the Beloved because the imagery of the scriptural texts upon which Gregory comments favour this. However, in the case of the bride it is less obvious that it is the Word who is speaking; one has to consider the effects that her discourse has on the daughters of Jerusalem to see that it is the same effect that the Word has on the bride. But in the case of Paul it is much more obvious that the Word is expressing itself.

Paul's encounter with the Word is depicted in the language of divine indwelling, and Gregory develops the *apophasis–logophasis* dynamic largely with the help of three texts from 2 Corinthians: 12: 4: 13: 3 and 2: 15. The *logophasis* of Paul is largely determined by these three pericopes. The vision of Paul caught up in the third heaven (2 Cor. 12: 4), is developed along decidedly apophatic lines. The indwelling Christ speaking in Paul (2 Cor. 13: 3) and Paul bearing 'the good odour of Christ' (2 Cor. 2: 15) become, then, the logophatic correlate tied to the apophatic experience of 2 Corinthians 12: 4.

These observations of the logophatic dimension of the apophatic experiences of Paul and the bride put us in a position to view Gregory's understanding of the encounter with God in bolder relief. We see, for example, that for Gregory of Nyssa union with God has a double face. There is the apophatic face of divine union characterized most typically by aphairetic gestures of letting go, only for this epistemological ascent to be crowned finally by the open-palmed grasp of faith. However, in many of the most apophatic of texts we see yet a taking on of discourse, of concepts rendered into speech. This taking on of discourse is paradoxically as much a part of the experience of union as the apophatic dimension. I say paradoxically because the apophatic dimension of Paul or the bride in ascent has entailed, on the one hand, the letting go of concepts, of knowledge, and therefore of speech. Paul or the bride *in*

---

[67] Pottier, *Dieu et le Christ*, 214–20, esp. 215; see also Desalvo, *L' 'oltre' nel presente*, 215–26.

ascent is characterized by *apophasis*. On the other hand, however, Paul or the bride *having ascended* on high is characterized also by *logophasis*.

While we can only agree with the many scholars who have drawn attention to Gregory's apophaticism and to the constitutive role this apophaticism plays in his thought, the logophatic dimension of his apophatic theology plays likewise an important role. It is only by focusing on the dual mediation of faith that this double face of union, apophatic and logophatic, stands out. From the perspective of the apophatic side of this dialectic, faith mediates union; from the perspective of the logophatic side of this dialectic, faith hands on to the mind something of what it has grasped of the Beloved; it mediates the drops of the night, the obscure knowledge from the locks of the Beloved, which in turn is rendered as fragrant Word-bearing speech and virtue.

Indeed it is the power of the Word and its dynamic tendency to become incarnate that constitute logophatic discourse. However, it is not a question of finding individual, logophatic words pronounced by either Paul, or the bride, or Peter, etc. The key, rather, is to observe in apophatic texts, which feature union or divine indwelling, the effect which the subsequent discourse has on those who witness it. Titus, Silvanus, and Timothy inhale the scent of Paul's speech and virtue and, because of the Word's presence in this scent, they too are transformed.[68] When Paul addresses Thekla and teaches her, she is transformed upon hearing these words from which truth shines; she, like Paul, becomes a dwelling place of the Word: 'after this teaching ... the Word alone lived in her'.[69] When the bride addresses her maiden companions, her words have the same effect upon them as the Word had upon the bride, namely, the enflaming of desire 'to know his substance and in what he consists'. This is because the bride's words are suffused in the Word. The bride's *apophasis* is her letting go of everything she had known; *logophasis* is seen in the effects of her Word-bearing speech on those around her, speech which proceeds from what the mind received from the grasp of faith. When the bride communes with the Word by placing her mouth on the fountain of the Bridegroom's mouth, her mouth is filled with words of eternal life.[70] Her heart becomes a treasure house of words, 'honeyed drops that the Word might be blended with milk and honey'.[71] 'They are not simply words but power.'[72] Because of her union with the Word by

---

[68] *In Cant.* III, GNO VI. 91. 17–92. 4.   [69] *In Cant.* XIV, GNO VI. 405. 7–9.
[70] See *In Cant.* I, GNO VI. 32. 9–33. 2.   [71] *In Cant.* IX, GNO VI. 270. 7–11.
[72] Ibid., 280. 3.

the grasp of faith,[73] a union which has required the letting go of all knowledge and speech, the power of the bride's exhortation of the daughters of Jerusalem is the fruitful productivity of the Word itself, 'a garden blossoming from her mouth'.

Logophasis is a manifestation of the Word in deeds and discourse that follows directly upon an apophatic experience of union with or indwelling of the Word.[74] It is precisely this logophatic dimension of Gregory's apophaticism that has not received sufficient scholarly acknowledgement. For if what we have seen of the role of faith is true, then there is no apophaticism in Gregory of Nyssa which supersedes or is unaccompanied by logophaticism. When considering the logophatic dimension of Gregory's apophaticism, however, it is important to distinguish this from the kataphatic element. Kataphatic speech is 'the likeness of gold and not the gold'.[75] Because the Bridegroom's beauty has become visible for our own benefit, the invisible being made visible, but without compromising the incomprehensible divine nature,[76] clues and traces of God are retained by creation and give our words the opportunity to speak of God as 'wise, powerful, holy, blessed, as well as eternal, judge, and saviour'.[77] *Kataphasis* is grounded in 'knowledge of God in his ἐνέργειαι, a knowledge of God deduced through his created effects'.[78]

Kataphatic speech may make assertions about God, which assertions bear a certain resemblance to God, like 'gold and the likeness of gold'. In logophatic speech, such as that evinced by Paul, the bride, Peter, the evangelists, and saints, any such assertion is grounded in an experience of apophatic union, and those words (or deeds), spoken on behalf of the transformation of others, manifest the power of the Word; *logophasis* is human discourse divinized.

This double face of union, *apophasis* and *logophasis*, mediated by faith, prevents, moreover, the possibility of discourse being emptied of all meaning, but instead assures that it is true expression of the Word. While for Gregory there is no question of comprehending the divine essence, there is nevertheless a certain grasp by faith which passes on to intellect,

[73] See *In Cant.* vi, GNO vi. 183. 7–10.

[74] As we endeavoured to show especially in Chapter 3, such experiences of union and indwelling are mediated by faith, whether or not faith is explicitly mentioned.

[75] See *In Cant.* iii, GNO vi. 85. 16–19.

[76] *In Cant.* xiii, GNO vi. 384, 13–19.

[77] *In Cant.* i, GNO vi. 37. 16–17.

[78] Carabine, 'Gregory of Nyssa on the Incomprehensibility of God', 79. See also idem, 'Apophasis East and West', *Recherches de Théologie ancienne et médiévale* 55 (1988), 5–29, esp. 11–15.

not torrents of knowledge, but obscure drops of insight from the locks of the Beloved. These drops of insight are concepts which can then be rendered as discourse. Hence, *logophasis* allows discourse, as Canévet has said, 'not to empty itself in a vain extension towards the infinite'.[79] Later Canévet asks, 'What is the source of religious language? Does it translate something other than the successive failures of an infinite quest?'[80] Based on what we have seen of the discourse of the bride, and of Paul, as well as Peter and the evangelists, we can say that the source is the Word itself as it is grasped by faith and mediated to the intellect, the *hegemonikon*, the heart. This discourse is the 'translation', to borrow Canévet's term, not of failure but of union with that fountain of Presence that has filled the bride's mouth with words of eternal life. The flow of her discourse bears witness to and manifests the flow of this Presence.

---

[79] Canévet, *Grégoire de Nysse et l'herméneutique biblique*, 57.
[80] Ibid., 62.

7

The Luminous Dark Revisited

Introduction

The purpose of this chapter is to redress the way in which scholarship on Gregory of Nyssa conceives of his theory of divine union. When considering Gregory's mystical theory, the great bulk of scholarship presents Gregory as a proponent of a mysticism of darkness and consequently extols him as one of the great 'mystics of darkness'. While I agree with the general lines of this position, I want to argue that Gregory of Nyssa's thought reveals no less what might be termed a mysticism of light. In what follows I shall first present the broad outlines of this so-called mysticism of darkness in order to demonstrate that it is tied exclusively to his interpretation of specific scriptural texts and has decidedly apophatic concerns. But this is not the only way in which Gregory expresses the experience of divine union. In the process of commenting on other scriptural texts, not part of that limited set of divine darkness texts, Gregory speaks of the bride's divinization in light. Moreover, the light in which the soul is divinized must ultimately be distinguished from that light which is overcome in the first stage of the divine-darkness motif. The light-of-divinization theme has different epistemological–ethical concerns which are themselves grounded in the exegesis of different scriptural *lemmata*. Just as Gregory's 'mysticism of darkness' reveals an important, indeed characteristic dimension of his thought, so Gregory's 'mysticism of light' reveals a likewise important, indeed characteristic dimension of his thought. For this reason I maintain that Gregory's so-called mysticism is no less one of light than one of darkness.

Preliminary Considerations

The question of Gregory's mysticism of darkness entered the scholarly arena with an essay by Henri-Charles Puech, 'La ténèbre mystique chez le Pseudo-Denys l'Aréopagite et dans la tradition patristique',[1] who said that the theme of the mystical dark finds its centre and its flowering in Gregory of Nyssa.[2] With the subsequent publication of Jean Daniélou's *chef d'œuvre*, *Platonisme et théologie mystique*,[3] the theme of darkness became something of a *carte d'entrée* for Gregory of Nyssa as the original and undisputed founder of mystical theology.[4] But indeed the claim was disputed several years later by Walther Völker in his *Gregor von Nyssa als Mystiker*,[5] a dispute subsequently made famous by the well-known article by Daniélou's Jesuit confrère, Henri Crouzel, who felt his Origen's spiritual genius besmirched:[6] Gregory can make no claim to be the founder of mystical theology, '*car tout l'essentiel se trouve déjà chez Origène*'.[7]

---

[1] In *En quête de la Gnose*, 2 vols. (Paris, 1978), vol. i, 119–41, esp. 136–9; the article appeared originally in *Études Carmélitaines* 23 (1938), 33–53; see also J. LeMaitre, 'Préhistoire du concept de gnophos', *Dictionnaire de Spiritualité, s. v.* contemplation, cols. 1868–72; *Reallexikon für Antike und Christentum*, vol. iv, s. v. Dunkelheit, cols. 350–8.

[2] Ibid., 136: 'Mais c'est en Grégoire de Nysse que toute notre tradition trouve son centre et son plus magnifique épanouissement.'

[3] Daniélou, *Platonisme et Théologie mystique*, esp. 175–314. See also Daniélou, 'Mystique de la ténèbre chez Grégoire de Nysse', *Dictionnaire de Spiritualité, s. v.* contemplation, cols. 1872–85.

[4] Ibid., 7.

[5] Wiesbaden, 1955. Völker announces in the preface his reservations regarding Daniélou's insistence on Gregory's originality. See Daniélou's review of Völker's book in *Recherches de Science Religieuse* 44 (1956), 617–20, where Daniélou admits to having exaggerated the differences between Origen and Gregory but at the same time insists that Völker minimizes their differences and thinks that Gregory is ultimately '*un plus grand mystique*'.

[6] 'Grégoire de Nysse est-il le fondateur de la théologie mystique?', *Revue d'Ascétique et de Mystique* 33 (1957), 189–202. One of Crouzel's chief objections is Daniélou's claim that Origen himself, along with the other Alexandrians, enjoyed no mystical experience (p. 189), claims which subsequently have been levelled against Gregory, which claims generate no interest for the present investigation.

[7] Ibid., 202. However, whether Gregorian darkness is actually present in Origen, as Crouzel seems to think, cannot be so easily solved by simply locating in Origen the existence of the theme of divine darkness. For the same theme is linked to the differing anthropological and theological presuppositions of each respective author. If God is difficult to know, or indeed cannot be known, for Origen it is due to the weakness of the human mind. For Gregory of Nyssa, however, God is unknowable in himself, irrespective of the mind's capacity. Therefore, even though the theme of divine darkness appears both in Origen (rarely) and in Gregory (more frequently but by no means ubiquitously), it is tied to different epistemological possibilities regarding the knowledge of God, who for both

This Scylla and Charybdis of who is original and who is derivative has largely determined the parameters of the debate which have consequently obscured the simple fact that for all Gregory's supposed concern for the divine darkness he is equally (if not more) concerned with the theme of light in describing the transforming experience of God, at least in the *Commentarius in Canticum canticorum.* The purpose of this chapter is to redress this balance.

Whatever Gregory's contribution, original or derivative, to the development of the theme of divine darkness, he (along with Denys the Areopagite) is identified with this theme more than any other Christian author in late antiquity.[8] It is precisely the identification of Gregory with this theme which I propose to controvert by arguing the following thesis: Gregory's so-called mysticism is no less a mysticism of light than of darkness. He invokes the theme of divine darkness relatively infrequently and then only while commenting on certain biblical texts, and these in quite specific apophatic contexts; he speaks more frequently of union by divinization in light. This is not to deny the existence of what might legitimately be called a 'mysticism of darkness', but rather to insist that Gregory speaks much more often of the further reaches of human participation in divine life in the language of light.

If Orthodox theologian Olivier Clément can call Gregory of Nyssa the 'poet and dramatist of darkness',[9] Gregory is equally the poet and dramatist of light. Indeed the most cursory reading of the *Commentarius in*

authors 'makes darkness his hiding place' (Ps. 17: 12). On this see the helpful article by A. Meredith, 'Licht und Finsternis bei Origenes und Gregor von Nyssa' in T. Kobusch and B. Mojsisch (eds.), *Platon in der abendländischen Geistesgeschichte* (Darmstadt, 1997), 48–59. Cf. J. Dillon, 'The Knowledge of God in Origen', in R. van den Broek, T. Baarda, and J. Mansfield (eds.), *Knowledge of God in the Graeco-Roman World* (Leiden, 1988), 219–28. For general background on the difficulty/impossibility of knowing God in Middle Platonism, see Dillon, *The Middle Platonists*; see also Carabine, *The Unknown God*, esp. 51–70; see also Lilla, *Introduzione al Medio Platonismo.*

[8] That the theme is a uniquely Judaeo-Christian theme rooted in the Bible was pointed out long ago by Puech, 'La Ténèbre mystique', 133. In *The Foundations of Mysticism*, 175, B. McGinn suggests that 'we should note that the mysticism of darkness is not found among pagan Neoplatonists. Indeed, we may even surmise that this distinctively biblical apophaticsim serves as a critique of late antique pagan theology with its heavy use of light imagery.' Cf. Carabine, *The Unknown God*, 65, who claims to find the theme of divine darkness also in Celsus; see Origen's *Contra Celsum*, VI. 36 [*sic*]; cf. VI. 17.

[9] O. Clément, *The Roots of Christian Mysticism*, trans. T. Berkley (London, 1993), 236. For another identification of Gregory with the mysticism of darkness as opposed to that of light, written for a largely popular audience, see the anthology prepared by L. Dupré and J. Wiseman (eds.), *Light from Light: An Anthology of Christian Mysticism* (Mahwah, N.J., 1988), 46.

Canticum canticorum reveals that Gregory is in fact more concerned with divinization in light than with encountering God in the darkness of unknowing, and this latter only within a quite limited set of exegetical and epistemological circumstances.[10]

From Light to Increasing Darkness

Of all the homilies in the *Commentarius in Canticum canticorum*, Homily 11, in which Gregory comments on Song 5: 2–7, is perhaps the clearest presentation of Gregory's doctrine on the noetic ascent as a movement from light to increasing darkness. Indeed there is much in this Homily which supports this view.[11]

It is important to note at the outset the scriptural *lemma* upon which Gregory comments in this important example of his doctrine on divine darkness: 'Open to me, my sister, my companion, my dove, my perfect one, for my head is filled with dew, and my locks with the drops of the night' (Song 5: 2). Words such as 'Dew' (δρόσμος, the night's moisture) and 'night' (νύξ)[12] encourage Gregory to interpret the theme of darkness in a positive, theological sense. Hence, the scriptural text itself encourages him to pursue a certain line of thought in the direction of the divine darkness theme.

Gregory reminds us of Moses' encounter with God. First God manifests himself to Moses through light (διὰ φωτός). After this God spoke

---

[10] Indeed Crouzel ('Grégoire de Nysse', 194) did his best to make it known that one of Völker's complaints, and a legitimate one in my opinion, against Daniélou's treatment of Gregory was an over-emphasis on the role of darkness in Gregory of Nyssa and that light plays a more important role in Gregory's thought than does darkness. While I agree with Völker that the theme of divine darkness in Gregory has been over-emphasized, I disagree with Völker that light is more important than darkness in Gregory. Indeed the theme of divinization in light occurs decidedly more frequently than the theme of divine darkness, but it would be misleading to conclude on the basis of this that light is therefore more important than darkness in Gregory's thought. I would argue that just as the fundamental structure of Gregory's thought holds virtue and knowledge on an even par, so the themes of divinization in light and the noetic ascent into divine darkness are likewise held on an even par.

[11] For a clear presentation of this theme see Louth, *Origins of the Christian Mystical Tradition*, 80–97, esp. 83–8; for a succinct statement of the relationship between Gregory's divine darkness and the allegory of the cave see idem, 'The Cappadocians', in C. Jones, G. Wainwright, and E. Yarnold (eds.), *The Study of Spirituality* (London, 1986), 161–8.

[12] It should be noted that as important as the term νύξ is for the theme of divine darkness in the *In Canticum* (e.g. GNO vi. 181. 4; 181. 14; 324. 8) Gregory usually employs the word in a negative sense (e.g. GNO vi. 48. 4; 70. 16; 77. 20; 192. 11; 196. 11).

to Moses through a cloud (διὰ νεφέλης). Then Moses saw God in darkness (ἐν γνόφῳ).[13] Indeed the ascent is one that begins in light and moves into progressive darkness.

Having identified Moses as revealing the master pattern of noetic ascent, Gregory then applies this pattern to us. First we withdraw from false opinions about God; this is a change from dark (σκότους) to light (φῶς). Next the soul moves from appearances to God's hidden nature, which is symbolized by the cloud that overshadows (ἐπισκιάζουσα) all appearances; thus the soul becomes accustomed to beholding what is hidden. Finally, journeying towards higher things and forsaking (καταλιποῦσα) what can be attained by human nature, everything that can be comprehended (καταλαμβανομένου), the soul penetrates the impenetrable and enters the sanctuary (ἀδύτων) of divine knowledge (θεογνωσίας) and is surrounded by the divine darkness (τῷ θείῳ γνόφῳ).[14]

Again the pattern of progressive darkness is evident, and Gregory finds this same pattern in the history of the bride's sojourn, as she progresses from ignorance and draws near the fountain of truth and is washed and made beautiful in the light of truth. She then moved with the speed of a horse, flying like a dove, through everything she understood, and rested under the apple tree's shadow (Gregory equates the shade of the apple tree with the cloud). Finally she was embraced by a divine night (θείας νυκτὸς).[15]

The pattern is clear: (1) from the darkness of sin and error to light; (2) from the light of knowledge to the cloud (or shadow of the apple tree), from the cloud to divine darkness (or divine night). It is clearly a movement from light to increasing darkness. However, it is worth emphasizing that the light that is part of this path of increasing darkness is the light of withdrawal from false opinions about God and not, as we shall soon see, the light of divinizing union, which is a path of increasing light and beauty. It is crucial to keep this distinction in mind when considering the relationship between light and darkness, especially in the *In Canticum*.

[13] *In Cant.* XI, GNO VI. 322. 9–12. Cf. *De vita Moysis*, SC, II. 162–4. Cf. also Philo, *De post. Caini* 4. 12–5. 16; *Vita Mos.* 1. 28. 158; *De mut.* 2. 7; and Clement, *Strom.* II. 2. 6; V. 12. 78.

[14] *In Cant.* XI, GNO VI. 322. 13–323. 9.

[15] Ibid., 323. 12–324. 9. The embrace by the divine night refers back to *In Cant.* VI (GNO VI. 181. 13–183. 10), where Gregory is interpreting Song 3: 1: 'I sought him on my bed at night but did not find him.' It is in the commentary on this passage that the bride finds the Beloved by the grasp of faith.

Gregory emphasizes on numerous occasions that the light that gives way to darkness is in some sense *epistemological* light. We see this both in *De vita Moysis* and in the *In Canticum canticorum*. At the first theophany of the Burning Bush, the truth shines upon (ἐπιλάμψει) us and illuminates (περιαυγάζουσα) the eyes of the soul.[16] This light of truth imparts knowledge of a discursive sort regarding the mystery of the Virgin, and that what the senses have come to understand and what was contemplated by the mind is nothing in comparison with the divine nature.[17] This is a discursive realization regarding the limits of human knowledge of God.

When Gregory alludes to this first theophany in *De vita Moysis* II. 162, he associates it once again with the light of knowledge, knowledge of a discursive order. He says that the text teaches that religious knowledge is at first light for those who receive it.[18] It is this light of knowledge that gives way to the increasing darkness of the cloud and the darkness where God is.

This association of the light of knowledge with the early movements of ascent is further evidenced by the bride's ascent in Homily 11 on the Song. Describing her ascent to the divine night where she is embraced by the Beloved, Gregory says she began her ascent by moving from the darkness of ignorance to the light of truth: she parted company with evil and approached the fountain of light and was illumined by the light of truth.[19] This light, however, gives way to darkness as she is embraced by the divine night and receives the drops of the night which flow down from the locks of her Beloved (Song 5: 2).

There is no need to belabour the point: the discursive knowledge that characterizes the early phase of an ascent is described in the language of light because Gregory is modelling the noetic ascent on Moses' sojourn which begins in light. Moreover, it is discursive knowledge and in no way approaches the loftier non-discursive encounters that will characterize Moses' movement beyond the cloud and into the darkness where God dwells.

---

[16] *De Vita Moysis*, SC, II. 19. 1–3.

[17] Ibid., 19. 21–4. Daniélou makes the interesting observation that Gregory appears to be the first to make a connection between the Burning Bush and Mary; see ibid., n. 3.

[18] Ibid., 162. 6–8: Διδάσκει γὰρ διὰ τούτων ὁ λόγος ὅτι τῆς εὐσεβείας ἡ γνῶσις φῶς γίνεται παρὰ τὴν πρώτην οἷς ἂν ἐγγένηται.

[19] *In Cant.* XI, GNO VI. 323. 20–324. 1: τότε καλὴ γίνεται τῷ φωτὶ τῆς ἀληθείας περιλαμφθεῖσα....

Before moving on to a consideration of Gregory's use of light imagery to describe the heights of the human encounter with God outside the divine darkness motif, let us keep in mind the following observations. The context in which we have seen the theme of divine darkness occur is specifically exegetical and epistemological. In introducing the theme of divine darkness Gregory is interpreting a scriptural text which lends itself to such an interpretation (Song 5: 2 and 3: 1). Apart from scriptural texts which lend themselves to such an interpretation, he does not introduce the theme of divine darkness.[20]

Moreover, the theme of divine darkness is tied to one of Gregory's preferred motifs for describing the human encounter with God: the epistemological ascent. For Gregory this typically involves *aphairesis* and apophatic language. In this text the gestures of *aphairesis* are seen in the images of letting go and forsaking: The soul forsakes appearances and comprehension; the bride, in Homily 6, lets go of everything she had previously understood.[21] The apophatic element, though not over-abundant, is provided not only by the imagery of darkness such as the cloud, divine darkness, divine night, and the shade of the apple tree, but also by such stock apophatic terms as ἄδυτον, ἀόρατον and ἀκατάληπτον. These apophatic terms and images combine with the aphairetic motif to characterize Gregorian epistemological ascents.

The pattern of epistemological ascent is clearly seen in the progression from discursive light of knowledge, having left the darkness of sin, to the non-discursive darkness of unknowing. Here light refers to knowledge of a discursive sort;[22] the movement into darkness (νεφέλη and γνόφος) is a movement into the non-discursive. Darkness surpasses light because in Gregory's noetic ascents the non-discursive apophatic always surpasses the discursive. Nevertheless, it is at the same

[20] Song 3: 1; 5: 2; 5: 5–6; Ex 20: 21; Ps. 17(18): 12.

[21] *In Cant.* vi, GNO vi. 183. 7–8: καὶ πᾶσαν καταληπτικὴν ἔφοδον καταλιποῦσα,... Because the image of the bride running (διαδραμοῦσα, *In Cant.* xi, GNO vi. 324. 5) like a horse through previous levels of understanding is parallel in structure to the more obviously aphairetic language of letting go both at *In Cant.* vi, GNO vi. 183. 7 and at *In Cant.* xi, GNO vi. 323. 3, I consider διαδραμοῦσα in this instance an aphairetic term.

[22] Later we shall see how important it is to distinguish the light of discursive knowledge, surpassed by the darkness of unknowing, from the light of divinized virtue, which is never surpassed by the darkness of unknowing but on an even par with it. Failure to identify and maintain this distinction risks leading to the erroneous conclusion that Gregory's theory of divine union is characterized *tout court* by a progression from light to increasing darkness instead of exhibiting this 'mysticism of darkness' *only* in certain exegetical and epistemological contexts.

time a faithful reading of the imagery of the texts which Gregory is interpreting; Moses encounters God in light (Exod. 19: 3), then in a cloud (Exod. 19: 16–19) and finally in darkness (Exod. 20: 21). This is another example of epistemology grounded in exegesis.[23]

On the basis of *In Canticum* XI, with support from *In Canticum* VI, *De vita Moysis* II. 162–3, and other texts, one can see why Gregory is considered one of the great fashioners of the mysticism of darkness. However, the ascent to God in the darkness of unknowing is not the only way in which Gregory describes the furthest reaches of the divine– human encounter. While the divine darkness theme, an interpretation of suitable Old Testament texts (Exod. 20: 21), is clearly one way in which Gregory does this, it is not the only way. He also describes the encounter in the language of light. In fact, the imagery of light far exceeds that of darkness in descriptions of communion with the divine. This is due to anthropological, sacramental, and pneumatological reasons.

Light unto Light

While it is true that Gregory describes the beginning of the noetic ascent as a conversion from the darkness of sin to the light of suitable ideas of and opinions about God, it is important to remember that Gregory

---

[23] In fact Gregory does force the text somewhat in order to make a smooth progression from light to darkness and thus serve his epistemological designs. At *In Cant.* XI, GNO VI. 322. 9–10, Gregory says that God appeared to Moses through light (διὰ φωτὸς). Langerbeck (p. 322) says this refers to Exod. 19: 3. However, when Moses begins his journey up Mt. Sinai at Exod. 19: 3, there is no mention of light. LXX simply reads: καὶ Μωυσῆς ἀνέβη εἰς τὸ ὄρος τοῦ θεοῦ · καὶ ἐκάλεσεν αὐτὸν ὁ θεὸς ἐκ τοῦ ὄρους λέγων. . . . The question suggests itself, why does Gregory appear to be supplying the imagery of light? Is he transferring to Sinai the fiery image of light in the theophany at Horeb (Exod. 3: 2)? Gregory seems quite keen to draw out the luminous qualities of fire when he describes the theophany at Horeb at *De vita Moysis*, SC, II. 22. 2 ff. (cf its slightly less luminous development at *In Cant.* XII, GNO VI. 355. 4). Gregory would seem to want this epistemological ascent to begin with light, knowing that the most famous ascent featuring light and darkness, the allegory of the cave (*Rep.* VI. 514a–516c) begins not in light but in darkness. A. Louth is probably correct when he says that, in describing the noetic ascent in terms of progressive darkness, Gregory is overturning Plato's cave; see his 'The Cappadocians', 167. As convincing as Louth's thesis is, and I believe it is correct, there are yet times when Gregory alludes to the famous allegory without controverting it. See e.g. *In inscrip. Psalm.* I. 6, GNO V. 41–2; *De beat.* III, GNO VII. ii. 104. 8–10; *In Cant.* VII, GNO VI. 212. 8. See the article by J. Daniélou, 'Le symbole de la caverne chez Grégoire de Nysse', in *Mullus: Festschrift Theodor Klauser*, Jahrbuch für Antike und Christentum 1, ed. A. von Stuiber and A. Hermann (Münster, 1964), 43–51, esp. 43–9, and Meredith, 'Licht und Finsternis'.

conceives the original condition of the human being as one of light. Moreover, the process of redemption flowers in a divinizing union that is also conceived of in terms of light. Let us consider some of these texts with a view to clarifying the relationship between light and dark, both of which are metaphors which describe the ultimate horizon of the divine embrace of humanity.

Original Condition of Light

Gregory of Nyssa conceives of the original condition of humanity as one of light and divine likeness. In *Oratio catechetica* he states the reason behind the creation of humanity. Safeguarding divine freedom, Gregory insists God did not create humanity out of necessity or compulsion, but freely and out of abundant love.[24] The reason Gregory gives is simply that God is light and that it is not fitting that light should be unseen, with no one to share or enjoy it.[25] Gregory then says that if humanity was created to enjoy and participate in this light, humanity must have been created in such a way as to be able to participate in this light and goodness. 'For just as the eye shares in light through having by nature an inherent brightness in it, and by this innate power attracts what is akin to itself, so something akin to the divine had to be mingled with human light.'[26]

For Gregory, then, there is something intrinsically luminous about human nature. Moreover, and this is crucial to the argument being pursued here, one cannot escape the epistemological implications of this language of light and vision which Gregory uses to describe this original created nature. Human nature has been created in such a way as to see and participate in that light which is God. Participation in and vision of divine light is in some sense an epistemological encounter. While this is not to say that this knowing implies a comprehension of the divine nature itself, a theme which plays surprisingly little role in the *Oratio catechetica* (written in roughly the same period as the *Contra Eunomium*, which is very much concerned with divine incomprehen-

---

[24] *Orat. cat.* V, GNO III. iv. 16. 22–17. 3.

[25] Ibid., 17. 4–7.

[26] Ibid., 17. 11–15: καθάπερ γὰρ ὁ ὀφθαλμὸς διὰ τῆς ἐγκειμένης αὐτῷ φυσικῶς αὐγῆς ἐν κοινωνίᾳ τοῦ φωτὸς γίνεται, διὰ τῆς ἐμφύτου δυνάμεως τὸ συγγενὲς ἐφελκόμενος, οὕτως ἀναγκαῖον ἦν ἐγκραθῆναί τι τῇ ἀνθρωπίνῃ φύσει συγγενὲς πρὸς τὸ θεῖον,... Translation by C. Richardson in *Christology of the Later Fathers*, ed. E. Hardy, Library of Christian Classics 3 (London, 1954), 276.

sibility), Gregory envisages a certain knowledge of God constitutive of the original nature of humanity, and this he describes in the language of light.

In Homily 4 on the Song Gregory likens the original condition of human nature to shining gold that resembles the undefiled good.[27] In Homily 12 he reflects on the extraordinarily beautiful character of all created things, among which is humanity; and this, being made beautiful by radiance (φαιδρῷ) of life, is bestowed with a beauty greater than that of all the others.[28] To this original condition, moreover, nothing needed to be added or acquired; all that was necessary was to safeguard this original condition of radiance. However, humanity did not guard this radiance that was given by God; rather this shining nature became discoloured and black by mixing with vice.[29]

In Homily 15, likening the soul to a garden, Gregory observes how the soul had been cultivated in paradise; the discolouring of the shining nature amounts to the devastation of this garden. To assist in the recovery of this garden Gregory says that God came down again with plants of virtues, virtues which are cared for and watered by the fountain of the Word.[30] For two reasons I draw attention to this text, which focuses on the role of virtues in recovering from the devastation of the garden or the obscuring of the brightness of our nature. First, we shall later see that the virtues play an important role in the bride's (soul's) transformation in light. Second, the Homily introduces the role of the incarnation in the restoration of this lost condition of light. With this in mind let us consider how the role of the incarnation and baptism carry on this theme of light.

Incarnation and Illumination

Having seen how Gregory conceives of the original created nature of the human person as one of light and that the fall obscures this light, it is not surprising, then, to see him clothe his descriptions of the incarnation in the same metaphor. For example, in Homily 2 Gregory says that humanity is light according to nature and then is subsequently obscured

---

[27] *In Cant.* IV, GNO VI. 100. 16–18: χρυσῖτις ἦν τὸ κατ' ἀρχὰς ἡ ἀνθρωπίνη φύσις καὶ λάμπουσα τῇ πρὸς τὸ ἀκήρατον ἀγαθὸν ὁμοιότητι, ...

[28] *In Cant.* XII, GNO VI. 348. 1–9.

[29] *In Cant.* II, GNO VI. 54. 7–9 and *In Cant.* IV, GNO VI. 100. 18–19.

[30] *In Cant.* XV, GNO VI. 437. 1–8.

through sin, but with the light of the incarnation, humanity becomes radiant.[31] Paraphrasing Paul, Gregory says that the reason for Christ's coming into the world was to make light (λαμπροὺς ποιῆσαι) those who were dark, whom Christ causes to shine (λάμπειν).[32]

In Homily 5 on the Song the theme of incarnation combines with that of union, and Gregory remarks that, after being prepared by the illumination of the prophets and the Law, the true light appears to those sitting in darkness and the shadow of death and through this unites with (συνανακράσεως) human nature. The Law and the prophets served to foster a desire to see the sun in the open air, which at last, with the coming of Christ, becomes a reality.[33] And again in Homily 15, speaking more remotely of incarnation, Gregory, citing Titus, says that the grace of the incarnation illumines: 'God's grace becomes manifest and enlightens (φωτίζουσα) us.'[34]

Within the context of incarnation as illumination Gregory locates an image of divine darkness, albeit subtle, that is often overlooked. It is nevertheless an occurrence which merits some consideration for it describes divine presence in the language of darkness, but a darkness that mediates and ultimately gives way to light.

In Homily 4 on the Song Gregory comments on Song 1: 16: 'Behold you are fair my Beloved and beautiful, overshadowing our bed.' He devotes special attention to the phrase, 'overshadowing our bed'.[35] This shadowing is an image of darkness which Gregory clearly aligns with incarnation and divine presence. Once again we see that for Gregory the incarnation is conceived of in terms of light, an 'unveiling of the pure rays of divinity'. But the brightness of divinity is shadowed over by the incarnation so as not to overpower us: 'For if while unveiling the pure rays of divinity you did not shade yourself over with the form of a servant, who would withstand your manifestation? For no one sees the face of the Lord and lives.'[36] Why is this shadowing necessary? Gregory tells us: 'you have come now as one who is beautiful, but also as one we

---

[31] *In Cant.* II, GNO VI. 48. 8–14.
[32] Ibid., 48. 18–49. 4: Χριστὸς εἰς τὸν κόσμον ἦλθε λαμπροὺς ποιῆσαι τοὺς μέλανας,... See Phil 2: 15.
[33] *In Cant.* V, GNO VI. 144. 19–145. 13.
[34] *In Cant.* XV, GNO VI. 448. 14.
[35] *In Cant.* IV, GNO VI. 107. 9: Πρὸς κλίνη ἡμῶν σύσκιος.
[36] Ibid., 108. 1–4: εἰ γὰρ μὴ συνεσκίασας αὐτὸς σεαυτὸν τὴν ἄκρατον τῆς θεότητος ἀκτῖνα συγκαλύψας τῇ τοῦ δούλου μορφῇ, τίς ἂν ὑπέστη σου τὴν ἐμφάνειαν; οὐδεὶς γὰρ ὄψεται πρόσωπον κυρίου καὶ ζήσεται.

can receive'.[37] But it is important to note that the darkness of this shadowing is subordinated to the divine light; Gregory says its role is to mediate light for us who live in darkness (σκότος). How else, he asks, could a mortal, perishable nature be joined in union (συζυγία) with what is pure and unapproachable?[38] Gregory says that this blending (ἀνάκρασιν) of divine and human natures is what is meant by the term 'bed' which the Beloved overshadows with his presence.[39]

Having seen, then, that our original condition is one of light and that the incarnation is viewed also in terms of light, we can see how this particular image of divine presence overshadowing the bed of human— divine union serves a general movement into increasing light: from the darkness of sin to the shadow of divine presence that mediates the unapproachable light. Reversing the light–cloud–darkness pattern of *De vita Moysis* II. 162, and of *In Canticum* XI, this passage reveals a pattern of darkness–shadow–light. The sequence is not one of increasing darkness but one of increasing light.

Shadow also gives way to light in Homily 5 when Gregory presents the broad movements of salvation history as a movement into increasing light. The Church has received the brilliant light of truth (τὴν τῆς ἀληθείας αὐγὴν) through the Law and the prophets. As bright as this revelation is, however, the Law is but a shadow (σκιὰν) of things to come, and with the dawning of the gospel, these shadows disperse, and the house which is the Church is fully illumined by the gospel.[40] Hence, for Gregory the broad movement of salvation history is itself one of increasing light in its movement towards the incarnation.

On the basis of these texts on creation and incarnation it is obvious enough that by the designation of that enlightenment consequent upon the incarnation Gregory does not envisage simply a movement out of darkness; it is more fundamentally a return to and an intensification of that luminous state which characterized the human condition before it was obscured by sin. Baptism returns one to this and is likewise described in the language of bathing and light. The bath of rebirth makes those darkened by sin 'to shine like the stars of heaven'.[41] When Gregory says that the Ethiopians washed off their darkness 'in the mystical water',[42] the luminous quality they knew was but a return to the luminous state of God's original, creative intention.

---

[37] Ibid., 108. 4–6.   [38] Ibid., 108. 7–10.   [39] Ibid., 108. 10–12.
[40] *In Cant.* V, GNO VI. 148. 7–20.
[41] *In Cant.* II, GNO VI. 49. 3: λάμπειν ὡς φωστῆρας ἐποίησε....
[42] *In Cant.* VII, GNO VI. 205. 12–16.

Light Communing in Light

Nor are we meant to believe that once returned from the darkness of sin through the enlightenment of baptism the sojourn then becomes one from light to increasing darkness. While this is without doubt an important way in which Gregory speaks of apophatic, epistemological ascents in the course of commenting on certain scriptural texts (as we have seen, for example, in Homilies 6 and 11), Gregory speaks frequently, indeed more frequently, of continual encounter with God in ever greater light and beauty. Homily 5 on the Song provides a clear example of this as he comments on Song 2: 13: 'Arise and come my companion, my beautiful one, my dove.'[43]

Gregory sees in this text important teaching regarding incessant growth which he describes as an ascent in light. We see the Word leading the bride up ascending 'steps of virtue'.[44] This ascent is described in imagery of increasing light. First 'through the windows of the prophets and the lattices of the law the word sends a beacon of light'.[45] The bride is then invited to approach the light and to become beautiful. In this light she is transformed into the image of a dove.[46] This transformation in light and beauty, moreover, does not come to an end, for Gregory introduces the theme of perpetual progress as the bride is continually drawn to participation in higher beauty. Even whilst being transformed and beautified in light she yet seems merely to be beginning her ascent. The image presented is clearly not one of movement from light to increasing darkness but one of perpetual transformation in light and beauty.

The text is noteworthy for its description of a luminous ascent in virtue, and there are a number of reasons for this, not the least outstanding of which is straightforward and exegetical. The better known ascents into darkness, such as those in Homilies 6 and 11, are commentaries upon scriptural texts which lend themselves to the theme of darkness. This text, however, does not lend itself to the theme of darkness. Moreover, the ascents into darkness have a decidedly apophatic thrust. This ascent focuses instead on increasing luminosity, growth in virtue and the divinizing role of the Holy Spirit. However, let us not forget the foundational character of this light and its epistemo-

---

[43] *In Cant.* v, GNO vi. 157. 7–8.   [44] Ibid., 158. 19–21.

[45] Ibid., 158. 21–159. 2.

[46] Ibid., 159. 2–4: καὶ προσκαλεῖται αὐτὴν ἐγγίσαι τῷ φωτὶ καὶ καλὴν γενέσθαι πρὸς τὸ εἶδος τῆς περιστερᾶς ἐν τῷ φωτὶ μορφωθεῖσαν.

logical nuances which we established earlier. With this in mind let us consider more closely this divinizing work of the Holy Spirit, symbolized by the dove.

The Light of Divinization

Long ago J. Gross identified Gregory of Nyssa as the *'témoin par excellence'* of the Greek doctrine of divinization.[47] However, I.-H. Dalmais claimed that Gregory, in contrast to other writers, presumably such as Clement of Alexandria, who introduced into Christian literature the term θεοποιεῖν,[48] is 'extremely reserved' in his use of the terminology of divinization.[49] Meredith would seem to agree with this view but adds an important qualification when he says: 'Although Gregory is less insistent, as far as vocabulary goes, on the divinization of man, this ought not to lead us to think that the reality contained in the idea was absent from or alien to his consciousness.'[50]

Indeed it is true that Gregory often explores the theme of divinization without using the vocabulary of divinization, but he does in fact use it with some ease and frequency and to such an extent that one questions the appropriateness of Dalmais's judgement of 'extreme reserve' in this regard. For example, in the *Oratio catechetica* Gregory describes the union between God and humanity in the incarnation with the technical language of divinization, evocative of the classical formulations of Irenaeus and Athanasius. He says God 'united himself with our nature, in order that by its union with the divine it might become divine'.[51] In his discussion on the Eucharist later in the *Oratio catechetica* Gregory distinguishes two types of union with God, due to humanity's twofold nature. The soul attains union through faith, but the body, says Gregory, experiences union in a different way. The body experiences union through

---

[47] J. Gross, *La Divinisation du chrétien d'après les pères grecs. Contribution historique à la doctrine de la grace* (Paris, 1938), 219. B. Studer holds a similar position in *Encyclopedia of the Early Church*, ed. A. Di Berardino, trans. A. Walford (Cambridge, 1992), *s. v.* divinization: 'But on the whole Gregory's [doctrine on divinization] remains the most considerable synthesis before the theology of Ps.-Dionysius and Maximus Confessor.'

[48] *Protrepticus* 11. 114; see McGinn, *The Foundations of Mysticism*, 107.

[49] *Dictionnaire de Spiritualité*, *s. v.*, divinisation, cols. 1382–3.

[50] Meredith, *The Cappadocians*, 83.

[51] *Orat. cat.* xxv, GNO iii. iv. 64. 7–9: κατεμίχθη πρὸς τὸ ἡμέτερον, ἵνα τὸ ἡμέτερον τῇ πρὸς τὸ θεῖον ἐπιμιξίᾳ γένηται θεῖον,... Trans. C. Richardson, in E. Hardy *et al.* (eds.), *Christology of the Later Fathers*, Library of Christian Classics 3 (London, 1954), 302. Cf Irenaeus, *Adv. haer.* v, pref., PG 7. 1120; Athanasius, *De incarn. verbi* LIV, PG 15. 192B.

reception of the Eucharist, the effects of which Gregory describes in the language of divinization: 'when the body which God made immortal enters ours, it entirely transforms it into itself'. When one receives the Eucharist, the Eucharist 'transforms his entire being into its own nature'.[52]

Another theme that typifies divinization in Gregory is the taking on of divine characteristics. An early example of this is seen in *De virginitate*. He says 'what greater praise for virginity than to show that in a certain sense virginity divinizes (θεοποιοῦσαν) those who participate (μετεσχηκότας) in its pure mysteries', for they participate in God's purity and commune (κοινωνούς) with his glory.[53]

Divinization as a consequence of union in which divine characteristics are taken on typifies Gregory's use of this theme whether or not the technical vocabulary of divinization is used. Indeed some of the most stirring examples of divinization occur with no recourse whatever to the vocabulary of divinization. Foremost amongst these is Gregory's commentary on Song 2: 5 in Homily 4 on the Song. As we saw in some detail in Chapter 3, the bride is wounded by the arrow of divine love. As a result of being wounded by this arrow she herself becomes an arrow, is raised, aimed, and sent forth deeper into God.[54] There are many more such examples of divinization, especially in the *In Canticum*, and Canévet has drawn attention to many of them in her examination of such symbols of interiority and union as divine perfume.[55] There is, however, another important manifestation of divinization in Gregory of Nyssa which is very important for our present argument, i.e. the life of virtue as a manifestation of divinization, or as Meredith has called it, 'progressive deification through virtue'.[56]

Gregory begins *De beatitudinibus* v with the suggestion that the beatitude, 'blessed are the merciful, for they shall obtain mercy', should be compared with Jacob's vision of a ladder stretching from earth to

---

[52] *Orat. cat.* XXXVII, GNO III. iv. 93. 21–94. 1: οὕτω τὸ ἀθανατισθὲν ὑπὸ τοῦ θεοῦ σῶμα ἐν τῷ ἡμετέρῳ γενόμενον ὅλον πρὸς ἑαυτὸ μεταποιεῖ καὶ μετατίθη σιν. See also ibid., 94. 4: πρὸς τὴν ἑαυτοῦ φύσιν καὶ τὸ πᾶν μετεποίησεν. Trans. Richardson, in Hardy *et al.*, *Christology of the Later Fathers*, 318.

[53] *De virg.* I. 20–4.

[54] See *In Cant.* IV, GNO VI. 127–9. On this image as an image of divinization see Daley, '"Bright Darkness"', 225.

[55] Canévet, *Grégoire de Nysse et l'herméneutique biblique*, 319–30.

[56] Meredith, *The Cappadocians*, 82. See also Canévet, 'Grégoire de Nysse', cols. 996–1001, who reminds us that for Gregory virtue is not a set of qualities we must acquire, but is God dwelling within us.

heaven, with God standing on the ladder (Gen. 28: 12). This ladder of ascension is the life of virtue,[57] And because God is standing on this ladder, 'participation (μετουσία) in the beatitudes means nothing else than to commune (κοινωνία) with God'.[58] These themes of participation and union lead Gregory directly to the theme of divinization, for through the effect of this beatitude, 'he divinizes after a fashion'.[59] He continues: 'If, therefore, the term "merciful" is suited to God, what else does the Word invite you to become but God?'[60] Virtue, then, in this instance mercy, is a manifestation of the effects of divine union.

Another clear example of this is seen in the *De oratione dominica* v. Gregory says that a person who is at the summit of virtue is 'almost no longer shown in terms of human nature, but, through virtue, becomes like God Himself, so that he seems to be another god, in that he does those things that God alone can do'.[61] Here the theme of ascent in virtue stands to the fore, and in this context mounting the heights of virtue implies or manifests a divinizing union in which the person becomes like God.[62] Gregory says that if a person imitates characteristics associated with God, that person becomes what he imitates.[63] For Gregory forgiveness is a virtue, a characteristic of God. By imitating this virtue we become like what we imitate. Virtue, then is both a manifestation of divine life and a means of divinization, or as Meredith has put it, 'progressive deification through virtue'.

Having situated the theme of virtue in the context of divinizing union I would like to look more closely at this theme, especially as it occurs in

---

[57] *De beat.* v, GNO vii. ii. 123. 20–124. 5.

[58] Ibid., 124. 13–14,

[59] Ibid., 124. 16: Δοκεῖ οὖν μοι θεοποιεῖν τρόπον τινὰ…

[60] Ibid., 124. 24–6: εἰ οὖν πρέπουσατῷ θεῷ ἡ προσηγορία τοῦ ἐλεήμονος, τί ἄλλο καὶ οὐχὶ θεόν σε προκαλεῖται γενέσθαι ὁ λόγος, οἱονεὶ μορφωθέντα τῷ τῆς θεότητος ἰδιώματι; Trans. H. Graef, *The Lord's Prayer, The Beatitudes*, Ancient Christian Writers 18 (New York, 1954), 131.

[61] *De orat. dom.* v, GNO vii. ii. 59. 4–6: …ἀλλα'αὐτῷ τῷ θεῷ διὰ τῆς ἀρετῆς ὁμοιούμενον, ὥστε δοκεῖν ἄλλον εἶναι ἐκεῖνον ἐν τῷ ταῦτα ποιεῖν ἃ τοῦ θεοῦ μόνου ἐστὶ ποιεῖν. Trans. Graef, 71, adapted.

[62] Gregory goes so far as to equate virtue with divine life itself at *In Cant.* ix, GNO vi. 285. 14–17: ἐλέσθω δὲ ἐξ ἑκατέρων ἢ τοῦ ἀκροατοῦ κρίσις ὃ βούλεται, εἴτε τὸ ἕτερον ἐξ αὐτῶν εἴτε ἀμφότερα· ἐν γὰρ τρόπον τινά ἐστιν ἀμφότερα ἥ τε τῆς τελείας ἀρετῆς καὶ ἡ τῆς θεότητος κτῆσις· οὐ γὰρ ἔξω ἡ ἀρετὴ τῆς θεότητος. See also *De beat.* vi, GNO vii. ii. 144, 2–4.

[63] *De orat. dom.* v, GNO vii. ii. 59. 9–11: εἰ τοίνυν τις ἐν τῷ ἰδίῳ βίῳ μιμήσαιτο τῆς θείας φύσεως τὰ γνωρίσματα, ἐκεῖνο γίνεται τρόπον τινὰ οὗτὴν μίμησιν ἐναργῶς ἐπεδείξατο.

the *In Canticum*, for it is here that we see the dominant role of the Holy
Spirit in this transformation, a role characterized notably by a luminosity
that never gives way to darkness.

Light of the Holy Spirit   In Homily 13 Gregory speaks of the Bridegroom as the bridal torch of the Holy Spirit's splendour.[64] It is just one
example among many pneumatological images of light throughout the
In Canticum. In Homily 7, for example, Gregory emphasizes the role of
the Holy Spirit, again in the imagery of light, as he comments on Song
4: 6: 'Until the day breathes and the shadows depart.'[65] Gregory means
us to associate the work of the Holy Spirit with illumination.[66] The
Holy Spirit breathes light that dispels error[67] and brings forth children
of light.[68] This association of the Holy Spirit with transformation in
light is something which Gregory does with some consistency throughout the *In Canticum*. It constitutes an important example of divine union
irrespective of both the notion of divine darkness and those scriptural
texts which undergird the theme of divine darkness.

In Homily 4 on the Song Gregory comments on a passage which
clearly lends itself to a description of divine communion in the
language of light: 'Behold, you are beautiful my companion; behold
you are beautiful; your eyes are doves' (Song 1: 15). This image of the
dove introduces the theme of the Holy Spirit which features prominently
in the soul's divinization in light.

Gregory says the text teaches us about the restoration of beauty which
the bride gained when she approached true beauty. It is important to
note that for Gregory this beauty which the bride acquires is not
something she has never before known; it is restoration of beauty. But
before going any further with this restoration of beauty, which Gregory
describes in terms of light, he situates this in his image theory and notes
how human nature is like a reflection that mirrors whatever is impressed
upon the free will.[69] Therefore when the soul has been purified by the

---

[64] *In Cant.* XIII, GNO VI. 388. 9–10.   [65] *In Cant.* VII, GNO VI. 239. 10–11.

[66] Ibid., 240. 3–4: χρὴ νοεῖν τὸ πνεῦμα τὸ ἅγιον ἢ φῶς καὶ ἡμέραν,...

[67] Ibid., 239. 13 and 18.

[68] Ibid., 240. 2. Gregory follows the other Cappadocians in associating the Holy Spirit
with light, divinization, beauty, and the bestowal of knowledge; for Basil see, for example
Ep. CCXXXIII. 1; *De spir. sanct.* XLVII; for Gregory Nazianzen see, for example *Orat.*
XXXI. 28–9 and *Orat.* XLI, *passim*.

[69] *In Cant.* IV, GNO VI. 104. 2–4: κατόπτρῳ γάρ ἔοικεν ὡς ἀληθῶς τὸ ἀνθρώ-
πινον κατὰ τὰς τῶν προαιρέσεων ἐμφάσεις μεταμορφούμενον· That Gregory
locates the divine image in the will is characteristic of his image theory generally

Word it receives in itself the orb of the sun and shines within the bride by means of this light.[70] The Word sees his own beauty shining from within the bride and says to her, 'you have become beautiful by drawing close to my light, by being drawn (ἐφελκυσαμένη) to me you commune with beauty'.[71]

Hence, while the bride has known the darkness of sin, she has moved into the light of communion with the Word and been beautified in this process. This text is significant, for while at first glance it depicts a movement from darkness to light, there is no hint of this light being superseded by subsequent movement into the divine darkness. However, the light that Gregory mentions in his interpretation of Song 1: 15 is not the same light which we saw superseded by divine darkness in Homily 11 on the Song and in the *De vita Moysis*. There the light superseded by divine darkness referred to a quite specific type of knowledge: withdrawal from false opinions about God and from what the senses have come to understand and consider.[72] Likely the principle reason why Gregory speaks of it in the language of light is the scriptural model on which he has grafted his notion of noetic ascent, namely the beginning of Moses' journey up Mount Sinai at Exod. 19: 3 (with possible support from the light of the Burning Bush at Horeb, Exod. 3: 2)[73] that constitutes the first stage of Moses' ascent in *De vita Moysis* II. 162 and repeated in Homily 11 on the Song. The light spoken of here, as Gregory comments on Song 1: 15, is a different sort of light altogether. Quite unrelated to the light of Horeb it is the light that results from communion with divine beauty, the light that results from divinization, the work of the Holy Spirit, already suggested by the word ἐφέλκω and especially by the image of the dove. For Gregory this light is never overcome by darkness.

---

and constitutes a notable departure from Origen, who locates it in the mind. The fact that the divine image is placed in the will implies the importance of the virtues in the restoration of the image and suggests in part why Gregory places the virtues on an equal par with knowledge.

[70] Ibid., 104. 10–13.   [71] Ibid., 104. 13–15.

[72] *In Cant.* XI, GNO VI. 322. 13–15; *De vita Moysis*, SC, II. 19. 21–9 and 162. 4–6. Viewing the matter from the perspective of the scale of knowledge which διάνοια is capable of performing, presented in Chapter 2, this level of knowledge would be rather at the lower end of the scale, just after διάνοια moves from things concerned with the world of the senses and turns towards the more discursive concerns of the mind, but far from the further reaches of διάνοια when it, for example, enters the Holy of Holies.

[73] See note 23 above.

The Word looks at the bride once again and sees her increased beauty and says, 'behold you are beautiful'.[74] The Word then looks into her eyes, sees the image of a dove and says 'your eyes are doves'.[75] Gregory explains how it is that the Word comes to see doves in the eyes of the bride. When someone's eyes are pure and clean one who looks into these eyes can see one's own face reflected in them. The eye, then, that gazes at an object receives in itself the image of that object.[76] In the present case it is the Word looking into the eyes of the bride, who, having been purified, has thus received this image. The image of itself which the Word sees is that of a dove, the Holy Spirit; the luminous beauty which the Word sees in the bride is the light and beauty of the Holy Spirit. But the bride too can look at the Word. How is this possible when only like can know, or in this instance see, like?[77] Gregory reminds us that the soul that is freed of bodily attachments, has in its eyes the image of the dove, that is to say, 'the seal of the spiritual life shines' within.[78] With this seal of the dove shining within, the soul is capable of gazing upon the beauty of the Bridegroom.[79]

The trinitarian context in which the bride finds herself stands in bold relief. The light and beauty which God the Word sees in the bride is God the Holy Spirit, which itself has rendered her capable of gazing upon the Word who gazes at himself (as Holy Spirit) in her. It is a profound experience of divinizing union in which the bride is suffused in divine characteristics of light and beauty. In the description of union Gregory has made no mention of the divine darkness; nor does this luminous state of the bride give way to any such darkness. The reason for his preference for light over dark in this description of union is twofold. First, the scriptural text which Gregory is interpreting (Song 1: 15: 'Behold, you are beautiful, my companion; behold you are beautiful; your eyes are doves') does not lend itself to commentary along the lines of divine darkness; irrespective of texts which lend themselves to interpretation along such lines (e.g. Exod. 20: 21; Ps. 17 (18): 12, etc.) Gregory does not concern himself with the theme of divine darkness. Second, in this commentary on Song 1: 15 he is not concerned with the knowability of the divine nature, which is always among his epistemological concerns in the interpretation of divine darkness texts. Instead Gregory is concerned with the role of the Holy Spirit in the bride's transforming union,

---

[74] See note 23 above. 105. 2.   [75] Ibid., 105. 4–5.   [76] Ibid., 105. 9–17.
[77] Gregory is generally faithful to this ancient principle.
[78] Ibid., 106. 3–4.   [79] Ibid., 106. 6–7.

which he tends to describe in language of purification, beauty, vision, and light.

The luminous quality of the bride's experience, and the fact that, because 'she has the dove in her eyes', she can gaze upon the Bridegroom's beauty, stands very much to the fore in this passage. The concerns for light and vision are evocative of Gregory's description in the *Oratio catechetica* of the original human nature created to participate in, to see, and to enjoy divine light and hence requires something of that light in its nature in order to do so. This light implies a certain knowing. From our discussions of union in Chapters 3, 5, and 6, we know that there is a tendency for Gregory to connect union and knowledge: faith gives something to mind. This should also be kept in mind when considering that union in light and beauty wrought by the Holy Spirit. The luminous quality of the bride and her capacity to see the beauty of the Bridegroom implies a certain knowledge also bestowed by the Holy Spirit.

What this shows is that Gregory has more than one way of describing union. There is that union in darkness beyond knowledge in Homilies 6 and 11 and there is divinizing union wrought by the Holy Spirit, bestower of light and knowledge. The one is described in the language of darkness, the other in the language of beauty and light. Let us consider some other texts which demonstrate this preference for light.

Ascent in Virtue   As we saw earlier in Homily 5, Gregory depicts the Bridegroom exhorting the bride to advance in virtue. This exhortation, as we noted, is set in a general context of salvation history, described in imagery of increasing light. The Church receives the ray of truth through the windows of the prophets and the lattices of the Law. Gregory likens the Law to a wall which forms a shadow (σκιάν) of things to come. The truth stands behind this wall. But when the revelation of the gospel comes, the wall is torn down and the darkness of the shadow gives way to the light of the gospel.[80] It is worth pointing out that Gregory has described the broad movement of salvation history in the language of increasing light. The only mention of darkness is the shadow employed as a metaphor for the Law, darkness that gives way to light with the full revelation of the gospel. Within this context of salvation history as increasing light, Gregory prepares to comment on the words of the Bridegroom addressed to the

---

[80]   *In Cant.* v, GNO vi. 148. 7–20.

bride in Song 2: 10: 'Arise, my companion, my beautiful one, my dove.' Because the words of the Bridegroom are efficacious,[81] she begins her ascent. Up to now this study has focused on the epistemological ascents of the bride, but here, in a general context of salvation history as increasing light, we see the bride called to ascend not to the darkness of unknowing but in greater virtue: 'Arise... and go forward through advancement in the good, finishing the race in virtue.'[82] In the context of this ascent in virtue, we see the bride transformed in light through divinization by the Holy Spirit. In response, then, to the efficacious power of the Word which bids her arise, the bride immediately does so and 'stands up, comes towards and is near the light'.[83]

Gregory sees in the very order of the words of Song 2: 10 an indication of the nature of her movement into light. 'She arises, approaches, draws near, becomes beautiful, is called a dove.'[84] As Gregory explains the bride's transformation, he introduces his image theory: human nature is like a mirror that became beautiful only 'when it drew close to beauty and was transformed by the image of divine beauty'.[85] He then equates this beauty with light and both of these with the presence of the Holy Spirit symbolized by the dove: 'Hence, by drawing close to the light, human nature becomes light and in this light it is moulded into the beautiful form of the dove, I mean that dove which declared the presence of the Holy Spirit.'[86]

Gregory's interpretation of Song 2: 10, therefore, presents us with an image of divinizing union, once again under the aegis of the Holy Spirit, in which human nature is transformed in divine light and beauty. Though no technical word is used for union, the sense of this passage is clearly in this direction, and if not union then something very close indeed, for by its proximity to this light human nature is transformed and takes on the qualities of the divine light in which it stands.

---

[81] *In Cant.* v, GNO vi. 149. 11–17.

[82] Ibid., 149. 4–6: οὐκ ἀρκεῖ δέ σοι, φησί, τὸ ἀνορθωθῆναι μόνον ἐκ τοῦ πτώματος, ἀλλὰ καὶ πρόελθε διὰ τῆς τῶν ἀγαθῶν προκοπῆς τὸν ἐν ἀρετῇ διανύουσα δρόμον. Cf. 2 Tim. 4: 7.

[83] Ibid., 150. 1–2.   [84] Ibid., 150. 7–8.

[85] Ibid., 150. 12–13: ἀλλ' ὅτε τῷ καλῷ ἐπλησίασε καὶ τῇ εἰκόνι τοῦ θείου κάλλους ἐνεμορφώθη.

[86] Ibid., 150. 18–151. 2: βλέπει δὲ πρὸς τὸ ἀρχέτυπον κάλλος. διὰ τοῦτο τῷ φωτὶ προσεγγίσασα φῶς γίνεται, τῷ δὲ φωτὶ τὸ καλὸν τῆς περιστερᾶς εἶδος ἐνεικονίζεται, ἐκείνης λέγω τῆς περιστερᾶς, ἧς τὸ εἶδος τὴν τοῦ ἁγίου πνεύματος παρουσίαν ἐγνώρισεν.

Gregory depicts the perfection of virtue along these lines because he thinks that the order of the words in Song 2: 10 suggests this itinerary of ascent and transformation in light and beauty.[87] The sequence of this itinerary is clearly one of increasing light. Moreover, Gregory has situated it in the context of salvation history, itself depicted as darkness that gives way to the full dawning of light. What needs especially to be emphasized, however, is the role of the Holy Spirit in facilitating this union in which human nature is 'moulded into the beautiful form of a dove', and it is important to observe that the virtues are the manifestation of this divinizing activity. Human nature becoming light should once again remind us of the light that characterized its original condition in which the light of God is seen and enjoyed. Hence, this light of divinized virtue should not be separated from, much less subordinated to, the light in which God is seen and in some sense known.

Not all transformation in light, however, is accomplished explicitly under the aegis of the Holy Spirit; but its presence should not be ruled out of the activity of purification. While these transformations are subtle indeed, they are no less important, for they pertain to the attainment of ἀπάθεια, and therefore are tantamount to becoming like God. For example, in Homily 8 Gregory comments on Song 4: 9: 'You have ravished our heart, our sister, our bride.' In order to lay the groundwork for the interpretation he wishes to pursue Gregory first draws a parallel between the creative power of the Word at creation and the Word's bidding the soul to draw close. As creation came into being at the Word's ordinance, in the same way when the Word bids the soul to draw close to him 'the soul is changed into something divine'. Hence, the glory that the soul already had is transformed into something even more glorious, divinized, 'changed into something divine'.[88] Therefore, the angels marvel at the bride. With Song 4: 9 on their lips as they say: 'You have have ravished our hearts, our sister our spouse.' He goes on to specify what precisely has happened in this transformation by identifying the meaning of 'sister' and 'spouse'. Because in this transformation she has taken on the divine characteristic of dispassion (ἀπαθείας) she is

---

[87] Gregory's exegesis of Song 2: 10 reveals a clear similarity to that of Origen, *Comm. in Cant.*, GCS, iv. 223. 21–5. Cf Canévet, *Grégoire de Nysse et l'herméneutique biblique*, 129. However, it is interesting to note that Gregory places more emphasis than Origen on the role of light and beauty.

[88] *In Cant.* viii, GNO vi. 253: 8–18, esp. 15–16: μεταποιηθεῖσα πρὸς τὸ θειότερον.

called 'sister' and because she attains union (συνάφειαν) with the Word she is called 'spouse'.[89]

Apart from the important connection Gregory draws between creation, the soul's divinizing union, and the mediation of both by the Word, what is important for the present purpose is to observe that this transformation of the passions into dispassion is described again in the language of light: 'for the seal of dispassion illumines the bride'.[90]

This connection between divinizing union and radiance is also seen in Homily 15 where Gregory comments on Song 6: 3: 'I am my Beloved's, and my Beloved is mine.' Gregory's interpretation of this passage reveals once again a description of divine union in the language of light. It is a text which easily lends itself to the ensuing presentation of divinization and virtue which emphasizes the indwelling presence of Christ and especially union with Christ, and the manifestation of this union.

Gregory begins by focusing on the words of the pure and undefiled bride ('I am my Beloved's, and my Beloved is mine') and immediately aligns this image of mutual possession with the notion of perfection in virtue.[91] Her perfection means that in conforming to Christ she is made beautiful according to the image and likeness of the original beauty in which she was created.[92] The soul, Gregory says, is a living mirror that possesses free will; when she beholds the face of the Beloved, his beauty is reflected in her face.[93] The divine presence of indwelling beauty Gregory likens to Paul's experience of being dead to the world, alive to God and having Christ alone living in him (Rom. 6: 11; Gal. 2: 20). Paul's statement in Philippians 1: 20 ('for me to live is Christ') is, according to Gregory, exactly what the bride means when she says, 'I am my

---

[89] *In Cant.* VIII, GNO VI. 254. 6–8.

[90] Ibid., 254. 1–2: ὁ γὰρ τῆς ἀπαθείας χαρακτὴρ ὁμοίως ἐπιλάμπων... Gregory makes a similar connection between ἀπάθεια and radiance (διαυγής) at *In Cant.* IX, GNO VI. 276. 13–15.

[91] *In Cant.* XV, GNO VI. 439, 5: κανὼν καὶ ὅρος τῆς κατ ἀρετήν ἐστι τελειότητος.

[92] Ibid., 439. 17–20. For another example of Gregory's image theory stated from the perspective of beauty see *De beat.* VI, GNO VII. ii. 143–4.

[93] Ibid., 440. 7–10. The phrase, 'τὸ προαιρετικόν τε καὶ ἔμψυχον κάτοπτρον' is a clear example that Gregory locates the divine image in the will and not in the mind as suggested by Gross, *Divinisation du Chrétien*, 223. See Meredith, *The Cappadocians*, 56–7: '[Gregory] came to see that the root of the image of God in us was not so much in the intellectual powers possessed by us as in the freedom of the will. However, this emphasis on the centrality of freedom seems to have been something Gregory grew into rather than began with.'

Beloved's and my Beloved is mine.'[94] This indwelling union with Christ, on the part of Paul or the bride, is what holiness is, says Gregory, and he goes on to describe it in the language of light.

The second half of the *lemma* upon which Gregory is commenting (Song 6: 3a: 'I am my Beloved's and my Beloved is mine') reads, 'he pastures me amongst the lilies'. The lilies, he tells us, symbolize the virtues which nourish the soul.[95] Lilies are radiant and, by implication, virtues too are associated with light; the virtues nourish the soul and make it likewise radiant.[96] This light that shines from within the virtuous soul is the divine presence itself, 'the radiance of the Lord' (Ps. 89: 17). In some of the Homilies we have considered (Homilies 4 and 5) the luminosity of divinized virtue occurs specifically under the guidance of the Holy Spirit. In other Homilies (8 and 15), the explicit role of the Holy Spirit is more difficult to discern, or is accomplished through union with the indwelling Word.

For Gregory, then, virtue is the outward manifestation of divinization, manifesting outwardly the divine presence in which it participates. Perhaps the finest example of this is seen in his likening the luminous lilies of virtue in the soul to a bouquet of lilies placed in a crystal vase. The lilies within the crystal vase can be clearly seen from without. Likewise, one who places the radiance of the lilies within the soul renders the soul diaphanous to the light shining from within.[97] The virtues, then, radiate outwardly the divine presence within the purified soul. Gregory's interpretation of this *lemma* that emphasizes indwelling communion draws to a close with the bride giving herself to the Beloved and being beautified in his beauty.[98]

Conclusion

(A) On the basis of the texts we have considered, chiefly in the *Commentarius in Canticum canticorum*, it is clear that for all Gregory's concern for what has been termed by Puech, Daniélou, Crouzel, and many others a 'mysticism of darkness', there is a consistent strand in Gregory's

---

[94] Ibid., 441. 1–3.

[95] Ibid., 441. 20: κρίνα δὲ κατονομάζει τὰς ἀρετὰς δι᾽αἰνίγματος

[96] Ibid., 442. 1–3.

[97] Ibid., 441. 15–18. On this image of the crystal vase employed by Gregory see Canévet, *Grégoire de Nysse et l'herméneutique biblique*, 328–30.

[98] Ibid., 442. 10–11.

thought that describes the heights of divine–human encounter in the language of light and beauty. If Gregory can be distinguished from Origen in his development of the theme of divine darkness,[99] he can likewise be likened to Origen in his concern for a 'mysticism of light'.[100]

(B) We have emphasized throughout this chapter the exegetical character of Gregory's doctrine on divine darkness and how this theme is linked to explicitly epistemological and apophatic concerns. Irrespective of texts which favour the theme of divine darkness, Gregory does not introduce the theme. Hence, we see it relatively infrequently and only in the course of commenting on such scriptural texts as Song 3: 1 ('By night on my bed I sought him whom my soul loves. I sought him but found him not'); Song 5: 2 ('Open, open to me ... for my head is filled with dew, and my locks with the drops of the night'); Song 5: 5–6 (' ... upon the handles of the lock. I opened to my Beloved. My Beloved was gone. My soul went forth at his word'); Exod. 20: 21; and Ps. 17: 12. In the exegesis of scriptural *lemmata* such as these, the apophatic ascent is the guiding motif, largely to emphasize the mind's inability to grasp God, an inability due not so much to the weakness of the mind as to the intrinsic unknowability of the divine essence itself. The theme of divine darkness, then, is limited to commentary on certain scriptural texts with specific epistemological and apophatic concerns regarding union with an unknowable God; apart from such texts and concerns Gregory tends to speak instead of the divinization of the soul in light.

(C) Moreover, it should be emphasized that Gregorian darkness is *epistemological* darkness. Hence, any comparison with the theme of darkness developed by later writers such as John of the Cross or Jacob Boehme, who give greater prominence to the emotional dimension and to the sense of divine absence, should exercise caution.[101] While Gregorian darkness knows well this play between presence and absence,

---

[99] Crouzel, *Origen*, 121.

[100] Many years ago Völker observed in his *Gregor von Nyssa als Mystiker* that Gregory shares with Origen, and indeed with other Alexandrians, a predilection for the symbolism of light: 'Noch in einem weiteren Punkte stimmt er [sc. Gregor] mit Origenes und den Alexandriner überhaupt überein, in seiner Vorliebe für die Lichtsymbolik' (p. 206).

[101] This is not to say that all subsequent writers on the theme of darkness do not emphasize darkness along the epistemological lines we see in Gregory. The final sections of Bonaventure's *Itinerarium mentis in Deum* would constitute a good example of the continuation of this theme in the mediaeval period; see Turner, *The Darkness of God*, esp. 102–34.

it is much more a metaphor of presence than one of absence, a metaphor which emphasizes the mind's capacity for union (supranoetic) with God, who is most intimately present, and yet who is not grasped by the mind in comprehension (grasped rather by faith). The *locus classicus* in this regard is perhaps the bride in Homily 11, who is embraced by the divine night; Gregory asks, How can the soul see what is invisible? The Bridegroom gives to the soul 'a sense of presence (αἴσθησιν... τῆς παρουσίας)'.[102] Gregorian darkness is a metaphor of union and presence.[103]

(D) When Gregory describes the divinization of the soul in light and beauty, often under the aegis of the Holy Spirit, he grounds this, like the theme of divine darkness, in scripture: Song 1: 15 ('Behold you are beautiful, my companion, behold you are beautiful; your eyes are doves'); Song 1: 16 ('Behold you are fair, my Beloved and beautiful, overshadowing our bed'); Song 2: 10 and 13 ('Arise, and come, my companion, my beautiful one, my dove; yes, come'); Song 4: 6 ('Until the day breathes and the shadows depart'); Song 4: 9 ('You have ravished our heart, our sister, our spouse'); Song 6: 3 ('I am my Beloved's and my Beloved is mine; he pastures me amongst the lilies'). These scriptural texts with their cluster of themes of beauty, ascent, the dove, light, and indwelling ground Gregory's teaching on the divinization of the virtues.

So as not to confuse exegetical lines, it is important to distinguish the light that is the first stage in the light–cloud–darkness sequence[104] from the light that is part of the ever-increasing-light sequence. This latter, the light and beauty of divinized virtue, evocative of the original condition of light in which humanity sees, and hence knows something of divine light, does not give way to divine darkness and rests on different scriptural *lemmata*, which are not used by Gregory to support the divine darkness theme. The light of divinized virtue, then, does not fit the pattern of increasing darkness (light–cloud–darkness) which not a few scholars have said defines Gregory's theory of the human experience of God. Indeed we have seen Gregory, speaking in the context of salvation

---

[102] *In Cant.* xi, GNO vi. 324. 10–11. See Canévet, 'La Perception de la présence de Dieu', 443–54.

[103] NB V. Lossky's observation in *In the Image and Likeness of God* (Crestwood, NY, 1985), 38: 'The infinite and never completed character of this union with the transcendent God is signified by darkness, which seems to be, for St. Gregory of Nyssa, a metaphor whose purpose is to remind us of a dogmatic fact.'

[104] e.g. *In Cant.* xi, GNO vi. 322. 9 and *De vita Moysis*, SC, II. 162.

history and the divinization of the virtues, present the pattern as one of increasing light.

(E) While Gregory can be likened to Origen in his use of light symbolism regarding knowledge, the Father, the Word, the Holy Spirit, an important distinction should be kept in mind particularly regarding the epistemological implications of light.[105] Both Origen and Gregory speak of knowledge as light.[106] But for Gregory the light of knowledge gives way to the darkness of unknowing in, and only in, divine-darkness texts. This is largely due to two exegetical reasons. First, Gregory adheres with singular fidelity to an inherited exegetical tradition regarding Exod. 20: 21 (*inter alia*). Puech indicated long ago the roots of this tradition in Philo and Clement, a tradition to which Origen does not adhere with any tenacity.[107] Second, following closely upon the first, Gregory's epistemology, especially the epistemological ascent, is very much an exegetical epistemology (especially in the *In Canticum*). Hence, when one considers a divine-darkness text such as *De vita Moysis* ii. 162 and *In Canticum* xi. 322, one should be aware that the ascent of Moses or the bride is described as a movement from light to dark, a description rife with apophatic terminology and motifs, because the vocabulary and imagery of the scriptural text lends itself to this.[108] In these darkness texts that feature an apophatic ascent, especially when based on Exod. 20: 21 (such as *De vita Moysis* ii. 162 and *In Canticum* xi. 322), light will relate to a

---

[105] For an overview of Origen's use of light symbolism see Crouzel, *Origène et la 'connaissance mystique'*, 130–54.

[106] Ibid., 130–1 and 152–3. As Festugière has noted, this association of light with knowledge characterizes the entire tradition, Christian and non-Christian; see *La Révélation d'Hermès Trismégiste*, 241.

[107] Puech, 'La ténèbre mystique'. I am not convinced by Crouzel's claim in 'Grégoire de Nysse' that Gregorian darkness is a development of what was already present, however incipiently, in Origen. The exegesis of, for example, Exod. 20: 21 is already well established by Philo and Clement. It seems more likely that Gregory is following (and developing) Philo and Clement than developing something that receives only minimal attention in Origen. It is Origen who departs from the Alexandrian tradition in this instance. See B. Otis, 'Nicene Orthodoxy and Fourth Century Mysticism', in *Proceedings of the XII International Congress of Byzantine Studies, Ochrid, 10–16 September 1961* (Belgrade, 1964), ii. 475–84, esp. 477–9. Speculation beyond that offered by Crouzel as to why Origen departs from Philo and Clement must await subsequent investigation. For Philo, Clement, and Origen on darkness see Puech, 'La ténèbre mystique', 133–6

[108] It might be asserted, and rightly so, that there is no Philonic-Clementine tradition on the darkness texts from the Song of Songs. However, the representative darkness texts in the *In Canticum* are riding on the shoulders of Exod. 20: 21 and Ps. 17(18): 12, which fall clearly within the Philonic-Clementine tradition.

relatively low noetic state (withdrawal from false opinions about God, withdrawal from what the senses have understood[109]) because this light is corresponding to the light that characterizes the beginning of Moses' sojourn, the scriptural model for the noetic ascent. Hence, instead of continuing in a transformation of ever greater luminosity (as we saw in *In Cant.* IV, V, VII, VIII, and XV), this 'first-stage' light gives way to the ever-increasing obscurity of cloud and darkness where God dwells simply because the sequence of scriptural images (Exod. 19: 3, 16 f.; 20: 21) undergirding the epistemological ascent dictate that it does so.

Moreover, while both Origen and Gregory speak of divinization, Origen tends to speak of the mind's divinization in the contemplation of God. In his *Commentary on John* Origen, thinking of the brilliant face of Moses descending Mount Sinai, speaks of the divinization of *nous*.[110] Gregory, by contrast, does not tend to speak of the mind itself as the subject of divinization. It is, rather, the virtues which are the subject of divinization. For Gregory the mind moves beyond the light of knowledge into the darkness of unknowing, and in this process the virtues, not the mind, are the subject of divinizing union. The mind attains to union by means of faith (and a possible way of conceiving the relationship between the mind and faith—for Gregory does not spell it out—was presented in Chapter 4); as explored in Chapters 3, 5, and 6, the mind yet receives something from this supramental union 'by faith alone'. Hence, the mind is certainly not abandoned. Knowledge and virtue participate in divine light: knowledge by means of faith, virtue by divinization.

Therefore, while we can agree with Völker that Gregory does indeed share, and in abundance, Origen's '*Vorliebe für die Lichtsymbolik*', there are subtle yet important distinctions that need to be maintained; the metaphor of the light of knowledge is a case in point, for it expresses

---

[109] See *In Cant.* XI, GNO VI. 322. 13–15; *De Vita Moysis*, SC, II. 19. 21–9 and 162. 4–6. It must be admitted that the bride's ascent at *In Cant.* XI, GNO VI. 323. 10–324. 9 does not fit as nicely into this pattern. However, this is because Gregory is presenting a summary of the growth of the bride in the previous Homilies. Hence, her ascent is stuctured by the various texts from the Song and not, as above, on the journey of Moses culminating in Exod. 20: 21.

[110] *In Jo.* XXXII. 27, GCS IV. 472. 31–4: λεκτέον τοιοῦτον εἶναι τὸ δεδοξάσθαι τὸ πρόσωπον τοῦ θεωρήσαντος τὸν θεὸν καὶ ὁμιλήσαντος αὐτῷ καὶ συνδιατρίψαντος τοιαύτη θέα, ὡς τοῦτο εἶναι τροπικῶς τὸ δεδοξασμένον πρόσωπον Μωϋσέως, θεοποιηθέντος αὐτῷ τοῦ νοῦ. Cf Gregory's treatment of Moses' descent from Mt. Sinai at *De Vita Moysis*, SC, II. 163. where there is a clear sense of the light of divinization but no sense that it was νοῦς that was divinized.

divergent positions (Gregory's from Origen's) regarding the knowability of God.

(F) Having seen that Gregory speaks of both light and darkness to describe the profoundest of divine–human encounters, and that the light that gives way to darkness in an ascent of ever-increasing darkness is not the same light of divinizing union which is never described as giving way to darkness, could not the argument still be advanced that this divine darkness must yet overcome the light of divinized virtue? For in the Platonic tradition, virtue (described by Gregory in terms of increasing light) is a means to the acquisition of knowledge and hence could be considered in the final analysis to be subordinate to knowledge. Therefore, viewing Gregory's thought as a whole, would not the light of divinized virtue be subordinate to the darkness of unknowing since virtue is a subordinated means to knowledge? Such would be a tempting position to adopt were it not for the convincing caveat established by Meredith on this very point.

In a paper given to the Seventh International Colloquium on Gregory of Nyssa, as well as in a more elaborated position taken in *The Cappadocians*, Meredith states that 'the close connexion between the love of and discovery of truth on the one hand and the reformation of life on the other owes much to the Platonic tradition, above all in the language which is used to express the upward search for the transcendent. The relation, however, between these two elements, the intellectual and the moral, has been significantly modified.'[111] Whereas 'the Platonist tradition had tended to subordinate virtue to knowledge, ethics to epistemology, while believing that there existed a close connection between the two',[112] Gregory does not show this subordination. Whilst Gregory likewise maintains a close relationship between the two, they are not cast in a relationship of subordination but kept on an equal level and in 'a two-way' relationship.[113] This may not illustrate Gregory's early view on the matter in *De virginitate*, arguably his earliest work, but it does characterize his later works; 'virtue is not only the condition of the possibility of knowledge, knowledge also serves as a step towards greater

---

[111] 'Homily One' in S. Hall and R. Moriarty (eds. and trans.), *Gregory of Nyssa: Homilies on Ecclesiastes* (Berlin, 1993), 146–7. Meredith has in mind certain texts which are particularly illustrative of the view that the Platonist tradition tends to subordinate ethics to epistemology; for Plato, Meredith cites *Phaedrus* 249d; *Symposium* 210a–211c; for Aristotle, *Nicomachean Ethics* 10. 7; for Plotinus, *Ennead* 6. 9. 11.

[112] Meredith, *The Cappadocians*, 59.   [113] Ibid., 61.

moral perfection. In other words there is a dialectical relationship between the two.'[114]

The fact that Gregory of Nyssa maintains virtue and knowledge on the same level, not subordinating one to the other, has clear implications for the respective roles of virtue and knowledge in his theory of divine union. Gregory's doctrine on union through the 'progressive deification through virtue' in light should not be subordinated to his theory of union in the darkness of unknowing. Moreover, purely within the context of the light imagery itself (i.e. the darkness texts aside) we have seen that for Gregory light embraces concerns for both knowledge and virtue: in the *Oratio catechetica* human nature was created that it might see, and therefore know in some sense, this divine Light; thus something of that light was in its original nature; in the ascents in virtue which we see in the *In Canticum*, human nature is 'transformed into something divine',[115] likewise characterized by light.

Therefore, Gregory's theory of divine union should be considered no less one of light than one of darkness. When considering passages which are particularly illustrative of Gregory's 'mysticism of darkness' one should avoid concluding that this encounter with God in increasing darkness characterizes Gregory's thought as a whole; it characterizes one part of the dialectic within which he clearly situates himself within the 'mysticism of darkness' tradition inherited from Philo and Clement, grounded in quite specific biblical passages and expressive of decidedly apophatic concerns. But it is not the whole picture.

(G) Perhaps the texts which scholars propose as particularly illustrative of Gregory's mysticism of darkness (one thinks principally of *De vita Moysis* II. 162; *In Cant.* VI and XIII) have been given too great an emphasis and have not been satisfactorily situated and interpreted in light of the general structure of his thought. Keeping in mind that the darkness of God is for Gregory a 'luminous dark' (λαμπρός

---

[114] Ibid. A very good example of this can be seen in the way in which Gregory uses the same symbol to speak of both knowledge and virtue in the space of a few lines. In Homily 15 on the Song Gregory tells us that the lily is symbol of a luminous pure mind (*In Cant.* XV, GNO VI. 438. 10–11: τὰ μὲν γὰρ κρίνα τοῦ λαμπροῦ καὶ καθαροῦ τῆς διανοίας αἴνιγμα γίνεται). However, some three pages on and still commenting on the same *lemma* Gregory says that the lilies are the virtues which nourish the soul (*In Cant.* XV, GNO VI. 441. 20: κρίνα δὲ κατονομάζει τὰς ἀρετὰς δι' αἰνίγματος). See Meredith for other texts illustrative of this point.

[115] *In Cant.* VIII, GNO VI. 253. 15–16: μεταποιηθεῖσα πρὸς τὸ θειότερον....

γνόφος),[116] perhaps the less-cited darkness-text in *In Canticum* XII is more representative of his position.

In the course of commenting on Song 5: 6, 'my soul went forth at his word', Gregory presents a catalogue of Moses' ascents in order to illustrate the incessant growth of the Patriarch.[117] At the end of this catalogue he says that Moses entered the cloud and then the darkness where God was. But Gregory does not stop here as he did in *De vita Moysis* II. 162 and *In Canticum* XI, when in the midst of an apophatic, epistemological ascent, he emphasized the pattern of increasing darkness. Here in Homily 12 Gregory adds that Moses becomes like the sun and is unable to be approached by those who are drawing near because of the light beaming from his face (cf. Exod. 34: 29–30).[118] This transformation in light occurs while Moses is in the darkness. Clearly light is not subordinated to darkness, just as for Gregory virtue is not subordinated to knowledge, even that knowledge which is an unknowing. Moses enters the darkness where God is but becomes luminous; he moves ever deeper in unknowing but grows increasingly in light. Whether the luminous quality surrounding the Patriarch is the light of knowledge consequent upon union beyond knowledge, or whether it is the light of divinized virtue, Gregory does not say with any precision. Based on what we have seen throughout this study regarding the relationship between union and knowledge, he would not want us to choose one to the exclusion of the other.

It has remained unquestioned throughout this chapter that Gregory of Nyssa is an exponent of the so-called 'mysticism of darkness', but he also expounds a 'mysticism of light'. To suggest that he proposes one as opposed to the other, as has been the decided tendency of twentieth-century scholarship on Gregory of Nyssa, not only reflects a hasty reading of one of his principle works on the matter in question, the *Commentarius in Canticum canticorum*, but obscures our understanding of the structure of his thought.

---

[116] *De vita Moysis*, SC, II. 163.

[117] *In Cant.* XII, GNO VI. 354. 13 ff.

[118] *In Cant.* XII, GNO VI. 355. 11–14: τὴν νεφέλην ὑπέρχεται, ἐντὸς τοῦ γνόφου γίνεται ἐν ᾧ ἦν ὁ Θεός, τὴν διαθήκην δέχεται, ἥλιος γίνεται ἀπροσπέλαστον τοῖς προσεγγίζουσιν ἐκ τοῦ προσώπου τὸ φῶς ἀπαστράπτων.

Conclusion

This study began with an attempt to determine the *status quaestionis* regarding Gregorian faith with a view to assessing what elements might sustain further development so that the current research might be advanced. Two authors, whose contribution to Gregorian scholarship is unquestioned, have, nevertheless, drawn conclusions regarding the relationship between knowledge and faith that stand in need of further nuance, indeed correction: Bernard Pottier has argued that 'the passage from knowledge to faith appears as a rupture'.[1] Moreover, he continues, 'faith, in the night, touches God as he is—but it is not knowledge'.[2] Walther Völker observed quite rightly that when Gregory spoke of faith in the exalted manner in which he did, supplanting knowledge by faith, he forsook the Alexandrian tradition in which faith was overcome by knowledge.[3] Völker also suggested, however, that Gregory, like Philo, gives faith no technical meaning.[4] Moreover, Völker maintained that Gregory has left to one side the question of the relationship between faith and knowledge and the relationship between

---

[1] *Dieu et le Christ*, 207: 'Le passage de la connaissance à la foi … se donne comme une rupture.' V. Harrison has a more cautious evaluation of this when she says that in the pilgrimage of the mind, faith 'surpasses' knowldege; see her *Grace and Human Freedom*, 68.

[2] Pottier, *Dieu et le Christ*, 209: 'la foi, dans la nuit, touche Dieu tel qu'il est—ce n'est pourtant pas une connaissance'.

[3] *Gregor von Nyssa als Mystiker*, 141 n. 7: 'In dieser hohen Wertung des Glaubens verläßt Gregor die Bahnen der christlichen Alexandriner'. In support of his view, which I share, Völker has in mind an important passage from Homily 3 on the Song, which this thesis has considered in some detail (*In Cant.* III, GNO VI. 87. 5–9, esp. the phrase, διὰ μόνης πίστεως.

[4] Ibid., 140: 'Könnten wir bei Philo beobachten, daß das Wort πίστις kein fester terminus technicus ist, sondern in verschiedenen Bedeutungen verwandt wird, so ist Gregor wenig interessiert.' Cf. idem, *Fortschritt und Vollendung bei Philo von Alexandrien*, 244 n. 1.

faith and grace.[5] By contrast, I have argued that the positions of Pottier and Völker on the matters stated are unsatisfactory.

In order to gain some insight into what exalted Gregorian faith is capable of and what it is not capable of, as well as some understanding of its relationship to knowledge, Chapter 2 followed with an examination of what Gregory said about the discursive and non-discursive activities of the mind. Amongst the various terms which Gregory can employ in this regard (*dianoia, nous, psyche*), *dianoia* was found to open up the field most satisfactorily. Whilst the intention of this chapter was largely by way of preparing to respond to Pottier and Völker, it was observed under the lens of *dianoia* that Gregory's notion of the mind was characterized by dynamism and flow.

We saw that Gregory parted company with the hierarchized epistemological structure of the Allegory of the Line. Instead, he used the same terms, whether *nous* or *dianoia*, in a fluid way, as we saw that the mind could flow from one state to another, according to the level of ascetic accomplishment: passionate struggle, tasks of ratiocination, discursive contemplation of the intelligibles; we even saw that *dianoia* could enter the non-discursive Holy of Holies, the darkness of God's presence. Each level of the mind was characterized by a certain state. The lowest state was characterized by passionate struggle and described as thick, dispersed, or grasping. We saw the grace of baptism to be particularly efficacious at this level as it unclenched the fists of the grasping mind. Nor did the mind enter the Holy of Holies unassisted by grace; we saw scripture lead *dianoia* into the sanctuary of divine presence. From the beginning, then, the noetic ascent is a graced one.

However, while it was important to notice that once in this sanctuary the mind did not grasp the Beloved in comprehension, the mind yet underwent something very important and very subtly expressed by Gregory. In Homily 11 on the Song, Gregory said that the Word touched the door of *dianoia* in its discursive search for what was ineffable. Through this same *dianoia* the sought-after Beloved came to dwell.[6] While the mind did not grasp the Beloved in comprehension, it allowed the Beloved to enter and take up residence. In this posture of receptivity the mind received something, a reception which Gregory described in the delicate imagery of dew drops. In the sanctuary of divine presence

---

[5] *Gregor von Nyssa als Mystiker*, 141.

[6] *In Cant.* xi, GNO vi. 324. 13–15: ἅπτεται τῆς θύρας ὁ λόγος. θύραν δὲ νοοῦμεν τὴν στοχαστικὴν τῶν ἀρρήτων διάνοιαν, δι' ἧς εἰσοικίζεται τὸ ζητούμενον.

the mind does not receive 'a swollen torrent of knowledge, ... but must be content if truth bedew one's knowledge with delicate and indistinct insights'.[7] Hence, the mind was capable of two things in the sanctuary of divine presence: (1) reception of indwelling presence, an aspect of which involves (2) a knowing encounter, in which the mind is somehow bedewed with indistinct insights.

As subtly expressed as this intimacy between the mind and the divine presence is, this intimacy received considerable emphasis in Chapter 2, for it prepared the way for Chapter 3's discussion of the grasp of faith. For though the mind received something from its encounter in the Holy of Holies, the darkness of God's presence, the mind did not grasp the Beloved. This function of union is reserved not to the grasp of comprehension but to the grasp of faith, which was examined in Chapter 3. We saw especially in Homilies 3 and 6 on the Song that one of the effects of union by the grasp of faith was the passing on to the discursive mind something of what faith had grasped in the darkness of divine presence. This placed *dianoia* and *pistis* in a very close relationship indeed, and for this reason I maintain that Völker's claim that Gregory did not consider the relationship between knowledge and faith and that Pottier's description of the distinction between knowledge and faith (and certainly there is one) as one of 'rupture' were not faithful to the texts themselves; for the texts consistently revealed what Canévet described as the tendency of faith to translate its intuitions into concepts.[8] While there is an important and consistent discontinuity between knowledge and faith, there is also an important and consistent continuity between the two.

How then to express this relationship between the mind and faith? It has to be said that Gregory does not always seem to be very clear on the matter. As we have seen, both *dianoia* and *pistis* can mediate the indwelling presence of God. In Homily 11 on the Song it was *dianoia* which stood as the door which the Word touches and through which the Word enters and dwells.[9] But in Homily 4, it was *pistis*, as the tip of the arrow, which mediated the indwelling presence.[10] Hence, both *dianoia* and *pistis*

[7] Ibid., 325. 21–326. 5: οὐ γάρ ἐστι δυνατὸν τὸν ἐντὸς τῶν ἀδύτων τε καὶ ἀθεωρήτων γενόμενον ὄμβρῳ τινὶ τῆς γνώσεως ἐντυχεῖν ἢ χειμάρρῳ ἀλλ᾽ ἀγαπητὸν εἰ λεπταῖς τισι καὶ ἀμυδραῖς διανοίαις ἐπιψεκάζοι τὴν γνῶσιν αὐτῶν ἡ ἀλήθεια διὰ τῶν ἁγίων τε καὶ θεοφορουμένων τῆς λογικῆς σταγόνος ἀπορρεούσης.

[8] Canévet, *Grégoire de Nysse et l'herméneutique biblique*, 63: 'Cette connaissance [sc. l'intuition de la foi] essaie cependant de se traduire en pensées, bien que l'infinité de l'essence divine soit incompatible avec le caractère défini de nos concepts.'

[9] *In Cant.* XI, GNO VI. 324. 13–15.   [10] *In Cant.* IV, GNO VI. 128 ff.

can mediate the same graced encounter. However, this is not to say that the two are synonymous. While the two can at times overlap, when Gregory wants to be quite specific and emphasize the experience of union, he will employ *pistis*. Herein lies the difference: both *dianoia* and exalted *pistis* can enter the Holy of Holies, the darkness wherein God dwells, but in this non-discursive sanctuary *dianoia* is purely receptive; it cannot perform its characteristic grasp of comprehension. *Pistis*, by contrast, can yet grasp; not a cognitive grasp of comprehension but a grasp of union beyond images and concepts. The bride herself has stated it perhaps the most succinctly: 'when I let go of every sort of comprehension, I found the Beloved ... by the grasp of faith'.[11] Hence, while both terms can be used to mediate divine indwelling, Gregory can also be more specific and indicate the difference between exalted *pistis* and *dianoia*. *Pistis* can do what *dianoia* cannot do: grasp the Beloved. Having grasped the Beloved it can then pass on to *dianoia* something of what it has grasped of the Beloved.[12] Between *dianoia* and *pistis*, then, there is as much rapport as rupture.

In contrast to Völker's claim that Gregory does not use the term 'faith' in a technical sense, this study argues the exact opposite. Based on an examination of representative texts in the *Contra Eunomium*, *De vita Moysis*, and *Commentarius in Canticum canticorum*, Gregory's reserved use of 'faith' can rightly be considered a *terminus technicus*. When used in certain apophatic contexts, whether or not there be an explicit epistemological ascent in which faith is always the summit, such as we saw in the migration of Abraham or in the case of the bride in Homily 6 on the Song of Songs, faith takes on a technical meaning which designates the means by which the soul attains to divine union. Such union, as we have seen, yields a number of results: faith renders the soul a dwelling place of God; faith expands the soul's desire for God even as the soul delights in God; faith does what the discursive mind can never do: grasp the incomprehensible nature of God; faith nevertheless passes on to the mind something of what it has grasped of the Ungraspable. These are the principal functions of faith when seen in its technical sense of bridging the gap between the mind and God.

Moreover, the technical meaning of faith is often rendered by a particular grammatical morphology. The mediational sense which technical faith serves is often expressed conveniently either as an

---

[11] *In Cant.* vi, GNO vi. 183. 7–9.

[12] Canévet, *Grégoire de Nysse et l'herméneutique biblique*, 63.

instrumental dative (πίστῃ) or governed by the preposition διὰ (διὰ[μόνης] τῆς πίστεως).[13] Hence, when faith is used in these conditions, it can rightly be said to have a technical meaning in the writings of Gregory of Nyssa.

The explicit concerns with divine union shown consistently by exalted faith were examined in detail, especially in the migration of Abraham as well as in Homilies 3, 4, 6, 9, 12, and 13 on the Song. Indeed, the theme of union is an important one especially in the *In Canticum*, which states early on that union with God is the very purpose of the Song.[14] This study of exalted faith affords a perspective on one of Mühlenberg's conclusions in his important study of Gregory.[15] Mühlenberg would deny that Gregory allows for the possibility of union with God, for union would imply knowledge, and this would be to enclose God in the grasp of comprehension. We have seen, however, that this is precisely what union with God through the grasp of faith does *not* involve. For it is not knowledge of a conceptual order but rather an unknowing which is higher than the conceptual grasp of mind. This union 'by faith alone' safeguards the distinction between finite creature and infinite Creator, for it is a union beyond knowledge.

By the same token it is important to respond to Pottier on this point. Quite rightly Pottier says that Gregorian faith 'touches God as he is'. However, he then goes on to say, 'but it is not knowledge'.[16] In a certain sense Pottier's point is well taken; it is not knowledge of a discursive sort. However, Pottier does not appreciate sufficiently the apophatic context of Gregory's noetic ascents, in which not-knowing is higher than knowing and continuous-yet-discontinuous with the mind's passionate search for the Beloved.

Whilst Mühlenberg is aware that Gregory has parted company with his master Origen on the notion of divine infinity, Mühlenberg is less aware that Gregory has also parted company with the general Alexandrian notion that faith is overcome in knowledge. For Gregory of Nyssa, on the basis of what we have seen in the migration of Abraham, Moses' ascent of the mountain of divine knowledge, and the bride's union with

---

[13] Obviously the phrase from *In Cant.* VI, GNO VI, 183, 9: τῇ τῆς πίστεως λαβῇ, should be understood as rendering this technical meaning of πίστις.

[14] *In Cant.* I, GNO VI. 15. 13–15: διὰ γὰρ τῶν ἐνταῦθα γεγραμμένων νυμφοστολεῖται τρόπον τινὰ ἡ ψυχὴ πρὸς τὴν ἀσώματόν τε καὶ πνευματικὴν καὶ ἀμόλυντον τοῦ θεοῦ συζυγίαν.

[15] Mühlenberg, *Unendlichkeit Gottes.*

[16] *Dieu et le Christ*, 209.

the Beloved by faith alone, it is knowledge that is overcome in faith. Both Dünzl and Desalvo observed that Mühlenberg did not consider in any detail the role of faith in Gregory's thought.[17] Mühlenberg's oversight prevents him from seeing the ontological function which faith serves. A strict boundary between finite creature and infinite Creator runs the risk of preventing any access to the Infinite without the loss of one's ontological status as a creature.[18]

Despite Daniélou's questionable threefold division of the ascent of the mind,[19] presuming, that is, that Daniélou intends it as more than a merely heuristic device, union with God is an explicit concern of Gregory of Nyssa, a concern which takes account in a fairly consistent manner of his overarching concern for protecting both the infinity and the incomprehensibility of the divine nature, and this union is very much the domain of the grasp of faith.

If Chapters 2 and 3 worked in tandem both to stabilize the technical meaning and to describe the precise functions which Gregory bestowed on exalted faith, Chapter 4 attempted to situate Gregorian *pistis* against the backdrop of the largely Neoplatonic concern for a faculty of supranoetic union. For although Gregory's exalted, technical sense of faith is rather idiosyncratic, the notion of a faculty continuous-yet-discontinuous with the mind, a supranoetic faculty that unites the soul to God, is something of a commonplace in Middle and Neoplatonic epistemology. Indeed the relationship between the mind and faith is roughly what we saw between the mind and the 'flower of the mind' or the 'crest of the wave of the intellect'. Our intention was not to suggest that Celsus or the *Chaldaean Oracles* or Plotinus exerted a direct influence upon Gregory of Nyssa but to establish these parallels in order to allow Gregory's exalted faith to stand in bolder relief. For while virtually no writer before Gregory spoke of faith in the apophatic manner in which he did, a number of authors spoke of a mediating supranoetic faculty of union. Gregory's innovation was to call it faith.

On several occasions in the course of this study attention was drawn to the fact that Gregory so often grounded his thought in exegesis that we could rightly speak of his epistemology as an exegetical epistemology, and this was especially true of the technical meaning of faith. Heb 11: 8; 2 Cor 5: 7; and Rom 4: 3 were never far in the background as Gregory

---

[17] Dünzl, *Braut und Bräutigam*, 326 n. 119; Desalvo, *L' 'oltre' nel presente*, 220.

[18] See Desalvo, *L' 'oltre' nel presente*, 221.

[19] Mühlenberg, *Unendlichkeit Gottes*, 25; Daniélou, *Platonisme et théologie mystique*, 146 ff.

commented on the Song of Songs or Exodus and found that with Abraham, Moses, or the bride it was their faith that allowed them to grasp the Ungraspable in the darkness of divine presence. In doing this Gregory draws out the epistemological implications of faith in terms and motifs consonant with the Neoplatonic *esprit du temps*.

Chapters 3 and 4 focused on the apophatic elements surrounding the ascent to the grasp of faith. It was only, or perhaps most characteristically, when faith appeared at the apex of an apophatic, epistemological ascent that it assumed its technical function and meaning. However, it was suggested that in order to understand other aspects of Gregory's exalted faith it was not enough to focus upon the primary function of union without also considering the effects of this union.

One of the advantages of studying this theme is that it has opened up a view onto a largely neglected dimension of Gregory's thought, a dimension which I have termed logophasis. Union with the Beloved through the grasp of faith characteristically occurs at the zenith of epistemological ascents, rich with apophatic terms and aphairetic gestures. Union followed upon the forsaking of all knowledge. In Chapters 5 and 6 we observed how in the context of union a paradoxical turn ensued. Having abandoned all language that searched for God, the figures of the bride and Paul assumed language that was full of God, and their words had the same effect upon others that the attractive power of the Word exerted upon them. Because the Word indwells them, the Word now speaks through them. Hence the term logophasis.

The grasp of faith, therefore, mediates in two directions. Along a fairly rigorously maintained apophatic trajectory, faith mediates union with God beyond all concepts. However, this union with the Word initiates another trajectory: the tendency of the Word to fill the mouth of the bride with words, to express itself in the words and deeds of those who attain union with the Word. Put another way, the words and actions of Paul, John, and the bride manifest the Word and bear witness to their adherence to the Word by faith. The grasp of faith grounds this coincidence of opposites and mediates both these trajectories, the one apophatic, the other logophatic. While the apophatic element is central to Gregory's thought, the dimension of logophasis is no less central; for it is the other side of union 'by faith alone'. But without a sufficient appreciation of the mediating role of faith in Gregory's thought, this complementary dimension of logophasis will most likely be overlooked.

Finally, while union by the grasp of faith took place in darkness, an attentive study of the role of faith led us paradoxically to texts that also spoke of knowledge and light. This occurred frequently enough that I grew increasingly convinced that the unequivocal identification of Gregory of Nyssa with the mysticism of darkness was decidedly mistaken: an attentive reading of the *Commentarius in Canticum canticorum* reveals that Gregory proposes no less a mysticism of light than one of darkness. Hence, Chapter 7 showed how both elements were present in the *In Canticum*. Gregory's doctrines on transformation in light and the entrance into the darkness of God's presence were each rooted in their own respective clusters of scriptural texts and had their own epistemological concerns.

BIBLIOGRAPHY

Lexica

Lampe, G. W. H., (ed.), *A Patristic Greek Lexicon*, Oxford, 1961.
Liddell, H. G. and Scott, R. (eds.), *A Greek–English Lexicon*, 9th edn., revised and augmented by H. Jones, Oxford, 1996.
Mann, F. (ed.), *Lexicon Gregorianum: Wörterbuch zu den Schriften Gregors von Nyssa*, Leiden, 1999–.

Primary Literature

Texts of Gregory of Nyssa

Editions
Commentarius in Canticum canticorum, GNO vi, ed. H. Langerbeck, Leiden, 1960.
Contra Eunomium Libri, GNO i–ii, ed. W. Jaeger, Leiden, 1960.
De anima et resurrectione, PG 46. 12a–160c.
De beatitudinibus, GNO vii, ii, ed. J. Callahan, Leiden, 1992.
De hominis opificio, PG 44. 124d–256c.
De oratione dominica, GNO vii. ii, ed. J. Callahan, Leiden, 1992.
De virginitate, SC 119, ed. and trans. M. Aubineau, Paris, 1966.
De vita Gregorii Thaumaturgi, GNO x. i, pars ii, ed. G. Heil, Leiden, 1990.
De vita Moysis, SC 1 *bis*, ed. and trans. J. Daniélou, Paris, 1955.
In Ecclesiasten, SC 416, ed. P. Alexander, and trans. F. Vinel, Paris, 1996.
In inscriptiones Psalmorum, GNO v, ed. J. McDonough and P. Alexander, Leiden, 1962.
Oratio catechetica, GNO iii. iv, ed. E. Mühlenberg, Leiden, 1996.
Vita S. Macrinae, GNO viii. i, ed. V. Woods, Leiden, 1952.

Translations
Callahan, V. Woods (trans.), *Gregory of Nyssa: Ascetical Works*, Fathers of the Church 58, Washington, DC, 1967.
Ferguson, E. and Malherbe, A. (trans.), *The Life of Moses*, Classics of Western Spirituality, New York, 1978.
Graef, H. (trans.), *The Lord's Prayer, The Beatitudes*, Ancient Christian Writers 18, New York, 1954.

Hall, Stuart G. (trans.), *Contra Eunomium I*, in L. Mateo-Seco and J. Bastero, (eds.), *El 'Contra Eunomium I' en la producción literaria de Gregorio de Nisa*, VI Coloquio Internacional sobre Gregorio de Nisa, Pamplona, 1988, pp. 247–68.

—— and R. Moriarity, (trans. and eds.), *Gregory of Nyssa: 'Homilies on Ecclesiastes': An English Version with Supporting Studies*, Proceedings of the Seventh International Conference on Gregory of Nyssa, St Andrews, 5–10 September, Berlin, 1993.

Hardy, E. *et al.* (eds. and trans.), *Christology of the Later Fathers*, Library of Christian Classics 3, London, 1954.

Heine, R. *Gregory of Nyssa's Treatise on the 'Inscriptions on the Psalms'*, Oxford Early Christian Studies, Oxford, 1995.

McCambley, C. (trans.), *Commentary on the Song of Songs*, The Archbishop Iakovanos Library of Ecclesiastical and Historical Sources 12, Brookline, Mass., 1987.

More, W. and Wilson, H. (trans.), *Selected Writings and Letters of Gregory, Bishop of Nyssa*, Library of Nicene and Post-Nicene Fathers of the Christian Church II. 5, Grand Rapids, Mich., 1892.

Moreschini, C. (trans.), *Teologia Trinitaria. Il 'Contra Eunomio' di Gregorio di Nissa*, Classici del Pensiero: Filosofia Classica e Tardo Antica, Milan, 1994.

—— *Omelie sul Cantico dei cantici*, Testi Patristici 72, Rome, 1996.

Musurillo, H. (trans.), *From Glory to Glory: Texts from Gregory of Nyssa's Mystical Writings*, Crestwood, NY, 1979.

Simonetti, M. (ed. and trans.), *La vita di Mosè*, Scrittori Greci e Latini, Milan, 1984.

Traverso, A. (trans.), *Sui titoli dei Salmi*, Testi Patristici 110, Rome, 1994.

Ancient Authors

Aristotle, *De anima*, SCBO, ed. W. Ross, Oxford, 1956.

—— *De partibus animalium*, LCL, trans. A. Peck, Cambridge, Mass., 1955.

—— *Ethica Nicomachea*, SCBO, ed. I. Bywater, Oxford, 1894.

—— *Metaphysica*, SCBO, ed. W. Jaeger, Oxford, 1957.

Athanasius, *De incarnatione verbi. Sur L'Incarnacion du Verbe*, SC 199, ed. and trans. C. Kannengieser, Paris, 1973.

Basil of Caesarea, *De spiritu sancto. Sur le Saint-Esprit*, SC 17 *bis*, ed. and trans. B. Pruche, Paris, 1968.

—— *Epistulae. Lettres*, 3 vols., CUF, ed. and trans. Y. Courtonne, Paris, 1957–66.

Chaldaean Oracles, *The Chaldean Oracles*, Studies in Greek and Roman Religion 5, trans. and ed. R. Majercik, Leiden, 1989.

—— *Oracles Chaldaïques*, CUF, trans. and ed. É. des Places, Paris, 1971.

Clement of Alexandria, *Protrepticus. Protréptique*, SC 2 *bis*, trans. C. Mondésert, Paris, 1976.

—— *Stromateis* II, SC 38, ed. and trans. C. Mondésert, Paris, 1954.

—— *Stromateis*, FC 85, trans. J. Ferguson, Washington, DC, 1991.

Damascius, *Traité des Premiers Principes*, 3 vols., CUF, ed. L. Westerink, trans. J. Combès, Paris, 1986–91.

Denys the Areopagite, *De divinis nominibus*, Corpus Dionysiacum I, Patristische Texte und Studien 33, ed. B. Suchla, Berlin, 1990.

—— *De mystica Theologia*, Corpus Dionysiacum II, Patristische Texte und Studien 36, ed. G. Hill and A. Ritter, Berlin, 1991.

—— *Epistulae*, Corpus Dionysiacum II, Patristische Texte und Studien 36, ed. G. Hill, and A. Ritter, Berlin, 1991.

Eusebius, *Praeparatio Evangelica. La Préparation Évangélique*, SC 206, ed. and trans. J. Sirinelli, and E. des Places, Paris, 1974.

Gregory Nazianzen, *Orationes. Discours* 27–31, SC 250, ed. and trans. P. Gallay, Paris, 1978.

—— *Orationes. Discours* 32–7, SC 318, ed. C. Moreschini, trans. P. Gallay, Paris, 1985.

—— *Orationes. Discours* 38–41, SC 358, ed. C. Moreschini, trans. P. Gallay, Paris, 1990.

Iamblicus, *De Mysteriis. Les Mystères d'Égypte*, CUF, ed. and trans. É. des Places, Paris, 1966.

Irenaeus, *Adverus haereses. Contre les Hérésies*, SC 100, 152, 153, 210, 211, 263, 264, ed. and trans. A. Rousseau *et al.*, Paris, 1965–9.

Origen, *Commentarius in Canticum canticorum*, GCS 8, ed. W. Baehrens, Leipzig, 1925.

—— *Commentarius in Johannis Evangelium*, GCS, ed. E. Preuschen, Leipzig, 1903.

—— *Contra Celsum*, rev. edn. trans. H. Chadwick, Cambridge, 1965.

—— *Contre Celse*, SC 132, ed. and trans. M. Borret, Paris, 1967.

—— *De principiis. Traité des principes*, SC 252, 253, 268, 269, 312, trans. and ed. H. Crouzel and M. Simonetti, Paris, 1978–82.

—— *Homilae in Genesim. Homélies sur la Genèse*, SC 7 *bis*, ed. and trans. L. Doutreleau, Paris, 1976.

—— *Homiliae in Numeros*, GCS 7, ed. W. Baehrens, Leipzig, 1921.

—— *In Lucam* fragmenta, GCS 9, ed. M. Rauer, Leipzig, 1930.

Philo, *De Abrahamo*, LCL, Philo vol. vi, trans. F. Colson, Cambridge, Mass., 1959.

—— *De decalogo*, LCL, Philo vol. vii, trans. F. Colson, Cambridge, Mass., 1958.

—— *De migratione Abrahami*, LCL, Philo vol. iv, trans. F. Colson and G. Whitaker, Cambridge, Mass., 1949.

—— *De mutatione nominum*, LCL, Philo vol. v, trans. F. Colson and G. Whitaker, Cambridge, Mass., 1949.

—— *De posteritate Caini*, LCL, Philo vol. ii, trans. F. Colson and G. Whitaker, Cambridge, Mass., 1950.

Philo, *De sacrificiis Abelis et Caini*, LCL, Philo vol. ii, trans. F. Colson and G. Whitaker, Cambridge, Mass., 1950.

—— *De vita Moysis*, LCL, Philo vol. vi, trans. F. Colson, Cambridge, Mass., 1959.

—— *Legum allegoriae*, LCL, Philo vol. i, trans. F. Colson and G. Whitaker, Cambridge, Mass., 1949.

Plato, *Epistula VII*, Platonis Opera V, SCBO, ed. J. Burnet, Oxford, 1907.

—— *Phaedo*, Platonis Opera I, SCBO, ed. J. Burnet, Oxford, 1900.

—— *Phaedrus*, Platonis Opera II, SCBO, ed. J. Burnet, Oxford, 1901.

—— *Res Publica*, Platonis Opera IV, SCBO, ed. J. Burnet, Oxford, 1902.

—— *Symposium*, Platonis Opera II, SCBO, ed. J. Burnet, Oxford, 1901.

—— *Timaeus*, Platonis Opera IV, SCBO, ed. J. Burnet, Oxford, 1902.

Plotinus, *The Enneads*, 7 vols., LCL, trans. A. H. Armstrong, Cambridge, Mass., 1966–88.

—— *The Enneads*, trans. J. MacKenna, abridged and introduced by J. Dillon, Harmondsworth, 1991.

Porphyry, *Ad Marcellam. Vie de Pythagore—Lettre à Marcella—frg. de l'Histoire de la philosophie*, CUF, ed. and trans. E. des Places, Paris, 1982.

—— *De abstinentia. Porphyre: De l'abstinence*, ed. and trans. J. Bouffartigue and M. Patillon, Paris, 1977.

—— *Porphyry the Philosopher: To Marcella*, Society of Biblical Literature Texts and Translations 28, Graeco-Roman Series 10, trans. K. Wicker, Atlanta, 1987.

Proclus, *Alcibiades I: A Translation and Commentary*, W. O'Neill, The Hague, 1965.

—— *De providentia. Trois Études sur la Providence*, 3 vols., CUF, ed. and trans. D. Isaac, Paris, 1977–82.

—— *In Alcibiadem*, ed. L. Westerink, *Proclus Diodochus: Commentary on the First Alcibiades of Plato*, Amsterdam, 1954.

—— *In Platonis Timaeum commentaria*, 3 vols., ed. E. Diehl, Leipzig, 1903.

—— *Theologia platonica. Théologie Platonicienne*, 6 vols., CUF, ed. and trans. H. Saffrey and L. Westerink, Paris, 1968–97.

Secondary Literature

Adam, J., *The Republic of Plato*, 2 vols., 2nd edn., Cambridge, 1963.

Armstrong, A.H., 'Platonic Elements in St Gregory of Nyssa's Doctrine of Man', *Dominican Studies* 1 (1948), 113–26.

—— 'The Nature of Man in St Gregory of Nyssa', *Eastern Churches Quarterly* 8 (1949), 2–9.

—— 'Platonic *Eros* and Christian *Agape*', *Downside Review* 79 (1961), 105–21; reprinted in *Plotinian and Christian Studies*, London, 1979.

—— 'Tradition, Reason and Experience in the Thought of Plotinus', in *Plotino e il Neoplatonismo in Oriente e in Occidente*, Atti del Convegno Internazionale dell' Accademia Nazionale dei Lincei (Rome 5–9 October 1970), Rome, 1970, 171–94.

—— 'The Way and the Ways: Religious Tolerance and Intolerance in the Fourth Century A D', *Vigiliae Christianae* 38 (1984), 1–17.

—— 'The Escape of the One: An Investigation of Some Possibilities of Apophatic Theology Imperfectly Realised in the West', *Studia Patristica* 13 (1985), 77–89.

Balás, D. *METOΥΣIA ΘEOΥ: Man's Participation in God's Perfections according to St Gregory of Nyssa*, Studia Anselmiana 55, Rome, 1966.

—— 'The Unity of Human Nature in Basil's and Gregory of Nyssa's Polemics against Eunomius', *Studia Patristica* 14 (1976), 275–81.

—— 'Plenitudo Humanitatis: The Unity of Human Nature in the Theology of Gregory of Nyssa', in D. Winslow (ed.), *Disciplina Nostra*, Philadelphia, 1979, 115–33.

Balthasar, Hans Urs von, *Présence et pensée: Essai sur la philosophie religieuse de Grégoire de Nysse*, Paris, 1942 (= *Presence and Thought: An Essay on the Religious Philosophy of Gregory of Nyssa*, trans. M. Sebanc, San Francisco, 1995).

—— *Origen, Spirit and Fire: A Thematic Anthology of His Writings*, trans. R. Daly, Washington, DC, 1984.

—— *Sponsa Verbi: Skizzen zur Theologie II*, Einsiedeln, 1961 (= *Spouse of the Word: Explorations in Theology II*, trans. M. Oakes, San Francisco, 1991).

Barmann, B., 'The Cappadocian Triumph over Arianism', Ph.D. thesis, Stanford University, 1966.

Barnes, M., 'The Polemical Context of Gregory of Nyssa's Psychology', *Medieval Philosophy and Theology* 4 (1994), 1–24.

Bebis, G., 'Gregory of Nyssa's "De Vita Moysis": A Philosophical and Theological Analysis', *Greek Orthodox Theological Review* 12 (1967), 369–93.

Behr, J., 'The Rational Animal: A Rereading of Gregory of Nyssa's *De hominis opificio*', *Journal of Early Christian Studies* 7 (1999), 219–47.

Beierwaltes, W., 'Exaiphnes oder: Die Paradoxie des Augenblicks', *Philosophisches Jahrbuch* 74 (1966–7), 271–83.

—— 'Reflexion und Einung: Zur Mystik Plotins', in *Grundfragen der Mystik*, Einsiedeln, 1974, 7–36.

—— *Denken des Einen: Studien zur Neuplatonischen Philosophie und ihrer Wirkungsgeschichte*, Frankfurt am Main, 1985.

Benko, S., 'Pagan Criticism of Christianity during the First Two Centuries', *ANRW* II. 23/2, ed. W. Haase, Berlin, 1980, 1053–1118.

Berchman, R., *From Philo to Origen: Middle Platonism in Transition*, Brown Judaic Studies 69, Chico, Calif., 1985.

Bernardi, J. *La Prédication des pères cappodociens: Le Prédicateur et son auditoire*, Montpellier, 1968.

Bertrand, F., *Mystique de Jésus chez Origène*, Théologie 23, Paris, 1951.

Bigg, C., *The Christian Platonists of Alexandria*, Oxford, 1913.

Böhm, T., 'Christologie und Hellenisierung: Der Fall "Arius". Eine Replik auf B. Studers Kritik', *Münchener Theologische Zeitschrift* 45 (1994), 593–9.

Böhm, T., *Theoria, Unendlichkeit, Aufstieg: Philosophische Implikationen zu 'De vita Moysis' von Gregor von Nyssa*, Supplements to *Vigiliae Christianae* 35. Leiden, 1996.

Bouchet, J.-R., 'Le Vocabulaire de l'union et du rapport des natures chez Saint Grégoire de Nysse', *Revue Thomiste* 68 (1968), 533–82.

Bregman, J., 'Elements of the Emperor Julian's Theology', in *Traditions of Platonism: Essays in Honour of John Dillon*, ed. J. Cleary, Aldershot, 1999, 337–50.

Bréhier, E., *Les Idées philosophiques et religieuses de Philon d'Alexandrie*, Études de Philosophie Médiévale 8, Paris, 1950.

Brightman, R., 'Apophatic Theology and Divine Infinity in St Gregory of Nyssa', *Greek Orthodox Theological Review* 18 (1973), 97–114.

Brown, P., *The Making of Late Antiquity*, Cambridge, Mass., 1978.

Bussanich, J., *The One and its Relation to Intellect in Plotinus: A Commentary on Selected Texts*, Philosophia Antiqua 49, Leiden, 1988.

—— 'Mystical Elements in the Thought of Plotinus', *ANRW* II. 36/7, ed. W. Haase, Berlin, 1994, 5300–30.

Cahill, J., 'The Date and Setting of Gregory of Nyssa's "Commentary on the Song of Songs"', *Journal of Theological Studies* NS 32 (1981), 447–60.

Callahan, J., 'Greek Philosophy and the Cappadocian Cosmology', *Dumbarton Oaks Papers* 12 (1958), 29–57.

Canévet, M., 'Grégoire de Nysse (saint)', s.v., *Dictionnaire de Spiritualité*, vol. vi, Paris, 1967, cols. 971–1011.

—— 'Exégèse et théologie dans les traités spirituels de Grégoire de Nysse', in *Ecriture et culture philosophique dans la pensée de Grégoire de Nysse: Actes du Colloque de Chèvetogne (22–26 septembre 1969)*, ed. M. Harl, Leiden, 1971, 144–68.

—— 'La Perception de la présence de Dieu. A propos d'une expression de la XIième Homélie sur le Cantique des Cantiques', in *Epektasis: Mélanges patristiques offerts au Cardinal Jean Daniélou*, ed. J. Fontaine and C. Kannengiesser, Paris, 1972, 443–54.

—— 'La Mort du Christ et le mystère de sa Personne Humano-Divine dans la théologie du IVième siècle', *Les IV Fleuves* 15–16 (1982), 71–92.

—— *Grégoire de Nysse et l'herméneutique biblique: Étude des rapports entre le langage et la connaissance de Dieu*, Paris, 1983.

—— 'Sens Spirituel', s.v., *Dictionnaire de Spiritualité*, vol. xiv, Paris, 1990, cols. 598–617.

—— 'L'Humanité de l'embryon selon Grégoire de Nysse', *Nouvelle Revue Théologique* 114 (1992), 678–95.

Carabine, D., 'Apophasis East and West', *Recherches de théologie ancienne et médiévale* 55 (1988), 5–29.

—— 'Gregory of Nyssa on the Incomprehensibility of God', in *The Relationship between Neoplatonism and Christianity*, ed. T. Finan and V. Twomey, Dublin, 1992, 79–99.

—— 'A Dark Cloud: Hellenistic Influences on the Scriptural Exegesis of Clement of Alexandria and the Pseudo-Dionysius', in *Scriptural Interpretation in the Fathers: Letter and Spirit*, ed. T. Finan and V. Twomey, Dublin, 1995, 61–74.

—— *The Unknown God: Negative Theology in the Platonic Tradition: Plato to Eriugena*, Louvain Theological and Pastoral Monographs 19, Louvain, 1995.

Cazelles, H. *et al.* (eds.), *Moïse: l'Homme de l'alliance*, Paris, 1955.

Chadwick, H., *Early Christian Thought and the Classical Tradition: Studies in Justin, Clement and Origen*, New York, 1966.

Cherniss, H., *The Platonism of Gregory of Nyssa*, Berkeley, 1930.

Clarke, M., *Higher Education in the Ancient World*, London, 1971.

Clément, O., *The Roots of Christian Mysticism*, trans. T. Berkley, London, 1993.

Corrigan, K., ' "Solitary" Mysticism in Plotinus, Proclus, Gregory of Nyssa, and Pseudo-Dionysius', *Journal of Religion* 76 (1996), 28–42.

Cortesi, A., *Le 'Omelie sul Cantico dei Cantici' di Gregorio di Nissa: Proposta di un itinerario di vita battesimale*, Studia Ephemerides Augustinianum 70, Rome, 2000.

Courcelle, P., 'Grégoire de Nysse, lecteur de Porphyre', *Revue des études grecques* 80 (1967), 402–6.

Cremer, F., *Die Chaldäischen Orakel und Jamblich de mysteriis*, Meisenheim am Glan, 1969.

Cross, R. and Woozley, A., *Plato's Republic: A Philosophical Commentary*, London, 1964.

Crouzel, H., 'Grégoire de Nysse est-il le fondateur de la théologie mystique? Une controverse récente', *Revue d'ascétique et de mystique* 33 (1957), 189–202.

—— *Origène et la 'connaissance mystique'*, Museum Lessianum Section Théologique 56, Paris, 1961.

—— 'Origene e l'origenismo: le condanne di Origene', *Augustinianum* 26 (1986), 295–303.

—— *Origen: His Life and Thought*, trans. A. Worrall, New York, 1989.

Daley, B., *The Hope of the Early Church: A Handbook of Patristic Eschatology*, Cambridge, 1991.

—— ' "Bright Darkness" and Christian Transformation: Gregory of Nyssa on the Dynamics of Mystical Union', in *Finding God in All Things: Essays in Honor of Michael J. Buckley, S.J.*, ed. M. Himes and S. Pope, New York, 1996, 215–30.

—— 'Divine Transcendence and Human Transformation: Gregory of Nyssa's Anti-Apollinarian Christology', *Studia Patristica* 32 (1997), 87–95.

Daniélou, J., *Platonisme et théologie mystique: Essai sur la doctrine spirituelle de Saint Grégoire de Nysse*, 2nd edn., Paris, 1953.

—— 'Grégoire de Nysse et Plotin', *Congrès de Tours, Association Guillaume Budé* (1954), 259–62.

—— 'Moïse exemple et figure chez Grégoire de Nysse,' *Cahiers sioniens* 2–4 (1955), 386–400.

Daniélou, J., 'Le mariage de Grégoire de Nysse et la chronologie de sa vie', *Revue des études Augustiniennes* 2 (1956), 71–8.

——— 'Le Symbole de la Caverne chez Grégoire de Nysse,' in *Mullus: Festschrift Theodor Klauser*, Jahrbuch für Antike und Christentum 1, ed. A. von Stuiber and A. Hermann, Münster, 1964, 43–51.

——— 'Mystique de la ténèbre chez Grégoire de Nysse', *s.v.* contemplation, *Dictionnaire de Spiritualité*, vol. ii. ii, Paris, 1953, cols. 1872–86.

——— *Le IVième siècle: Grégoire de Nysse et son milieu*, Paris, 1965.

——— 'La Chronologie des œuvres de Grégoire de Nysse', *Studia Patristica* 7 (Texte und Untersuchungen 92, Berlin, 1966), 159–69.

——— 'Grégoire de Nysse et le néo-Platonisme de l'école d'Athènes', *Revue des études grecques* 80 (1967), 395–401.

——— *L'être et le temps chez Grégoire de Nysse*, Leiden, 1970.

Davis, S., *The Cult of Saint Thecla: A Tradition of Women's Piety in Late Antiquity*, Oxford Early Christian Studies, Oxford, 2001.

De Andia, Y., *Henosis: L'Union à Dieu chez Denys L'Areopagite*, Philosophia Antiqua 71, Leiden, 1996.

Des Places, E., *Syngeneia: La Parenté de l'homme avec Dieu d'Homère à la patristique*, Études et Commentaires 51, Paris, 1964.

Desalvo, C., *L' 'oltre' nel presente: La filosofia dell'uomo in Gregorio di Nissa*, Platonismo e filosofia patristica, Studi e testi 9, Milan, 1996.

Di Berardino, A., 'La Cappadocia al tempo di Basilio', in *Mémorial Dom Jean Gribomont*, Studia Ephemerides Augustinianum 27, Rome, 1988, 167–82.

———. (ed.), *Encyclopedia of the Early Church*, trans. A. Walford, Cambridge, 1992.

Di Berardino, A. and Studer, B. (eds.), *Storia della Teologia*, vol. i: *Epoca Patristica*, Casale Monferrato, 1993.

Dihle, A., *The Theory of the Will in Classical Antiquity*, Berkeley, 1982.

Dillon, J., *Middle Platonists*, London, 1977.

———. 'Iamblichus of Chalcis', *ANRW* ii. 36/2, ed. W. Haase, Berlin, 1987, 863–909.

———. 'Looking on the Light: Some Remarks on the Imagery of Light in the First Chapter of the *Peri Archon*', in *Origen of Alexandria: His World and His Legacy*, ed. C. Kannengieser and W. Petersen, Christianity and Judaism in Antiquity 1, Notre Dame, 1988, 215–30.

———. 'Plotinus and the Chaldaean Oracles', in *Platonism in Late Antiquity*, ed. S. Gersh and C. Kannengeiser, Notre Dame, 1992, 131–40.

———. 'Rejecting the Body, Refining the Body: Some Remarks on the Development of Platonist Asceticism', in *Asceticism*, ed. V. Wimbush and R. Valantasis, Oxford, 1995, 80–7.

———. ' "A Kind of Warmth": Some Reflections on the Concept of "Grace" in the Neoplatonic Tradition', in *The Passionate Intellect: Essays on the Transformation of Classical Traditions Presented to Professor I.G. Kidd*, ed. L. Ayres, New Brunswick, 1995, 323–32.

Dodds, E. R., 'Theurgy and its Relationship to Neoplatonism', *Journal of Roman Studies* 37 (1947), 55–69; reprinted in *The Greeks and the Irrational*, Boston, 1957, 83–311.

——. 'New Light on the "Chaldaean Oracles"', *Harvard Theological Review* 54 (1961), 263–73; reprinted in H. Lewy, *Chaldean Oracles and Theurgy: Mysticism, Magic and Platonism in the Later Roman Empire*, new edition by M. Tardieu, Paris, 1978, 693–701.

——. *Pagan and Christian in an Age of Anxiety*, Cambridge, 1965.

Dunstone, A., 'The Meaning of Grace in the Writings of Gregory of Nyssa', *Scottish Journal of Theology* 15 (1962), 235–44.

Dünzl, F., *Braut und Bräutigam: Die Auslegung des Canticum durch Gregor von Nyssa*, Beiträge zur Geschichte der Biblischen Exegese 32, Tübingen, 1993.

Dupré, L. and Wiseman, J. (eds.), *Light from Light: An Anthology of Christian Mysticism*, Mahwah, N.J., 1988.

Elliot, M., *The Song of Songs and Christology in the Early Church 381–451*, Studien und Texte zu Antike und Christentum 7, Tübingen, 2000.

Fédou, M., *Christianisme et religions païennes dans le Contre Celse d'Origène*, Théologie Historique 81, Paris, 1988.

Fedwick, P., 'The Knowledge of Truth or the State of Prayer in Gregory of Nyssa', *Polyanethema: Studi di Letteratura Cristiana offerti a Salvatore Costanza. Studi Tardoantichi* 7 (1989), 349–71.

Ferguson, E., 'God's Infinity and Man's Mutability: Perpetual Progress according to Gregory of Nyssa', *Greek Orthodox Theological Review* 18 (1973), 59–78.

Festugière, A.-J., *La Révélation d'Hermès Trismégiste*, vol. iv: *Le Dieu Inconnu et la Gnose*, Paris, 1954.

Figura, M., 'Mystische Gotteserkenntnis bei Gregor von Nyssa', in *Grundfragen christlicher Mystik*, ed. M. Schmidt and D. Bauer, Stuttgart, 1987, 25–38.

Gain, B., *L'Eglise de Cappadoce au IVe siècle d'après la correspondance de Basile de Césarée (330–379)*, Orientalia Christiana Analecta 225, Rome, 1985.

Gaïth, J., *La Conception de la liberté chez Grégoire de Nysse*, Paris, 1953.

Gargano, I., *La Teoria di Gregorio di Nissa sul Cantico dei Cantici: Indagine su alcune indicazioni di metodo esegetico*, Orientalia Christiana Analecta 216, Rome, 1981.

Gillet, R., 'L'Homme divinisateur cosmique dans la pensée de saint Grégoire de Nysse', *Studia Patristica* 6/4 (1962), 62–83.

Girardi, M., 'Annotazioni al *De beatitudinibus*', *Augustinianum* 35 (1995), 161–82.

Gregory, John, *The Neoplatonists: A Reader*, 2nd edn., London, 1999.

Gross, J. *La Divinisation du Chrétien d'après les pères grecs: Contribution historique à la doctrine de la grace*, Paris, 1938.

Grube, G.M.A., *Plato's Thought*, London, 1935.

Hadot, P., 'Fragments d'un commentaire de Porphyre sur le *Parménide*', *Revue des Études Grecques* 74 (1961), 410–38.

——. 'Bilan et perspectives sur les *Oracles Chaldaïques*', in H. Lewy, *Chaldean Oracles and Theurgy: Mysticism, Magic and Platonism in the Later Roman Empire*, new edition by M. Tardieu, Paris, 1978, 703–20.

——. 'Les Niveaux de conscience dans les états mystiques selon Plotin', *Journal de Psychologie* (1980), 243–66.

——. 'The Spiritual Guide', in *Classical Mediterranean Spirituality*, ed. A. H. Armstrong, World Spirituality: An Encyclopedic History of the Religious Quest 15, New York, 1986, 436–59.

——. 'L'Union de l'âme avec l'intellect divin dans l'expérience mystique plotinienne', in *Proclus et son Influence*, ed. G. Boss and B. Seel, Actes du Colloque de Neuchâtel, juin 1985, Zurich, 1987, 3–27.

——. 'Structures et thèmes du Traité 38 (vi. 7) de Plotin', *ANRW* ii. 36/2, ed. W. Haase, Berlin, 1987, 624–76.

——. *What is Ancient Philosophy?* trans. M. Chase, Cambridge, Mass., 2002.

Hanson, R., *The Search for the Christian Doctrine of God: The Arian Controversy 318–381*, Edinburgh, 1988.

Harl, M., 'Recherches sur l'origénisme d'Origène: la satiété (*koros*) de la contemplation comme motif de la chute des âmes', *Studia Patristica* 8 (1966), 374–405.

——. ' "From Glory to Glory": L'interprétation de II Cor. 3,18b par Grégoire de Nysse et la liturgie baptismale', in *Kyriakon: Festschrift Johannes Quasten*, ed. P. Granfield and J. Jungman, Münster, 1970, 730–5.

Harrison, V., *Grace and Human Freedom according to Gregory of Nyssa*, Studies in Bible and Early Christianity 30, Lewiston, NY, 1992.

Hart, M., 'Reconciliation of Body and Soul: Gregory of Nyssa's Deeper Theology of Marriage', *Theological Studies* 51 (1990), 450–78.

——. 'Gregory of Nyssa's Ironic Praise of the Celibate Life', *Heythrop Journal* 33 (1992), 1–19.

Heine, R., *Perfection in the Virtuous Life: A Study in the Relationship between Edification and Polemical Theology in Gregory of Nyssa*, Patristic Monograph Series 2, Philadelphia, 1975.

——. 'Gregory of Nyssa's Apology for Allegory', *Vigiliae Christianae* 38 (1984), 360–70.

——. 'Cappadocia', in *Encyclopedia of the Early Church*, ed. A. Di Berardino, and trans. A. Walford, Cambridge, 1992, s.v.

Henry, P., *Plotin et l'Occident*, Louvain, 1934.

Horn, G., 'Le "Miroir", la "nuée", deux manières de voir Dieu d'après S. Grégoire de Nysse', *Revue d'Ascetique et de Mystique* 8 (1927), 113–31.

Hübner, R., *Die Einheit des Leibes Christi bei Gregor von Nyssa: Untersuchungen zum Ursprung der 'physischen Erlösungslehre'*, Leiden, 1974.

Inge, W., *The Philosophy of Plotinus*, Gifford Lectures at St Andrews 1917–19, 2 vols., London, 1918.

Jaeger, W., *The Theology of the Early Greek Philosophers*, Gifford Lectures at St Andrews 1936–37, Oxford, 1947.

——. *Paideia: The Ideals of Greek Culture*, trans. G. Highet, 3 vols., Oxford, 1939–44.

——. *Two Rediscovered Works of Ancient Christian Literature*, Leiden, 1954.

Jones, A.H.M., *The Cities of the Eastern Roman Provinces*, Oxford, 1937.

Kannengieser, C., 'L'Infinité divine chez Grégoire de Nysse', *Recherches de Science Religieuse* 55 (1967), 55–65.

Kobusch, T., 'Name und Sein: Zu den sprachphilosophischen Grundlagen in der Schrift *Contra Eunomium* des Gregor von Nyssa', in *El 'Contra Eunomium' I en la producción literaria de Gregorio de Nisa*, ed. L. Mateo-Seco and J. Bastero, Pamplona, 1988, 247–68.

Ladner, G., 'The Philosophical Anthropology of Saint Gregory of Nyssa', *Dumbarton Oaks Papers* 12 (1958), 58–94.

Langerbeck, H., 'Zur Interpretation Gregors von Nyssa', *Theologische Literatur-zeitung* 82 (1957), 81–90.

Leisigung, H., 'La connaissance de Dieu au miroir de l'âme et de la nature', *Revue d'histoire et de philosophie religieuses* 17 (1937), 145–71.

LeMaitre, J., 'Préhistoire du concepte de gnophos', *Dictionnaire de Spiritualité*, vol. ii. ii, Paris, 1953, s.v. contemplation, cols. 1868–72.

Lewy, H., *Sobria Ebreitas: Untersuchungen zur Geschichte der antiken Mystik*, Giessen, 1929.

——. *Chaldean Oracles and Theurgy: Mysticism, Magic and Platonism in the Later Roman Empire*, Cairo, 1956; new edition by M. Tardieu, Paris, 1978.

Leys, R., *L'Image de Dieu chez Saint Grégoire de Nysse*, Museum Lessianum Section Théologique 49, Paris, 1951.

Lieske, A., 'Zur Theologie der Christusmystik bei Gregors von Nyssa', *Scholastik* 14 (1939), 495–514.

——. 'Die Theologie der Christusmystik Gregors von Nyssa', *Zeitschrift für Katholische Theologie* 70 (1948), 49–93, 129–68, 315–40.

Lilla, S., *Clement of Alexandria: A Study in Christian Platonism and Gnosticism*, Oxford, 1971.

——. 'La teologia negativa dal pensiero greco classico a quello patristico e bizantino', *Helikon* 22–7 (1982–7), 211–79; 28 (1988), 203–79; 29–30 (1989–90), 97–186; 31–2 (1991–2), 3–72.

——. 'Diogini', in *La Mistica: fenomenologia e riflessione teologica*, 2 vols., ed. E. Ancilli and M. Paparozzi, Rome, 1984, 381–7.

——. 'Platonism and the Fathers', *Encyclopedia of the Early Church*, ed. A. Di Berardino, trans. A. Walford, Cambridge, 1992, s.v.

——. *Introduzione al Medio Platonismo*, Sussidi Patristici 5, Rome, 1992.

Lindsay, D. *Josephus and Faith: πίστις and πιστεύειν as Faith Terminology in the Writings of Flavius Josephus and in the New Testament*, Arbeiten zur Geschichte des antiken Judentums und des Urchristentums 19, Leiden, 1993.

Lloyd, A. C., *The Anatomy of Neoplatonism*, Oxford, 1990.

Lossky, V., *In the Image and Likeness of God*, Crestwood, NY, 1985.

Lot-Borodine, M., *La Déification de l'homme selon la doctrine des Pères grecs*, Paris, 1970.

Louth, A., *Origins of the Christian Mystical Tradition: From Plato to Denys*, Oxford, 1981.

——. 'The Cappadocians', in *The Study of Spirituality*, ed. C., Jones, G. Wainwright, and E. Yarnold, London, 1986, 161–8.

——. *Denys the Areopagite*, Outstanding Christian Thinkers, London, 1989.

Macleod, C., 'ΑΝΑΛΓΣΙΣ: A Study of Ancient Mysticism', *Journal of Theological Studies* NS 21 (1970), 43–55.

——. 'Allegory and Mysticism in Origen and Gregory of Nyssa', *Journal of Theological Studies* NS 22 (1971), 362–79.

——. 'The Preface to Gregory of Nyssa's *Life of Moses*', *Journal of Theological Studies* NS 33 (1982), 183–91.

Mamo, P., 'Is Plotinian Mysticism Monistic?' in *The Significance of Neoplatonism*, ed. R. Harris, Norfolk, Va., 1976, 199–215.

Marrou, H. I., *Histoire de l'Education dans l'Antiquité*, Paris, 1948.

May, G., 'Die Chronologie des Lebens und der Werke des Gregor von Nyssa', in *Écriture et culture philosophique dans la pensée de Grégoire de Nysse*, ed. M. Harl, Leiden, 1971, 51–67.

McClear, E., 'The Fall of Man and Original Sin in the Theology of Gregory of Nyssa', *Theological Studies* 9 (1948), 175–212.

McGinn, B., *The Foundations of Mysticism*, vol. 1: *Origins to the Fifth Century*, London, 1992.

McGrath, C., 'Gregory of Nyssa's Doctrine on Knowledge of God', Ph.D. thesis, Fordham University, 1964.

Melling, D., *Understanding Plato*, Oxford, 1987.

Meloni, P., *Il profumo dell' immortalitá: L'interpretazione patristica di Cantico 1,3*, Verba Seniorum NS 7, Rome, 1975.

Meredith, A., 'Orthodoxy, Heresy and Philosophy in the Latter Half of the Fourth Century', *Heythrop Journal* 16 (1975), 5–21.

——. 'Porphyry and Julian against the Christians', *ANRW* II. 23/2, ed. W. Haase, Berlin, 1980, 1119–49.

——. 'The Pneumatology of the Cappadocian Fathers', *Irish Theological Quarterly* 48 (1981), 196–211.

——. 'Gregory of Nyssa and Plotinus', *Studia Patristica* 17 (1982), 1120–26.

——. 'The Concept of Mind in Gregory of Nyssa', *Studia Patristica* 22 (1989), 35–51.

——. 'The Good and the Beautiful in Gregory of Nyssa', in *EPMHNEYMATA: Festschrift für Hadwig Hörner zum sechzigsten Geburtstag*, ed. H. Eisenberger, Heidelberg, 1990, 133–45.

——. 'Homily 1', in *Gregory of Nyssa: 'Homilies on Ecclesiastes': An English Version with Supporting Studies*, Proceedings of the Seventh International Conference on Gregory of Nyssa, St Andrews, 5–10 September, ed. and trans. S. Hall and R. Moriarty, Berlin, 1993, 145–58.

——. *The Cappadocians*, Outstanding Christian Thinkers, London, 1995.

——. 'Origen's *De Principiis* and Gregory of Nyssa's *Oratio Catechetica*', *Heythrop Journal* 36 (1995), 1–14.

——. 'Licht und Finsternis bei Origenes und Gregor von Nyssa', in T. Kobusch and B. Mojsisch (eds.), *Platon in der abendländischen Geistesgeschichte*, Darmstadt, 1997, 48–59.

——. *Gregory of Nyssa*, The Early Church Fathers, London, 1999.

Merki, H., $OMOI\Omega\Sigma\Sigma$ $\Theta E\Omega$: *Von der platonischen Angleichung an Gott zur Gottähnlichkeit bei Gregor von Nyssa*, Fribourg, 1952.

——. 'Ebenbildlichkeit', *Realexikon für Antike und Christentum* 4 (1959), 459–79.

Merlan, P., *Monopsychism, Mysticism, Metaconsciousness*, The Hague, 1963.

Moingt, J., 'La Gnose de Clément d'Alexandrie dans ses rapports avec la philosophie', *Revue de Science Religieuse* 37 (1950), 398–421; 37 (1950), 537–64; 38 (1951), 82–118.

Mortley, R., *Connaissance religieuse et herméneutique chez Clément d'Alexandrie*, Leiden, 1973.

Mosshammer, A., 'Disclosing but Not Disclosed: Gregory of Nyssa as Deconstructionist', in *Studien zu Gregor von Nyssa und der christlichen Spätantike*, ed. H. Drobner and C. Klock Leiden, 1990, 99–122.

Muckle, J., 'The Doctrine of Gregory of Nyssa on Man and the Image of God', *Mediaeval Studies* 7 (1945), 55–84.

Mühlenberg, E., *Die Unendlichkeit Gottes bei Gregor von Nyssa: Gregors Kritik am Gottesbegriff der klassischen Metaphysik*, Forschungen zur Kirchen- und Dogmengeschichte 16, Göttingen, 1966.

——. 'Synergism in Gregory of Nyssa', *Zeitschrift für die neutestamentliche Wissenschaft und die Kunde der älteren Kirche* 68 (1977), 93–122.

Nock, A., *Early Gentile Christianity and its Hellenistic Background*, New York, 1964.

Norris, R., 'The Soul Takes Flight: Gregory of Nyssa and the Song of Songs', *Anglican Theological Review* 80 (1998), 517–32.

O'Daly, G.J.P., 'The Presence of the One in Plotinus', in *Problemi Attuali di Scienza e Cultura* 198, Atti del Convegno Internazionale sul tema: Plotino e il Neoplatonismo in Oriente e in Occidente (Roma, 5–9 ottobre, 1970), Rome, 1974, 159–69.

Osborn, E., *The Philosophy of Clement of Alexandria*, Texts and Studies: Contributions to Biblical and Patristic Literature NS 3, Cambridge, 1957.

Osborne, C., *Eros Unveiled: Plato and the God of Love*, Oxford, 1994.

Otis, B., 'Cappadocian Thought as a Coherent System', *Dumbarton Oaks Papers* 12 (1958), 97–124.

Otis, B., 'Nicene Orthodoxy and Fourth Century Mysticism', in *Proceedings of the XII International Congress of Byzantine Studies (Ochrid, 10–16 IX 1961)*, vol. ii, Belgrade, 1964, 475–84.

Pelikan, J., *Christianity and Classical Culture: The Metamorphosis of Natural Theology in the Christian Encounter with Hellenism*, Gifford Lectures 1992–93, New Haven, 1993.

Pépin, J., *Théologie cosmique et théologie chrétienne*, Paris, 1964.

——. '"Image d'image", "Miroir de miroir", (Grégoire de Nysse, *De hominis opificio* xii, PG 44, 161c–164b)', in *Platonism in Late Antiquity*, ed. S. Gersh and C. Kannengiesser, Christianity and Judaism in Antiquity 8, Notre Dame, 1992, 217–38.

Peroli, E., *Il Platonismo e l'antropologia filosofica di Gregorio di Nissa. Con particolare riferimento agli influssi di Platone, Plotino e Porfirio*, Platonismo e filosofia patristica: Studi e testi 5, Milan, 1993.

Phillips, J., 'Plotinus and the Eye of the Intellect', *Dionysius* 14 (1990), 79–105.

Pietrella, E., 'L'antiorigenismo di Gregorio di Nissa', *Augustinianum* 26 (1986), 143–76.

Placida, R., 'La presenza di Origene nelle *Omelie sul Cantico dei cantici* di Gregorio di Nissa', *Vetera Christianorum* 34 (1997), 33–49.

Pottier, B., *Dieu et le Christ selon Grégoire de Nysse: Etude systématique du 'Contre Eunome' avec traduction inédite des extraits d'Eunome*, Ouvertures 12, Namur, 1994.

Pouchet, J.-R., *Basile le Grand et son univers d'amis: Une stratégie de communion*, Studia Ephemerides Augustinianum 36, Rome, 1992.

Puech, H.-C., 'La Ténèbre mystique chez le Pseudo-Denys l'Aréopagite et dans la tradition patristique', in *En quête de la Gnose*, 2 vols., Paris, 1978, vol. i, 119–41.

Rist, J., 'Mysticism and Transcendence in Later Neoplatonism', *Hermes* 92 (1964), 213–25.

——. *Plotinus: The Road to Reality*, Cambridge, 1967.

——. 'Basil's "Neoplatonism": Its Background and Nature', in *Basil of Caesarea: Christian, Humanist, Ascetic. A Sixteen Hundreth Anniversary Symposium*, ed. P. Fedwick, Toronto, 1981, 137–220.

——. 'Back to the Mysticism of Plotinus: Some More Specifics', *Journal of the History of Philosophy* 27 (1989), 183–97.

——. 'Plotinus and Christian Philosophy', in *The Cambridge Companion to Plotinus*, ed. L. Gerson, Cambridge, 1996, 386–413.

Ritter, A., 'Die Gnadenlehre Gregors von Nyssa nach seiner Schrift "Über das Leben des Mose"', in *Gregor von Nyssa und die Philosophie*, ed. H. Dörrie, M. Altenburger, and U. Schramm, Leiden, 1976, 195–239.

Rondeau, M.-J., 'Exégèse du Psautier et anabase spirituelle chez Grégoire de Nysse', in *Epektasis: Mélanges patristiques offerts au Cardinal Jean Daniélou*, ed. J. Fontaine and C. Kannengiesser, Paris, 1972, 517–31.

——. 'D'où vient la technique exégétique utilisée par Grégoire de Nysse dans son traité "Sur les titres des psaumes"?' in *Mélanges d'histoire des religions offerts à Henri-Charles Puech*, Paris, 1974, 263–87.

Rosán, L., *The Philosophy of Proclus*, New York, 1949.

Rousseau, P., *Basil of Caesarea*, Transformation of the Classical Heritage 20, Berkeley, 1994.

——. *The Early Christian Centuries*, London, 2002.

Saffrey, H., 'Les Néoplatoniciens et les *Oracles Chaldaïques*', *Revue des Etudes Augustiniennes* 27 (1981), 209–25.

——. 'The Piety and Prayers of Ordinary Men and Women in Late Antiquity', in *Classical Mediterranean Spirituality*, ed. A. H. Armstrong, World Spirituality: An Encyclopedic History of the Religious Quest 15, New York, 1986, 195–213.

——. 'Neoplatonist Spirituality II: From Iamblichus to Proclus and Damascius', in *Classical Mediterranean Spirituality*, ed. A. H. Armstrong, World Spirituality: An Encyclopedic History of the Religious Quest 15, New York, 1986, 250–65.

Sells, M., *Mystical Languages of Unsaying*, Chicago, 1994.

Shaw, G., *Theurgy and the Soul: The Neoplatonism of Iamblichus*, University Park, Pa., 1995.

——. 'Divination in the Neoplatonism of Iamblichus', in *Mediators of the Divine: Horizons of Prophecy, Divination, Dreams and Theurgy in Mediterranean Antiquity*, ed. R. Berchman, South Florida Studies in the History of Judaism 163, Atlanta, 1998, 225–67.

Sheppard, A., 'Proclus' Attitude to Theurgy', *Classical Quarterly* 32 (1982), 212–24.

Siorvanes, L., *Proclus: Neo-Platonic Philosophy of Science*, Edinburgh, 1996.

Smith, A., *Porphyry's Place in the Platonic Tradition*, The Hague, 1974.

Smith, R., *Julian's Gods: Religion and Philosophy in the Thought and Action of Julian the Apostate*, London, 1995.

Srawley, J., 'St Gregory of Nyssa on the Sinlessness of Christ', *Journal of Theological Studies* 7 (1906), 434–41.

Stead, G. C., 'Ontology and Terminology in Gregory of Nyssa,' in *Gregor von Nyssa und die Philosophie: Zweites Internationales Kolloquium Gregor von Nyssa (Münster 18–23 September 1972)*, ed. H. Dörrie, M. Altenburger, and U. Schramm, Leiden, 1976, 107–19.

——. 'The Concept of the Mind and the Concept of God in the Christian Fathers', in *The Philosophical Frontiers of Christian Theology*, ed. B. Hebblethwaite and S. Sutherland, Cambridge, 1982, 39–54.

——. *Philosophy and Christian Antiquity*, Cambridge, 1994.

Stefano, T., 'La libertà radicale dell'immagine secondo Gregorio di Nissa', *Divus Thomus* 75 (1972), 431–54.

Theiler, W., *Die Chaldäischen Orakel*, Halle, 1942.

Turner, D., *The Darkness of God: Negativity in Christian Mysticism*, Cambridge, 1995.

Valantasis, R., *Spiritual Guides of the Third Century: A Semiotic Study of The Guide— Disciple Relationship in Christianity, Neoplatonism, Hermeticism, and Gnosticism*, Harvard Dissertations in Religion 27, Minneapolis, 1991.

Verhees, J., 'Die ENEPΓEIAI des Pneumas als Beweis für seine Tranzendenz in der Argumentation des Gregor von Nyssa', *Orientalia Christiana Periodica* 45 (1979), 5–31.

Völker, W., *Fortschritt und Vollendung bei Philo von Alexandrien*, Texte und Untersuchungen der altchristlichen Literatur 49.1, Leipzig, 1938.

——. *Der wahre Gnostiker nach Clemens Alexandrinus*, Texte und Untersuchungen der altchristlichen Literatur 57, Berlin, 1952.

——. *Gregor von Nyssa als Mystiker*, Wiesbaden, 1955.

Wallis, R., 'Nous as Experience', in *The Significance of Neoplatonism*, ed. R. Harris, Norfolk, Va., 1976, 121–54.

——. 'The Spiritual Importance of Not Knowing', in *Classical Mediterranean Spirituality*, ed. A. H. Armstrong, World Spirituality: An Encyclopedic History of the Religious Quest 15, New York, 1986, 460–80.

——. *Neoplatonism*, 2nd edn., London, 1995.

Ware, K., 'My Helper and My Enemy: The Body in Greek Christianity', in *Religion and the Body*, ed. S. Coakley, Cambridge Studies in Religion 8, Cambridge, 1997, 90–110.

Watson, G., 'Gregory of Nyssa's Use of Philosophy in the *Life of Moses*', *Irish Theological Quarterly* 53 (1987), 100–12.

Weiswurm, A., *The Nature of Human Knowledge according to Gregory of Nyssa*, Washington, DC, 1952.

Whitaker, J., Ἐπέκεινα νοῦ καὶ οὐσίας', *Vigiliae Christianae* 23 (1969), 91–104.

Wilken, R., *The Christians as the Romans Saw Them*, New Haven, 1984.

Williams, J., *Denying Divinity: Apophasis in the Patristic Christian and Soto Zen Buddhist Traditions*, Oxford, 2000.

Williams, R., 'Macrina's Deathbed Revisited: Gregory of Nyssa on Mind and Passion', in *Christian Faith and Greek Philosophy in Late Antiquity*, ed. L. Wickham and C. Bammel, Leiden, 1993, 227–46.

Wolfson, H., *Philo: Foundations of Religious Philosophy in Judaism, Christianity, and Islam*, 2 vols., Structure and Growth of Philosophic Systems from Plato to Spinoza, Cambridge, Mass., 1947.

——. *The Philosophy of the Church Fathers*, Cambridge, Mass., 1956.

Wörmer, A., 'Die Verborgenheit Gottes im Hohenliedkommentar Gregors von Nyssa und ihre Rezeption durch Pseudo-Dionysius Areopagita', *Ephemeriedes Theologicae Lovaniensis* 77 (2001), 73–107.

INDEX

Abraham: as example of faith 16–17, 19, 39, 93, 116, 127
  and faith as bridge between mind and God 22, 68–77, 104–5
  and faith and justification 1, 74, 106
  as 'father of the faith' 70, 72, 106
  and unknowing 71–2, 100
  see also ascent; faith and knowledge
Adam, J. 56–7 n.136
Alexandrian theology: and exegesis 69, 75
  and faith 19, 22–3, 26, 102, 103, 205, 209
  and light symbolism 198 n.100
  and perpetual movement 37
alpha privatives 66, 81, 84
anabasis 71–2
anthropology, theological 54, 58, 59–61, 69, 175 n.7, 187–8, 194–5
  and original condition of humanity 182–3, 185, 193, 195, 203
  of Plotinus 121 n.60
aphairesis 65, 90, 110, 144, 170
  and Abraham 71–2, 74, 116, 131–2
  and the bride 52–3, 88, 109, 117, 127, 130, 165
  in *Chaldaean Oracles* 116, 130
  and darkness theme 48, 180
  and Moses 83
  and Paul 157
  in Plotinus 119, 127, 130
apophasis 17–18, 19–20, 25, 31–2, 43, 144
  and faith 2, 65–6, 68, 71–3, 79–84, 131–2, 210–11

  and language 20, 51 n.113, 65–7, 71, 72–3, 76, 82–4, 87, 180
  and *logophasis* 153, 156–7, 165–9, 170–2, 211
  and mysticism of darkness 174, 176–8, 180, 198
  and positive knowledge 132, 133–5, 155
  see also aphairesis; ascent of the mind
archer: bridegroom as 94–5, 128
  God as 91–5, 101, 105, 168–9
Arianism 69, 75–6
Aristotle 35, 80, 149
Armstrong, A.H. 6, 118–19 n.48, 120 n.53, 121 n.60
arrow: bride as 91, 93–5, 105, 128, 169, 188
  faith as tip 92, 96, 98, 100, 105, 128, 168, 207
  Son as 91–2, 95, 98, 101, 105, 168–9
ascent of the mind 43–4, 45–6, 48–9, 52–3, 60, 108
  and Abraham 25, 30, 70–4, 76, 84, 93, 105, 110, 116, 126
  and the bride 17, 87–91, 100, 105, 116–17, 125–6, 130, 165, 178, 201 n.109
  in *Chaldaean Oracles* 115–16
  and darkness 48–55, 177–81, 198, 200–1, 204
  and David 43
  and faith and knowledge 50, 59, 74, 83–5, 86–9, 102, 109–11, 165, 211
  and justification 74
  and light 186

Index compiled by Meg Davies (Registered Indexer, Society of Indexers).